D1737026

Hollywood's War with Poland

Hollywood's War with Poland
1939–1945

M. B. B. BISKUPSKI

THE UNIVERSITY PRESS OF KENTUCKY

Copyright © 2010 by The University Press of Kentucky

Scholarly publisher for the Commonwealth,
serving Bellarmine University, Berea College, Centre College of Kentucky,
Eastern Kentucky University, The Filson Historical Society, Georgetown
College, Kentucky Historical Society, Kentucky State University,
Morehead State University, Murray State University, Northern Kentucky
University, Transylvania University, University of Kentucky, University of
Louisville, and Western Kentucky University.
All rights reserved.

Editorial and Sales Offices: The University Press of Kentucky
663 South Limestone Street, Lexington, Kentucky 40508-4008
www.kentuckypress.com

Library of Congress Cataloging-in-Publication Data

Biskupski, Mieczyslaw B.
  Hollywood's war with Poland, 1939–1945 / M. B. B. Biskupski.
    p. cm.
  Includes bibliographical references and index.
  ISBN 978-0-8131-2559-6 (hardcover : alk. paper)
  1. Poland—In motion pictures. 2. Polish people in motion pictures.
3. World War, 1939–1945—Motion pictures and the war. 4. Motion pictures—
Political aspects—United States. I. Title.
  PN1995.9.P54B57 2009
  791.43'658438053—dc22   2009031481

This book is printed on acid-free recycled paper meeting the requirements of
the American National Standard for Permanence in Paper for Printed Library
Materials.

Manufactured in the United States of America.

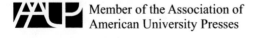 Member of the Association of
American University Presses

Matce swej ukochanej, swiętej pamięci Wirginii Biskupskiej, która mnie nauczyła kochać filmy lecz Ojczyznę jeszcze bardziej poświęcam.

Contents

Preface   ix

Introduction   1

1. The Polish Presence in American Cinema before 1939   11

2. Poland in the Second World War   45

3. Radical Hollywood and Poland   57

4. The Roosevelt Administration and Film during the War   67

5. Hollywood's Version of the War: The Polish Films   83

6. Poland: Fleeting, Ambiguous, or Omitted   119

7. Hollywood and the American Poles during the War   169

8. Why Hollywood Was at War with the Poles   201

Conclusion   229

Notes   231

Bibliography   331

Index   345

Photos follow page 168

Preface

Hollywood presented a fundamentally distorted and negative portrayal of Poland and the Poles during the Second World War. An American citizen whose knowledge of the war was derived exclusively from the movies would be unsympathetic if not hostile to Poland and understanding if not supportive of Soviet policies directed against Poland's sovereignty and territorial integrity. The number of Americans who fell into this category is impossible to determine, but it was doubtless large. Moreover, even for those for whom the movies were but one source of information, films had at least some effect, and for the Poles that effect was negative.

This conclusion is based on a careful consideration of scores of films and on the reconstruction of the evolution of stories from literary property through various "treatments" into ever changing scripts. This reconstruction has been supplemented by evaluations of the films and their political content provided by governmental agencies. In addition to studying the films closely, I have consulted many memoirs, letters, diaries, and memoranda by screenwriters, directors, studio heads, actors, and other film employees.

Discussions of Slavs in American cinema are few, and of the Poles, very few. All of them are characterized by sweeping allegations based on a small sample of films. For the average American, "going to the movies" usually meant watching cheap and artless efforts, not just attending a few major productions. It is thus only by considering a great many films, not just a handful of lasting impression, that we can sense the cumulative effects of the films on the public. Hence my examples are many and far ranging.

That Poland was treated very negatively is beyond question. Why this was so is more difficult to determine. The principal factor was the desire by the political Left, especially the Communist Party, to gain sympathy for, and promote the foreign policy interests of, the Soviet Union. Undermining Poland's claim on the support of the American public was a direct contribution to promoting Soviet political and territorial ambitions. That Poland had long been regarded by the political Left as an inveterate enemy of the Soviets made this effort more passionate. In Hollywood, the Left, therefore, was ideologically anti-Polish.

This disposition complemented the foreign policy of the Roosevelt administration, which regarded close wartime cooperation with Moscow as fundamental. Poland had very considerable grievances against the Soviets, and any consideration of them complicated relations with Moscow. Simply put, the American government could be either pro-Russian or pro-Polish; there was no compromise position. For reasons of realpolitik, it chose the former. This made it a functional ally of the Hollywood Left. Much has been written about the relations between New Deal liberalism and the radical Left. In Hollywood, at least over Poland, they worked in tandem.[1]

These are the main factors that explain Hollywood's treatment of Poland and the Poles during World War II. But they are merely the central features of a complex landscape. Poland was presented the way it was as a result of the interaction of many factors imbedded in the ethnic mosaic of the United States, including the Poles' relationship with other minority groups, especially the Jewish community. Polish-Jewish relations haunt the story even though they were rarely specifically addressed. That World War II brought both the Holocaust of the Jews and the ruination of Poland, themes Hollywood avoided, makes this discussion especially sensitive and significant.

Finally, the American conception of World War II as "the good war," in which villains and heroes were clearly distinguished and moral ambiguity was banished, required avoiding radical doubts about the worthiness of the Soviet Union as an ally of the United States. Norway and France, Czechoslovakia and England were all victims of Nazi rapacity. Discussing any of them merely underscored the moral clarity of the war. Poland, however, was different. It was invaded, occupied, and abused by both Germany and Russia. Poland raised the radical question about the Soviet Union's place in the coalition of the righteous.

But since the Soviets were obviously paying the largest price in the struggle to defeat Nazism, entertaining doubts about their fitness raised awkward questions about the cynicism and ruthlessness of American foreign policy. Such questions could not coexist with the self-confident rectitude of a country off to war singing "Onward Christian Soldiers." Poland had to be ignored to salve the American conscience. At base, Poland's fate in Hollywood reflected the Americans' need to feel good about themselves.[2]

In 1989 I was invited to comment after a public screening of Frank Capra's wartime propaganda film *The Nazis Strike*. When I noted that the depiction of the war grossly misrepresented both Poland and Soviet Russia, a member of the audience rose in passionate protest. It was simply too painful for this veteran of American service to hear criticism of a film that he remembered as symbolizing national unity and purpose. He was virtually in tears at what he regarded as a blaspheming of his memories. Ironically, he was an American Pole known for his patriotic attachment to his ancestral homeland. The possibility that the United States had done a disservice to the Polish cause was more than he could bear; it thus could not be true. However, it was true. This is not a book about Poland but about how America viewed and represented Poland as a result of the interplay among ideology, nationality, and politics.

By focusing on the Polish issue, this book throws considerable light on the question of what the Left was about in wartime Hollywood and whether it had any effect on films—a passionate topic long debated. The "red menace" may well have been more effective than many believe if we focus on its geopolitical propagandizing and not its social message. We also are able to consider from a new perspective the question of whether Hollywood really was the source of pro-Russian propaganda during the war. Everything that hurt Poland helped Russia. Omitting, or providing an inaccurate portrayal of, Poland damaged its ability to gain the sympathy and attention of the American public.

I should like to thank the friends and colleagues who have offered helpful suggestions: Piotr S. Wandycz and Jadwiga M. Biskupska of Yale University, Piotr Wróbel of the University of Toronto, and Anna Cienciala of the University of Kansas, all of whom provided important advice; Robert Szymczak of Pennsylvania State University for his help regarding population figures; Irene Tomaszewski of the Canadian

Foundation for Polish Studies for early encouragement; Jay Bergman for his good judgment and many kindnesses, and Ewa Wołyńska and Renata Vickrey for their research skills, all three at Central Connecticut State University; James S. Pula of Purdue University for his invaluable help regarding the Poles in America; Dominic Pacyga of Columbia College for his knowledge of Chicago; Stanislav Kirschbaum of York University for his help with Slovak; Michael Alfred Peszke for his advice about matters pertaining to the war; and my brother, John R. Biskupski, for his extraordinary assistance in unearthing sources. My greatest debt is to Anna Laura Bennett for her superb editing. The University Press of Kentucky has been a pleasure to work with, and I owe Anne Dean Watkins my sincere gratitude for her patience and consideration. My wife, Virginia R. Mitchell, was, as always, a source of wise counsel, which I usually ignored, a decision I always later regretted. My two youngest children, Misia and Staś, helped Daddy more than they know. In addition, Kate Farley, Paul Hermann, Anne Marie Incorvaia, and Melissa Macko, my former students at St. John Fisher College in Rochester, New York, brought many matters to my attention regarding American films of this era while participating in the class Hitler and Hollywood during the autumn 2001 semester. They have my thanks for their help and their support. The book is dedicated to my mother, whom I love more with the years.

Introduction

FILMS IN THE ERA BEFORE TELEVISION were a significant source of information as well as entertainment, and their influence on popular attitudes, though impossible to quantify, was considerable.[1] Let us remember that in the 1939–1945 era Hollywood released five hundred films yearly and that the decade beginning in 1935 saw a phenomenal increase in American film attendance: 74 percent of the population of the country went to the movies at least once a week; many, especially in urban areas, went more often.[2] Attendance at films surpassed 85 million a week, and the industry exceeded $1 billion in annual receipts.[3] Films mattered; their "manipulative qualities" shaped taste and attitude. They made things important by their attention, and they rendered them marginal by their neglect.[4] "An average feature film," Melvin Small notes, "reached more people than any single book, newspaper, or magazine."[5] American films not only sought to portray the conflict but, as Arthur F. McClure notes, also "tried to define the objectives of the war." In fine, they attempted to create policies, or at least mold popular support for them.[6] For good or ill, Hollywood was, in Carl Sandburg's words, "the foremost educational institute on earth."[7]

American public opinion demonstrated a marked shift during the war in its perceptions of Poland. Whereas Poland was always a marginal concern for Americans, the general impression of the country in the immediate aftermath of the September invasions was sympathetic, though not supportive enough to disturb isolationist inclinations.[8] However, after 1941 and the Soviet Union's entry into the war against Germany, this situation changed. Support for Soviet Russia grew—including support for its political and territorial designs on Poland—and the popular image of Poland deteriorated. As Richard C. Lukas notes,

"One of the most remarkable phenomena of World War II was the dramatic change in American attitudes towards the Soviets and the Poles. . . . [Whereas the Soviet Union] emerged by the end of the war as an admired and respected nation . . . Poland . . . came to be characterized as the enfant terrible of the Allies, threatening to wreck their wartime alliance."[9]

This situation deteriorated still more in the spring of 1943 when the Germans discovered thousands of Polish corpses at Katyń on the eastern front. The Russians, who had perpetrated the crime, blamed the Germans. American public opinion largely shared the Russian view. The Poles, who knew the truth, were in a quandary. To many Americans, the Poles were damaging Allied unity by not accepting German guilt. When the Russians broke diplomatic relations with the Polish government soon after, the Poles were isolated. American public opinion almost certainly blamed the Poles for this state of affairs.[10]

Both Hollywood leftists and members of the Roosevelt administration frequently claimed that positive portrayals of Russia, however inaccurate, were justified because of the enormous prejudice the American public had felt toward Soviet Russia. Hence, though they were propaganda, pro-Russian efforts were in effect counterpropaganda to undue years of ignorance and prejudice. That this claim is without foundation was known at the time. A widely reported Gallup poll in July 1941 made it clear that the American public favored a Soviet victory over Nazi Germany by a gigantic disparity, 72 percent to 4 percent. Soviet war relief was popular in the United States; public declarations of support for the Russians from prominent figures were frequent.[11] To be sure, isolationism was widespread until Pearl Harbor, but there was absolutely no need to "sell" the Russian war effort, which had overwhelming American support even before Washington and Moscow became formal allies.

The extraordinary growth of popular Russophilia, including the proliferation of pro-Russian and pro-Soviet films, has been well studied.[12] A 1943 public opinion survey noted that one of these films, *Mission to Moscow,* "raised pro-Soviet sentiment . . . among those who saw it."[13] Small concludes, "Public opinion polls tell us that Americans became increasingly friendly towards the Soviet Union during the period, and Hollywood undoubtedly had something to do with this shift in attitude."[14] However, less attention has been devoted to the concomitant deterioration of American support for Poland. There is a valuable study by David Januszewski of American press treatment of the Polish-Soviet imbroglio.[15] But Hollywood's portrayal of Poland has not heretofore received extended scholarly analysis. Given the significance of the movies for the formation of the modern American mind, this is a noteworthy lacuna.

The American film industry produced a large number of films in the 1939–1945 era that were completely or substantially devoted to the war.[16] However, virtually none of them concerned Poland. The reasons for this are difficult to understand. Kathryn Kane has suggested that, whereas the Pacific theater of the war began dramatically for the Americans with the Pearl Harbor attack, the origins and early stages of the European conflict were confusing and ambiguous. Moreover, whereas American troops were at once in action in the Pacific, involvement in the European theater was delayed until the fall of 1942, with the North African landings. Only in 1943, with the Italian campaign, did American troops fight on the continent.[17] These facts would explain the initial paucity of films devoted to Europe in general, but they would have no bearing on which theaters of the European conflict were emphasized.

This takes us to the first of several perplexing questions. Hollywood was at pains to serve the national interest by portraying the Germans as barbarians determined to conquer the world. Their uncivilized methods of war and unspeakable occupation policies made them an implacable enemy of all decent people. One would think, in light of this, that the best illustration of this dichotomy would be the Polish example: a military campaign distinguished by great sacrifice and gallantry; a huge, resourceful underground offering unyielding resistance; and, of course, an occupation regime of unparalleled savagery. Hollywood, however, devoted no cinematic attention to Poland whatsoever until 1942, when it released a single film set there, the controversial *To Be or Not to Be.* Two years passed before two additional films about Poland, *In Our Time* and the obscure, low-budget *None Shall Escape,* were released. These were Hollywood's last "Polish" films of the war.[18]

By comparison, Norway, where armed resistance to the 1940 German attack had been brief and a collaborationist regime under Vidkun Quisling was installed, was a subject of endless attention by Hollywood. There were many films devoted to Norway, five appearing in a period of several months after late 1942, many featuring major stars and representing considerable budgets.[19] France was also the subject of lavish attention. As Bernard F. Dick notes, "Hollywood's Franco-philia during the war even surpassed its pre-war Anglophilia. France . . . became a symbol of freedom in chains."[20] Unlike Poland's, France's military defeat was far more rapid than was anticipated or justified by circumstance. Moreover, the Vichy regime under Marshal Pétain was collaborationist, and French troops even fired on Americans disembark-ing in North Africa in Operation Torch in November 1942.[21]

Finally, there were at least six cinematic depictions of Czechoslo-vakia during World War II, perhaps more. All are complimentary to the Czechs.[22] This despite the fact that there was no military opposition to German occupation, and the relative docility of the population led Vojtech Mastny to refer to it as "the failure of national resistance."[23] Indeed, the most famous resistance fighter in the history of Hollywood's reconstruction of the war is, mirabile dictu, a Czech, Casablanca's Vic-tor László. Thus the travail of continental Europe is presented to Ameri-can audiences not through a depiction of Poland, which would prove a handy and, indeed, eloquent example, but through Czechoslovakia, Norway, and France, whose service in this role is awkward at best.[24] Hence Hollywood chose to ignore Poland even when it was, seem-ingly, in its cinematic interest to do otherwise.[25] Even the federal office assigned to monitor the film industry was perplexed by Hollywood's ignoring of Poland during the war.[26]

As we shall see, the overall negative portrayal of Poland and the Poles by Hollywood was a combination of factors. These include, at base, the absence of a tradition of interest in Polish subjects in Ameri-can culture as a whole and the insignificant presence of Poles in the United States and hence of Poland in the mental world of the American government and its people. These are large factors long in place. How-ever, if we consider just the war years and the motives of the studios, we discern more specific factors. Chief among these is the powerful pro-Soviet disposition of many in Hollywood, especially the screenwriters, among whom membership in the Communist Party was quite common. Party members, by the estimate of Paul Buhle, who is certainly sym-pathetic to the political Left, were "creatively critical" for between one thousand and fifteen hundred films in the years before 1947.[27] Films that portrayed Poles negatively, presented Soviet designs against Poland favorably, or omitted Poland from the story at critical moments were almost always the work of writers of the radical Left. This leftist campaign against Poland was not motivated by anti-Polish prejudice but by the need to protect Soviet interests, which required Poland to be either denigrated or removed from popular discourse. This project was easy to accomplish because it largely complemented the foreign and domestic policies of the Roosevelt administration, which saw in Poland a trifling ally whose contribution to the war was far less significant than its role in promoting frictions with Moscow.

In simple terms, the Soviet Union pursued a policy inimical to the sovereignty and territorial integrity of Poland. This was quite obvious by 1941, if not before. Although Washington bore the Poles no ill will, it did not regard the defense of Polish interests as important. Poland had not been significant in American policy before 1939 and was not a major force in the war. By contrast, close cooperation with Moscow was the basis of wartime strategy and fundamental to the creation of a postwar world. Hence, for the Roosevelt administration, Moscow would be accommodated as regarded Poland. Any public discussion of this fact would inconvenience Washington's policy toward Moscow. American films were to present the war in a manner that facilitated the public's acceptance of administration policies. Hence the governmental agency that monitored the film industry, the Bureau of Motion Pictures (BMP) of the Office of War Information (OWI), was very careful that Russia be presented positively and that issues that might cast the USSR in a negative light be eliminated. Because Russian actions regarding Poland were a catalog of outrages, the Polish issue was especially sensitive. Hence the Roosevelt administration and the Hollywood Left had identical goals as regarded Polish issues in American films.

This returns us to the controversial question about Communist influence in Hollywood. The 1947 congressional investigations into alleged Communist infiltration of the motion picture industry produced publicity and melodrama but certainly did not prove the existence of serious and effective Communist subversion of Hollywood. The witnesses who tried to discern Communist influences in wartime films are often dismissed. "The proceedings," as Victor S. Navasky wrote, "had comic overtones."[28] The very idea that Hollywood films could contain Communist propaganda was "laughable."[29] William Triplett concludes, "The Communist Party certainly had a Hollywood presence. Its effectiveness, however, within the film industry in the 1930s was almost nil," and subsequently, during the war years, "no pro-Communist passage . . . ever made it past the editing hatchet of the producer."[30] This is corroborated by the detailed accounting of screenwriter Albert Maltz, himself a party member, of the difficulty of inserting propaganda into films.[31] Party chief William Z. Foster told a secret meeting in 1946, "We can't expect to put any propaganda in the films."[32] Indeed, Triplett argues that Communists in Hollywood had their hands full just blunting the anti-Communist propaganda in films.[33] The issue is closed. The Communist Party realized it was not possible to use films to advance the party program and hence did not do so.[34]

This argument, however, is seriously in need of reexamination. If we look for supposed "Communist subversion" in films by anticipating long passages from Karl Marx or calls for a workers' rebellion in the United States or for the overthrow of capitalism, the argument is entirely valid. However, such insertions would have been easily cut, and they would have been bootless even if allowed. The United States was obviously not on the brink of social revolution. However, the main task of the party was to advance the foreign policy agenda of the Soviet Union, to rally support for it during the war with Germany and facilitate its geopolitical designs.[35] In their important study on politics in the film community, Larry Ceplair and Steven Englund note, "Although Party rhetoric was replete with revolutionary phraseology, most adherents—including the vast majority of Hollywood screenwriters—did not perceive themselves as the vanguard of violent upheaval or, still less, of a dictatorship of the proletariat. . . . Party members uncritically supported the U.S.S.R. in the public and tended to confuse [in Paul Jarrico's words] 'the national interests of Russia with those of the United States' . . . in private."[36]

Here Poland plays a crucial role. The re-creation of an independent Poland, within its historical frontiers, under its legal government, would have been an insuperable obstacle to Soviet expansion in Europe. By contrast, the replacement of a sovereign Poland with a Soviet satellite would be the basis for a forward policy for the Soviets in Europe. It was Stalin himself who said in 1945 that "Poland has always been a corridor for attack on Russia. . . . It is not only a question of honor but of life and death for the Soviet State."[37] Hence undermining the Polish cause in the United States was an important goal for supporters of the Soviet Union, including, preeminently, members of the party, who were bound to promote the vital interests of Soviet Russia. That this goal was easily within reach in the United States was because of a host of reasons explored in the present work. However, it is precisely here, in the party's role in facilitating Soviet strategic aims by undermining the position of Poland, that we may look to discover the real focus of party efforts in Hollywood in the war era. And, unlike the 1947 investigations, this analysis discovers a considerable effort and considerable results.

Evidence of the efforts by the party and its sympathizers to denigrate Poland and promote Soviet claims to Poland's detriment must be sought in the material they produced by analyzing the scripts and the evolution of the films they worked on from initial studio interest to finished release. We shall not find party directives to say nasty things about Poles or memoranda from screenwriters explaining how they wished to portray Poland in an unsympathetic light. In large part this reflects a recent observation by Dan Georgakas that, for all of the memoir literature, much of it by repentant ex-Communists, we know virtually nothing of what went on at party meetings in Hollywood.[38] Many note that these gatherings were frequent and interminable, but we have absolutely no inkling of whether they discussed how specific scripts would be handled and themes developed.[39] In other words, we can discern only from the work of the party and their many ideological sympathizers what they wished to say about Poland and the Poles; they do not tell us directly.

These political factors, particularly the congruence of the U.S. administration policy with the pro-Soviet agenda, explain much of Hollywood's approach to Poland and the Poles in the war years. But there are additional elements. It was really quite easy to use the cinema to convey an unsympathetic image of Poland because a number of factors were already in place to facilitate that design. First, Hollywood was almost devoid of significant Polish voices, either émigré or American born. Whereas there had been a number of prominent Poles in the film industry earlier, by 1939 Poles were almost completely absent from Hollywood's creative roles, studio executives, and featured players. What few Poles were in Hollywood were effectively invisible, using changed names, avoiding any contact with the Polish community, and not publicly associating themselves with Poland or Polish issues. There was, simply, no group available that would instinctively defend the Polish cause. A powerful Irish lobby in the 1920s, exploiting its predominating position in the American Catholic Church, had been remarkably effective in forcing Hollywood to treat the Irish—and the church—with care by the 1930s. Unlike the Irish, the Poles were not a community capable of pressuring Hollywood. And the Polish government-in-exile (established after the occupation of Poland in 1939) was painfully aware of its diplomatic weakness. Forced into the role of supplicant for American favor, it could not supplement this effort.

A second and paradoxical factor affecting the Polish issue in Hollywood was that Hollywood was heavily populated by Jews, most of Eastern European origin, for whom Poland was not a sympathetic topic. For them, Poland represented a past best forgotten. This is a sensitive and elusive matter usually "nervously avoided," as Peter Novick argues—but it cannot be ignored.[40] Unlike the Poles of America, who considered their ancestral homeland with affection and loyalty, Polish Jews associated the country with discrimination and barriers to personal and community advancement. That many Poles came to the United States intending eventually to return whereas most Jews planned to stay and build radically new lives is a significant differentiation. The war only magnified this disparity. In the years before the war, the Polish Republic was marred by considerable anti-Semitic prejudice, which became more marked and more pervasive in the 1930s. Whereas the extent and depth of such prejudice in prewar Poland remains controversial, there is no doubt that elements of Polish society harbored anti-Semitic views. American Jews were doubtlessly aware of these facts, which would understandably affect their attitudes toward Poland.

Once the war began, American Poles wanted to see Poland's efforts praised and its trials presented with sympathy. But for the Jews, the Second World War was inextricably intertwined with the Holocaust. For Hollywood's Jews, discussing anti-Semitism in Europe had traditionally been a dangerous and painful topic. The war exacerbated this. Poland was the main site of the Holocaust, and hence after 1939, Jewish moguls of Hollywood were even more reluctant to discuss Polish themes. This inclination was reinforced by the Roosevelt administration, which did not want specifically Jewish issues raised in presenting the war.[41]

Finally, the discussion of Hollywood's treatment of Poland is part of a larger theme concerning the Polish presence in America. In recent decades a number of scholars have noted that in many ways American culture has been uncongenial to the Poles. American literature has largely dismissed the Poles from its explorations, and when they do appear, they are usually marginal or unsympathetic. Polish writers in America are few and unheralded. They have done little to add their community's story to the national epic, and the absence has not been regretted. The Polish community in America enjoys scant prestige, and Polonia has often felt disdained by its fellow citizens. Poland, so dear to the hearts of the Poles in America, has never been significant to Washington, which has traditionally relegated Poland to a matter of minor concern, worthy only of symbolic and often insincere gestures. If the Poles of America have long suspected that America does not regard them highly, a consideration of the American cinema is a most appropriate place to test that assumption. Siegfried Kracauer observed a generation ago a "permanent interaction between mass dispositions and film content." Hence, though "American audiences receive what Hollywood wants them to want . . . in the long run audience desires, acute or dormant, determine the character of Hollywood films."[42] Hollywood had a great many reasons for presenting Polish themes in the manner it did during World War II. If these dispositions have retained their resonance in American culture, however, it is because the images are what the public finds pleasing or at least verisimilar. This is the largest and the most depressing theme suggested by this study, but I shall leave it unexamined. We have enough to do.

1

The Polish Presence in American Cinema before 1939

POLAND, RETURNED TO THE MAP at the end of the First World War, mattered little to the United States after 1918. This was true in both political and cultural matters. American films reflected this lack of interest. Indeed, the Polish population in the United States was also largely an unknown community to the American public, who regarded this newly created minority group with a mixture of disdain and indifference. It is not surprising that few films produced in the silent era or later in the 1930s featured Polish themes or explored the lives of Polish immigrants to America. The relative insignificance of the Polish presence was in contrast to the considerable attention devoted to other large ethnic groups.

A few Poles enjoyed brief careers in Hollywood. None—with one exception—were identifiable as Poles.[1] Marianna Michalska and Apolonia Chałupiec, both born in Poland, were stars of the silent screen under the pseudonyms Gilda Gray and Pola Negri, but neither enjoyed a long career.[2] This was particularly unfortunate for the Poles as regarded Negri, who, for all her notorious personal behavior, was outspokenly patriotic and cultivated the Polish community in America. In 1923, for example, five years after Poland was restored to independence, she placed a wreath at the monument to Polish national hero Tadeusz Kościuszko in Chicago, to the delight of the local Poles. She announced, "I have come here not seeking personal acclaim or fortune, but to bring glory to our people. I wish to contribute however insignificantly to the renown of our reborn beloved Fatherland." Later she was the benefactor of a Polish Roman Catholic parish in Texas. In the 1930s she refused to perform in a German film because she regarded it as insulting to Poland. Briefly she was the highest-paid actress in Hollywood; in a few years in the mid-1920s, she earned a reported $6 million.[3] Never before or since did a Pole combine such popularity and power in Hollywood with such open devotion to her country.[4] However, her career in Hollywood was over by the 1930s.

Gilda Gray's Hollywood years were also very short; she had a few major roles in the 1920s that were huge box office successes. However, she suffered a heart attack and went bankrupt in the next few years, effectively ending her career, which included only one additional film in 1936. During World War II, she dedicated herself to the Polish cause and was decorated for her efforts to raise money. As a Hollywood figure, however, she had already disappeared.[5] Even briefer was the career of Warsaw-born Estelle Clarke (Stanisława Zwoliński). Though she made ten films, with increasingly large roles, between 1924 and 1928, her career ended that year, when she was twenty-nine.

The life of Lyda Roberti (daughter of a Polish mother and a German father, both circus performers) was tragic. Born in Warsaw but raised in Shanghai and other exotic locales, she had a precocious career culminating as a talented and popular comedy actress in Hollywood. In at least two of her roles, she apparently played Polish characters: *Dancers in the Dark* (Paramount, 1932) and *George White's 1935 Scandals* (Fox, 1935). She is perhaps best known for an inspired comic creation, Mata Machree, of uncertain ethnicity, in the eccentric 1932 Paramount comedy *Million Dollar Legs.* However, bending to tie her shoe, she died of heart failure in 1938. Barely out of her twenties, she had been, after a series of successful films, at the peak of her career.[6]

A career also foreshortened by tragedy was that of Miliza Korjus (Korcjusz).[7] She was born in Warsaw in 1909 of Lithuanian-Polish noble stock (Gintowt) on her mother's side; her father's family was Estonian. She spent her childhood in Soviet Ukraine but defected as a teenager to Estonia in 1927. On the basis of a brief sojourn in Germany, she was later billed in Hollywood as the "Berlin Nightingale." A gifted coloratura soprano, she made a fine impression in her first film, MGM's major 1938 release *The Great Waltz,* and was nominated for an Oscar for best supporting actress. Signed for a major role in a new film with Robert

Taylor and Hedy Lamarr, she was grievously injured in an automobile accident just before the film was to be shot. She spent the war years in Mexico for obscure reasons and never resumed a career that had started spectacularly. In any event, by the outbreak of World War II, she was another very youthful Polish has-been whose Hollywood career was a single film. Her contribution to the Polish presence in Hollywood was further diminished because Korjus was usually regarded as an Estonian, despite her place of birth and her mother's family.[8]

Raised by her Polish mother after being abandoned by her Norwegian father, Carole Landis appeared in several films in the late 1930s, including a very minor role in *The Emperor's Candlesticks,* which was set in Poland. One of the legendary screen beauties, she managed to reach minor stardom but died by her own hand at twenty-nine after her career failed during World War II after a few notable films. She was probably the best-known actress of Polish descent during the World War II years.[9] However, she was from an impoverished background, and her tumultuous personal life and series of film failures prevented her from becoming an established figure. The facts that she performed under a pseudonym and that her birth name was Norwegian also attenuated her connection to Polonia.[10]

Jean Parker occupies a similar niche in the history of Poles in Hollywood. Born in 1915 in rural Montana as Lois Zelinska, the child of a Polish-French marriage, Parker was raised by foster parents not of Polish origin. A multitalented young woman, she was an accomplished artist and student of Sanskrit. In a long career, she made several dozen films, often in starring roles, particularly in Poverty Row productions, in which she did much of her work. Beautiful and vivacious, Jean Parker was not associated with the Polish community, and her ethnic ancestry was disguised beneath layers of false biographies that she or the studios devised. Because of her childhood circumstances, it seems doubtful that she retained any loyalty to her Polish origins.[11]

Hardly tragic, though still brief, was the American screen career of the operatic tenor Jan Kiepura.[12] Although he had a beautiful voice and considerable charm, he was quite wooden as an actor, and he spoke very little English. Each of his several pre-1939 films was merely a series of arias loosely held together by an insignificant script. Although several of his European films were released in the United States—where they were distributed by Gaumont British Picture Corporation of America—

only the obscure 1936 release *Give Us This Night* was a completely American production.[13] Kiepura was usually cast as an Italian to comply with the ethnic stereotype of a singer. Though Kiepura had rather little exposure to wider American audiences, he was known to Polish audiences as both a Pole and a patriot, and he long enjoyed a devoted following as a result.

Beyond any doubt, the most successful film career of any American Pole was that of Tom Tyler, born in 1903 as Wincenty Markowski in a small village in upstate New York but raised in heavily Polish Hamtramck, Michigan.[14] Tyler was a handsome man of titanic strength, a boxer and Olympic weightlifter who was billed in his youth as the strongest man in the United States. He spoke with a heavy Polish accent early in his career and overcame it only with some difficulty. Tyler played in over two hundred films, often as a cowboy, in which role he unfailingly was given an Irish name, probably one of the reasons his true nationality remained unknown to the public. He worked for many studios, primarily the denizens of Poverty Row, and was uniformly badly paid. His powerful physique explained his casting as Captain Marvel in the eponymous serial of 1941 and later as both the Phantom and the dreaded Mummy. Tyler's legendary strength failed him in the late 1940s, when he was stricken with rheumatoid arthritis and rapidly became crippled. He died penniless and forgotten in Hamtramck at fifty, on the eve of the Polish national holiday, May 3. Ironically, shortly before he died, Tyler's "fame began to soar" because his old films were appearing frequently on television, but, as his obituaries noted, he gained nothing from them, as he had "neglected to buy the rights to his old pictures."[15]

Tom Tyler was briefly an American matinee idol, but few knew of his Polish origins, and he seems not to have associated himself with Polish causes in the United States or with Polonia in general. Never a serious actor, Tyler was primarily an action hero in inexpensive productions or a secondary player in more lavish releases. It is characteristic of Hollywood that in his many screen roles, he never portrayed a Pole.[16] Many aspects of his biography are very sketchy, and even his nationality is occasionally misreported as Lithuanian.[17] Tyler, like so many other Polish performers in Hollywood, did nothing to increase the visibility of his nationality.

Even more egregious health problems severely limited the career of Robert Donat, one of the most celebrated actors in film history despite his appearing in only a handful of films.[18] Born in Manchester, England, to a Polish immigrant father, Donat was always in fragile health, which prevented him from appearing in many films despite his uniformly outstanding performances. Virtually all of Donat's roles were in British productions. He visited Hollywood briefly and appeared in only one film produced there, Universal's 1934 *The Count of Monte Cristo.* Hence one can scarcely speak of Donat as a Hollywood Pole, though he certainly was a major star. In the United States he was regarded as archetypically English, and his Polish origins were not known. It is perhaps not a coincidence that in one of his greatest roles, the romantic hero of Hitchcock's 1935 masterpiece *The 39 Steps,* Donat's character resides at Poland Place.[19]

We may well add to this list the name of John Gielgud, scion of a distinguished eastern Polish family. A celebrated Shakespearean actor, Gielgud is another figure whose Polish ancestry is not widely known. Unlike Donat, Gielgud did not appear in any American productions before 1945.

Beyond these we have minor players only, and not many of them. Edward Kucharski was born in Warsaw in 1900 and made a number of films in the interwar years and even later. For some reason he billed himself as "Raquello" and often portrayed Latinos or Italians. (Of what nationality someone named Raquello might be is a good question, but Polish is not a candidate.) His pictures were unimportant and his roles less so, peaking with the major role of Emilio Cervantes in the embarrassing 1928 film *South of Panama* by the forgotten Chesterfield Motion Picture Corporation. By the 1930s, working for larger studios, the best he could do was such roles as "Rodolfo, who bets with El Rayo" in RKO's very low budget *The Girl and the Gambler.* By the outbreak of the war, his career was over, though he was still quite young.

By the late 1930s, Michal Mazurkiewicz from Tarnopol, in southeastern Poland, began a long career playing thugs and criminals. A huge, homely professional wrestler, Mazurkiewicz acted under the name Mike Mazurki in many films almost until his death in 1990. Though usually cast as a loutish villain, Mazurkiewicz was well educated and something of an intellectual. Before World War II he had only very small parts, and he never became a major player, though his roles grew after 1945. There is much confusion about his nationality because he was born before Poland regained its independence in 1918, and his birthplace was incorporated into the Soviet Union after World War II. As a result he was almost never referred to as a Pole. Sources inevitably garble his name and refer to him as Austrian, Hungarian, Ukrainian, or Russian.

John Hodiak, born in Pittsburgh of a Ukrainian father and a Polish mother, played in only two major films during the war (1944's *Lifeboat* and 1945's *A Bell for Adano*). He had a number of major parts later, though his film career was interrupted by several years when he concentrated on the stage, where he displayed considerable talent. Unfortunately he died young, ending a promising career. Tall, handsome, and athletic, Hodiak was one of the very few actors of Polish origin to play romantic leads. He may be the best-known Polish actor of the war era, and he was certainly the only star whose ethnicity was obvious because of his Slavic name.

Janina Walasek, born in Chicago in 1923 to Polish immigrant parents, appeared in four films during the war years. In three of these her role was uncredited, and in the fourth she was called only a "Louisiana Belle." Thereafter she became a minor star under the name Jean Wallace. She was surrounded by coincidental Polish attachments: Her first husband, the near-star Franchot Tone, was widely misreported to be of Polish origin as well, probably because his real first name was Stanislas.[20] Years later, Wallace married Cornel Wilde, who played the part of the Pole Chopin in the 1944 MGM film *A Song to Remember.* Wilde, of Hungarian origin, was also not a Pole. These are but curiosities, however.

Turning from actors to directors, Ryszard Bolesławski (Bolesław Ryszard Średnicki), a former Polish cavalryman, directed a handful of major films, but he died in 1932. Bolesławski had produced an early Polish documentary chronicling the victory over Soviet Russia in 1920 (*Cud nad Wisłą*). He arrived in Hollywood in 1929 after a brief sojourn in Germany. Within a few years, Bolesławski not only directed a number of important films but also published a series of books. Among these are two volumes of memoirs, which discuss his extraordinary military adventures in combat against the Russians and reveal Bolesławski as an ardent Polish patriot. Among his major films were *Les Miserables* (1934) with Frederic March, *The Garden of Allah* (1935) with Charles Boyer and Marlene Dietrich—one of the first color films—*Men in White* (1934) with Clark Gable, and *The Painted Veil*

(1934) with Greta Garbo. He was a major established figure when he died in his forties.[21]

His countryman Ryszard Ordyński was a highly acclaimed pioneer director in Poland before World War II who was responsible for such important films as *Pan Tadeusz* (1928) and the superb 1928 documentary film *Sztandar wolności* (The Standard of Freedom). Ordyński had been in the United States during World War I, where he served as stage director for the New York Metropolitan Opera and was deeply involved in patriotic and relief work for Poland. He returned in the 1920s to his native land.[22] No longer young when he again found himself in America as a refugee during World War II, he had a very minor Hollywood career indeed, consisting almost exclusively of invisibly small character parts and service as a technical adviser.

Poland had no major artistic figure in Hollywood during the war years, 1939–1945, although there had been some in the earlier decades and would be again in the postwar years. There were, however, a great many Polish Jews in Hollywood, including Jack and Harry Warner (from central Poland), Samuel Goldwyn (born in Warsaw as Szmuel Gelbfisz), and Louis B. Mayer (from near Minsk in the eastern borderlands, an area now in Belarus), as well as "German" director Ernst Lubitsch (whose family was from Grodno, in eastern Poland).[23] The list includes such major stars as Paul Muni (born Mehilen Weisenfreund in Lwów, Austrian Poland), Al Jolson (born in the northeastern borderlands of historic Poland as Asa Joelson), and Illinois-born Jack Benny. To these we may add a large number of minor players like Maurice Cass from Wilno, Leo White from Grudziądz, Jesse de Vorska from Kowno, Kurt Katch from Grodno, George E. Stone from Łódź, Alexander Granach from Galicia, and Baruch Lumet, Freddie Rich, Camille Astor, Anna Held, and Marek Windheim from Warsaw.[24] Molly Picon, who was better known for her work in the Yiddish theater, also had a number of films to her credit. Her father was from Warsaw. These actors appeared in scores of films. None of them, however, seem to have associated themselves with the Polish community in America or stressed their attachment to Poland after 1918.[25] This is a complicated theme we shall address later.

Whereas films about Poland or the Polish community in America were exceedingly rare, there were many films with a rather powerful Russian theme. Hollywood was fascinated with Cossacks and revolutionaries.[26] Early in the silent era, such veterans of the Russian stage as Alla Nazimova attracted a devoted following and were much admired for their training and technical prowess.[27] Soon after, Hollywood began producing a large number of films devoted to the tsarist era or to the Russian Revolution. This trend crested in 1928 when MGM released a major film, *The Cossacks,* based on the Tolstoy novel, that cost almost a million dollars—then an enormous sum—and employed a great many Russians.[28] This was merely the most significant of what a Russian émigré referred to a "downpour" of films about Russia being produced by Hollywood.[29] Jeff Peck has even discerned a genre of "heroic Russian films" in the 1920s that emphasize the attractive qualities of the Russian people and feature a sympathetic Russian as the main character.[30] Hollywood, before World War II, had created a Russian type that populated many films and was a part of the variety expected by viewers.[31] Moreover, many of these Russian roles were played by Russians whose nationality was public knowledge.

Indeed, a large number of Russians worked throughout the industry, and several had long careers, albeit usually as minor players. Perhaps the best known of these who were still active in the World War II era are Mischa Auer, Maria Ouspenskaya, the aging veteran Nazimova, Leonid Kinskey, Akim Tamiroff, Michael Chekhov, Mikhail Rozumny, Michael Visaroff, and Vladimir Sokoloff.[32] Whereas none were performers of the first rank, they appeared in many films, and Chekhov, Tamiroff, and Auer were all nominated for Academy Awards. Olga Baclanova, from Moscow, was a minor star in the 1930s.[33] So large was the Russian presence in American films that the *New York Times* reported, erroneously as it turned out, that there were no fewer than fifteen hundred Russian émigrés in Hollywood.[34]

In the 1930s American recognition of the Soviet Union prompted a sudden interest in Soviet films. Frank Capra, Cecil B. DeMille, and Lewis Milestone (himself a Russian émigré) were among the directors who wanted to experiment with Soviet themes, stories, and cinema styles. The celebrated director Sergei Eisenstein briefly worked in Hollywood (for Paramount in 1929–1930), further enhancing the prestige of Russian cinema. A number of rather large projects were under way in the 1930s, though none were ever realized. Nonetheless, at least eleven more "Russian" films were released in the 1930s.[35] Hence, Brian D. Harvey writes, there was a "longer trajectory" behind the pro-Soviet

Hollywood propaganda films of World War II, based on decades of Russian themes and actors later complemented by a fascination with Soviet cinema.[36] Hollywood thus had a well-developed tradition of favorable and sympathetic depictions of Russians to utilize when it embarked on its wartime celebration of the Soviet Union.[37]

By 1939 there was a virtual Russian network in Hollywood, including many actors and such studio chieftains as producer Gregory Ratoff and director Milestone. This was convenient. For example, the émigré actor Michael Chekhov had a job waiting for him when he arrived in Hollywood thanks to the intervention of Ratoff and composer Sergei Rachmaninoff. Chekhov, in turn, quickly established a popular acting class frequented by many major players.[38]

Although many of the Hollywood Russians derived from an earlier, anti-Communist emigration, after 1941 the war did a great deal to submerge old political divisions. Events held at the Soviet Consulate in Los Angeles or designed to raise money for the Red Army were attended by old émigrés in a show of Russian patriotism transcending differences. The fact that after 1941 the Soviet Union was widely and correctly regarded as playing the principal role in defeating Nazi Germany understandably endeared it to the many Jews in the industry despite their established misgivings about Communism and distaste for traditional Russian anti-Semitism.[39] "American Jews," writes Novick, "were the Red Army's greatest cheerleaders during the war."[40] For the Poles who knew what the Red Army had done to the Poles, this was appalling.

During the war, films about Russia often had huge numbers of ethnic Russians portraying characters of their own nationality. For example, *Song of Russia* (MGM, 1944) featured at least thirty actors born in Russia. By contrast, even the few Polish characters Hollywood presented were almost never portrayed by Poles. Long before World War II, both Hollywood and the American public were far more familiar with Russians and Russia, no matter how depicted, than with Poland and the Poles—including the Poles in America. Poland was a virtual terra incognita.[41] In 1943 Warner Brothers claimed that it had difficulty in rendering a putative Warsaw street scene because the studio was unsure what Poles looked like.[42]

Hollywood's fascination with the Russians may be explained by the fact that they represented a major world power, though they were a very small minority in the United States. However, of all the major European immigrant communities to arrive in turn-of-the-century America—the Irish, the Jews, the Italians, and the Poles—it is only the last group that was ignored by Hollywood.

After the mid-1920s, there was a flood of films about the Irish in America; there is nothing comparable regarding any other ethnic group. *The Shamrock and the Rose* (1927), *Underworld* (1927), *The Racket* (1928), *Smiling Irish Eyes* (1929), *Clancy at the Bat* (1929), *O'Malley Rides Alone* (1930), *Clancy in Wall Street* (1930), *The Public Enemy* (1931), *The Last Mile* (1932), *Me and My Girl* (1932), *Clancy of the Mounted* (1933), *King Kelly of the USA* (1934), *Irish Hearts* (1934), *The Irish in Us* (1935), *We're Only Human* (1935), *Princess O'Hara* (1935), *Dublin in Brass* (1935), *The Irish Gringo* (1936), *O'Malley of the Mounted* (1936), *Boulder Dam* (1936), *San Francisco* (1936), *Irish for Luck* (1936), *Kelly of the Secret Service* (1936), *Kelly the Second* (1936), *Rose Bowl* (1936; also released as *O'Riley's Luck*), *Youth on Parole* (1937), *Clancy in Wall Street* (1937), *The Great O'Malley* (1937), *Irish and Proud of It* (1938), *Sergeant Murphy* (1938), *In Old Chicago* (1938), *Irish Luck* (1939), *Torchy Blane . . . Playing with Dynamite* (1939), *Three Cheers for the Irish* (1940), *Knute Rockne All-American* (1940), *Bullets for O'Hara* (1941), and *Ride, Kelly, Ride* (1941)—each of these films, produced by Hollywood in the years before Pearl Harbor, depicts an Irish main character or is substantially devoted to the Irish in America, often with a cast heavily composed of Irish actors. This is not an exhaustive list; it omits shorts, serial episodes, and many releases by minor studios. But, among other things, it demonstrates the large number of Irish performers available to cast.

Irish films were a major genre; indeed the Irish were the most prominently featured ethnic minority in America. Unlike Italians, who are often portrayed as thugs and gangsters, the Irish characters are usually cast in a sentimental and charming light or as admirable figures, like policemen, athletes, and witty reporters. Roman Catholic clergy are almost exclusively Irish in films.

There seems little doubt that the Irish were the favorite "other" ethnic for the heavily Jewish motion picture studios of the prewar era. Indeed, Stuart Samuels concludes from the large number of Irish-Jewish films that "the Jews felt" that, "to 'make it' in America," they had to "change their name and to marry the Irish girl or boy next door," and they made films symbolically conjuring this vision.[43] Stephen J. Whitfield observes that "the Irish represented the ethnic group at whom the Jewish hunger for acceptance was most often directed."[44] Certainly the Irish were the only Catholic community frequently and almost always positively presented. This tradition of regular and prominent Irish roles continued during the war years, in which hardly any film failed to feature at least one Irish character, often in a leading and heroic role. Hollywood treated the Irish with enormous and flattering attention.[45]

This phenomenon is easy to explain. Most important, the Irish came earlier to the United States and arrived in larger numbers than did the Poles. They also had the considerable advantage of speaking English. The Irish played a major role in vaudeville, which later was translated into Broadway and radio. Vaudeville had been replete with both Irish performers—the Four Cohans are merely a convenient example—and Irish-Jewish combinations, of which Gallagher and Shean is the best known. By comparison the Poles, like the Italians, both members of a later immigrant wave, did not have an established role in American entertainment culture by the dawn of the motion picture age. Vaudeville's ethnic tradition did not include Poles.[46] Films were just another step for the Irish along a path virtually untrodden by Poles.

With the film age came a well organized and ultimately effective Irish campaign against what they regarded as Hollywood's derogatory presentation of Irish Catholics in America. The effort, which crested in the late 1920s, led to the decision by Hollywood to establish the Production Code, which was written by two Irish Catholics, and enforced by another, the anti-Semitic Joseph I. Breen.[47] Although the issue is often presented as a compromise between Hollywood and Catholic America, this is rather misleading. The major force that convinced Hollywood to concede to this organized censorship was an almost exclusively Irish lobby.[48] A particular target of Irish animosity was the Warner Brothers studio, which epitomized the "'Jewish Trust' hell-bent on destroying the Irish."[49] In Hollywood after 1930, propitiating the Catholics became in effect patronizing the Irish. Before the late 1920s, Hollywood had occasionally portrayed the Irish as drunks and hooligans; that changed markedly thereafter. Other Catholic communities in America, the Italians and Poles for example, only much later launched efforts to defend their communities' image; both were insignificant. The Irish in America were able to use their dominant position in the Catholic Church to force

Hollywood to a lasting and very rewarding compromise.[50] Michael Freedland, the Warners' biographer, notes that Jack's most frequent concern about a film was "What would the Catholics say?"[51] Functionally that became, What would the Irish say?

This sensitivity was accompanied by a notion that the Irish were peculiarly sympathetic to Jews because they had similarly experienced racial and religious persecution, which became axiomatic in Hollywood.[52] Lester D. Friedman notes that "Hollywood, from its earliest days, happily paired the Jews and the Irish" and cites a popular slogan in the industry: "The sun cannot shine in Ireland when it's raining in Jerusalem."[53]

During World War II, efforts by the Polish community to protest what it regarded as Hollywood's insulting treatment of Poles were little more than a minor nuisance to the studios. The Italians, stigmatized by Mussolini's alliance with Hitler, were silent. Hollywood continued its established pro-Irish tradition increasingly reinforced by inertia. If "the representation of ethnicity" in films reflected "power," the Poles would be invisible.[54] Ana M. Lopez argues that ethnic groups had a "golden moment" in Hollywood when film become "temporarily more sensitive" to them.[55] The Poles are an exception.

Indeed, there is a subgenre of Irish-Jewish film in which both ethnic groups are featured in comic but affectionate juxtaposition. These Irish-Jewish stories are symbolic reconciliation films for two major immigrant groups, with the Catholic community represented exclusively by the Irish.[56] The "Jewish boy falls in love with Irish girl" story is frequently and symbolically repeated.[57] There is no equivalent Italian-Jewish or Polish-Jewish subgenre.[58] With the Irish functioning as the representatives of all Catholics in America, non-Irish Catholics were reduced to insignificance. The best-known example of the reconciliation subgenre is *The Cohens and Kellys* series of seven films released in the late 1920s and early 1930s, but there were a number of others, many from the silent era. D. W. Griffith alone was responsible for several of these in the pre–World War I years. Later the trend continued, even increasing, including such films as *Second Hand Rose* (1922), *Fool's Highway* (1924), *The Rag Man* (1925), *Old Clothes* (1925), *One of the Bravest* (1925), *Sweet Daddies* (1926), *Izzy and Lizzie* (1926), *Clancy's Kosher Wedding* (1927), *Sally in Our Alley* (1927), *Sweet Rosie O'Grady* (1927), *A Harp in Hock* (1927), *For the Love of Mike* (1927),

Frisco Sally Levy (1927), the often remade *Abie's Irish Rose* (1928), *Kosher Kitty Kelly* (1926), *Pleasure before Business* (1927), *Around the Corner* (1930), *Princess O'Hara* (1935), and two George Jessel vehicles, *Private Izzy Murphy* and *Sailor Izzy Murphy*. Perhaps the ultimate exemplar of this theme is Irish Jimmy Cagney bursting into Yiddish in 1932's *Taxi!*[59] Samuels observes that the number of films of this genre is "staggering."[60]

Compared to the omnipresence of the Irish in Hollywood films, Jewish characters were rarer in major roles, though very frequently portrayed. *The Jazz Singer* (1927) is a famous example. We should note that in this film the cantor, Rabinowitz, becomes enamored of an Irish girl (May McAvoy as Mary Dale). Nonetheless the number of films devoted to the Jews is very large, and they are almost without exception sympathetic. There were a considerable number of silent films with Jewish themes and characters, and then an explosion occurred in the 1920s, when, according to one scholar's count, there were ninety-five Jewish portrayals.[61] Jewish characters are significant cast members, or there are multiple lesser Jewish characters, in a great many films: *Love 'Em and Feed 'Em* (1927), *Why Girls Say No* (1927), *Cheaters* (1927), *Sunshine of Paradise Alley* (1927), *The Shamrock and the Rose* (1927), *The Last Parade* (1931), *Symphony for Six Million* (1931), *Cimarron* (1931), *Women of All Nations* (1931), *The Spider* (1931), *Are You Listening?* (1932), *Blessed Event* (1932), *Hypnotized* (1932), *The World Gone Mad* (1933), *Pilgrimage* (1933), *Girls' Dormitory* (1936), *Roamin' Wild* (1936), *The Little Red Schoolhouse* (1936), *Star for a Night* (1936), *Make Way for Tomorrow* (1937), *That I May Live* (1937), *Our Daily Bread* (1937), *George White's 1935 Scandals* (1935), *23½ Hours Leave* (1937), *Man of the People* (1937), and *Gateway* (1938). There are doubtless others.[62] Although the characters may not be referred to as Jewish in the scripts, they are given names like Solomon Levy, Mr. Chutzpah, and Cherokee Cohen and are portrayed almost exclusively by Jewish émigré actors from Central and Eastern Europe who speak (after the silent era) with strong accents.

In addition to these Jewish characters scattered about, we have specific films in which Jews or Jewish settings are fundamental to the story. These include the several Irish-Jewish films mentioned earlier as well as *Jewish Prudence* (1927), *Don't Tell Everything* (1927), *Jake the Plumber* (1927), *The Ghetto* (1928), *Jazz Mad* (1928), *The*

Younger Generation (1929), *Around the Corner* (1930), *Uptown New York* (1932), and, perhaps most prominent, the affectionate evocation of the Jewish Lower East Side in Warner Brothers' *The Heart of New York* (1932), as well as the hagiographic historical epic by Twentieth Century *The House of Rothschild* (1934). There were two biographies of Disraeli (1921 and 1929), and even a film called *George Washington Cohen* in 1928. We should also note the production *Dr. Ehrlich's Magic Bullet,* which was released just after the war began in 1940, among several others. In sum, identifiably Jewish characters appeared in scores of Hollywood productions before World War II, and there were a number of films about Jews and Jewish themes. None of these films portray them in a negative light.

The relatively large number of Jewish films reflects the facts that the Jewish immigration to the United States preceded the Polish arrival by perhaps a generation and that the Jews—like the Irish—quickly established themselves in the entertainment industry. Later immigrants, Eastern and Southern Europeans, arrived at a time when certain ethnic types were already created by vaudeville, Broadway, and later radio. Hence they did not figure in the pre–motion picture world of popular culture. There were no Polish equivalents of the Marx brothers, Al Jolson, Eddie Cantor, Burns and Allen, or Jack Benny. The Yiddish theater also acted as a link to the American stage for Jews. Karen Majewski, in a pioneering study, shows that a Polish-American literature did develop to impressive dimensions among the immigrants, but it was a parochial culture that did not escape the ethnic community.[63] The Irish and the Jews, by comparison, made successful transitions to a wider American presence. As Albert McClean notes, films were "not prepared to initiate the Italian or the Slav directly into the American way of life."[64] There was no Polish stereotype in entertainment that film could inherit.

Among the turn-of-the-century immigrants, the Italians are a much more frequent presence than the Poles, though still insignificant compared to the Irish and Jews. Certainly, it took many decades for the *Godfather* genre to make the Italians a major ethnic presence in film, but already during the silent film era, Italians were featured in an "impressive number" of films. George Beban virtually made a career of Italian roles in a series of early releases.[65] Carlos E. Cortés has discovered quite a number of Italian films from the silent era, a few condescending, but others, like *The Italian* (1914), sympathetic.[66] Luis Alberni, born in

Catalonia, played no fewer than forty-three roles as an Italian (often named Luigi).[67] Thus Alberni alone accounts for more Italian characters in prewar Hollywood films than all the Polish characters in all prewar Hollywood films combined.[68] But Alberni was not alone; there were several actors who repeatedly appeared as Italians: Harry Semels, for example, who also occasionally played Jewish characters, and J. Carrol Naish, who played at least seven Italian roles in the 1930s alone.[69] We should not forget that one of the Marx brothers, Chico, was presented as an Italian in the comedies he and his brothers produced in the 1930s. Positive, if minor, roles for "Italians," often employing heavy accents and much gesticulation, were thus a commonplace in prewar Hollywood.[70]

Though negative Italians appeared in a few post–World War I films,[71] *Song of the City* (1937) is set among the Italian community of San Francisco, which is portrayed affectionately. *Winterset* (1936) also focuses on the Italians in America, though it is rather darker. The main characters are Italian in *The Bride Wore Red* (1938), *Love, Live, and Laugh* (1929), *A Lady to Love* (1930), *Street Scene* (1931), and *Kid Galahad* (1937). In the latter there is even an extended scene in which the characters converse in Italian. A similar theme, Italians in boxing, is the theme of *Golden Boy* (1939) and of *East of the River* (1940), which featured a great many putative Italians.[72] *They Knew What They Wanted* (1940) is a touching portrayal of a noble Italian farmer (Charles Laughton, perhaps strangely cast) in California.[73] *The Florentine Dagger* (1938) is set, appropriately, in Florence. Other films set in Italy include *The White Sister* (1923, remade in 1933) and *The Wages of Virtue* (1924).

Beyond this, there were leading Italian characters, albeit of a negative sort, in the spate of crime films that made Italians regular Hollywood players in the 1930s.[74] Even the Italian-as-gangster film, however, usually included other Italians who were more admirable or even portrayed the gangsters as "basically decent people who chose criminality out of frustration over the apparent obstacles to legitimately-attained success."[75] The Italian characters were not always the positive figures that the Irish and Jewish characters were, but they were a visible part of the American scene.

Hence audiences became used to ethnic characters sprinkled about, but even in films that for obvious reasons wish to emphasize the ethnic variety of the country, Poles are conspicuously absent. Examples of this are numerous. The Warner Brothers crime comedy *A Slight Case of Murder* (1938) is dominated by the villainous (yet lovable) Italian mobster Marco and his henchman Giuseppe, joined by characters named Rosenbloom and Cohen and also Gallagher and Ryan. Ironically, a minor part in the film is played by the Polish Carole Landis, but her character is known only as "the blonde" and has no indicated ethnicity. *I Hate Women* (1934), by obscure Goldsmith Productions, features a leading character named McGuire and lesser players Casey and Flanagan, joined by a Cohen. There are, again, no Poles. *High Pressure* (1932), a Warner Brothers film, features an Irishman (Mike Donahay), an Italian (Colombo), a Jew (Colonel Ginsburg), and even a Greek (Poppolus), but no Poles. The cast of the 1937 MGM exploration of urban corruption, *Man of the People,* is almost exclusively supposed Irish and Italians with a Jewish character or two. In 1938 Paramount released another of the crime-comedy films, *You and Me,* featuring every imaginable urban ethnic type, including a Mr. and Mrs. Abie Levine and even a character identified as a Swede. Again, neither film contains Poles, even in the most minor roles. The Twentieth Century–Fox service film *Sub Patrol* (1938), directed by the Irish John Ford, features a heavily Irish crew (Quincannon, Haggerty, McPeek, McAllison, Duffy, and Kelly) but also a Goldfarb, a Luigi, and an Olaf. There are, however, no Central or Eastern Europeans at all.

Crime films, so popular in the 1930s, were usually heavily ethnic. United Artists' famous gangster film *Scarface* (1932), for example, is replete with Italian characters. Ironically, they were played by a Polish Jew (Paul Muni), a Czech (Anna Dvorak), and a German (George Raft), among others, and the film also has a Jewish character, Epstein. Both the gangsters and the police in Warner Brothers' *Public Enemy* (1931) are mostly Irish, with one possibly Jewish character (Nails Nathan).[76] Edward G. Robinson's career-launching *Little Caesar* (Warner Brothers, 1931) was largely a matter of Italian thugs and Irish police, but it had a Russian (Olga Strassoff) added for variety. Republic's slapdash gangster saga *The Return of Jimmy Valentine* (1936) has a large cast of characters, almost all Irish or Italian. Most of the inmates and their warders in both *The Racket* (1928) and *The Last Mile* (1932) are Irish or Italian, though a few other nationalities are depicted. However, no Poles are included in any of these films on either side of the law. In

Hollywood, it seems, Poles literally could not even get arrested.[77] This list, and this characterization, could be extended almost limitlessly. The absence of Polish images in the films of prewar Hollywood is striking.

The ethnic theme in American films visibly faded in the 1930s. The resurgence of nativism and pressure to assimilate played a considerable role, especially for an industry like Hollywood, in which the foreign-born constituted a large percentage of the workforce.[78] Organized anti-Semitism, both in Europe and in the United States, and the trepidation of Jewish studio moguls certainly explain the sudden decline in Jewish films by the mid-1930s.[79] Fascism in Italy probably contributed to the drop in Italian films, though the number here was always quite modest. Crime films, unusually urban and ethnic, also peaked in the mid-1930s and faded thereafter; as a result, fewer Italians were depicted. As Kracauer observes, the early period in which Russian films were quite positive, or at least nostalgic, was followed by a brief era in which the only Russian films were a handful satirizing the Soviets, *Comrade X* and *Ninotchka* being the best known.[80] As for the Poles, as we have seen, they never were a major theme for Hollywood, and this did not change.

Although the World War II period produced no films focused on the Polish, Italian, or Jewish community or its major figures, it did include *The Sullivans,* about Irish in the navy, and two films about the Irish in World War I (*The Fighting 69th* and *The Iron Major*), as well as biographies of two Irish American prizefighters, James J. Corbett (*Gentleman Jim*) and John L. Sullivan (*The Great John L*), the vaudevillian George M. Cohan (*Yankee Doodle Dandy*), the thug Roger Touhy (*Roger Touhy, Gangster*), the saloon keeper Mary Louise Cecilia "Texas" Guinan (*Incendiary Blonde*), and the aviator "Wrong Way" Corrigan (*The Flying Irishman*), among others. This is in addition to the endless production of Irish-themed fictional films.

One of the major reasons for the absence of Polish themes in wartime American films is that there was no tradition of such depictions from the preceding era. Polish observers of film were concerned about the virtual absence of Poland, Poles, and Polish themes from the world's cinema, especially Hollywood productions. Things Polish rarely appeared, and when they did they were often presented inaccurately, unflatteringly, or incomprehensibly. Warsaw film commentator Jerzy Bossak wrote exasperatedly in 1938, "In these circumstances the Polish theme in foreign films frequently takes the form of propaganda directed against Poland and the Poles. Consciously and targeted libels do less damage than a film made without hostile intention which makes its way around the globe propagating everywhere its irresponsible ignorance."[81] Hence it is important to consider the very few exceptions in the pre-1939 era. The Polish motif in Hollywood consists of only a handful of examples. Films devoted to Poland are almost nonexistent. The Polish community in America is the focus of a few films, but even here Poles are usually treated marginally or their nationality is ambiguous.[82] Whereas there are Jews, Irish, and Italians in films, the Poles, to use Ella Shohat's expression, were "subject to homogenization."[83]

Probably the only major silent film to feature Poles was the 1924 D. W. Griffith melodrama *Isn't Life Wonderful.*[84] Although usually described as the saga of Polish refugees trying desperately to survive in Berlin after World War I, the film is really not about Poles at all.[85] To be sure, the refugees have arrived from Poland, but they are almost certainly to be understood as Germans leaving Poland. Not one has a Polish name, a picture of the kaiser is featured in the family home, and all seem to speak German. Of course, why Poles would seek refuge in Germany at a time of intense Polish-German antagonism is the most obvious question. Only a slightly ridiculous traveling entertainer who boards with the family refers to himself as having performed in Poland; that is the limit of the main characters' Polish credentials. Hence, even in what is probably the most significant silent film devoted to Poles, there are probably no Poles at all.

Perhaps the earliest sound film version of the ambiguous Polish presence is the 1934 *Palooka,* released by Reliance Pictures and distributed by United Artists, based on the long-running comic strip by Ham Fisher.[86] Palooka is a huge and rather slow-witted farm boy who becomes heavyweight boxing champion. Though cloddish, he is kind and gentle and, on balance, a positive character. The film mentions nothing about Palooka's ethnicity; nonetheless, his name suggests Eastern European origin, as it approximates "Pakula," a not uncommon Polish surname, particularly for Polish Jews. Curiously, in both the original comic strip and the 1934 film, Palooka is fair and blond, unlike the usual later Hollywood Pole, who is short and swarthy. Wagner and Buhle contend that Palooka was understood to be Polish (even though they offer no proof for the assertion) and a rather demeaning reference at that, as Palooka was obviously intended to be a simpleton.[87] This is more than plausible, as Ham Fisher invented the original character on the basis of a "big, burly, and inarticulate boxer" he met outside a poolroom in his native Wilkes-Barre, Pennsylvania, home to a substantial community of Poles (and other immigrants). Fisher originally named the character Joe Dumbelletski, which tells us much of both what the character was to be and Fisher's taste.[88] Hence the prototype of the cinematic Palooka was probably supposed to be a Pole, perhaps the first "dumb Polack" stereotype that Hollywood later did so much to propagate. Though there were postwar screen versions of Palooka, during World War II he was exclusively a comic strip character after this 1934 release.[89]

Rather more serious is the 1935 Warner Brothers film *Black Fury,* set contemporaneously in the Pennsylvania coalfields.[90] Like a number of other Warner Brothers films of the era, it explores the pathetic lives of the underclass in America, here focusing on the poor wages, wretched conditions, and dangerous lives of the miners. Though a few of them are obviously supposed to be Irish, Italian, or African American, the bulk are vaguely Eastern European, though that term is very elastic for Warner Brothers.

The film was based on a combination of two literary properties. The first, a play titled *Bohunk: A Melodramatic Comedy,* was the work of Harry R. Irving in 1932.[91] Set in a squalid house in Pottsville, it is replete with Polish characters, all of them similarly primitive and repulsive. Mrs. Mancaweitz, for example, is charmingly described by Irving as "a Pole . . . masculine in a foreign way. A perfect slatternly type that has worked hard all her life."[92] However, although this creature and a few others are Poles, the hero is Joe Radek, a "stolid Hungarian" who quite clearly regards himself as superior to his fellow immigrants on the basis of his Magyar descent.[93] He is a charming ignoramus who prevails after a series of complex and windy scenes.

Warner Brothers also possessed another property, "Joe Volkanik," written by Judge M. A. Musmanno, which Warner Brothers immediately renamed "Black Hell."[94] This story, rather more serious than the Irving piece, is much less specific about the nationalities of the cast of generic Eastern Europeans. It begins with a long preamble about labor unrest and the dangers and privations endured by the miners. The protagonist, the volcanic Mr. Volkanik, "heavily built, stodgy," is a cheerful primitive who inadvertently injures his fellow miners through his "doltishness."[95]

Warner Brothers assigned Abem Finkel to combine these quite different sources into a script originally titled "Black Hell," the first draft of which was available by April 1934.[96] The main setting has become the home of a miner named Shemanski, probably a Pole but not specifically so identified. His boarder is Joe Radek, whose Hungarian nationality has not accompanied his name from the Irving script.[97] He now has no specific nationality at all. After several drafts Radek emerges as an ignorant and stupid though genial man. The story hinges on his cloddishness, which produces a major strike with accompanying violence, which he regrets and eventually, miraculously, rights.[98] He speaks an idiolect largely composed of mangled clichés. His culture is indicated by his wistful hope that "now maybe Annah and me go raise pigs and kids."[99]

By the fall of 1934, screenwriter Carl Erickson had joined Finkel, and the script gained sharper focus. Key action is set in Moravia Hall. The Novak family, which has a major role (Joe is infatuated with Annah Novak), is identified as Slovak.[100] No other characters have defined nationalities. However, the writers provided an ethnographic analysis of the population they sought to conjure: "In the faces of the miners we see the heterogeneous mixture of race and nationality which is characteristic of the Pennsylvania coal fields. Stolid, high-cheek-boned Poles; docile Lithuanians; and rugged, smiling Slovaks predominate. Interspersed with these are the swarthy, excitable Italian, and the meek, wide-eyed Negro. Here and there are some Nordic faces, mostly Welsh and Irish, descendants of the men who first worked these coal fields."[101]

Released in 1935 as *Black Fury,* the film starred Paul Muni as the generic Eastern European Joe Radek. Muni had a central role in the birth of the film: he had bought the rights to the Irving play and provided them to Warner Brothers.[102] Muni, a Polish Jew from Lwów, in Austrian Galicia, was a veteran of the Yiddish stage and came from a theatrical family.[103] Muni obviously regarded the Radek character he portrayed as a Pole. In preparing for the role, he dyed his dark hair blond and had the studio makeup artists provide him with what was described as "a typical 15-cent Pennsylvania coal-town haircut," achieved by fitting his head with a "cereal bowl." The result satisfied Muni, who announced, "That I guarantee you is a Polock, born and reborn."[104] We may assume that screenwriter Finkel shared Muni's conception of the character. Finkel was Muni's brother-in-law and owed his position at Warner Brothers to the actor's intervention. Finkel was known at the studio as "Muni's writer" because he would doctor scripts to suit the actor's fancy. It is thus inconceivable that Finkel would not adopt Muni's view that Radek was Polish.[105]

However, in the film, Radek's Polishness is ambiguous at best. The only references to nationality issues are Moravia Hall and a Slovak dance hall; there are no Polish locales. Muni twice sings ostensibly Slavic ditties, but they are virtually incomprehensible and include only a few Western Slavic words. His accent is not Polish but rather Czech or Slovak, as indicated by his tendency to pronounce names with initial rather than penultimate accentuation, the major phonological difference between Czech and Slovak on the one hand and Polish on the other. Indeed, despite Muni's rather crude reference about his appearance, a viewer would conclude that Radek is probably intended to be a Slovak for most of the film. This, however, is complicated by a sequence near the conclusion in which Muni beats a foul thug who has murdered his friend while repeatedly referring to him as a Cossack, an opprobrious reference that would be quite logical for a Pole but not at all for a Czech or Slovak.[106] The mining police refer to the miners generically as "Hunkies" and "Hunyaks"—vague terms of, it seems, ethnic-cum-occupational derision employed in more than one Warners Brothers film.[107]

Hence Paul Muni's Radek is perhaps meant to be a Polish character—certainly Muni saw him as that—but that is hardly clear to viewers.[108] It is noteworthy that the Slovak community in America was certain that Radek was intended to be one of their number. The contemporary Polish-language press does not seem to have made a similar claim for this dubious attribution.[109]

Black Fury is replete with Eastern Europeans, but they are not differentiated. Indeed, the story seems purposely to obfuscate nationality issues. Radek is on balance an ambiguous figure. He is a loyal friend with a primitive but real sense of decency and fairness. When sober, he behaves well and is liked and respected by his fellows. However, he is also crude and ignorant. He is reckless and easily manipulated, childlike in his simplicity. People like him could never be given positions of authority or responsibility. They must be led, controlled, and watched. Strong and tough, they are ideal for manual work but racially predestined for the lower orders. Muni—who often descended to gross overacting—played his role with a perpetual look of vacuity, frightened and disoriented when faced with even simple questions. As a reviewer noted, Muni rendered Radek an "inspired interpretation of the moronic Slav" with "physical Newfoundland dog roughness," exhibiting "the dull workings of his childlike mind."[110] *Black Fury* gives us a valuable insight into Hollywood's vision of the American Slav, including the Pole, in the 1930s. We also learn perhaps how Muni saw Poles, but that is a minor matter.

In the mid-1930s, there were two explorations of Poles in rural America. The 1934 Warner Brothers film *As the Earth Turns* was based on a novel by Maine localist Gladys Hasty Carroll.[111] This, her first novel, was both a popular and critical success, and Warner Brothers rushed it into production. The story is quite simple and rather tedious. A family of Poles—the Janowskis—takes possession of a dilapidated farm in rural Maine. The local population, though initially suspicious of such exotics, gradually learns to see them as hardworking and earnest, though most peculiar. The oldest son, Stan, wins the affection of Jen Shaw, the admirable daughter of an old Yankee family. The Janowskis decide to abandon their Maine farm for Boston. Stan, however, has developed a great love of farming and has decided to stay. He is virtually adopted by the Shaws, and, as the novel concludes, all the auguries are that Stan and Jen will soon wed and rural Maine will have assimilated a Pole with many fine qualities.[112]

Despite the fact that the Poles were a major element of her story, Carroll admittedly knew nothing about them, and her portrait of them is preposterous.[113] One of the Poles is named Manuel, a Spanish name; another is called Ondia, which Carroll concocted; and a third, a girl, is Marion, a version of which could only be a man's name in Polish.[114] The family is, apparently, traditionally in the garment business—which would have been highly unusual for Polish gentiles—but they decide to become farmers.[115] This notion is obviously necessary to show the Poles, an agricultural people, to be quite unfamiliar with basic farming techniques in their new setting. Although presumably Roman Catholic, they assimilate effortlessly into a Protestant milieu—not a reasonable assertion. The Polish characters have no identifiable characteristics except an inability to control themselves when music is played, unleashing primitive passions that cause them to jump about quite madly. They speak like vaudeville comedians (and never employ a single Polish word), except for Stan, who has neither accent nor residual Polish lexical elements. It is very important to the author to stress that all of them have "black eyes," in contrast to the blue-eyed Americans. Hence the children have "fat, dark . . . faces . . . with shoe-button eyes."[116] The only other thing we learn about the "Polocks" is that they are tough and powerful; their imperviousness to pain and suffering disconcerts the more civilized Americans.[117] Unfortunately, they are also quite stupid; hence Mrs. Janowski, though she is the mother of a large family, has no idea how to care for a sick child, and Jen, a mere girl, has to give her basic guidance.[118]

In addition to the Janowskis there is another Pole—there are vague allusions that he is Jewish—who, though loyal to his countrymen, is virtually a crook.[119] Though he is called Keele, his real name is "something unpronounceable," and the author suggests that his surname is so astounding that even he cannot remember it.[120] He is also named Manuel.[121]

Stan is obviously the key to the Poles' function in the story. He, inexplicably, has blue eyes, unlike his swarthy family, and the locals conclude that he does not "look much Polish."[122] He is assimilated into the community; the departure of his family is the symbolic extirpation of his Polish roots. He becomes an American by ceasing to be Polish. He is useful breeding stock for the melting pot; the others are jettisoned.

Warner Brothers, wishing to capitalize on the book's popularity, hurried production of the film version. A huge publicity effort accompanied the release in 1934, with a "special campaign" orchestrated from Chicago.[123] Warner Brothers stressed that this was to be a "realistic" film, one "with as little change as possible from the original text." As a result, "this film reflects Truth" and is a "bunkless picture" with "utter freedom from hokum." Indeed, Warner Brothers piously claimed that it cared not at all for the "entertainment" aspects of the film. To bear witness to its efforts, the studio distributed opinion cards in theater lobbies to compass viewers' reactions to their bunkless efforts.[124] This campaign attracted wide attention in the press, and the film was positively reviewed. Its debut in Dallas—an oddly chosen site—was much ballyhooed.[125]

Carroll was not pleased with the result. She was in Hollywood during the film's production and offered a great many suggestions, all of which were apparently ignored. She found the "no hokum" campaign ridiculous and the film an "absurdity." However, in the detailed critique she sent to producer Hal Wallis, all her complaints concerned minor matters of local color: diction, lexicon, agricultural terminology.[126] Regarding the film's fidelity to her novel in terms of the story and characters, she had no criticism. The Polish aspects of the story were never mentioned in her correspondence with Warner Brothers; evidently they were as she wished them to be.

The film, unfortunately, retains the implausible features of the book. Stan wishes to be a farmer but is also a violinist; his family fails at farming because they are really practiced in the garment trade. The notion of Polish tailors and violinists seeking to be farmers strains credulity. The Poles are portrayed as hardworking and stalwart and rather less "fat and dark" than Carroll indicated.[127] In general they are a minor element of the film, though they are pleasantly primitive and addicted to dance.[128] Stan, played by the handsome minor star Donald Woods, wins the affections of more than one local Yankee girl in the film, a rarity among Hollywood's Polish portrayals. He is probably the most positive major Polish character in prewar American films.

Reviewers of the film—like those of the book—virtually never mentioned the Poles, which certainly reflected Carroll's indifference. For her, as for the critics, this is a story about life in Maine, and the Poles are simply a handful of exotics who allow us to better appreciate Maine's foibles. The huge collection of reviews and comments Carroll assembled about her cinematic triumph contains virtually no mention of the film's (or the book's) Polish elements.[129]

The most elaborate exploration of the Polish community in America was the 1935 United Artists melodrama *The Wedding Night,* which gives us another portrait of rural Poles.[130] Here, however, they appear not as harmless aliens but as repulsive barbarians. Gary Cooper stars as a novelist, Tony Barret, who, after an initial success, has produced increasingly bad and repetitive books. His literary descent is accompanied if not facilitated by a life of sybaritic self-indulgence. Penniless when his latest novel is rejected by his publisher, he and his frivolous wife Dora (Helen Vinson) are forced to abandon Manhattan for his long-forgotten family home in rural Connecticut. Here a local informs him that the area has recently become crowded with Polish tobacco farmers. Tony becomes fascinated by his "Polock" neighbors, whom he considers "something out of another world," and decides to portray them in his new novel. In particular he is enchanted by the bright, attractive Manya Novak (Anna Sten), with whom he quickly becomes infatuated. His attentions are resented by Manya's father (Siegfried Rumann), who has already promised the girl to Frederik Sobieski (Ralph Bellamy), a loutish neighbor.

Tony's wife quickly tires of rural life and returns to New York. Unencumbered, Tony ardently pursues Manya. A blizzard traps Manya at Tony's house, where she chastely spends the night. Her reputation is nonetheless compromised, and her father insists she marry Sobieski immediately to save what is left of family honor. In the meanwhile, Tony's wife returns and reads his new Connecticut novel, which is a thinly disguised account of his rejuvenation as a man and a writer inspired by the fresh charm of the beautiful Manya. The story comes rapidly now to denouement. Manya is forced to marry Sobieski after a grotesque celebration. (Here too the Poles are given to savage dancing.) Tony is close enough to hear the raucous sounds of the Polish revelry. After much anguish, he becomes drunk and, uninvited, intrudes on the reception, causing a scene. Sobieski, hopelessly inebriated, realizes that his new wife loves Tony and decides to kill him. He follows Tony back to his house; a fight ensues on the staircase. Manya tries to intercede and falls over backward in the attempt. She is fatally injured. After a few hours she dies, leaving Tony bereft. Dora behaves handsomely in observing the final hours of the dying and quite innocent Manya and the agony of Tony.[131] How the Poles are affected is not shown.

Although the film was well crafted and Cooper, never a versatile actor, gave an unusually nuanced performance, it was not successful. Its depressing conclusion is often blamed for this; audiences found it unsatisfying despite generally positive reviews. Director King Vidor regarded the film very highly, though it was on balance "a flop."[132] Producer Samuel Goldwyn demonstrated his legendary incomprehensibility by describing the romantic interlude of the two principals thus: "If this scene isn't the greatest love scene ever put on film, the whole goddamned picture will go right up out of the sewer."[133]

The Poles emerge in this film as a completely unpleasant community. Manya's father, Jan Novak, is a cold, domineering tyrant who is also a cunning and dishonest businessman. Manya's intended, Sobieski, is revolting: vulgar, drunken, and stupid. The other Poles are merely a blur of oddly costumed peasants. The film is at pains to differentiate the Poles from the dissolute but nonetheless genteel Barrets. The adult Poles, for example, dine like beasts, and their children eat what leavings they can find, a Polish family tradition not known beyond the confines of the United Artists studio. A long scene is devoted to the grotesque gluttony of the Poles, observed with fascinated revulsion by Tony. The most striking characteristic of the Polish men is their abominable treatment of women. They never refer to their wives as "wives" but only and disdainfully as their "women." The poor souls are forced to work like cattle and are treated with brutality by their husbands. Indeed, Polish men and women are portrayed rather differently: The men are uniformly vile, without any redeeming virtue. By contrast, the women are merely pathetic. The local Yankees are appalled by the Poles, whom they regard as incomprehensible primitives; the viewer is enjoined to adopt a like attitude.

Raymond Durgnat and Scott Simmon make a perceptive observation concerning the film's depiction of the Poles as central to the story:

> It is hard to say how far Goldwyn, or Vidor, wanted Polish "alienness" to bear the brunt of the blame [for the tragic denouement]. Our suspicion is that spectators whose immigrant family experience is fresh in memory would treat Manya's fate as a tragic anomaly, while authors (and there will be the majority) would have veered nearer the anti-Polish response. To wit: While Polish immigrants may eventually be capable of aspiring to Americanism, as young Manya does, old Polish ways are not merely different, or out-of-place, but in themselves bad. . . . Her plight comes over as entirely her community's fault.[134]

Polish film critics lamented the gross inaccuracies in the film's portrayal of their countrymen. They wear exotic costumes, a mélange of styles. Similarly, they speak a sort of common Slavic, with elements from Russian and Ukrainian thrown about for linguistic seasoning, all of it enunciated with much gesticulation and rolling of eyes. Their names are a grab bag of strange sounds. Hence Tony's novel—supposedly based on the local Poles, with Manya the invaluable native informant—features principals named Sonya and Henirich, neither of which is Polish. Sobieski, the name of the Polish hero king of the seventeenth century, is given to Manya's cloddish suitor, a reference that still makes Polish viewers wince.

The Wedding Night was based on a story by Edwin Knopf and written for the screen by Edith Fitzgerald. Neither knew anything about the Polish community in America. The director, King Vidor, was a Texan of radical leftist inclination.[135] Among the principals, Cooper, Vinson, and Bellamy were Americans. Siegfried Rumann, who later shortened his name to Sig Ruman, by which he is better known, was an Austrian expatriate. Sten is a curious figure. Little is known of her biography except that she was born in Kiev in 1908, supposedly of Swedish-Ukrainian origin. Her original name was reportedly Anel Sudakevich, which appears to be a garbled version of a Polish name.[136] Indeed, she correctly pronounces the few Polish words she speaks in the film.[137] Supposedly she could not speak English until the early 1930s. Her first films were not successful. Though she had a handful of subsequent roles, her costarring billing with Cooper in *The Wedding Night* was the zenith of her career, which quickly thereafter declined.

The film presents no positive Polish characters, and the Poles' culture and behavior are repulsive. Only Manya is an exception, and she, symbolically, wishes to leave her community for the company of Tony, the "other." Indeed, in a key scene, her father beats and denounces her for wishing to be an "American girl" when she must remain a "Polish girl"—not a difficult choice for her in this film or for its audience: Polish women's lives are presented as consisting of degradation, backwardness, and drudgery.[138] The plot device of a character trapped between two worlds is, of course, a common one, but here the conflict is a caricature. There is nothing about the Polish alternative that is remotely attractive. Lest this demonstration be lost on the viewer, there is more than one scene in which Manya and Tony ridicule at length the accent, manners, and behavior of her Polish family. The Poles are at best ridiculous and at worst barbarians. This film, we should remember, is set contemporaneously; it does not evoke Polish immigrants of a generation or two earlier but depicts the Polish community of the Connecticut valley in the 1930s. A similar plot element is employed in *The Jazz Singer,* but there the contrast between Americanization and Jewish tradition presents the latter with great dignity and respect.[139] When the alternative to complete assimilation is Polish, however, United Artists presents it as an obviously ridiculous and repellent option. For Hollywood, *The Wedding Night* provided the American film audience with their Polish fellow citizens, a few years before the war, as bizarre primitives.[140]

If the Polish community of America was a rare setting for Hollywood, even more exotic was Poland itself. Among the few films of the 1930s devoted, even partially, to Polish affairs was the 1937 MGM melodrama *The Emperor's Candlesticks.*[141] William Powell is cast as an elegant Polish nobleman (with the misspelled name Baron Stephan Wolensky) who is involved in a convoluted plot against tsarist rule.[142] His nemesis and eventual romantic partner is Countess Olga Mironova (Luise Rainer), a Russian agent. Wolensky, an attractive character, gains the viewer's sympathy for the Polish cause, which, however, is not even superficially explained and is thus without meaning. The film purposely obfuscates time and place, and no historical characters are either represented or implied. The screenplay was based on a novel by the Hungarian writer Baroness Orczy, best known for *The Scarlet Pimpernel.* There were no Poles in any part of the creation of the film, which explains why the Polish aspects of the film are few, superficial, and incidental. Essentially the film is a costume drama and romantic vehicle for the two leads then at the heights of their careers. In sum, the use of the word "Polish" in this film is meaningless.

Rather more noteworthy is *Conquest,* also a 1937 MGM release, set in early-nineteenth-century Europe.[143] Based loosely on a novel by the popular Polish writer Wacław Gąsiorowski, *Pani Walewska,* this lavish production features Charles Boyer as Napoleon in one of his best, and certainly least restrained, performances.[144] Greta Garbo's portrayal of the unfortunate Countess Walewska emphasizes her patriotic motivations. The film depicts the affair between Napoleon and Walewska as being arranged by Polish nobles to gain the favor of the Corsican for the Polish cause, which places the romantic theme of the movie in a sordid light. Polish film critics were pleased that the producers actually sent a team to Poland to inspect portions of Warsaw and gather materials to design the sets.[145] This may well have been the only time Hollywood took such pains regarding a film set in Poland until recent years. Unfortunately, the film was not popular, and it became one of MGM's major financial disasters of the era. It has also not fared well at the hands of critics.

Conquest was probably the only Hollywood film set in Poland made before the outbreak of the Second World War, which is surprising given the country's turbulent and romantic history and the large immigrant population it sent across the Atlantic. Even among the nations of Eastern Europe—substantially neglected in American films—this is striking. Not surprisingly, it disconcerted Polish observers. By comparison, there was, as we have seen, a significant genre of Russian films, and even tiny Hungary was the setting for no fewer than seven films before 1939.[146]

By the mid-1930s, the deteriorating European situation and the rise of Nazism were beginning to attract Hollywood's attention, though the studios reacted with great reluctance. Most studios, even those led by Jews, were hesitant to criticize the German regime, reflecting their "sensitivity that such scripts would call attention to their Jewish origins, problematical in an era of increasing anti-Semitism in both Europe and America where isolationism was popular."[147] This caution reflected the disposition of the Roosevelt administration.[148] Moreover, offending Germany meant losing a lucrative export market for American films.[149] An exception was Warner Brothers. President Harry Warner was an early and passionate opponent of Nazism and openly endorsed exposing and denouncing the anti-Semitism of the Hitler regime, a view regarded as incautious in the Hollywood of the early 1930s. Harry was convinced that Warner Brothers could portray the evils of Nazism and alert the American public to the double menace of an aggressive Germany in Europe and pro-Nazi sympathies in the United States.[150]

In part this position was an extension of what had become the hallmark of Warner Brothers films in the 1930s: exposés of social ills. The studio made films about crime and gangsters, prison abuse, and the seamier side of urban life. Racism and nativism in America, like the rise of fascism abroad, were yet more themes Warner Brothers regarded as worthy of cinematic exposure and social commentary.[151] Harry's anti-Nazi campaign, which predated World War II, reflected his view that films could be a potent means of alerting and enlightening the public, a polite definition of propaganda.[152] Thus Warner Brothers was the only major studio to release films openly critical of Nazism, the famous *Confessions of a Nazi Spy* being the first.[153]

In 1937 Warner Brothers made another film designed to alert the public to the dangers of domestic fascism, a rather self-aware didactic effort titled *Black Legion,* starring a rising young star, Humphrey Bogart.[154] The story is the account of a decent but rather unintelligent factory worker—Frank Taylor, an American of no discernible ethnicity and neither Jewish nor Catholic—who is passed over for promotion in favor of a more able colleague who happens to be a member of an ethnic minority. Enraged and frustrated, he becomes convinced that "foreigners" have cheated him out of what is rightfully his, and he falls in with a radical group of fascist thugs who encourage his paranoid delusions. He participates in a number of criminal activities, notably the beating of his antagonist, whose home he also helps burn down. The man and his elderly immigrant father are driven from the town. Frank's career briefly prospers, and he exults in the feeling that real Americans can defend their interests against cunning foreigners. However, Frank's victory is short-lived. His personal life collapses, his new colleagues are shown to be repulsive, and he repents ever joining them. He denounces them in court during a trial in which he and his erstwhile band are sentenced to prison. The judge lectures them, and the audience, on the dangers of prejudice and the threat of domestic fascism.

In Robert Lord's original story, dated June 1936, the precipitating event in Frank's descent into fascism is the success of a Jewish coworker, Hirsh, at his factory. In this version, Frank is shown to be both an anti-Semite in his reaction to Hirsh and, immediately thereafter, an anti-Catholic when he denounces an Irish Catholic neighbor.[155] However, the Warners decided to remove the anti-Semitic element in the film, and when screenwriter Abem Finkel joined Lord in July, they replaced Hirsh with Sam Dombrowski.[156] In making this change, the Warners created probably the most positive Polish character in the history of their films. However, that conclusion may be more apparent than real.

Frank Taylor, the protagonist eventually played by Bogart, is a machinist; Dombrowski is his coworker. The latter, we are told, always has "his nose in a book on mechanical engineering," works with a slide rule, and attends night school. He has already made recommendations that have benefited the company's production techniques and resulted in considerable efficiencies. Hence, when an opening for a promotion appears, it is he rather than the affable but far less ambitious and talented Frank who gains the promotion. Dombrowski is an impressive character. Immensely diligent and able, he is also kind and generous. He personifies the American dream of advancement through hard work.[157] When Frank fails, he grumbles about "foreigners" in general and ironically laments that if his name were "Taylorinsky," he would have been successful. Frank specifically denounces the Irish in the Lord and Finkel treatment but never mentions Poles, even in reference to Dombrowski.[158]

Finkel refined the script in July and essayed a description of Dombrowski: "dark, swarthy, and obviously of foreign extraction." Dombrowski's father is described as a "kindly old fellow with a rugged peasant face" who speaks with "a Slavic accent."[159] This is the closest we ever get to a nationality for the Dombrowski character. By the autumn of 1936, William Wister Haines joined the screenwriting effort. Archie Mayo, known charmingly as the "fat slob" in Hollywood, was selected to direct the film. Dombrowski is now Joe, and his appearance is still described as "dark, swarthy." The script makes only a few passing references to his nationality, which is never specifically indicated. At one point an antagonistic fellow worker mocks Dombrowski's use of a slide rule: "Hey, Dombrowski! What you got there? A Hunyak back scratcher?" The same worker later discusses Dombrowski with Frank and refers to him as a "grease-ball"—dark and swarthy—and, again, as a "Hunyak."[160] These references, which were added to the script in November 1936, represent the film's only elaboration of Dombrowski's ethnicity. The terms, we should remember, were also used in the studio's film *Black Fury* to refer to Eastern European miners.

In sum, the character was originally Jewish and then was transformed into a "swarthy" foreigner of indeterminate nationality.[161] His religion is never indicated, and the only Catholic references involve an Irish character. Twice he is referred to as a Hunyak, which at the very least suggests a Hungarian. Why, if he is a Pole, is he not called a Polack by his cloddish detractors? Only a passing reference to his father's accent suggests his Slavic ancestry, but that is not developed. Repeatedly he is referred to as "dark" and "swarthy," hardly characteristic features of Poles. For much of the time, the character was named Sam, a name very rarely used by Poles. Early in the script, a fellow makes a reference to Dombrowski's having a large nose, a common caricature of a Jew, but not of a Pole. Hence, though the name Dombrowski certainly suggests a Polish character, Warner Brothers did nothing to make this clear, and indeed, script emendations seem to suggest he is Hungarian.[162]

This lack of clarity is unfortunate because Dombrowski is certainly a more positive character than any Pole Warner Brothers presented during the war years. He is intelligent, hardworking, and successful, a victim of discrimination quite undeserved. In a brief exchange later in the film, we learn that the Dombrowskis are regarded as honest and upright people by their neighbors as well. But *Black Legion* obfuscates Dombrowski's nationality, either through ignorance or in an effort to suggest a general category rather than limn a national type. In fact, Nick Roddick is convinced that Dombrowski was intended to be a Jewish character, though the references are much muted.[163] This is quite possible; it would mean that the studio never really removed Hirsh but merely disguised him. Dombrowski may be positive only because he was not really intended to be Polish in the first place. Regardless, Dombrowski demonstrates that for Hollywood, as in *Black Fury,* the population of Eastern Europe is a mass of dark foreigners without specific characteristics. Hence elements can be attributed at random as long as the result is, as Finkel noted, "obviously of foreign extraction."[164]

By contrast, a character named Mike Grogan (Clifford Soubier), who, like Dombrowski, is victimized by the Black Legion, is specifically referred to as being Irish.[165] He speaks with a brogue, unlike Dombrowski, who curiously has no accent; his family refers repeatedly to church; and his wife speaks to the Irish Mrs. Riley by phone. In short, even though Grogan is a less significant character for the story, his Irish ethnicity is specifically named and developed, whereas the featureless Dombrowski is merely a mysterious "Hunyak."[166]

Dombrowski is played by the émigré actor Henry Brandon (born in Berlin as Heinrich von Kleinbach). Although Brandon performed in a variety of roles, he was often cast as an American Indian, Persian, or Arab because of his dark hair and features.[167] Warner Brothers' casting of Brandon may have been one of the few times it chose a tall, physically impressive actor to play a Pole—if Dombrowski was indeed a Pole. The traditional Hollywood versions of the Pole were Edward G. Robinson, Peter Lorre, and John Garfield, all very short, swarthy, and "obviously of foreign extraction."

As small as this sample of films is, it is even less significant than it seems. Radek is probably supposed to be a Slovak in *Black Fury* or to have no particular ethnic background other than generic Eastern European. Similarly, *Black Legion*'s Dombrowski may be purposely indeterminate, with some attributes of his original Jewish designation partially obfuscated by a Polish name without attendant ethnic characteristics. Palooka's status as a Pole is questionable at best. This means that Hollywood's entire representation of the Polish community before World War II consisted of the strange Janowskis of *As the Earth Turns* and the barbaric intruders in the Connecticut valley of *The Wedding Night.*

Beyond this, we have only a handful of ambiguous possibilities in minor roles. There is a character named Stanislaus in the obscure 1934 Chesterfield film *Sons of Steel.* The role was played by the German émigré Adolph Milar, who had portrayed various nationalities in a long career in Hollywood. Whether he was intended to be a Pole in this film or not is unanswered. The 1935 Warner Brothers film *Stranded* includes a character named Stanislaus Janauschek as the fifth featured role, played by Robert Barrat, who also had a long career, often portraying military leaders—he was later twice Douglas MacArthur. The character's name may well have been one of Hollywood's clumsy attempts to render a Polish name, but little more can be said about this film. Ward Bond's Wynkoski in the 1934 Columbia release *Girl in Danger* may also be a Pole, but that is not a certainty.[168] Kay Francis gives a memorable performance as Vera Kowalska, ostensibly a Pole, in the 1937 Warner Brothers melodrama *Confession.* However, most of the other cast members have Russian names, and thus her nationality is not definite. This film was largely a remake of the German film *Mazurka,* starring the Polish actress Pola Negri, so it has some Polish attributes in any case. Curiously, three 1932 films (*Flesh, Uptown New York,* and *Deception*) include, in a very minor role as a nameless wrestler, the Polish strongman Władysław Zbyszko. It is unclear whether he was identified as a Pole. In any event, these were very small parts. Ironically, in *Deception,* a real German wrestler, Hans Steinke, has a rather larger role as Ivan Stanislaus, a name possibly intended to be Polish. Obviously, even if all of these were supposed to represent Poles, the number of Polish characters in pre–World War II American cinema was exiguous, far smaller than the number of Russian, Italian, and Jewish film characters and the merest fraction of the gigantic Irish presence in American films.

A special category of Hollywood production is composed of the popular serials, twelve or thirteen (more rarely fifteen) episodes of perhaps twenty minutes each designed to be shown weekly in theaters as additional attractions along with the main film. The serials, which were made cheaply and quickly, were famous for their liberal use of stock footage and their stilted dialogue in stories filled with action sequences. Many were tales of espionage and crime, featuring the exploits of heroes, often with extraordinary powers. They were very popular in the 1930s through the war years. Serials were the specialty of Poverty Row studios, but major companies also produced a great many.

A careful evaluation of the serials made before the war began in 1939 produces useful results. Though the sample I have compiled does not exhaust the category, it is a large one and hence deserves consideration as an accurate reflection of the whole. I have isolated fifty-eight serials, a total of about 750 episodes, all released between 1929 and 1939. They were produced by Universal and Columbia, by such smaller companies as Republic and Principal Picture Corporation, and by independents Romance, Weis Serials, Mascot Pictures Corporation, and Victory Pictures. The sample represents the work of many screenwriters over a decade and features a range of characters, including cowboys, assorted Asian villains, marines, clever dogs, Boy Scouts, crazed scientists, and assorted government agents. The serials are set in every locale from the tundra to the jungle and lost islands.

Among the more than 2,300 characters, there are considerable numbers of Irish and Germans and even many Italians. We also have a sprinkling of Russians. However, there is not a single Polish character in any episode of any of these serials. Not only are there no Poles or Americans of identifiable Polish ancestry among the featured detectives, soldiers, criminals, and others, but there is not a single Polish name among the identified roles (those not called merely, for example, "thug" or "man in bar"). The serials are completely without Polish references of any kind; according to them, there are no Poles in America. If we remember that the Polish population in the United States in the 1930s is reckoned at more than 4 million, we could reasonably expect at least 3 percent of the characters to be Polish. This would mean that of the 2,319 characters in the serials in our sample, there should be at least 70 Poles. There are, however, none—or, at most, there is one. In the 1939 Universal serial *Buck Rogers,* Henry Brandon appears briefly as Captain Laska, possibly a Pole, assuming he is an earthling.[169]

2

Poland in the Second World War

BEFORE WE CONSIDER WHAT HOLLYWOOD said about the Poles during World War II, it would be useful to present a brief outline of the events to which the film industry was reacting. Two themes are particularly noteworthy. The first is that many of the significant aspects of Poland's involvement in the war were ignored by Hollywood. The second is that the film industry made certain references to Poland that were entirely without foundation but nonetheless figure prominently in Hollywood's version of the war. In other words, Poland in World War II and Hollywood's Poland have little in common.

Germany invaded Poland early in the morning of September 1, 1939. A few days previously, on August 23, the famous Hitler-Stalin pact was signed in the Kremlin, pledging mutual neutrality in the event of a war. Soviet neutrality was vital to Hitler's strategy of isolating Poland before the invasion, as he had assumed that Britain and France, ostensibly Poland's allies, would not respond. Poland, thus isolated, would be easily defeated. The Nazi-Soviet pact included a secret protocol that detailed far-reaching economic cooperation and carefully delineated a future partition of Poland that would divide the country roughly equally between Russia and Germany. Additional paragraphs specified zones of influence for each country in the Baltic.[1] By these secret aspects, the Soviets and Nazis conspired against the sovereignty and territory of their neighbors. Only by ignoring these aspects of the treaty can one interpret it as designed to preserve peace in Europe—an interpretation that was basic to the presentation by Hollywood Communists.

Although the Poles had anticipated a war for some time, they were well aware that their military position was far weaker than that of Germany or Russia. As a result, their strategy was based on a long-term view of the war in which Poland would emerge victorious only after prolonged efforts. In fine, Warsaw planned to resist Germany with all of its strength until France and England could mount a major offensive on the western front, a period anticipated as lasting perhaps two weeks. During this interval, Poland would face Germany alone and, being hopelessly overmatched, could anticipate enormous casualties and much destruction. Poland would have to hold as much of its national territory as possible. Once the western front became active, the pressure on the Poles would greatly lessen, and Germany would face a two-front war in which Poland would have some chance of victory. The larger the territory Poland controlled, the more rapidly and effectively it could serve as a second front.

The German onslaught was even more powerful than the Poles had feared, and despite heroic resistance, the front was broken in many places after a week of intense combat. The Polish counteroffensive of September 6, the Battle of the Bzura, delayed but did not deflect the forward impetus of the Wehrmacht. German military efforts included indiscriminate bombing of civilian targets and wholesale terror directed against the population. By mid-September the Polish situation was desperate, and only a rapid French offensive could have brought significant relief. No such offensive took place, and the British also made no contribution to Poland's defense. The strategic prewar plans collapsed, and Poland's position was dire.

On September 17, a massive Soviet invasion flooded into eastern Poland. Polish defense had to be improvised using border guards and other lightly armed units, as the bulk of the main forces were engaged against the Germans. The Soviet invasion force included twenty-four infantry divisions, fifteen cavalry divisions, two tank corps, and additional units, the whole accompanied by a vast air armada. The troops numbered between 500,000 and 1 million, accompanied by at least two thousand tanks.[2] Fighting was ferocious, with fire and police departments, scouts, and schoolchildren joining in a desperate defense of eastern Poland. Troops at Dzisna suffered 50 percent casualties in a few hours; at Grodno the local population fought Soviet tanks on the streets with homemade weapons. The Soviets later massacred many of the city's defenders. This was repeated at Sarny, where many Poles were murdered after surrendering; the rest were beaten and robbed. Similar massacres occurred throughout the vast territory. The Russians suffered heavy casualties at a number of fierce encounters—the precise number has never been ascertained, but estimates range from 2,500 to 10,000— plus the loss of one hundred tanks. This was a massive invasion conducted with unusual barbarism.[3] It did not exist for Hollywood.

The Polish government characterized the Soviet invasion as a violation of the Polish-Soviet pact of 1932, as well as a perfidious act given Poland's war with Germany. British scholars, among others, have concluded that the Soviet act was a violation of international law as well as a contravention of a number of existing treaties.[4] The Soviet response contended that the war against Germany had been lost by Poland within days and hence "the Polish state no longer exists." Thus the Soviets were justified, for reasons of their own security, to come to the aid of their "blood brothers" in eastern Poland.[5] By this logic the invasion was not an invasion at all but merely a postwar rescue operation. Thereafter the notions that the war was over in just a few days and that the Soviets did not invade Poland became axiomatic in the Communist presentation of the September campaign. They also appear repeatedly in Hollywood representations of the war.

The Soviet offensive was followed by terror and massacres; arrests were carried out on a mass scale. War crimes were committed from the first hours. For example, prisoners were often executed. Faced with this double invasion, Polish military resistance became disorganized into a number of isolated units, and overall command broke down. Political and military leaders rushed to the southeast to cross the Romanian border to organize resistance from abroad. No surrender was ever signed, and the Poles regarded the war as a continuing struggle against two enemies, the Germans and the Russians, who had collaborated in destroying their country.

Contrary to the subsequent Hollywood presentation, fighting actually intensified during September, with major actions on the Bzura River and several other places. By September 28, after an extended siege, Warsaw fell to the Germans. Prominent leaders were arrested and imprisoned; many were later executed. The last field units surrendered at Kock on October 6. The campaign had lasted five to six weeks and resulted in approximately fifty thousand German casualties. The Germans' material losses were heavy: one thousand tanks and armored cars, almost six hundred aircraft, twelve thousand trucks and other vehicles, and much additional equipment.[6] These losses matched or exceeded those the Germans endured during the 1940 campaign in Western Europe, when they defeated the combined armies of France, Holland, Belgium, and Britain in roughly the same time as the September campaign against Poland. When we remember that the Poles were attacked without warning, were able to mobilize only a fraction of their forces, and were forced to depend on obsolete equipment—whereas the Western European allies in 1940 had nine months to prepare, had the advantage of having observed German military technique in operation, and fielded a force roughly equal to that of the Germans in number and actually superior in certain key materiel components—the performance of the Poles is impressive. Still, Hollywood ignored the campaign or implied that it was over in a few days after token resistance.

Polish casualties, however, were gigantic, more than two hundred thousand, with more than six hundred thousand taken prisoner. Civilian losses and damage inflicted by the Soviets were integral parts of the Polish trial of September 1939. Indeed, resistance did not really end in October 1939: Major Henryk Dobrzański withdrew his unit to the Świętokrzyska Mountains and fought on till his death in late 1940. By then an underground army of many thousands was already formed. No observer of American cinematic re-creations of the war would realize any of this.

From the beginning of the war, the Soviet press had adopted a tone hostile to Poland.[7] As Poland was in ferocious combat, the Soviet government and the Comintern issued a series of pronouncements explaining the war and their participation. Poland "shared [the] blame for the war," announced Comintern chief Georgi Dimitrov. The country was a "prison of peoples" that practiced "terror" against its national minorities and, as a result, "fell to pieces in some two weeks."[8] Foreign Commissar Molotov rejected the very idea of a war on fascism and ridiculed the western powers. Poland was caricatured as a feudal state dominated by a reactionary landed aristocracy.[9] Hollywood would soon depict 1939 Poland as a feudal society with serfs whipped by their lords.

Poland's defeat was the result of overwhelming numerical inferiority and gross deficiencies in key categories, particularly communications, transportation, armor, and aircraft. There were certainly errors in civilian administration and military planning, but these were not significant causative factors. Poland could not have survived invasions by the two largest military powers in the contemporary world no matter what government had been in power or what strategy had been adopted.

The widespread myths that Poland hastened if not caused its own defeat by using massed cavalry formations to attack German armored columns and by allowing the bulk of its air forces to be destroyed on the ground are without foundation. The air force was secretly moved and hidden before the German attack and thus survived to oppose the invasion with full force. It fought with skill and intrepidity until supplies were exhausted and the German advance prevented further sorties. Flying obsolete aircraft and operating under difficult and rapidly deteriorating conditions, the Polish air force matched the vaunted Luftwaffe and downed as many planes as it lost.[10] Hollywood, nonetheless, repeated the myth that the Polish air force was destroyed on the ground.

Cavalry is central to the long history of Polish military glory. The Poles were not, however, deluded about its usefulness in modern warfare. Mechanization of the cavalry was proceeding as fast as the state could afford it, and there were no plans to mount mass charges against armored attacks. In the September 1939 campaign, cavalry was used to bring mounted units into proximity to the enemy, where they fought as infantry. Reconnaissance was also often a cavalry responsibility. In those few instances when Polish cavalry opposed German units in field operations, it performed well. In American films, however, the Poles blindly charge into German armored units, with predictable results. This suicidal proclivity is presented as part of the country's dysfunctional inappropriateness for the modern world.

At the time of the invasion, the Polish government was largely composed of men of humble origin, many of them former military officers. The president was a prominent scientist, the commander in chief a child of poverty, the foreign minister a soldier whose father was a provincial lawyer. There were no landed aristocrats within the cabinet and only a handful in the diplomatic service; aristocrats' role in public affairs was marginal. Most of the prominent members of the government were political moderates, and many were former socialists. By comparison, the Roosevelt administration, to say nothing of the British government, was a collection of the rich and privileged. In addition, though the majority of the Polish population was Roman Catholic, the government was not conspicuous for the religiosity of its leaders, who were at most only nominally Roman Catholic. In the fall of 1939, the Polish government was reassembled as an exile authority in Paris under the leadership of General Władysław Sikorski, also a man of humble social origins and a political moderate. A similar profile extended to his administration. The charge that Poland was dominated by religious fanatics or by aristocrats who were out of touch with the average Pole is baseless.

Pro-German sentiment was almost nonexistent in prewar Poland, fascist parties were fringe groups, and appeasement was rejected as incompatible with national honor. Appeasement was the policy of the British and French governments, but Hollywood later attributed this instead to Warsaw.[11] Ethnic minorities, despite strained relations in the interwar era, served loyally, and the population, excepting some Germans and Ukrainians, was resolute and united. Polish Jews, like Ukrainians, Belarusians, and others, served loyally in Polish ranks in September and later in other theaters. Polish military cemeteries are dotted with the Stars of David and Orthodox crosses of the Jews, Ukrainians, and Belarusians who died for Poland. The suggestion that Poland was rife with fifth columnists, offered in more than one Hollywood film, is untrue.[12]

The Germans divided their portion of Poland into two zones, one of which was directly annexed to Germany. There all signs of Polish culture and history were obliterated rapidly. Poles living there were herded together and dumped into the remaining portion of the occupied country, the so-called Generalgouvernement. The conditions of the Poles there were abominable. Arrests of prominent citizens, executions of leaders from all walks of life, forcible labor drafts, and random brutality were the features of life under a German occupation that was far more severe than any subsequent occupation regime in Western Europe. The Germans ruled conquered Poland directly; there was no puppet regime, and collaborators were almost nonexistent. Again a comparison to Western Europe is to Poland's credit. Czechoslovakia, seized by the Germans without resistance after March 1939, experienced a far milder occupation that led to widespread collaboration. The later German occupations of France and Norway were also comparatively mild. Both countries provided numerous and active collaborators and volunteers for German military service, including the SS.[13] Despite these facts, the depiction of life in occupied Poland is rare in Hollywood films, which spent much more time and sympathy on France, Norway, and Czechoslovakia.

A special feature in Poland was the rapid segregation of the large Jewish population, which before the war counted one Polish citizen in ten. Though extermination began only in 1941, early in the war Jews were subjected to intense discrimination, mistreatment, and random violence more severe than that endured by the gentile majority. Although the ghastly fate of the Jews is now widely known, it was almost completely ignored by wartime Hollywood.

By prearrangement the Soviets occupied all of eastern Poland and worked closely with the Germans in suppressing the Polish population.[14] Thirteen million Polish citizens came under Soviet control. The Gestapo and its Russian counterpart, the NKVD (People's Commissariat of Internal Affairs), functioned harmoniously in joint efforts at hunting down and arresting potential members of the opposition. The Soviets immediately began wholesale reorganization of the country: mass population relocations, confiscations of property, arrests, systematic looting of cultural artifacts, and a series of huge deportations that eventually sent more than 1 million Polish citizens, including many Jews and Ukrainians as well as ethnic Poles, into the farthest reaches of Siberia and the Soviet Arctic for slave labor. Ethnic hatred was promoted and nationality conflict encouraged in a policy of *divide et impera*.[15] The eventual casualties from these operations were large.[16]

The Red Army had taken 200,000 to 250,000 Polish prisoners of war, and most were held in bad conditions. Thousands were transferred to Gestapo care; a large number perished during the move.[17] On March 5, 1940, Stalin ordered the murder of 14,700 Polish POWs and 11,000 additional political prisoners; the executions were carried out by the NKVD.[18] Many of the officers thus condemned were brutally butchered at a number of mass murder sites, of which Katyń (where approximately 4,500 were shot and bayoneted in 1940) is only the best known. Waves of subsequent arrests included major political leaders, many of whom were prominent Jewish figures. Two hundred thousand men were forced into service in the Red Army and given onerous duty. Whereas for Jews the Nazi regime was an unsurpassed horror, Christian Poles often fled from Soviet to Nazi occupation zones because the Russians' behavior was worse than the Germans'. The Jews shared with all other citizens of the Polish Republic the deportations of 1940–1941, in which a huge number were scattered about the Soviet Union. Of these about 60 percent were Polish speakers and 20 percent were Hebrew or Yiddish speakers; the remainder were from the Ukrainian and Belarusian minority populations of eastern Poland. The totals are still controversial, but estimates range from 1.2 million to 1.6 million. The mortality rate exceeded 30 percent.[19] Hollywood has never addressed this theme; it remains one of the major forgotten tragedies of the war. Nothing in occupied Norway or Czechoslovakia is remotely comparable, though Hollywood devoted many films to those countries.

Organized Polish resistance appeared immediately after the September defeat, though its density and size were far greater in the German zone than in the Soviet. The military created a complex web of units engaged in intelligence, sabotage, and propaganda—eventually called the Armia Krajowa (Home Army)—while an elaborate civilian administration featuring a complete judicial and educational system emerged. Both the civilian and military networks were headquartered in Warsaw and recognized Sikorski's government-in-exile as the legal continuation of the prewar authorities. The Polish government-in-exile enjoyed almost universal loyalty both abroad and in Poland. In size and effectiveness, no occupied country rivaled Poland in creating a network of opposition. Poland functioned as a legal entity uninterruptedly throughout World War II.

The exile government was able to create a fighting force of eighty thousand by 1940, and these troops fought in the defense of France against the German invasion of May–June 1940. After France's defeat, Sikorski and his government—and a remnant of the Polish military—evacuated to London, where they resided for the rest of the war. New forces were rapidly raised, and Polish units briefly composed a significant percentage of anti-German forces, eventually numbering two hundred thousand soldiers and suffering more than forty thousand casualties. There were Polish naval and air units as well; the latter destroyed almost one thousand German planes.[20] These were Polish troops, fighting under Polish command, not Poles serving in British units, as Hollywood repeatedly insisted. Polish pilots played a distinguished role in the Battle of Britain in the summer of 1940, outclassing both the Germans and their own British colleagues in combat effectiveness. Polish pilots destroyed a disproportionate number of German planes over London with few losses. Indeed, one-eighth of the planes defending

London were flown by Poles. Polish troops also played a role in the ill-fated British effort to stop the German invasion of Norway (the Narvik campaign) and fought in the defense of France and Belgium in 1940 and later in North Africa, everywhere distinguishing themselves. The only Hollywood reflection of this contribution to Allied victory is a Polish airman depicted in the 1942 film *Eagle Squadron*. He is mentally disturbed.

By the summer of 1941, after almost two years of close cooperation, Germany and the Soviet Union were at war. Their cooperation had enabled both to profit in the mutual despoilment of Europe. Germany had been free to invade Poland, Norway, Denmark, France, Holland, and Belgium, as well as Greece and Yugoslavia, without fear of an eastern front. At the same time, Stalin seized eastern Poland, a large portion of Romania, the three Baltic states, and a substantial portion of Finland through either invasion or political blackmail. The last was particularly outrageous, as tiny Finland fought against an unprovoked attack by its huge neighbor. German blueprints, prototypes, and machine tools flowed into Soviet Russia while raw materials from Stalin supplied the German war machine. It was an arrangement of mutual advantage.

The German invasion of Russia in June 1941 changed the war fundamentally. Thereafter, the bulk of the German military effort was directed against the Russians, who were forced to expend blood and treasure to escape defeat, which, until 1943, seemed likely. Given the incomparable importance of the Soviet front in the struggle against Germany, Stalin was presented with formidable political leverage in dealing with Great Britain and, after the attack on Pearl Harbor in December 1941, the United States. Both Washington and London were aware of the collapse of Russia in World War I and of the seeming invincibility of the Wehrmacht thus far in World War II. Hence they were willing to pay virtually any price to propitiate the Soviets to maintain them in the war. By comparison, Poland was an occupied country, and the Sikorski government had only perhaps a hundred thousand men, widely scattered, at its disposal. Poland's military contributions to the war were only a small fraction of the Soviet total.

By 1943 the German onslaught against Russia had crested, and thereafter it was the Soviet army that gradually assumed the offensive. The British and American combat contributions to the war against Hitler were comparatively small. The North African landings of November 1942, the first direct actions against German positions, proved slow and cumbersome. The subsequent campaign against Italy—the Sicilian invasion of July 1943, followed by the attack on the mainland in September—made ponderous progress against the skillful and determined German resistance. During the Italian campaign, significant Polish units fought under British command and were responsible for a number of victories, including the famous capture of the German position at Monte Cassino, which was vital to the Allied advance. Hollywood depicted this episode in one film, *The Story of G.I. Joe,* but gave credit for the victory to the Americans and omitted the Poles.

While the western powers crept north through Italy, Soviet forces gained momentum in driving the Germans westward. The Soviet zone of political influence expanded with the advance of the Red Army. It was only the Normandy landing of June 1944 that established a real second front, when the war had less than a year to go.

Poland's geopolitical position, always weak, deteriorated markedly in 1943–1944. In April 1943, the discovery of the thousands of Polish graves at Katyń—obvious evidence that the Russians had perpetrated atrocities—caused a break in relations between the Sikorski government and Moscow. Thereafter, Washington and London continued to deal with the Poles but found them an obstacle to smooth relations with Moscow, which they considered of much greater moment. Hence they urged the Poles to accommodate the Soviets and were very concerned about any Polish criticism of Russian actions that might arouse public suspicion that Russia was not a fit partner for the West but an ally of necessity. In early July 1943, Prime Minister Sikorski was killed in an airplane crash. His death badly affected the Polish exile government, which now fell to the leadership of lesser men without Sikorski's stature or influence with London and Washington. Thus by 1944 the Americans and British would have preferred to see Poland disappear from public attention.

By the spring of 1943, the Jewish population of Poland had suffered systematic annihilation for almost two years; already at least 1.5 million were dead. Efforts by the Polish government to bring the horror of the Jewish situation to the attention of both London and Washington were largely ignored as a distraction from wartime strategy. In their agony the remaining Jews of Warsaw launched a heroic rising in April 1943 that lasted weeks and resulted in massive casualties but only delayed further annihilation. The Holocaust, like Poland itself, was largely ignored in the West.

Late that year, when Russian troops approached the Polish border, the full dimensions of Soviet political and territorial appetites quickly became obvious. Polish efforts to assert sovereignty over its prewar territory were ignored by the Russians, who annexed as they advanced and brought a puppet regime with them to install in Warsaw in place of the legal authorities. The western powers largely abandoned defense of Poland's political independence and territorial integrity. They acquiesced in Soviet demands in both particulars at the Tehran conference of November 1943, at which Poland's fate was decided with no Poles present. This was an eerie recapitulation of the Munich conference of 1938, at which appeasement had been to the benefit of the Germans and at the expense of the Czechs. The Munich conference was often denounced in Hollywood films, but when it was repeated five years later in Tehran to propitiate Russian aggrandizement at Polish expense, Hollywood did not mention it. After 1943 the Kremlin adopted an increasingly abusive tone in dealing with Polish issues, which was not countered by London or Washington. Poland's efforts to defend its position were unwelcome by the western powers.

Because films devoted to occupation and resistance were a Hollywood staple, it is important to consider the size and achievements of the Polish underground in comparative perspective. Of all the activities of the various resistance movements, the most significant for the war were gathering intelligence and passing it to the West. The Polish intelligence network after 1939 was gigantic and included operatives throughout the world. In occupied Poland alone perhaps as many as 40,000 agents were at work, furnishing many reports to London, a quarter of which the British rated as of "extraordinary value." The next largest intelligence system was maintained by the French and numbered a mere 2,500. Czech and Norwegian operations were insignificant in size and consequence.[21] Polish intelligence operations reported the preparations for the attack on the Soviet Union in 1941 and the German development of the V1 rocket at Peenemünde; they even later retrieved a V2 rocket. The Polish underground numbered more than 1 million, of which 600,000 were in armed units. During the course of the war, these forces carried out 10,000 military attacks, several hundred of large scale; 800,000 sabotage operations; 280 attacks on railroads; and several hundred assassination attempts on German officials. It is estimated that half a million German troops were occupied in combating Polish efforts.[22] There is virtually no echo of this in Hollywood films; the only reference to the Polish underground (in *To Be or Not to Be*) describes it as being directed by the British.

By early 1944, Soviet troops were on Polish soil, and the very future of Poland was in limbo. In a last-ditch effort to assert Polish claims to control the fate of their country, the underground army, with the compliance of the Polish leaders in London, launched the massive Warsaw Rising on August 1, 1944, which lasted for more than two months and resulted in almost a quarter million Polish casualties, approximately the total of all American casualties on all fronts in the entire war. The Soviets not only furnished no serious aid to the uprising but also blocked the western powers' efforts to provide assistance, efforts they made tardily and without much force.

The defeat of the Warsaw Rising left the once huge Polish underground army shattered and the exile government politically powerless and emotionally spent. The last months of the war saw the complete occupation of Poland by the Soviet army, the formal annexation of eastern Poland, and the installation of a Soviet puppet government. Widespread persecution of the most devoted and patriotic elements of the population was carried out on a mass scale by Soviet authorities and their Polish Communist assistants. The war had been for Poland an unmitigated disaster.

Polish casualties were proportionally the highest of any nation in the Second World War: perhaps 6 million Polish citizens died, about 20 percent of the prewar population. This included almost the entirety of Polish Jewry. Polish military losses were triple those of the United States.[23] Material damage was extensive, and many cities, including Warsaw, were virtually leveled. The government-in-exile became a pathetic remnant of a seemingly lost cause as the country returned to peace as an occupied province of the Soviet empire. Given the Polish sacrifices in the war, proportionally greater than British or American losses and even exceeding those of the Soviets, Poland's fate in the war was bitter indeed. The loss of lives, treasure, territory, and freedom meant that Poland ended the war as the only completely defeated nation among the victors. This story, with its innumerable poignant episodes, including the Holocaust of Polish Jewry, was virtually ignored by American films.

3

Radical Hollywood and Poland

THE FBI TRACED THE COMINTERN'S determination to establish a presence in American films to articles by Willi Münzenberg in the *Daily Worker* in 1925 that extolled the significance of motion pictures as a means of political propaganda and hence the need for the Communist Party of the United States of America (CPUSA) to control their production.[1] The accuracy of this genealogy is problematic, as it was several years before the party undertook concrete steps to gain a foothold in the entertainment industry. In 1934 the total party membership in the Los Angeles area was estimated by the FBI to be a paltry three dozen,[2] but in that year a special "Hollywood studio section" was organized, and it grew rapidly thereafter.[3]

Party headquarters in New York sent the Polish-born party intellectual Isaac Romaine (using the name Victor Jerome) as "cultural commissar" to the fledgling operation in California.[4] It was Jerome who decided that "Hollywood luminaries" would constitute a unique section, separate from the local party rank and file, linked directly to headquarters in New York, bypassing the normal hierarchy. Writers—not actors, whom the party regarded as "99 percent political morons"—were the emphasis.[5] Members of the section would be protected by having party membership books destroyed.[6]

Jerome apparently had the playwright John Howard Lawson sent from New York to become the permanent head of this effort, and when Jerome returned to New York, Lawson became the undisputed master of the Hollywood Communists.[7] FBI informants insisted that the party had a definite plan of infiltrating and gaining an influential position in the movie industry, which it put into operation in the mid-1930s.[8] In 1934 Lawson joined Samuel Ornitz, Dudley Nichols, Guy Endore, and Harry Carlisle to form the Screen Writers Guild, with Lawson as its first president. All were party members except Nichols, who was a fellow traveler.[9] Soon after, party member John Weber founded the Screen Readers Guild, whose members—most aspiring screenwriters—were to analyze potential scripts. They were notoriously, and predictably, dominated by the Screen Writers Guild.[10] Lawson noted, "The Communist Party exerted a good deal of influence in Hollywood."[11]

As early as 1934, Lawson declared, "My aim is to present the Communist position and to do so in the most specific manner," a credo he never renounced.[12] It was Lawson's party assignment to recruit and organize Hollywood screenwriters and then enforce the party line, disciplining those found to be wavering. Doctrinaire and arrogant, Lawson was described by a party comrade as speaking "with the voice of Stalin and the bells of the Kremlin."[13] His own son noted that Lawson turned "a blind eye to Soviet reality."[14] Held in awe by many young radicals in Hollywood, Lawson assumed that others would bring their work to him for ideological imprimatur.[15] Lawson's respect for the truth is well indicated by his explanation that freedom of speech was to be protected for Communists in the United States but denied to fascists because the former spoke the truth and the latter lied.[16] Lawson later explained that a screenwriter should try to insert a few minutes of party propaganda into a film, best placed in an expensive scene, lessening the likelihood of reshooting.[17] Lawson's devotion to propaganda is obvious in his admonition to young actors in 1946: "Unless you portray any role given to you in a manner to further the Revolution and the Class War, you have no right to call yourself an artist or an actor. . . . You must do this regardless of what the script says and what the director tells you."[18]

The next year, 1935, Comintern agent Otto Katz arrived incognito in Hollywood to organize front organizations as part of the energetic cultural work then being conducted by the Comintern throughout the world. Katz, who later boasted that, whereas "Columbus discovered America," he had "discovered Hollywood," was instrumental in creating the Hollywood Anti-Nazi League, described recently as "the key Communist front around which the work of Stalinist politics was accomplished in Hollywood during the Popular Front" era.[19] The league appeared in 1935 and grew rapidly to almost three thousand members, the vast majority of them not Communists at all but those concerned about Nazi anti-Semitism. It published a weekly newsletter, *Hollywood Now,* which circulated about four thousand copies (virtually all in Los Angeles) and enjoyed generous contributions from many wealthy supporters. The FBI considered the league a Communist front and followed its actions closely.[20] Suspicions that Communists played a dominant role in the league caused studios, with the exception of Warner Brothers, which remained steadfast, gradually to distance themselves from it.[21]

The key to understanding the CPUSA's agenda in Hollywood is realizing that fighting fascism was not the party's goal but only its later boast. Rather, the mission of the party was to support the foreign policy of the Kremlin and to advance Soviet interests. Fighting fascism was occasionally congruent with this motivation; other times it was not. From 1935 to 1939, the Communist strategy of collaborating with other political factions in opposition to Nazi Germany, the so-called Popular Front, reflected Moscow's interests and was thus supported by the CPUSA. Poland, when mentioned at all, was derided as a fascist state and an ally of the Nazis.[22] The Hollywood Anti-Nazi League, among many other front organizations, reflected this.[23]

This strategy had considerable success in both Europe and the United States, where party membership crested in the summer of 1939 at near one hundred thousand. The party "had taken some major steps toward becoming 'a mass organization' and . . . it was now a powerful force in the CIO, the youth movement, the intellectual world, and in a few large cities."[24] Since the mid-1930s, the CPUSA had championed an active united front against Hitler on the international scene and a domestic coalition in favor of Roosevelt. Both had gained it much sympathy on the left, especially in Hollywood, where Communists were seen as the most vociferous opponents of fascism both abroad and at home.[25]

However, in 1939, this changed quite suddenly with the announcement of the Hitler-Stalin pact of August 23. There is no doubt that the pact was a terrible blow for party loyalists in Hollywood, as it was for them everywhere. It made nonsense of years of rhetoric and organization; in an instant the party line had changed. Denunciations of Nazism werc to ccasc, and calls for American intervention were to be replaced by attacks on those very actions as warmongering. The party went from chief antagonist of Hitler to his apologist, from advocate of preparedness to promoter of American isolationism.[26] John Howard Lawson advised that events required "flexibility" from party members.[27] The party's support in Hollywood, especially among industry Jews, had rested in good part on its championship of the anti-Nazi cause, which it now abandoned. Not until the German invasion of Soviet Russia in June 1941 could the party readopt the cry of anti-Nazism as its motto.

At first the CPUSA did not know how to react to the pact, and it thrashed about in confusion.[28] The *Daily Worker* even praised the pact as contributing to Poland's security in a front-page editorial.[29] The propaganda journal *Soviet Russia Today,* issued in New York, cobbled together a defense of the pact, but it clumsily mentioned that the USSR had had a "non-aggression agreement" in place with Poland since 1932—a most awkward datum once the Soviets invaded Poland on September 17.[30] No instructions from Moscow reached the CPUSA for several days after the pact was announced.[31]

The CPUSA was still in a quandary as to how to respond when news broke of the German invasion of Poland on September 1. At first, the party supported Polish resistance. The *Daily Worker* even editorially applauded Poland's fight; it was, after all, quite obviously a war against fascism, supposedly the party's cause. The editorial assured people that Moscow would provide beleaguered Poland with arms and possibly even come to its defense.[32]

However, soon the tone changed radically.[33] On September 12 the party said both sides in the conflict were "equally guilty" and stopped praising Polish efforts. On September 15 the *Daily Worker* approvingly reprinted an editorial from *Pravda* denouncing the government of Poland as "an oppressor of the people." On September 18, the day following the Soviet invasion, Poland was referred to as a virtually fascist country; the Soviet invasion was hailed as an effort at rescuing the population of the Polish east and hence "another triumph for human freedom." The next day the National Committee of the CPUSA condemned support of the war against Nazi Germany and rejected the idea that opposition to Germany was tantamount to opposing fascism.[34] This meeting, held in Chicago, adopted resolutions that heaped abuse on "fascist" Poland, then still fighting a double invasion, and demanded that the United States do nothing against Nazi Germany.[35]

CPUSA chairman Earl Browder rushed a pamphlet into print that explained the German invasion of Poland not as facilitated by the Hitler-Stalin pact but rather as a result of the fact that London, Paris, and Warsaw had "sabotaged" Moscow's efforts for peace in Europe. In response to the question "Can Poland be saved?" Browder responded that it was possible, but only if the Polish people forced their own government to "collaborate with the Soviet Union," an indirect and very early call for the repudiation of the legal government of Poland and the creation of a regime subservient to Moscow. The United States, warned Browder, must not "take sides" in the war.[36] On September 30, *Pravda* announced that "the German-Soviet friendship is now established forever."[37]

In late September, detailed instructions from the Comintern finally arrived at CPUSA headquarters. They provided the framework for the party's attitude toward Poland for the rest of the war. The Popular Front was dead; the western powers were greater enemies of the USSR than was Germany. Poland was a "reactionary multinational state built on the oppression of Ukrainians, Belorussians, and Jews. It decayed because of the corruption of the ruling classes. The international proletariat has no interest in the existence of such a parasitical state." Like England and France, Poland was a "reactionary imperialist state" run by an "imperialist clique." There was no Soviet invasion of Poland in September; rather the Russians "came to the aid of western Ukrainian and Belorussian workers, saved 11 million people from a capitalist hell, brought them into the ranks of socialism, assured their national and cultural development, and with all of its might secured them from foreign enslavement." Hence the task now was to "fight against the war."[38]

On October 13, the CPUSA dutifully issued a resolution: "Since the outbreak of the present war, the Soviet Union has continued to exert all of its mighty proletarian influence in the cause of peace, democracy, and liberty. When the fascist government of Poland collapsed and abandoned its peoples to the [sic] fate at the hands of the imperialist robbers, the Soviet Union . . . in order to protect the lives and welfare of the people, occupied West Ukrainia [sic] and Byelo-Russia, related to the peoples of the Soviet Union by nationality, and forcibly torn away in 1920 by Polish imperialism." This occupation occurred not as a result of the September 17 invasion but from "a situation arising from the collapse of the Polish state and the establishment of peace in Eastern Europe."[39] The Jewish section of the CPUSA even endorsed the invasion of Poland, arguing, with grotesque logic, that delivering a large number of Jews to Soviet control was "good for the Jews." Other Jewish groups read this argument with incredulity and outrage.[40] Indeed, the party line was that the so-called Russian invasion was in reality a "humanitarian act undertaken to safeguard the rights of Polish workers." After September 1939, the CPUSA ceased to be an antifascist force and actually impeded the struggle against German aggression.[41]

This 1939 indictment of Poland, even the vocabulary, can be found in later references to Poland and the war and to the Polish-Russian relationship in the Hollywood films written by party members and fellow travelers. Hence Poland was a fascist state, no better than and little different from Nazi Germany. The party began shopping a few clichés to describe prewar Poland; references to the domination of "corrupt nobility" were popular.[42] Poland did not deserve any sympathy as a result of the German attack in September, and thus the event could be largely ignored. The Soviet invasion later that month did not in fact occur; rather, there was a border adjustment in Eastern Europe that redounded to the advantage of the millions of people who had been mistreated by the Polish government. Indeed, this territory was not really Polish at all but occupied, having been unjustly seized from the Russians in 1920 in an earlier war of aggression. Poland had to be fundamentally reformed; a new government with a radically different attitude toward the Soviet Union was the only hope for the country. Party member and prominent screenwriter Ring Lardner Jr. listed as one of the articles of faith "to remain a Communist" after 1939 the conviction that there had been no Soviet aggression against Poland in 1939.[43] Even years later, John Howard Lawson denied the existence of a Hitler-Stalin pact as "irrational" and insisted that the Soviet invasion of September 17 was the movement of Russian armies "forward to face the Germans."[44]

The party did nothing to support the final stages of the Polish war effort or to organize succor for its troubled population. Quite the contrary: Poland and its plight were either ignored or ridiculed. By May 1940, the CPUSA's position on Poland had been fully formed and was announced at a major conference. Poland was denied the status of a national state; it was merely a land mass with "artificial borders." The invasion by Germany had nothing to do with fascism, and the Hitler-Stalin pact that enabled it was "a great landmark in the struggle against war."[45]

The Hollywood Anti-Nazi League was thrown into immediate crisis by this madcap logic. The careful alliance between the party minority and many left-liberals, which had developed rapidly in the late 1930s, was shattered by the party's volte-face regarding Germany.[46] The league's perfervid denunciations of Nazi Germany were first muted and then replaced by a campaign against domestic fascism, which was identified as the moving spirit behind the preparedness movement and any calls for intervention in Europe. Because the Russian invasion of Poland was an absolutely taboo subject, the earlier German invasion of Poland on September 1, 1939, itself became impossibly awkward because it implicated the Soviets in Poland's despoilment. For the party, there was no war in Europe. Hence a league ostensibly organized to combat the evils of Nazism said virtually nothing about Nazism's first great outrages, the invasion of Poland and its ghastly behavior toward the population.

No group now opposed war against Nazi Germany more vociferously than the Hollywood Communists and their front organizations like the league. It is telling that in December 1939 the league, at the insistence of its Communist members, renamed itself the Hollywood League for Democratic Action.[47] Its newsletter struggled on for a few months but was terminated in the summer of 1940. One of its last acts was to denounce American conscription as "the core of fascism."[48] Thereupon a new organization appeared, the Hollywood Peace Forum, which went through a series of names, always prominently featuring the word "peace." It also expired by the end of 1940. A series of front organizations opposing war appeared in 1940–1941, all ephemeral.[49] As late as June 1941, the party was supporting a National Peace Week and launching peace initiatives of all kinds. The FBI considered the league (in its evolving embodiment) to have become effectively "pro-Hitler" after September 1, 1939, as a result of its frantic opposition to the war.[50] In the summer of 1940, league events featured condemnations of Roosevelt as a "traitor" and denunciations of the B'nai B'rith for "espionage."[51] As late as August 1940, the league proudly listed all the "homeless and refugees" it had aided in "China, Spain, Germany, Austria and Czecho-Slovakia" and all it had done to oppose war in Europe. Poland and the invasion of 1939 were not mentioned.[52] So vociferous was the league's chairman, director-screenwriter Herbert J. Biberman, in denouncing the American preparedness campaign and the Roosevelt administration that a disgruntled former member of the organization suggested Biberman might be a Nazi.[53] Even mentioning Poland brought risks of being denounced as a "warmonger" by party members and their allies.[54]

With the German invasion of the Soviet Union on June 22, 1941, all of these peace efforts suddenly vanished.[55] The same organizations and people who had denounced war now called for rapid mobilization, intervention, and "all-out aid to Russia." Opposition to fascism was a mutable tactic; support for Soviet policy was a strategic constant. Arthur Koestler's remark that the party did not represent the Left but the East was reified.[56] Party member and screenwriter Donald Ogden Stewart began to sob tears of joy on hearing the news of the German invasion because he was able to "fight Fascism" again.[57] The invasion made Stewart euphoric because it allowed him to continue "believing in . . . the leadership of the great Stalin."[58] Denunciations of the Roosevelt administration and warnings of incipient domestic fascism were replaced by jingoist patriotism and perfervid Americanism. The relocation of Japanese Americans, for example, was applauded by the CPUSA in its new orientation.[59] By late 1941, to paraphrase Moran and Rogin, Hollywood was mobilizing the country for war with a hastily reconstructed Popular Front of New Dealers and Communists exploiting "celebratory nationalism" to launch an antifascist crusade.[60]

Poland was thus at the center of the most agonizing moment in the party's history. The invasion of Poland coincided with the commencement of Nazi-Soviet collaboration and the brief history of the party as an apologist for German aggression in Europe and an opponent of any critique of militant fascism on the march. Any mention of the 1939 Polish campaign recalled the twenty-one months of Soviet-Nazi collaboration. The Polish case was dangerous, as it exposed the cynicism of the party line and made into nonsense the claim that both Russia and the party were stalwart opponents of Nazism. Hence, for Hollywood's Communists, Poland was a topic best ignored. Since Poland could not be safely discussed, it was consigned to oblivion or, on those few occasions when it was mentioned, presented in a manner so unappealing as to elicit no sympathy. There was a well-prepared series of tropes and conventions in place to discredit Poland's prewar regime and to ridicule or disparage its government-in-exile.

4

The Roosevelt Administration and Film during the War

POLAND'S TRAVAILS HAD NO CONSEQUENCES for American policy, and public opinion continued to oppose active American involvement in the war after the September campaign. By the time the United States entered the war, the major opponent of Nazi Germany was the Soviet Union, and Poland was a weak member of the anti-German coalition. Propitiating the Russians was the preemptive concern of American policy regarding Poland and Polish-Russian difficulties after 1941. The idea of a free Poland may have been theoretically American policy, but it was completely subordinated to whatever was required to maintain "cordial relations" with the Russians.[1]

Within months after the attack on Pearl Harbor, Washington quite obviously had no intention of opposing Soviet territorial expansion at Polish expense and was unconcerned about the protection of Polish sovereignty.[2] In April 1942, Roosevelt told Under Secretary of State Adolf Berle that he "would not particularly mind" if Russia seized all of eastern Poland—without any consultation with the local inhabitants. This was a direct contradiction of the Atlantic Charter he had signed only weeks before.[3] Besides, as Roosevelt told Francis Cardinal Spellman, the people of eastern Poland "want to become Russian."[4] This was particularly callous as that area had been subjected to massive forcible migrations. The most charitable observation is that Roosevelt simply did not know what he was talking about.

So solicitous was the Roosevelt administration of the Russians that in 1943 the president dismissed out of hand overwhelming proof of Russian guilt for the Katyń massacre and insisted without any explanation that the charge was "German propaganda." His administration threatened and coerced Polish-language broadcasters into silence when they sought to present evidence of Russian guilt, actions later denounced by Congress.[5] Roosevelt informed an aide that he had no intention of negotiating with Poland; it would get what he decided.[6] In disgust, the Polish ambassador in Washington characterized the Roosevelt administration as practicing a "New Deal form of Machiavellian naiveness."[7]

Roosevelt grew demonstrably impatient with Polish issues as the war continued, regarding them as a nuisance to the unfolding of his Russian policy. In 1945 he blithely opined that Poland had had no government since 1939, denying the legal and moral authority of the Polish government-in-exile. A few months earlier, he had told Ambassador Averill Harriman that he was completely unconcerned about the postwar fate of Poland.[8] This combination of capricious disdain for Polish interests and solicitude for the Russians characterized the administration's policy regarding Polish-Russian issues. It is not surprising that the idea that Roosevelt had "betrayed Poland" was "pervasive" in the Polish community of America by the end of the war.[9]

The Roosevelt administration was keenly aware of the influence of film in rallying public opinion and maintaining domestic unity. Hence it took rapid steps to involve the film industry in the war effort.[10] Hollywood, early in the war, was designated an "essential war industry."[11] By executive order, the president created the OWI on June 13, 1942, consolidating "several prior information agencies."[12] The OWI was "the chief government propaganda agency during World War II."[13] Reporting to its director, Elmer Davis, was the mousey and insignificant Lowell Mellett, chief of the BMP. The BMP "monitored the content of every film coming out of Hollywood."[14] All of the key administrators were journalists by profession and ardent liberals by creed, devoted to Roosevelt and the New Deal.[15] Davis regarded the "entertainment picture" as the "easiest way to inject propaganda" into Americans' lives.[16] This in turn reflected the keen interest in molding public opinion that was characteristic of the Roosevelt administration.[17] The movies, an OWI official explained, "can give the public understanding."[18]

Even before the OWI was constituted, the Roosevelt administration was informed that the Polish government was aggrieved at the neglect of Polish suffering in American information and propaganda efforts. The Poles were convinced that the inattention to German atrocities in Poland—the absence of "any moral support"—"encourages [the] Germans to believe" they could act "with impunity." The Roosevelt administration admitted that the "Poles' lot is by far worse than that of the populations in occupied Belgium, Holland, Norway and France."[19] Key presidential adviser Harry L. Hopkins was sufficiently troubled by the virtual inattention to Poland that he urged more "publicity" for it in late 1941, though he muted the significance of this by dissolving Poland among an unspecified group of "the smaller countries," which deserved an occasional mention.[20] Hopkins was also aware that surveys compiled by the Office of Facts and Figures (one of the OWI's predecessors) in March 1942 indicated that the American people were very well disposed toward the Soviet Union and that even Stalin enjoyed a favorable rating from the public.[21]

The OWI was accused, deservedly as it now appears, of employing a large number of Communists in key positions. Several of the employees of the Polish section, for example, later figured in the postwar Communist government in Warsaw. The presence of Communists in sensitive positions in the OWI was well known during the war, but the efforts of Poland's ambassador to Washington, Jan Ciechanowski, to bring this to the attention of the Roosevelt administration were denounced as meddling in American affairs by Davis, who similarly rejected efforts by Representative John Lesinski, Democrat from Michigan, to alert him to this fact.[22] The Hollywood Left rallied to the OWI's defense, correctly discerning that an ideological soul mate was under attack.[23]

The Poles' conviction that the OWI was inveterately hostile to Poland and extraordinarily pro-Russian is corroborated by the reminiscences of Phillip Dunne. Dunne had cofounded the Screen Writers Guild and was appointed chief of production of the OWI's Overseas Operations Branch in 1942. A major figure at Twentieth Century–Fox, Dunne was also a powerful member of the BMP. Though never a party member himself, Dunne was politically on the left and close to many party members in Hollywood. Dunne had little sympathy for Poland during the war. For him it was simply a fascist and anti-Semitic country, and Soviet designs on its territory were completely justified by both history and ideology.[24] Dunne's Overseas Operations Branch was criticized in Congress in 1943 by Lesinski and others for its pro-Soviet and anti-Polish activities.[25] The BMP was equally uncongenial to the Poles.

BMP chief Mellett established a Hollywood office under Nelson Poynter, who had a staff of reviewers working under him. Many of the films dealing with Russian and Polish topics were reviewed by Lillian Bergquist, who provided commentaries and suggestions. She was not only a key figure in the BMP but was also vice president of the Screen Readers Guild and a member of the Communist Party.[26]

The OWI quickly established clear ideological guidelines for Hollywood. They were enforced by Poynter, who furnished the studios with a widely distributed manual for their political guidance—the "clearest possible statement of New Deal liberal views on how Hollywood should fight the war." The guide insisted that the building of a "new world order" be presented as the goal of the war. Indeed, neither fascism nor Nazism was the real enemy; rather, the struggle was against "militarism . . . the doctrine of force"—an extraordinary vague formulation hardly more appropriate for Germany than for Soviet Russia. If "the doctrine of force" was the ultimate enemy, and Russia was a specifically designated ally, logically the Soviet Union could not be characterized as a regime based on force. The ideological definition of the war was contradictory and could be maintained only by fiat. Questions of traditional power politics were not considered germane, and both the United States and its allies were to be treated with "uncritical adulation."[27]

The manual repeatedly raised the question of Russia. The charge that "the Russians were going to sell us down the river" was attributed to "the enemy," suggesting that all criticism of Russia was highly suspect. Studios were enjoined to "emphasize the might and heroism" of the Allies, specifically "all the victories of the Russians," Chinese resistance, British fortitude, Dutch naval efforts, and the "resistance" in Norway and Yugoslavia and "other parts of occupied Europe." Obviously the Polish struggle against the Germans was insignificant. Studios were warned to be on their guard for "lies" about Russia and England and were asked, rhetorically, "So we reject Communism, but do we reject Russia as an ally?"[28] Communist screenwriter John Howard Lawson was warm in his praise for Poynter.[29]

No film "that had Anti-Semitism at its core" was to be produced lest it complicate the administration's pursuit of the war. Hence, in 1942–1943, the OWI was able to face down an enormous campaign by the American Jewish Congress to force Hollywood to depict the Holo-caust.[30] Only at the war's end, when the OWI's "influence was fading due to budgetary cutbacks," did the Germans' persecution of the Jews gain Hollywood's attention. Robert Fyne considers the OWI to have been very effective in shaping the ideological content of Hollywood's efforts: "For a four-year period the motion picture industry followed the OWI's edicts, producing every title in a standard format. The results were an effective combination of information, patriotism, hero-worship, and propaganda."[31] The OWI realized the potential of films to shape public attitudes. It was relentless in ballyhooing what it regarded as the correct Hollywood view of the war. It issued a weekly newsletter, widely distributed in a great many languages, titled *Letter from America.* The OWI was very open about the importance of providing accept-able motion pictures for the public. *Letter from America* explained that films were "a weapon of unexpected importance on the home front, among the fighting forces, and in the occupied territories." This article cited, as examples of such "weapons," *Action in the North Atlantic* and the occupation films *Hangmen Also Die* and *The Moon Is Down.*[32] Later issues mentioned favorably such pieces of pro-Russian propaganda as *The North Star* and Capra's *Battle of Russia.*[33]

Not content to merely review films for their content, Poynter and his staff pressed themes and ideas on the studios and were withering in their criticism of films that fell afoul of their guidelines. Indeed, Poyn-ter boasted in his first annual report to Mellett that the "large num-ber of valuable picture ideas" he had "suggested to producers" was his major accomplishment.[34] Poynter regular used terms like "atrocity" and "libel" for films he did not like and went so far as to suggest specific lines of dialogue he wished to be inserted. As a colleague noted, the voluble Poynter had a "tendency to talk too big" and "over-step your authority" and was "careless about facts."[35]

The BMP insisted on seeing scripts before production and interpos-ing itself between the studios and other governmental agencies, whose cooperation was vital for the many films that contained military aspects. Mellett later insisted that even this was not enough and demanded that the studios furnish preliminary drafts of possible films.[36] This out-raged some in Hollywood: Walter Wanger, president of the Academy of Motion Picture Arts and Sciences, publicly denounced the OWI for seeking "to dominate [film] production" by going beyond censoring to actively trying to "write things into scripts." The OWI "continually urged [the studios], under pressure, to make so-called propaganda pictures." Wanger fulminated that the OWI regarded the American people as "boobs."[37]

In November 1942, Ulric Bell joined the Hollywood staff. He represented the Overseas Operations Branch of the OWI and could threaten to prevent the foreign distribution of a film if the BMP objected. The financial implications of such a verdict were daunting. By 1942 the BMP already had significant influence over the content of all Hollywood war films, but it lusted for still more capacity for intervention. By early 1943 Poynter and Bell were in an acrimonious debate over the OWI's power to emend and censor scripts. Bell was aggressive and sought, successfully, more power to intervene.[38] The result was that the OWI exerted even greater influence over motion picture production.

It is perhaps surprising, given its arrogant meddling, that the OWI prompted so little resistance from the notoriously independent moguls, apart from public complaints such as that by Wanger. The reasons for this are complex. First, certainly, was the studios' desire to be seen as patriotic and engaged in war work, for reasons both sincere and commercial. Wanger himself boasted that the studios were churning out "several hundred" pictures specifically designed to "induce war enthusiasm, comprehension and kinship with our allies" quite independent of OWI promptings.[39] Second was the fact that the ideological content so vehemently required by the BMP was identical to the Left-progressive views of the great majority of the Hollywood screenwriters.

The BMP's manual was prefaced by a "yardstick" of seven points, which commenced with "Will this picture help win the war?" and included a proviso that the film not "create a false picture of America [or] her Allies." Specific guidelines for the portrayal of "The United Nations" stated, "Above all avoid disparaging portrayals of Allied types." The war was to be presented as "a people's war" stressing the importance of "the man on the street." As regarded immigrants, films were to "show aliens aiding the war effort."[40]

These general suggestions were given greater precision in a lengthy memorandum drafted by Poynter in October 1942 that included a section titled "We Can Do Business with Russia." This document described the types of films Poynter wanted the studios to make in the future. It began by noting that "there is still widespread distrust and misunderstanding" regarding Soviet Russia among the American people. "We must overcome this feeling," he noted. The idea that "Russia and Communism" were threats to "world peace and stable world order" were "Axis propaganda" that had to be counteracted.[41]

To demonstrate his point, Poynter insisted that Soviet war aims were "essentially . . . the same" as those of the United States. Russia had promised to "seek no territorial gains and to refrain from interference in the internal affairs of other countries." Moreover, Russia was no threat to the world because its wartime exertions would render it harmless for "at least a generation"; it did "not need more territory," and in any event "since the end of the last World War Russia has the best record of seeking to preserve the peace of any major power in the world except the United States." Proleptically he noted that the "attack on Finland . . . [was] strictly defensive and justifiable." He concluded by asking, "Will Russia try to Sovietize Europe?" He answered piously, "The Russian government's stated policy says no." But "there will be revolution in Europe," and "the revolution will be to the left, since governments in Europe today are as far to the right as they can go, being fascist." As for Communists in the United States, they were a "threat" only if "our system fails."[42]

This memorandum was a pastiche of gross naiveté, prevarication, and nonsense. One can only wonder, for example, what the reference to all European governments' being fascist could conceivably mean. That such a combination of Soviet apologetics and unsophisticated geopolitical notions formed the basis of the BMP's preferences for Hollywood films is breathtaking.

In late 1942 a BMP memorandum included this extraordinary pronouncement: "A study of Russia's diplomatic history since the last war shows that she perhaps more than any other nation has stood by her diplomatic agreements."[43] Robert Mayhew understandably concludes that "the New Dealers reviewing films for the OWI [in Hollywood] followed a line that was virtually indistinguishable from the Soviets."[44]

In fact, even those Hollywood writers who were party members regarded the OWI as relentlessly pro-Soviet. Paul Jarrico, author of the panegyric *Song of Russia,* recalled that "Hollywood was more than willing to do war films, but it took a lot of pressure by Roosevelt and the OWI to get the major studios to celebrate our alliance with Russia."[45] MGM's Louis B. Mayer, for example, produced the film only reluctantly and under administration pressure.[46] Mayhew observes that BMP reviews were "slanted [and] propagandistic" to an "amazing" degree.[47]

It is therefore not surprising that Poynter worked closely with the Hollywood Writers Mobilization to produce a series of short films "for use in industrial plants and Army camps." An FBI informant noted that Poynter "demanded a pro-Russian slant as a prerequisite to acceptance" of the films and worked most closely with screenwriters known for their party membership.[48] In 1942 Poynter explained to Robert Buckner that they agreed that the Soviets had essentially the same objectives as the United States, that Stalin had been forced to purge fascists in the 1930s, and that by opposing fascism in the war, the Russians were demonstrating their opposition to militarism, as extolled in the OWI manual.[49]

As regarded Poland, the OWI had very clear guidelines. The central goal of American propaganda and management of the news and motion pictures was to promote allied unity. This required the most favorable possible portrayal of the Soviet Union and the avoidance or deemphasis of anything that might disrupt that unity, for example suggesting to the American public that Russia was anything other than a virtuous and honorable ally.[50] Unfortunately, as is well known, Soviet-Polish relations were a series of outrages visited on Poland by the Russians from the September 17 invasion to the imposition of a Communist regime six years later. To make this palatable required a herculean effort: producing a barrage of pro-Soviet propaganda—witness the stream of Russophile films—and either ignoring Poland or presenting it in an unfavorable light to vitiate the Polish case against Russia.

As a result, the occupation subgenre of the war film was most often set in Norway or France, two Western European countries whose depiction, whether favorable or not, had no consequence for American audiences' attitude toward the Soviet Union. To engage in a counterfactual exercise, we can well imagine how a series of films showing a heroic resistance effort in Poland would have raised a host of awkward issues. Half of Poland was, after all, under Russian occupation. Moreover, the Soviets clearly coveted Polish territory and regarded the country as within their sphere of influence. It would have been difficult to celebrate Polish valor while selling the Soviet Union as a champion of democracy. Hence Hollywood followed the Roosevelt administration's lead in deemphasizing, if not ignoring, Poland, which raised unpleasant issues in the area of manipulating public sentiment about the war.

The Czechs were a much less difficult problem. There were no territorial issues between the Czech government-in-exile, led by the pliable Eduard Beneš, and Soviet Russia. Indeed, the Czech government was warm in its praise for Moscow, unlike the London Poles, for whom the Soviet Union was at best an ally of necessity.[51] Hence *Casablanca*'s Victor László could never have been a Pole, but as a "Czechoslovakian" he was suitably exotic without raising criticism of Soviet Russia.[52]

No studio enjoyed more cordial relations with the BMP and its Hollywood office than Warner Brothers. "There is a grip of Rooseveltian loyalty about Warners," Ethan Mordden notes.[53] In August 1940, "Jack Warner . . . offered to produce any film the administration wanted regardless of cost," and in the fall, Mellett and Harry Warner discussed the outlines of Hollywood's future cooperation with the government. Both were ardent supporters of Roosevelt's reelection. Mellett sent Leo C. Rosten to Hollywood as the "authorized representative of the National Defense Commission" to meet with studio heads. Mellett was particularly anxious that Warner share with Rosten his "very considerable thinking" on the nature of government-Hollywood relations.[54]

When Mellett became director of the BMP, the Warner Brothers director of advertising and publicity, Charles Einfeld, was delighted: "How long we have hoped for just your kind of guy!"[55] Mellett regarded Harry Warner and his studio as his principal allies in the film community. One of his first letters after assuming the directorship of the BMP was to Harry, whom he referred to as "the pioneer among those in the motion picture industry who grasped the significance of world events" and "the first to talk with me about it and to indicate the part pictures could play."[56] Einfeld informed director Frank Capra in early 1942, "Frankly and sincerely we consider our whole Warner Bros. setup as another agency of the government."[57] Harry Warner was truly "Roosevelt's man in Hollywood."[58]

This mutual affection became much greater when Poynter arrived in Hollywood and predictably gushed over every Warner Brothers war film. He was often on the set during production.[59] Poynter regarded himself as the major figure behind Warner Brothers' infamous *Mission to Moscow*. As a result, the BMP and Warner Brothers were virtually a united front in promoting and later defending the film from its critics.[60] When the film's Stalinist screenwriter Howard Koch replied to the mounting attacks in the *New York Times,* Poynter sent Koch an effusive letter of support and wrote to the Warner Brothers publicity department, urging it to reprint Koch's letter and send it to "an enormous list of writers, scholars, publicists, editors, etc.—including the whole theatrical fraternity."[61] The Hollywood office of the BMP was aghast that this film, which Poynter had praised unstintingly as a refutation of "isolationists and appeasers," would suffer any criticism. For the BMP this exercise in propaganda was "a great impetus to our whole job of getting this industry into a realm of really important issues."[62]

The consequences for Poland and the Poles of OWI policy, and of the work of such zealous pro-Soviets as Poynter, were baleful. Fundamentally, the BMP was committed to presenting a dishonest portrayal of the Soviet Union in which its geopolitical benignity was central. When Hollywood issued such propaganda films as *Mission to Moscow, The North Star,* and *Song of Russia,* Poynter wrote to Mellett in absolute delight, "Our knowledge of Russia will be strengthened" by these films, which constituted an "enormous contribution toward post-war collaboration of peace-loving peoples."[63] This was a private memorandum; hence Poynter cannot be excused by the oft-cited post-1945 explanation that portraying the Soviet Union to the public in false colors was necessary for the war effort. Either Poynter regarded these propagandistic exercises as fundamentally accurate, in which case he was a man of unusual naiveté, or he knew that they were misleading and approved of the effort to deceive his fellow citizens.

In 1943 the OWI compiled surveys of public opinion regarding the war and popular attitudes toward various countries. The results are fascinating. One question asked, Which country is "trying hardest to win the war?" The percentage choosing Great Britain was low, 5–8 percent. However, the number choosing Soviet Russia doubled between May and November from 22 percent to 44 percent. Similarly, those who regarded Russia as "dependable" after the war rose from 38 percent in May, to 51 percent in August, during the same period that the numbers for Britain declined from 76 percent to 72 percent.[64] Obviously, selling Stalin's Russia was a successful operation in 1943, and the BMP was a major part of it. However, we should remember that the Soviet military effort was always popular in the United States, and no propaganda was needed to convince the public of it.

Because the Russian invasion of Poland occurred shortly after the war began, it would be impossible to portray the Soviet Union in such positive terms if its relationship with Poland were noted, even in passing. Hence the BMP placed structural impediments before Hollywood to ensure that any portrayal of Poland did not reflect badly on Moscow. Characteristically, the BMP insisted in late 1942 that because the American public did not "well understand" Soviet actions of the recent past, MGM should interpose in the *Song of Russia* script certain interpretations of Soviet foreign policy to enlighten them: that the Hitler-Stalin pact was only an expedient, as Moscow regarded war with fascism as inevitable; that the Soviet invasion of Finland in November 1939 was a defensive gesture dictated by war; and that the September 17 invasion of Poland was also a gesture of self-defense, aimed at "extending her [Soviet Russia's] frontiers soon after Germany's invasion of Poland in 1939."[65]

To strengthen the OWI's argument, Mellett sent the MGM script to the first secretary of the Russian embassy in Washington, Vladimir Bazykin, who offered specific wording for the film's dialogue so that the Soviet position on the Hitler-Stalin pact would be presented according to the Kremlin's line.[66] BMP reviewer Lillian Bergquist also specifically requested that studios provide Soviet officials with copies of scripts before a film's release so they could review content.[67] No such request was made in conjunction with any film depicting Poland, and the BMP seems never to have consulted the Polish authorities regarding the accuracy or content of any film in which Polish issues were portrayed. It perhaps need not be said that the BMP found every complimentary film made about the Soviet Union during the war to be extraordinarily fine and objected only that the films were not sufficiently exuberant in their praise.[68]

However, the guidelines about presenting the Allies—usually referred to as the "United Nations"—in a flattering light were enforced unevenly. The BMP disliked scripts that were even mildly critical of the British. Thus Columbia's 1943 film *Appointment in Berlin* was scolded for an unflattering remark regarding British policy at Munich in October 1938.[69] The same studio's 1942 release *Counter Espionage* was attacked because it suggested that Scotland Yard was inept in the handling of a fictitious investigation. British officials, including the police, were not to be portrayed unflatteringly.[70] Twentieth Century–Fox was similarly criticized because its 1943 film *Diplomatic Courier* adverted to prewar British policy in a negative manner.[71] The BMP was even queasy over the fact that the MGM compilation of patriotic episodes *American Cavalcade* made a reference to the American Revolution: would mentioning this episode of discord with London make Americans "unsympathetic to the British"? the BMP agonized.[72]

A similar protective mantle was cast over the French by the BMP, which did not like that the trivial films *Blonde Fever* and *Block Busters* contained passing remarks that the French might find disparaging.[73] It also found that *Assignment in Brittany* was insufficiently positive in its portrayal of the French people. The film showed a Frenchman "grousing" when "his devotion to the cause of freedom should be a primary part of him coloring all his actions."[74] The OWI wrote indignantly to Republic Pictures about what it thought was an uncomplimentary reference to the French in its film *Secrets of the Underground.*[75] The OWI did not argue that any of these films were critical or nasty toward England or France, merely that the portrayals were not uniformly positive.

Czechs and Norwegians were the objects of special BMP solicitude. Commenting on the film *Hitler's Madmen,* the BMP reviewer included the obiter dictum that, "since most Czechs are militant warriors," the film was commendable for celebrating the Czech underground.[76] The portrayal of Czechs as "militant warriors" was scarcely justified by the developments since 1938. The BMP also commended *Hangmen Also Die* for its pro-Czech tone.[77] Similarly, Paramount's *Avengers,* a British import, was commended for depicting the Norwegians as "anything but a defeated people."[78]

These responses were as nothing compared to the special solicitude for the Russians. The BMP was preternaturally sensitive regarding any film that mentioned Russians or had even minor Russian characters. Hence it was very concerned that the Soviet agents depicted in *Background to Danger* were not presented in a sufficiently positive light and that the Russian woman in *Bomber's Moon,* though completely positive, was shown without a sense of humor; this was to be remedied: Americans could not be presented with a Russian who did not have a sense of humor.[79] A character in the B film *Miss V from Moscow,* released by the minor studio Producers Releasing Corporation, though positive (and even presumably possessing a sense of humor), concerned the BMP because she was insufficiently "Russian." More should have been done to make the ethnicity of the role real to the audience.[80] In perhaps the most extreme case, the BMP insisted that what it admitted was a "minor character" identified as of Russian ethnicity be removed from the film *Destroyer* because he was included as a comic foil. Russians were much too important to be cast in trivial roles. The comment is telling: "It is of extreme importance at present to maintain confidence in and achieve understanding of our Russian ally; [hence] the character of Yasha is an unfortunate choice." If the story required a clownish character, "make him an American."[81] Yasha was removed. Obviously, "understanding" was equated with a presentation that was uniformly exemplary; Russians could not even be silly.

In the spring of 1943, MGM supplied the Hollywood office with a novel by Frederick Hazlitt Brennan and a long synopsis intended to provide the basis for a film script.[82] The story, episodic and complex, was an imaginative though not particularly intelligent fantasy version of the war in which the Soviet Union deserts the anti-German coalition and a 1942 peace conference results. Although most of the characters are, for reasons unclear, Irish, there is a "fiery young Polish girl escaped from Germany, where she had participated in an un-realized scheme to kill Hitler" who plays a significant and positive role. The facts that this Pole for some reason bears the quite impossible name of Karen Laurencos and seems to reside in Lisbon are among the story's oddities, but they are perhaps not of moment. The BMP was horrified by the MGM proposal and responded with an inordinately long response full of melodramatic phrasing. A film that portrayed the Soviet Union "negatively"—by, in effect, repeating its 1939 maneuver of joining with Germany—was outrageous: "The suggestion that our valiant Russian ally is planning to sell out the United Nations is gravely detrimental" to the war effort; worse, it was an "injustice." The BMP was indignant. It did not analyze films; it bore witness to the interests of the Soviet Union.[83]

As we have seen, the OWI consulted Russian diplomatic officials regarding films portraying Russia and even urged the studios to confer with other governments over foreign topics. For example, when Columbia proposed to make a film titled *Doughboys in Ireland,* the Hollywood office of the OWI suggested that the studio consult "some Irish authority" to assure "no errors in the presentation of Irish people and customs." Although Ireland was neutral during the war and pro-German sympathies were not uncommon there, Hollywood maintained its traditional favorable disposition toward the Irish.

Curiously, this concern for the positive portrayal of foreigners and their government did not extend to Poles.[84] When Columbia prepared *None Shall Escape* and Warner Brothers produced *In Our Time,* both set in Poland and presenting Polish "people and customs" in profusion, the BMP did not suggest that any Polish authorities be consulted, though certainly Poland was a far more exotic and less known locale than Ireland.[85] Even extremely negative portrayals of Poland, its government, its military, and its general population never elicited a rebuke from the BMP. Poles regularly—indeed, almost invariably—were portrayed in American films as mentally unstable, incompetent, vicious, and vacuous scoundrels, cowards, traitors, buffoons, and Nazi sympathizers, and the Polish government was accused of appeasement and fascism, all without a murmur of protest from the BMP. Kracauer's notes that Hollywood's goal of "endearing everything British to the American masses" could be expanded to cover all the Allies—save Poland, which was an exception to the policy enforced by the OWI.[86] It is inconceivable that the BMP would have allowed this passage from *None Shall Escape* to be uttered about any nationality other than the Poles: "These aren't people, they're dogs. But good dogs. You can train them."[87] This difference is particularly noteworthy given Ana M. Lopez's conclusion that "Hollywood does not represent ethnics and minorities; it creates them."[88]

Contrast the BMP's indifference to Poland and Polish issues with its angry reaction to MGM's planned 1943 film tentatively titled "The White Cliffs." The BMP was very unhappy that the film alluded gently to social and class frictions in Great Britain. Such themes should not be raised. However, an even greater transgression was that the film discussed the 1942 Dieppe Raid without mentioning the Russians. Of course, no Russians participated in the Dieppe Raid, but this was not of moment to the BMP. The film should have gotten around that awkward reality by demonstrating that "had it not been for the heroic battles of the Russian army . . . the British might have been fighting the Nazis on British soil."[89] The Dieppe Raid could have a Russian perspective if you only tried hard to find one. Indeed, by such logic, everything had a Russian aspect. Ironically, Polish naval and ground forces did fight at Dieppe and suffered considerable casualties, but the BMP, so concerned about placing Russians at Dieppe, did not notice the Poles' omission from the film.

Poles in Europe could be depicted in any manner whatever, but the BMP was concerned about positive portrayals of the various ethnic communities in America, including the Poles. It regularly lauded positive portrayals of Italian Americans and Greek Americans and even complained when Polish Americans were not shown in a positive light, though its main concern was the manner in which African Americans were portrayed. Here we have a curious distinction. Whereas the BMP was unconcerned about unflattering—indeed, vicious—portrayals of Poland or the Poles of Europe, it showed some concern for the sensibilities of Polish Americans. Although we must speculate on the factors at work, it is probable that the former issues automatically carried with them foreign policy matters, especially the BMP's sensitivity over extraordinary Russian matters, whereas the latter almost certainly did not and could be considered more a question of national unity among Americans of various backgrounds rather than any particular concern for those of Polish origin.

By comparison with the activities of the BMP, the monitoring of films carried out by the Motion Picture Producers and Distributors of America (MPPDA) and the application of its famous Production Code, established in 1930, were devoid of geopolitical significance. The office's reviews focused heavily on the moral contents of the films, being very concerned about the depiction of illicit sex and the use of suggestive or even mildly profane language. One film was criticized because a soldier thumbed his nose. The association's occasional forays into a film's political implications were perfunctory at best. Hence the reviewer of the Stalinist *North Star* said nothing about its favorable portrayal of the Soviet Union; the reviewer of *Edge of Darkness* said nothing about the depiction of a Pole as a Nazi camp follower; the reviewer of *Tomorrow the World* failed to notice that there is a symbolic clash between a Pole and a German in the United States with the Pole bearing the name of the hero of Poland's national anthem; and the reviewer's only comment on *Desperate Journey* was that, since the film "reflects favorably upon the English . . . we think you don't have to submit it to the War Department."[90]

The MPPDA's script reader filed a daily production report that included "War Angle" as the third most important category, immediately following the title and producer of a film. This seemingly important category asked whether the film involved U.S. forces or "British, Canadian, Australian, Chinese, Russian, Italian, Japanese or Miscellaneous."[91] Polish forces did not even exist as a category for the MPPDA.

5

Hollywood's Version of the War: The Polish Films

HOLLYWOOD HAD MUCH MATERIAL to use but created only three films set in Poland. Two of them deal with the last days of peace and the immediate aftermath of the invasion. Only *None Shall Escape*, made in 1944, focuses on the occupation. Certainly the inattention to Poland reflected the fact that, by the time of American belligerency, the September campaign was more than two years past. By late 1941, the war seemed largely an affair of Britain, Russia, and the United States.

Life under German occupation was another matter, however. Unprecedented in its brutality, this was a story of contemporary relevance. Hollywood showed interest in Czech, French, and Norwegian occupation, but the situation in Poland was virtually ignored. Poland's contribution to the war effort after 1939 also went unnoticed. The systematic extermination of Poland's Jews was also not presented. Certainly nothing of Russia's invasion and seizure of eastern Poland ever was mentioned by Hollywood.

Apart from the failure to exploit abundant material, how did Hollywood present the Poles? Let us consider its modest repertoire of three films.[1] The first, most expensive, and by far best-known American wartime film devoted to Poland was the 1942 United Artists release *To Be or Not to Be,* set in occupied Warsaw early in the war.[2] Its main characters are a group of actors, one of them an understandably morose Jewish performer. In a convoluted story line involving multiple impersonations, the Poles uncover a German spy, save their colleagues from the clutches of the Gestapo, and eventually escape to England. The performances, led by Jack Benny at the height of his career and Carole Lombard in her last role before an untimely death, are excellent.[3] Director Ernst Lubitsch, a German émigré renowned for his sophisticated comedies (*Ninotchka* is perhaps his best-known work), has received retrospective glowing reviews, and critical appreciation for the film has grown with the years.[4]

However, the film's satirical approach to the grim subject—occupied Warsaw and the consequent plight of the Jews—and the presence of the well-known comedian Benny perhaps explain why it initially appeared "to a barrage of hostile notices which found the film to be in the grossest bad taste," one even deeming it "propaganda for Goebbels" that "reduced the war in Europe to a bad joke." Lubitsch and producer Alexander Korda were "shocked by the reaction," which indicated that certain topics, particularly the German persecution of the Jews, could not be safely addressed, especially as comedy.[5] Reviewers focused specific attention on an exchange between the doltish but vicious Colonel Eberhard of the Gestapo (Sig Ruman) and a vain Polish actor named Josef Tura (Benny).[6] Tura, in disguise, asks Eberhard whether he has ever seen Tura act. The colonel responds, "What he did to Shakespeare, we are now doing to Poland." Whereas *Time* magazine found the line hilarious, many people then and now regard it as grotesque. Even Lubitsch's wife asked him to cut it from the film.[7]

The *New York Times'* influential Bosley Crowther was so appalled by the film that he wrote a lengthy reconsideration after his initial, rather brief evaluation. Crowther's principal objection was that "setting a fantastic comedy against a background of contemporary woe" was tasteless to the point of incomprehensibility. Crowther denounced the film's "disregard of sensibility" and was perplexed by the absence of "outrage" at some of the sequences. It was "callous" to provide Warsaw's anguish as a backdrop for such antics. In perhaps the most sympathetic limes he ever wrote about Poland, Crowther reminded readers that a comedy was inappropriate commentary for "the anguish of a nation which is one of the great tragedies of all time."[8] A few months later, Theodore Strauss, Crowther's *Times* colleague, listed *To Be or Not to Be* as one of the worst films of the year, commenting that the film was "offensively conceived."[9] Even the leftist Hollywood Writers Mobiliza-

tion, which generally was indifferent to the portrayal of Poland, retrospectively referred to the film as "callous."[10] Most of the contemporary
reviews were in a similar vein.[11]

The film remains controversial. It was the first Hollywood consideration of the plight of Poland, and it raised, however tangentially, such
powerful issues as the terror of German occupation and the persecution
of the Jews. To be sure, the film was produced before some of the worst
aspects of Nazi occupation became common knowledge. Nonetheless,
no other Hollywood film about German occupation is in the form of a
satire. There is no comedy about the horrors of German-controlled Norway, Czechoslovakia, or France. Only in Poland is the situation made
the backdrop of clever jokes and recherché bedroom farce.[12] Films that
depict the German occupation of Russia uniformly present the Germans
as fiends; there is no buffoonish Sig Ruman in *The North Star* or *Song
of Russia.* Had there been a number of films about the German occupation of Poland, the fact that one used this circumstance as a frame
for comedy would still make the Lubitsch film controversial. However,
the fact that this was the first of only two films exploring the subject
(and the second, as we will see, was a rather minor production late
in the war) adds considerably to the controversy attaching to the film.
Crowther asked rhetorically why the public was not outraged that Hollywood did this to Poland. Lubitsch later commented that a comedy was
"the only way to get people to hear about the miseries of Poland." If
true, this tells us a good deal about both Hollywood's and the American
public's level of interest in Poland.[13]

How does this film portray the Poles? According to the British film
historian Colin Shindler, Lubitsch and Korda intended to offer a portrait
of the Poles that emphasized their "obstinacy and idiocy."[14] However, a
closer look does not support this conclusion. The Poles are resourceful
and clever, and they repeatedly outwit the Nazis in a series of daring
if improbable episodes.[15] One of them, played by Robert Stack in one
of his earliest performances, is a heroic pilot flying with the Royal Air
Force. Stack, who would become a leading man in B films and then
enjoy a long television career, is handsome and dashing. Other Poles
are played by Lionel Atwill, Tom Dugan, and Charles Halton in uniformly good performances. Even the vainglorious Benny, playing an
incompetent actor and a cuckolded husband, is a devoted patriot quite
ready to die for his country.[16] Moreover, the sympathetic Jewish mem-

ber of the acting troupe, Greenberg (Felix Bressart in an outstanding performance), is completely integrated into the company, the friend and colleague of the other actors. Whereas German anti-Semitism makes him live in terror, he is completely safe among his fellow Poles, who are devoted to him.[17]

However, several features of the Poles are presented to parody or at least question certain supposed Polish traits. Their patriotism, though sincere, is a bit ridiculous; their bravery is ostentatious. They belong, in fine, to a theatrical nation that, though quite charming, is not really appropriate for the modern world.[18] Even though the film acknowledges the existence of an underground movement in Poland, it is portrayed as being directed by the British, who refer to it as "our organization." Hence a Polish soldier reports his suspicions regarding a possible German spy not to his own government but to the British authorities.[19] Indeed, there is no Polish government at all in this film. Hollywood never recognized the Polish government-in-exile.

The government of Poland on the eve of the war is presented briefly, and unflatteringly: a government censor demands that the Warsaw theater troupes cancel a performance ridiculing Hitler. The implication is that the Polish government is either craven or inclined to appeasement; neither reading is accurate or generous. Hollywood would repeatedly charge Warsaw with appeasement; this is perhaps the earliest example of the practice. Though the scene is seemingly insignificant, Lubitsch obviously regarded it as important. He even briefly considered titling the film *The Censor Forbids*.[20]

Moreover, the September campaign is presented in such a way as to suggest that the country was overcome in days, perhaps hours. In the opening moments of the film, a narrator explains that the German invasion found the Poles "stunned and helpless," an inaccurate description that does not cast the Poles in a heroic light. This is a far cry from Hollywood's standard adulatory depiction of Russian, Norwegian, and Czech resistance.

In praising the later Polish resistance to the Nazis, a voice-over explains that the "real struggle" is being waged neither by the home army nor by the forces serving the government-in-exile but by the nonexistent "Polish squadron of the RAF." This reduces the entire Polish military effort to a minor footnote.[21] Therefore, whatever the intentions of Korda and Lubitsch, their film suggests unmistakably that Poland was not a serious focus for American attention. Even when heroic, Poles are insignificant, and the important decisions are left to the British.[22] This conclusion, and the fact that unpleasant issues were raised that complicated the American perception of the war, are the most important consequences of the film's impact on the theater audience.

To Be or Not to Be was based on a story by the Hungarian-born Melchior Lengyel as rewritten for the screen by the fellow traveler Edwin Justus Mayer.[23] Lengyel also wrote, or cowrote, two other films in the same era. The first was 1939's gentle parody of Russian Communism, *Ninotchka*—in which he worked again with director Lubitsch—and the other was the wartime drama *Days of Glory* (1944), perhaps the least crude of the several pro-Soviet propaganda films of the era. It is noteworthy for its implication that Moscow was tolerant regarding matters of religion.[24]

Korda, the producer, was also born in Hungary but was a passionate, perhaps fanatical, propagandist for his adopted home, England. Korda's ambition, according to biographer Bruce Eder, was "selling the British Empire all over the world."[25] Korda, who dominated the British film industry in the 1930s, devoted his cinematic career to a mélange of glorification of British imperialism, fervent anti-fascism, and marked sympathies for the political Left, even inserting positive portrayals of pro-Communist Britons into his films. During the war Korda apparently was closely involved with British intelligence, though this remains rather murky.[26] Korda's ideological fancies aside, his views were decidedly Left.

Almost no one of Polish origin was involved in the production of *To Be or Not to B*e or was featured among the performers. There were two exceptions: One was Ryszard Ordyński, who served as technical adviser. It is probably thanks to him that the Polish signs displayed in the film are spelled properly and most names are correct.[27] The other was Benny, the child of Jewish immigrants from Poland. He was active in Jewish causes during the war, but his views on Poland, if he had any, cannot be reconstructed.[28]

Two years later, the same dubious Polish virtues were stressed in a far different film, the vicious *In Our Time.*[29] Despite its focus on a touching romance that overcomes all obstacles, the film is in reality a vehicle for a propagandistic assault on Poland. The influential screenwriter Howard Koch arranged to have his old friend political radical

Ellis St. Joseph provide the script, but St. Joseph, by his own admission, was "fired 3 or 4 times" for producing a script too left-wing even for Warner Brothers. St. Joseph contended that Jack Warner considered replacing him with Albert Maltz.[30] This is most revealing, because Communist Maltz, later one of the Hollywood Ten, was one of the most leftist writers in town. Eventually, after months of delay, Koch himself intervened and produced the final script. St. Joseph claimed that Koch's real contribution to the story was "zilch," a claim largely corroborated by an analysis of the Warner Brothers script files.[31] Koch added only a few insignificant scenes; the story, characterization, and major plot elements were all set before Koch penned a word.

Koch is a most controversial character. Like many Hollywood writers, he was a clever man who mistakenly believed he was brilliant, a failing perhaps more pronounced than usual in his case. After a series of major wartime scripts, he was fired from Warner Brothers and denounced by Jack Warner as a Communist before Congress.[32] Koch later claimed that he was not a Communist, which may have been technically correct, and that he was rather apolitical, which was nonsense.[33] As a matter of fact, Koch was one of the most pro-Soviet leftists in Hollywood. A student of the era described him as a "Stalinist." Koch was often asked to rewrite stories for the screen to give them a specific political coloration, as when the script for *Casablanca,* originally the work of the Epstein twins (Julius and Phillip), was reworked by Koch to include "more political elements."[34] Koch admitted many years later, in a 1984 letter to Bernard Dick, that he had altered the script of the film to give it what he deemed "political depth."[35] His particular intent, he wrote in 1973, was that the film depict "the world struggle against fascism."[36] Koch, whose sympathies for the Soviets were open and ardent, also made political contributions to, among other films, United Artists' mawkish *Three Russian Girls.*[37] Recent investigations conclude that Koch "was probably a Party member for some time in the 1930s; and if not, he was clearly a fellow traveler of the Communists and the Soviet Union."[38] Many of his correspondents addressed him as "Comrade Koch."[39] His wife, Anne, was a party member.[40] No matter who was ultimately responsible for writing *In Our Time,* Warner Brothers evidently was dedicated to producing a film from the perspective of the radical Left.

The cast was led by Austrian exile Paul Henreid, an active member of several major leftist organizations (he was, for example, like Koch, a member of the National Council of American-Soviet Friendship[41]) who was later, by his own claim, blacklisted. Costar Ida Lupino's political activities are identical.[42] Lesser roles were played by two members of the large Russian émigré community in Hollywood, Michael Chekhov and the bizarre Nazimova.[43] Director Vincent Sherman, the child of Russian Jewish immigrants, was not highly regarded either then or later. He claimed later that his reading of Polish history had taught him that "Poland . . . was a lot like the South just before the Civil War—landed gentry and large estates being run on the backs of a peasant work force."[44]

In the film, Jennifer Whittredge (Lupino) is a simple shopgirl in London who, in early 1939, finds herself quite unexpectedly transported to Warsaw to accompany her employer on a buying trip. While there she accidentally meets the handsome Count Stefan Orvid, portrayed, in his usual wooden fashion, by Paul Henreid.[45] The couple fall quickly in love, but their marriage is opposed by the Count's family, which consists of a vapid and self-indulgent sister and mother, both oblivious to the world around them, and an insufferably pompous Uncle Pavel, played by the Belgian former stage actor Victor Francen. Francen decided that a Polish aristocrat was best captured by adopting a sinister manner and "the heaviest, darkest scowl you ever saw."[46]

Only the slightly ridiculous Uncle Leopold (Chekhov) is a sympathetic character. His main function is to point out, as though it were not already obvious, that the family is a nest of prejudice and fatuousness.[47] What makes the Orvids more than just a group of unpleasant Poles is that revolting Uncle Pavel is a high (but unidentified) member of the Polish foreign ministry whose personal idiosyncrasies reflect his larger political and geopolitical prejudices: he is devoutly and delusively pro-German, and the clear implication is that in this error he symbolizes the Polish government and Polish society—both of which are dominated by these wrong-headed fossils.

Over the objections of the family, the young Count marries Miss Whittredge, and they settle down to run his vast estates. Quickly we are presented with a catalog of Polish national faults. It is this young English shopgirl who introduces machinery to the estate: previously the Count regarded mechanization as impossible given the backwardness of the peasantry (a feudal setting is implied in rural Poland). The farmers themselves are uncomprehending at the sight of a tractor, and only Jennifer's perseverance allows them to realize the benefits of modernity. Indeed, this young woman, who has no background in agriculture, transforms the estate, simply because, being English (the traditional stand-in for American in Hollywood's depiction of Europe), she is sensible and hardworking in comparison to the antediluvian Poles. It is she who, over shocked and intransigent objections, allows the peasants into the manor to share in its cultural life. Only the young Count, now thoroughly henpecked, shows any hope for Poland. He, of course, has to break with his family—which represents Poland—to accomplish anything. Incidentally, the film's writer, St. Joseph, described this aspect of the film as celebrating democratic values by depicting "serfs" glimpsing the modern world thanks to an English girl.[48] Serfdom still existed in 1939 Poland, according to Hollywood. As a matter of fact, this portrait of rural Poland is completely false: manors were islands of modernity in Polish agriculture of the era, and the nobles were civic minded. As a major study concluded, even without English shopgirls, "interwar landowners played an important role in the agricultural societies and farmers' circles, while their estates were frequently centers for advanced agricultural technology. The manor houses were traditional centers of the countryside cultural life, while their owners frequently sponsored social and cultural activities."[49]

Even Polish patriotism is questionable. A Warsaw shopkeeper (played by Marek Windheim, a Polish Jew from Warsaw) makes elaborate boasts about the historic value of his wares, punctuated by statements of exalted national pride.[50] However, he is willing to sell these presumed emblems of national tradition for whatever prices the sharp English merchant offers. He is, in essence, a fraud, hiding behind pompous claims that are essentially efforts to inflate the prices. This national type is designed to demonstrate that Poland is a country of meaningless symbols based on a distant past of no relevance yet readily available to the highest bidder. The English buyer comments that she will turn these relics of ancient Polish glories into ashtrays and umbrella stands: finally, practical use will be made of Polish vanities.

The dichotomy between hopeless Polish obscurantism, quite unreformable, and the modern world is given a geopolitical turn when we are treated to a scene depicting prominent Nazis visiting Poland. The Polish government, led by the reactionary Count Pavel, is obviously pro-Nazi. However, young Jennifer is instinctively repulsed and adopts an attitude of hostility. Here the American audience is given a surrealistic lesson in the geopolitics of the 1930s: the resolutely antiappeasement British try desperately to alert the pro-Nazi Poles to the error of their ways.

The film concludes with the September campaign. The Orvid clan, disoriented and indicted by history for their fatuity, flee the country to continue their parasitic existence elsewhere. They are the stand-in for the Polish government-in-exile. The virtuous Jennifer is unflinching: she passionately decides to burn the fields and defy the Nazis to the end. Her feckless husband, a shattered veteran of the first week's fighting, has an epiphany. After explaining to Jennifer (and the audience) how the Poles' military efforts consisted of massed cavalry charges, which they had been told would be effective against German tanks, he now realizes that all he has been led to believe was nonsense. Again following his wife's lead, he presides over the destruction of his estate to deny its benefit to the invader. Hence it is the English who teach the Poles the value of resistance in the face of their own inclination to flee. The Poles' sad fate is the result of being misled by a worthless government.

In addition to being a piece of historical rubbish, this film is unremittingly nasty toward the Poles and goes out of its way to paint an inaccurate picture of the geopolitics of the wartime era. Reactionary Poland, dominated by hopeless dinosaurs and tainted by class prejudice, has plunged Poland into a war despite the best efforts of the West. Poland's only hope is to restructure itself, but this will require a complete abandonment of everything previously associated with the country and its traditions. It is no wonder that this film was hailed by the Communist *Daily Worker* as having "exposed the reactionary forces represented by the Polish Government-in-Exile." The only fault the paper found with the film was its "inattention to the plight of the Jews."[51] The star, Paul Henreid, understandably did not think highly of the film, which he dismissed in his memoirs with this telling summary: "We're married, and she teaches me 'the Democratic Way.' I try to change my family estate with all its serfs into a democratic enterprise, but one of my uncles, a Nazi sympathizer, forces me to give up the idea. The film ends with the Nazis taking over Poland and Ida and me staying on to fight with the peasants—another piece of pseudo-historical romance concocted by Howard Koch and another writer in the heat of World War II."[52]

The earliest version of the story was a brief treatment by St. Joseph written late in September 1942. In a clumsy foreword, St. Joseph insisted that the essential "theme" of the story was twofold: *In Our Time* was to be "a documentary of a woman's heart" but also a demonstration that "there can be no peace in our time except by facing the reality of life. . . . There can be no peace or happiness for any of us unless we fight for peace and happiness for others. To secure these things we must fight for the four freedoms not only for ourselves but for men and women everywhere."[53] This is a rambling means of arguing for yet another attack on appeasement. However, since appeasement was not a motif in Polish foreign policy—as it was in, for example, British—why a film set in Poland would be an appropriate venue to explore the ramifications of such a wrong-headed political disposition is very hard to understand. Indeed, if Warner Brothers wished to make a film about appeasement as late as 1943, Poland was perhaps the most inappropriate setting imaginable. Indeed, by the time St. Joseph sketched the story, the costs Poland was paying for its failure to practice appeasement were painfully obvious. Contrarily, if Warner Brothers wished to make a film about Poland, there were a host of subjects worthy of exploration. We are forced to conclude that the film was designed to say something negative about Poland, and "appeasement" was by 1943 sufficiently disreputable a term that applying it to Poland would appear promising.

If we examine the original treatment, it is immediately obvious that St. Joseph knew nothing about Poland; even the nomenclature is hopelessly wrong. The Henreid character is originally named Stefan Polinaff (St. Joseph inexplicably changes this name to Polianoff a few pages later; neither is Polish) and he is "of royal birth," which is impossible.[54] The royal gentleman with the Russian name lives, St. Joseph explains, in a house "two hundred years old," which would have been a new dwelling for real Polish aristocrats. He is surrounded—in 1939, let us remember—with serfs who are ancient property of the family. Of course serfdom had ended in Poland three generations earlier, approximately when slavery ended in the United States. These benighted serfs are completely oblivious of the modern world—though they are close enough to Warsaw to see its flames at the end of the film—and live in what the author describes as a "feudal aristocratic setup."[55]

Originally Stefan is a reserve air force officer—only later is he transformed into a cavalryman, doubtless to make his inappropriateness for the modern world more obvious. The family objects violently to his marriage to Jennifer because, as St. Joseph explains, "the Polish aristocracy is even more rigid than [the] English aristocracy." St. Joseph next proposes a long interlude following their initial courtship in which growing tension in the marriage is suggested as a device to reflect the European situation—with Jennifer facing reality and her Polish husband "putting a lid on a growing war tension," which of course is the appeasement theme. Stefan is to represent "paternalism," his wife "modernism," and the two must inevitably clash. Somehow, Jennifer, a poor shopgirl, has developed a sophisticated understanding of international politics that her husband cannot grasp, despite that he is of a family of prominent diplomats and scholars; the two thus become estranged. He is incapable of a modern view of gender roles, agricultural management, military preparedness, or international relations. London shopgirls are, however, masters of all these matters. After Stefan goes off to war, his return is to represent not just personal trial but national ruin: "Like Poland, he is broken, defeated, in tatters."[56] Jennifer must take command. As it has foolishly allowed itself to be crushed and humiliated, Poland, symbolically, must be led by England. *PM* cleverly described the film as "Cinderella Plots a Better Poland."[57]

St. Joseph was not content with this treatment; he originally wanted the film to go on much longer. He had many additional scenes in which the family flees to Warsaw, confronts chaos and panic, and separates. Stefan, who has been transformed from a vile aristocrat to "a man of the people," thanks to his wife, remains to defend the capital alongside the "common people," whom he did not know or understand—but the others flee to Lithuania. However, after some unclear contrivances, the family members die off, leaving only husband and wife. Stefan renounces his old ways, having realized that "his former aristocratic attitude was only a mask for weakness, but now he is truly strong." Having been reborn by shedding his Polish delusions, Stefan is worthy of "a bigger fight—the people's war."[58] St. Joseph is again speaking in metaphors: the September campaign is unimportant, the death of a worthless regime; the current war is the real struggle, and it is joined for different reasons. In other words, Poland is not a serious cause but only a disreputable memory. Stefan in exile joins the Polish air force in England. His wife, now freed from the restrictions of Poland, bears a child. The future is assured; Poland has been left behind in the rubbish bin of history.

Here the script, substantially done, remained for several months while a director (Vincent Sherman) and producer (Jerry Wald) were named. Sherman was, in his own words, a "left-wing liberal" who was active in many radical organizations.[59] Hence the screenplay by Koch and St. Joseph would be in politically friendly hands. A much more detailed version of the story now evolved. Stefan is not "politically enlightened" in the second treatment, from April 1943, but he "unconsciously" is moving toward a break with the "feudal set-up." The vile Uncle Pavel is not a Nazi but a "secret monarchist," and he opposes all reform and "fosters a reactionary party." He is also now elevated to being a prince.[60] Here St. Joseph's political prejudices have led him into utter chaos. Perhaps to him monarchists and Nazis are all members of the same consortium of foulness, but in Polish politics the combination is fantastic.

The author's characterizations of the other players are also available by April. Stefan's mother represents the "ignorance and superstition of the old world." His sister Janina is a "spinster" and "intensely religious"; we later are told that she is repulsive and virtually crazed, typical attributes for Polish Catholicism's only representative in the film. Uncle Leopold is a decent man, wise and tolerant, because he studied abroad and "became influenced by progressive and liberal-minded friends."[61] Such influences could obviously not be found in Poland.

St. Joseph now wanted the film to begin with a presentation of a map of Poland in the sixteenth century that, for some reason, catches fire and is burned to ruin, all obscured by dark smoke. This curious cartographic exercise is apparently intended to explain that Poland was ruined not by its rapacious neighbors in the eighteenth century, the partitioning powers, but by some internal problem two hundred years earlier. In fact the sixteenth century was the golden age in Poland, and the dominant political faction was the very numerous and impressive nobility. When the smoke disperses, the writer wants the borders that were created after World War I—in other words, the frontiers of the Polish Second Republic—to be revealed, a chronological leap of many centuries that neatly avoids Russia's role in partitioning and occupying the country for four generations. However, this Poland, the one of 1939, is to be portrayed by a map that is "fly-specked—old and streaked," obviously a disgusting thing.[62] The Poland invaded in 1939 is unworthy of preservation or restitution. For the writer to engage in such elaborate contrivances for a few seconds of symbols is quite striking. It is obvious that a very clear vision of Poland was being marketed, and no opportunity was to be lost. If the film was really intended to be about Jennifer and her beneficial effect on Stefan, why do we need this symbolic commentary on Polish history that concludes by denigrating the Poland of 1939?

In addition to this rather heavy-handed use of symbolic geopolitics, St. Joseph has added a few more touches. In an early scene depicting Nazi officials hunting in Poland before the war, smiling Polish governmental officials—all snobbish aristocrats—are to be contrasted with humble Poles, who gaze on the Nazis with suspicion and unease. Later, when Henreid and Lupino visit an antique dealer in Warsaw—who is an empty boaster it will be remembered—it is important that among his worthless curiosities are to be included various "religious paintings, carved effigies, ivories, etc." In this way Catholicism is linked symbolically with Poland's most unhelpful past. The shopkeeper vaingloriously is made to say, regarding the Germans: "We beat them then [Grünwald in 1410] and we'll do it again."[63] He is another Polish absurdity.

A few days later St. Joseph added a few more touches. Stefan is now a cavalry officer. However, Jennifer, who also seems to be well informed about military technology, argues that reliance on mounted cavalry is dangerous in the modern world. Stefan is foolishly unpersuaded.[64]

Stefan is given a particularly repulsive speech early in the film when he casually explains that the architect of the Łazienki Palace in Warsaw, which he proudly shows to Jennifer, had his eyes put out by Poland's seventeenth-century king "so he couldn't repeat such perfection." The palace was actually built a century later, and the monarch, the gentle intellectual Stanisław Poniatowski, never ordered any such barbarism. Mercifully, this disgusting passage was later altered. When the couple drives through the countryside near Warsaw, the script notes that the farmers work "by hand just as they have since the Middle Ages."[65] The Polish rural population is presented repeatedly as downtrodden, ignorant, and primitive, in stark contrast to Hollywood's portrayal at exactly the same time of Russian peasants in such films as *Mission to Moscow* and *The North Star,* where the rural folk are happy, self-confident, and quite well equipped with modern technology. Poland, we are repeatedly told by this Warner Brothers film, is hopelessly backward, trapped in a system that does not allow its poor millions to move into freedom and modernity as exemplified by the Soviet Union.

In this treatment a few dreadful speeches are inserted. In the first, saintly Uncle Leopold condemns Poland for having "promised Germany" that it will "stand by while Hitler gobbles the rest of Czechoslovakia."[66] The setting of the scene is unclear, but it logically must have taken place after October 1938, when the Munich conference initiated the dismemberment of Czechoslovakia, but before March 1939, when Germany occupied the remainder of that country. But Jennifer arrives only in the spring of 1939, after both these events have taken place. Leopold could not denounce Pavel for making a wicked deal with Berlin because Czechoslovakia was already gone, and hence Poland was not "standing by" to help Germany. Indeed, Poland was at the time the target of increasing German political pressure, and Great Britain, ostensibly Poland's ally, was urging appeasement on Warsaw. However, presenting these facts would require the film to portray Poland as opposing the Germans and the British as abetting them. These facts were most inconvenient for the screenwriters, who had quite another project in mind. But this scene, which seemed designed exclusively to embarrass Poland by making it complicit with Germany in the ruination of Czechoslovakia, was later cut, probably because it made no sense chronologically. Hence St. Joseph's effort to remind American audiences of Poland's unfortunate role in the destruction of Czechoslovakia had to be sacrificed to the demands of common sense. That he wished to include such a scene in the first instance, however, is noteworthy. Also, having Jennifer—the stand-in for England—be present at a discussion of the destruction of Czechoslovakia was probably unwise, as the Chamberlain government played an awkward role in the affair, and St. Joseph was at pains to make Poland, not England, the bête noire of Europe.

A long speech by Jennifer in this version was also cut from the final film. Originally Jennifer was to have said immediately after Leopold denounces Pavel's diplomatic machinations, "Daddy didn't approve of appeasement either. . . . He used to say Mr. Chamberlain was so afraid of communism that he preferred the treachery of Hitler to the friendship of Russia, or even of his own English people." At this a horrified

Zophiya (Stefan's mother) exclaims, "Your father was a Bolshevik?" This altogether reasonable query was here meant to identify the woman as a mindless reactionary. In a bit of sloppy editing, Jennifer's speech was cut, but the reaction of the mother remains; without any prompt from Jennifer, it is an incomprehensible ejaculation. The excised speech may well have been one of those leftist flourishes that St. Joseph thought Warner Brothers could not stomach. To complete this very thorough political exercise, St. Joseph also has Leopold tartly comment, regarding Stefan's sister, "It's a good thing she's so religious, or she'd poison us all." Later she is shown doing a needlepoint of the sacred heart, lest we forget she is a Roman Catholic. At the end of this scene, St. Joseph wrote in pencil, "Never completed."[67] It is just as well, because in a film already laden with political propaganda, such additional weight would perhaps have been too much, even for Warner Brothers.

In May, probably embarrassed by the relentlessly anti-Polish nature of the film, St. Joseph altered the opening sequence to eliminate the burning and fly-specked maps and inserted a dedication to "the men, women, and children of Poland, first to take up arms against Nazi aggression."[68] The reference to King Stanisław Poniatowski's having blinded his architect is also gone. The denunciation of Poland over its complicity in the dismemberment of Czechoslovakia is drastically cut, as is the speech Jennifer makes about her father and appeasement.[69]

Approximately a week later, the "revised final" version was ready. This adds a few curious turns. Stefan is about to whip his "peasants" in one scene, suggesting quite clearly that in 1939 Polish lords flogged their serfs. Evil Uncle Pavel is overheard conversing with General Breck in the summer of 1939, urging him not to modernize the army lest it upset the Germans. There was no General Breck in pre-1939 Poland, but there was a Colonel Beck, and the similarity was a convenience for St. Joseph. Pavel fatuously expatiates to Breck on the centrality of cavalry to Poland's military plans and the superiority of the horse over mechanized weapons. St. Joseph is obsessed with counterposing Polish cavalry and German mechanization; doubtless he saw this as a handy way of depicting the Poles as fools and enemies of modernity. The final scenes of the film are also altered. In a previous version, we are told that Stefan left to join his regime the day of Germany's attack on Poland, hence September 1, 1939. Now we are told he has returned, a beaten man in a beaten country, after "a week and a half."[70] The viewer thus would conclude that Poland was defeated in just a few days. In fact the war lasted over five weeks.

Pavel's final scenes are most unpleasant. While his country is collapsing, he airily discourses about his "villa at Monte Carlo," whither he invites Stefan to "sit under the jasmine trees." This reference provokes the following exchange:

> STEFAN: You were responsible [for Poland's defeat].
> PAVEL: You're confusing me with the Germans.
> STEFAN: I admit there isn't much to choose between you.
> PAVEL: You're feverish, rambling.
> STEFAN: You're a traitor.

Stefan denounces his uncle for "appeasement" and a desire to "deceive and suppress the people" and then bodily ejects him from the house. Jennifer meanwhile explains, "I can speak better than you for the Polish people," a rather pointed symbolic version of the western powers' presuming to decide Polish issues without consulting the Polish government then in London. The foul Orvids then escape on a luxurious private railway car—surrounded by their grand possessions—to Romania, where Pavel notes that he will "help negotiate a peace." This is not a daunting task, as the "Germans won't be unreasonable."[71]

Lest the viewer not understand the political conniving of St. Joseph, the vapid Zophiya proposes a toast: "May the future be like the past." However, just as they drink, a German plane blows them up, and they all die quite badly. St. Joseph could not decide whether he wanted them killed on a bridge or a trestle but generously noted that he would accept "whatever is available."[72]

Having cleared the stage of the evil Poles, St. Joseph finally turns to those few redeemed, Stefan and his wife. In a particularly nasty bit of mischief, he enlists the by-then dead mayor of Warsaw, the heroic Stefan Starzyński, to give a completely fictitious speech. Starzyński, identified by name in the script, is made to say, "The rulers of our city have fled. In their absence the men and women of Warsaw have taken over, and set up a people's government. As their mayor I speak for them."[73]

Starzyński not only never said this but never would have. Starzyński's movingly patriotic addresses to the beleaguered people of Warsaw in 1939 called for selfless support of the military and civil authorities. He was a loyal member of the very government he is made to denounce in the film. No "people's government"—whatever that is—was organized in Warsaw in 1939. This is propaganda on St. Joseph's part as he prostitutes the dead for his own political purposes and turns a brave man against his friends and colleagues to embroider his class-warfare explanation of Polish history. The real last words of Starzyński to the people of Warsaw were this moving farewell: "Though where there were fine orphanages is now rubble; though where there were parks, there are today barricades, covered with dead; though our libraries burn, and our hospitals, it will not be in one hundred years, but today that Warsaw, by defending the honor of Poland, stands at the pinnacle of its greatness and glory."[74] Alas, Starzyński was not in a position to defend himself or his country from St. Joseph's ideological mischief; he was tortured to death by the Germans in 1943, perhaps at the time Hollywood was exploiting him.[75]

To revise St. Joseph's amorphous script with its unclear ending, Warner Brothers briefly assigned Albert Maltz to the project. Maltz's contributions were brief and insignificant and, not surprisingly, reflected his Communist Party affiliation. He suggested that Stefan denounce the Polish nobility as "wrapped in ten centuries of dry rot" and implied that the Poles were ready to cede Danzig to the Germans before the war—another effort to paint the Poles, inaccurately, as appeasers. Stefan was also given a grotesque speech at the conclusion of the film in which he exhorts, "We shall build a better Poland—a people's Poland." Maltz, however, later noted that none of these notions were incorporated.[76] Their omission is of no consequence, however, because they only repeated themes already included.

Thus by late summer 1943, *In Our Time* was already a very nasty bit of work. Things, however, got worse. The film was also greatly behind schedule, and Jack Warner sent characteristically rude and threatening memoranda to director Sherman.[77] After a few months, a new writer, St. Joseph's patron Howard Koch, was recruited, and the script underwent revisions. Utilizing the St. Joseph script, Koch began inserting scenes in July and August 1943.[78] These include a speech by Pavel in which he announces, "Democracy is a contagion," and suggests troops be used to suppress student demonstrations in Poland. Warming to the theme of whipping peasants introduced by St. Joseph, now Koch adds Pavel to his list of floggers.[79]

Koch's first full treatment, from October 1943, has a great many small changes, mostly improving the clumsy story line. However, Koch also unwisely decided to add plot elements to what was already a very muddled account. Pavel, whom Koch makes even more repulsive, is now made to decide to flee Poland *before* the German invasion.[80] He is thus the ultimate appeaser, a virtual German agent. He is obviously concerned only with his personal safety and has no regard for his country. Next Koch turned to the Orvid family. They are made to host a large and grotesque party, which is interrupted by the German invasion, dramatized by the dawn bombing of Warsaw—a further indication of their obliviousness.[81]

Jennifer is enlarged in her dominating role. Not only is she the voice of modernity and agricultural innovation, as well as an expert on military tactics, but she now also becomes an inspiring leader of farm laborers, whom she directs personally after Stefan departs. Indeed, earlier, the peasants—impossibly ignorant—are saved solely by Jennifer's intervention when Stefan's bumbling efforts to teach them the values of the tractor are fruitless. Koch notes that the Poles' reliance on horse labor instead of tractors should be emphasized as a reminder of the Poles' foolish insistence on the use of cavalry instead of tanks.[82]

Koch also added a few overtly political scenes. Soon after Jennifer and Stefan's marriage, when the issue of German efforts to gain the "Polish corridor" is broached, wise Jennifer realizes the importance, whereas foolish Stefan "is not too concerned." Again the Poles are shown to be a nation of political naifs inclined toward appeasement who have to be instructed by the vigilant English. Jennifer makes an embarrassingly self-important speech to Pavel that "his tactics are merely paving the way for the eventual collapse of all Poland and of all freedom-loving people." By contrast, Stefan supports his uncle and regards Polish-German relations as being on a good course—this in the late summer of 1939.[83] Of course, Polish-German relations were very strained by this time, and to suggest that Poland was still fecklessly pursuing a pro-German orientation is a gross misrepresentation of events. Finally, Jennifer confronts Pavel and overpowers him by sheer force of righteousness. Koch notes, "He speaks for the old Poland and she for the new."[84] Why a young English girl a few weeks in the country has the right to "speak for Poland" is a good question. Indeed, what right Koch had to limn a "new Poland" is also an apt question.

In a crowning touch, Koch elaborated the huge and grotesque ball at the Orvids' home the night before the war begins. It is horrible because Jennifer "must formally receive the [Polish] nobility" for the first time. They intersperse dancing "old-fashioned polkas and mazurkas" with demonstrations of "snobbery, backwardness, and unrealistic confidence in the face of impending war." Stefan, really a fool, gets drunk and "toasts the Cavalry and military glory of Poland," an act that Koch revealingly states is "more than Jenny can endure."[85] Why should a reserve officer not drink a toast to his country's army at a moment of national crisis? Why would Jennifer be appalled that her husband, a soldier, is devoted to his country's defense? Why should a scene in which the Poles demonstrate pride in their old glories and resolution about the impending danger be anything other than positive? Jennifer is the representative of the audience; she is the American public. She is repulsed by this; the audience is to be repulsed. Why did Warner Brothers produce and the OWI endorse a film that did not celebrate an ally's courage and defiance in the face of a common enemy?

The irresponsible Poles drink and carouse till the break of day and are only roused from their revelries by the German invasion of their country. Janina prays; Stefan begs for rain; the others are in chaos.[86] Thus Poland faces war.

After four days, the Polish army is defeated in Koch's revision of World War II, which is reduced to endless repetition of the fatuity of Polish cavalry's charging tanks. We are told that the radio reports that the "Polish Army is putting up a stiff resistance; that the Polish Air Force is heroically fighting the enemy," but wise Uncle Leopold reacts with contempt and despair. Polish claims to a brave defense in 1939, Koch teaches us, are propaganda. Leopold is right; Poland is a fraud. Indeed, Stefan soon returns in ruins and explains the war in a manner most unflattering to Polish military pride. He "practically weeps." Jennifer, of course, sustains him, as has been the case throughout the film. In distress the Orvids are ridiculous cowards; a useless priest flutters about doing no good. So much for the national faith of Poland for a millennium. Koch adds several very extensive scenes in Warsaw after the Orvids flee. All show the Poles in frantic chaos. This alone is an important point of comparison to Hollywood films' portrayal of the Russians, who receive the German invasion with resolution, bravery, and intrepidity. By comparison, the Poles are a pack of scoundrels. Stefan, now redeemed, explains to the audience that Polish "appeasement" has brought the world to this misery.[87]

In his late October script, Koch included a scene in which Pavel tries to surrender to the Germans, as well as a very extended final sequence in Warsaw, showing the chaos and disorder of the war, with people "running for their lives." As a matter of fact, the army defended the city with gallantry and was aided by civilian volunteers. More than twenty thousand soldiers fell in defense of the capital, and twice that number of civilians died. One hundred thousand prisoners were taken, and a large number of officers committed suicide rather than accept the ignominy of surrender.[88] None of this could be guessed from the script, which presents the defense of Warsaw as a brief mob scene. Koch even included an episode in which Stefan meets Mayor Starzyński. As a closing episode, Koch had Stefan and Jennifer in England, with him joining the "Polish branch of the Royal Air Force," which of course did not exist, though there were units of the Polish air force fighting alongside the RAF.[89]

Many years later, Koch described *In Our Time* as "an antifascist film set in Poland during the Mannerheim, pro-Nazi regime before the war broke out."[90] Because the film says virtually nothing about Germans or Italians, it seems clear that to Koch, it was the Poles who were both fascists and pro-Nazi. The film is thus about Polish fascists invented by the screenwriters to discredit Poland by associating it with the most repulsive term in the political lexicon of the Left. Who in Poland was pro-Nazi? And what Marshal Mannerheim, a Finn, had to do with the subject is more difficult to explain. What was important to Koch was to attack fascists, real or imaginary.[91] By referring to prewar Poland, Koch echoes the Comintern's nomenclature noted earlier. Had the OWI previewed a film about pro-Nazi Russians, it would have been livid.

While screenwriters St. Joseph and Koch were developing the story, the studio was devoting considerable time and effort to delving into the events portrayed in the film. There is a disparity between the dispassionate and energetic efforts by the studio's research department and the obvious ideological project of the screenwriters. Already in January 1943 Warner Brothers had obtained the services of two technical advisers, later joined by two or even three others. The first was Stephen Barasch, who, Warner Brothers claimed, was a "Polish attorney who was a militia man in the siege of Warsaw" and later "escaped from the Nazis" through the Baltic, the Soviet Union, and China before arriving in Hollywood.[92] Though Warner Brothers promoted his role in the film to suggest its timeliness, he remains a shadowy figure, and his role seems to have been negligible.[93]

Barasch was joined in January by Felix Faust, who is also mysterious. Warner Brothers then assigned the competent and industrious Herman Lissauer, head of the research division, to prepare a detailed chronology of the war "from the invasion of Poland to October 7, 1940," an odd assignment, as the film ends with the September campaign.[94] Lissauer's document is completely unlike the story eventually filmed in both detail and spirit. Lissauer emphasizes the fierce and prolonged fighting throughout September, the first stages of guerrilla warfare, and the creation of an underground government. He makes much of the Soviet invasion of September 17 and the subsequent partition of the country. He also refers pointedly to the efforts of the Red Army to "hunt down and liquidate Polish troops."[95] What is more, he reminded producer Wald that Warsaw held out for one month and did not fall in a few days, as the script implied.[96] Lissauer apparently consulted members of the Polish community to provide rather specific notes on the sights of Warsaw, biographies of famous Poles, and other materials.[97] Lissauer also prepared a detailed discussion of the diplomacy of the 1930s, which is quite balanced and accurate.[98]

The Polish Information Center in New York provided Lissauer with detailed information.[99] In exchange for his assistance, T. Strzelecki of the center insisted on being given specific information about *In Our Time* while it was in production.[100] The Poles were furious over the recently released Warner Brothers film *Edge of Darkness,* which contained very unflattering references to Poles, and they were determined to avoid a repetition.[101] Strzelecki wrote Lissauer a very pointed letter accusing Warner Brothers of already having done "harm to the Poles" and having offended Polish "dignity and honor." He forecast "great indignation" among the Poles of America if the new film contained similar abuses, and he rather grandly deemed his views a "protest" in the name of the Polish government.[102] Lissauer assured the Poles that the film "will avoid giving offense to the Poles in any way" but told them nothing of it. However, he told producer Wald to approach Strzelecki "if you want support for your picture from the Polish people in this country."[103] In an effort to remove some of St. Joseph's more objectionable notions, Lissauer urged Wald to cut the reference to the Polish king's gouging out an architect's eyes and the ridicule implied in the scene in which Polish historical treasures are to be converted to bric-a-brac. The Poles, Lissauer warned, were already "raising a miniature storm" and would be deeply offended by these passages—which he had already assured Strzelecki did not exist.[104] Strzelecki also wrote to Jack Warner, explaining the Poles' keen interest in the project, a point emphasized when the Polish consul in Los Angeles, Lech Niemo-Niemojowski, also told Warner that the Poles would be watching the film with unusual interest.[105]

In the autumn, Warner Brothers was shaken by a barrage of letters from Polish organizations in the United States denouncing what they regarded as an anti-Polish film in preparation. The Polish Roman Catholic Union of America, a large Chicago-based fraternal organization claiming 150,000 members nationwide, wrote to Warner Brothers that "word had reached" them that the yet unreleased *In Our Time* "portrays Poland in a most horrendous way." Prewar Poland, they had heard, was depicted as a virtually "feudal system," and the aristocracy and government were described as "pro-German." Such a film was, in the union's view, "biased" and harmful.[106] A few days earlier, a similar protest had arrived at Warner Brothers from the Polish Refugee Association, which claimed that the "grape-vine" had alerted them that *In Our Time* "presents Poland and the Polish people in a terrible and insulting way."[107] Both letters demanded the film be radically altered and reminded Warner Brothers of Poland's sacrifices in the war. Other Polish organizations sent similar protests. One rather pathetically asked, "Why are you doing this and what are your motives for depicting such a faithful ally of the USA in such a scandalous way?"[108]

The Warner Brothers director of publicity, Charles Einfeld, told Jack Warner that letters were "pouring in," including those from "fairly important" organizations. But, Einfeld assured Warner, like previous Polish protests in conjunction with *Edge of Darkness,* the letters seemed to be from only a few sources.[109] Einfeld, a man famous for his willingness to do anything for the studio, proposed a form-letter response, which Warner subsequently sent to the Poles.[110] The Einfeld letter begins with the dismissive observation that the complaints were "all from Chicago" and goes on to characterize the criticisms as "baseless" and inaccurate. Indeed, Einfeld describes the film as a tribute to

Poland and its struggle against the German invaders. Warner Brothers, Einfeld assures recipients, had only "sympathy and admiration for our Polish ally," which was, indeed, the reason that it made the film. The film cast Poland "in a favorable light," and "the total effect of the picture is to glorify the heroic resistance and sacrifice of Poland and its people."[111]

Warner was right to deem Einfeld's response clever. It avoided confronting any of the charges of the protests, all of which were absolutely accurate. The film presented Poland in an appalling light, which was precisely as the screenwriters had intended. Warner, who paid extraordinarily close attention to the production—even providing detailed comments on minor scenes and involving himself in the phrasing of the few introductory words—knew that the film showed prewar Poland as a corrupt feudal society under the sway of a government of appeasers and scoundrels.[112] His film almost literally calls for the overthrow of the government of Poland. His Polish critics described exactly what *In Our Time* was. Einfeld's letter was shameless.

The BMP logically classified the film as IIIA, "the United Nations and peoples—Poles," the only such film Hollywood made during the war.[113] BMP reviewers' reaction to the script in development is unknown, but they were well pleased with the finished work, regarding it, essentially, as a celebration of "the common man, his character, his aspirations, the justices of his cause."[114] This rather baldly echoed Warner Brothers' own publicity release describing the film as designed to "pay tribute to the common people of Poland."[115] It is a most peculiar evaluation, as the film's only "common man" is Jennifer, who is, of course, not a Pole. All the Polish characters depicted are aristocrats, save a tiny handful of minor players whose lives are not developed at all, many of whom do not even have specific names or dialogue. What "cause" of the "common man" is mentioned, let alone developed in the film? Only the decision to mechanize the Orvid estate and share in the profits could be understood as a populist idea. But this requires us to assume that the estate was feudal and the peasants held in serfdom—one of the several implications of the film that the BMP, to its discredit, did not seem to notice. The bureau's summary does, however, coincide nicely with a reading of the film as an indictment of prewar Poland and the implied message that once the social order depicted in the film is ousted, the country can be delivered into the hands of the "common man." This, of course, specifically reflects the September 1939 programmatic statement issued by the CPUSA's Earl Browder.

This strange evaluation is explained in the lengthy essay the BMP's Eleanor Berneis included in her remarks. Berneis notices with satisfaction that the "common people are not fighting merely to preserve the world they knew but are united in a determination to crush the enemy and to bring about a better world."[116] Why should the BMP be pleased that a film argues in favor of the radical restructuring of one of the "United Nations"? Quite apart from whether prewar Poland deserved demolition and reconstruction, was it Warner Brothers' function to advocate sociopolitical revolution in an Allied country, even a country in which it thought serfdom existed in 1939? William Donati correctly summarizes the film as demonstrating "the corruption of the Polish aristocracy and the consequent demise of the nation."[117] The problem was that putative aristocratic corruption had nothing to do with the Polish defeat in 1939.

Concluding her evaluation, Berneis becomes carried away with her own rhetoric when she denounces the "appeasers among the aristocrats," whom this film "exposes." Of course, since there were no aristocratic Polish appeasers in the 1939 government, this function of the film is hard to appreciate. There were "appeasers" in the prewar British government and in Washington, for that matter, but the most mildly unflattering reference to them was rebuked by the BMP. However, a film that invents Polish appeasers in order to denounce them was not only not criticized but extolled.[118]

In closing, Berneis remarks, "The story is particularly valuable in that it emphasizes that a 'new Poland' will be born of the violent changes of the war, and identifies the interests of the Polish people with those of the ordinary people all over the world." The charge that the government of pre-1939 Poland and its successor in London exile were creatures of a corrupt aristocracy, without representation of the majority of the population, was Soviet propaganda repeated since 1939 as a justification for its invasion of the country. The legal government of Poland, the "old Poland," was in exile; it had the support of the vast majority of the population. That an American film reviewer should celebrate the possibility of its being overthrown is noteworthy, especially because no such advocacy of political revolution would have been tolerated by the BMP in the case of any other ally.

Berneis's superior at the BMP Hollywood Office, Ulric Bell, was delighted with the film. He wrote to all the main figures at Warner Brothers, "I am getting hoarse from shouting hurrah for Warner Brothers pictures." *In Our Time,* he assured the studio, was in the BMP's view "one of the finest things that has come along. It is certainly swell from our standpoint."[119] Two days later, the deputy chief of the Hollywood office, William S. Cunningham, wrote to Warner Brothers with renewed praise: "We are particularly enthusiastic about *In Our Time,*" he began, and continued by summarizing Berneis's remarks. Among the many wonders of the film, Cunningham concluded, was that it "clearly shows the manner in which the Nazis set out to conquer Europe."[120] Insofar as that sentence means anything, it suggests that the BMP's deputy chief thought that blaming World War II on corrupt Polish aristocrats who collaborated with the Nazis was a salutary and edifying lesson for American film to convey to the public concerning the geopolitical history of the 1930s. That it slandered an ally while conveying a falsehood did not matter.

The political implications of a film released in early 1944 set in Poland are obvious. Polish-Soviet relations had become very embittered during the preceding year, especially after the Germans announced the discovery of mass graves of Polish soldiers at Katyń—a massacre that they correctly attributed to the Russians. This led to an acrimonious dispute between the Poles and the Russians resulting in Moscow's refusing to recognize the legal government of Poland in April. The Americans were now under pressure to abandon the Polish government as well, an action whose justification is implied by this film. On July 3 General Sikorski, the Polish prime minister and by far the most prominent and respected Polish political figure, had died in a plane crash. In November vital Polish interests were discussed at the diplomatic summit in Tehran by Churchill, Roosevelt, and Stalin without the Poles' being present or even invited. In fine, the Polish position in international affairs had declined precipitately, and Poles were fighting a losing battle to retain any control over their own destiny. By contrast, the Soviet victory at Stalingrad had turned the course of the war on the eastern front, and 1943 saw Soviet military and hence political fortunes increase. When *In Our Time* was released in February 1944, Poland's position vis-à-vis Russia was weak and declining, and determined support from Washington and London was really the only hope the Poles had to protect their national interests. Hence the sympathetic support of the American public was vital to Poland's fortunes. *In Our Time* was a blow aimed at a cause in distress.

Koch, who piously claimed to be apolitical, was well aware of the political significance of his film and the effect it might have on public opinion. He wrote to his close friend party member Jay Leyda in 1944 that "this would be a grand time to release" what he called "our Polish film" because it "says some pretty plain things about Polish landowner fascism and the stupid appeasement policy of the govt. before the war. I hope Warners brings it out soon—and I think they will."[121] When it indeed was released in February, Koch noted to Leyda that the film's "chief contribution is political rather than artistic."[122]

Given these circumstances, the reaction to *In Our Time* is noteworthy. Michael Chekhov, who played Uncle Leopold, regarded the script as having no value and the director, Vincent Sherman, as even less worthy of praise. Paul Henreid, who played the leading role of Stefan, did not consider the film significant. Sherman claimed he did not want to do the film because "I didn't think we had a good story, and we *didn't*."[123] These, however, are artistic and not political evaluations.[124]

Contemporary critical reaction is striking. Virginia Wright regarded *In Our Time* as intended to "pay tribute to an ally and still face facts." The "facts" that Wright regarded the film as exposing were that prewar Poland, though not without "heroes and . . . democrats," also featured "a decaying aristocracy, an illiterate peasantry, an outmoded army and a pervading sense of compromise." The last phrase is especially noteworthy. It was, of course, Poland's unwillingness to compromise in the face of German demands that distinguished it most starkly from Czechoslovakia. Nonetheless it was Poland that was criticized by Hollywood and Czechoslovakia that was praised. Wright concluded that Poland, as the film teaches us, had "the seeds of destruction . . . within itself." Thus, for Wright at least, appeasement is a Polish attribute, not the private folly of Count Pavel. Stefan is "one of Poland's aristocracy who doesn't run away"—running away being, apparently in Wright's mind, the typical behavior of the Polish upper classes. This in turn implies that the members of the government-in-exile are not noble exiles but a pack of cowards who have fled rather than fight. How an American should view the government of Poland presented in such a light is obvious. Lest any viewer be disquieted by this negative view of the Polish government and its social elite, Wright assured readers that "there is nothing heavy-handed" in the script, for this is a "good picture."[125]

For the *Los Angeles Times*' Edwin Schallert, the film's significance was the light it cast on current developments by its "attempt to penetrate the inner psychology of Poland." The events were not as remote as they first seemed, Schallert noted delphically; he even pronounced the film "carefully analytical." Since the film shows prewar Poland to be corrupt and hypocritical, Schallert's unwritten conclusion can scarcely be positive.[126]

A similar conclusion was made by the *New Yorker*, which told its readers that Warner Brothers, "the studio . . . with the social conscience," had made a film whose "conclusions . . . are that Poland was not the most progressive state in the world and that Fascism was not altogether foreign to it."[127] This conclusion was "disquieting" to critic Lowell Redelings, for whom the film showed that "even before the Nazi invasion there were those Fascists inclined enough to compromise with Germany."[128] In other words, the St. Joseph–Koch tale of the crafting of Polish appeasement by a nest of landowning fascists had not escaped these shrewd analysts.

The *New York Herald-Tribune*'s Otis L. Guernsey Jr. applauded the release of such a "timely" and "informative" film to tell the American public much about Poland just as that country's "affairs are in the spotlight." For Guernsey, prewar Poland had "two political groups": "the Fascist-minded nobility" and "the peasants"—a handily streamlined guide to the complexities of Polish politics for the American public. Guernsey lamented the "ponderous" development of the story, laden with many minutes of dialogue and a general lack of action. But he espied the essential political motives of the film: "an indictment of the Polish ruling class" that "ends on a note of warning that the leaders who found it most easy to escape are the least to be trusted."[129] This is another inculpation of Poland's exile government that echoes the analysis of the *Daily Worker* cited earlier.

For Bosley Crowther of the *New York Times,* this exercise in anti-Polish propaganda is reduced to "the old and the new social orders . . . contrasted in pre-war Poland." In fact, as he noted in a characteristically badly written review, "It may be that Polish society was medieval before this war, oppressed by a class of landed gentry, as suggested in the Warners' *In Our Time*. It may be that Polish aristocrats were pompous and full of gab. . . . [But] why try to beat the dead animals as they do in this new film . . . ?"[130] Syndicated columnist Walter Winchell grasped the social message of the film at once, though he either ignored or missed its geopolitical import. In his characteristically colloquial brevity, he summarized the film as follows: "Ida Lupino, who hails from south of the railroad tracks, weds a Polish blueblood . . . and peasantizes him."[131] Many years later, the *Los Angeles Times* summarized a television presentation of the film as "Polish Count turned Resistance fighter."[132] Obviously, service in the Polish army did not constitute resistance.

John T. McManus of the radical New York *PM* was one of the very few who demonstrated that he had actually understood the film as its creators intended: it showed a "typical Polish minister of state," an "appeaser" friend of Nazis, and a "dinosaur" who represents the "whimpering class" who fled Poland because "his Poland is now dead." The major value of the film, McManus explained, was that it helped viewers understand "claims now being asserted by the Polish Government in Exile." Like the cowards and villains seen escaping in the film, the Polish government in London was a band of rogues who deserted Poland in its travail. The film "leaves no room for doubt as to who should inherit the Polish earth after the war." McManus was grateful that finally a "popular medium" has exposed "the old ruling class of Poland." The film was a brief against the government of Poland in favor of a Soviet-sponsored regime, what McManus aptly called "plot[ting] a better Poland."[133]

These reviews make it very clear that St. Joseph and Koch may not have combined to produce a particularly entertaining film, but their political indictment was unequivocal. At the very time when the American public was being presented with Warsaw and Moscow as alternative possibilities of support, Hollywood offered a damning vision of Poland: The prewar Polish Republic was ruled by reactionaries and fascists who had foolishly appeased Germany and then fought incompetently or fled. Indeed, this same parasitic class abandoned the country after the war began and was now claiming to speak for it in London. Poland's history was a tradition of such feckless nobles' betraying the national interest by their self-indulgence. The London government was thus just the latest in a grotesque cavalcade. Poland deserved something radically different. The real Poland was composed of the humble and downtrodden who had been exploited before 1939. Hence, for

Poland to be free, it must not be restored but re-created along entirely new lines.

In Our Time is an attack on the government of Poland and a justification for its replacement. It is partisan propaganda, and it was delivered at a crucial moment in the war. This version of events reflected in all its analytic particulars the Comintern line on the war. The reviewers realized that the film had clear and significant political implications and either were untroubled or persuaded by them. Buhle and Wagner correctly deem *In Our Time* a "work of popular explanation."[134]

Even if the film's depiction of the social foibles and political errors of the prewar government were accurate, why subject Poland, an ally, to so embarrassing a rumination, especially in 1943–1944, when it was obviously suffering and its exile government was laboring under the greatest burdens? At the same time Warner Brothers was preparing this film about Poland, it was also readying *Mission to Moscow,* which was at pains to present a flattering view of another American ally, Soviet Russia. Shortly before writing *In Our Time,* St. Joseph collaborated in the writing of another film about the early war, *Joan of Paris.*[135] Here the French are portrayed very flatteringly—indeed the film is a piece of pro-French propaganda—and there is no effort to indict their prewar government.[136] Only the government of Poland was subjected to a harsh inculpation by Hollywood; no other Allied country was so treated. Indeed, an enemy power, Mussolini's Italy, probably received a more generous portrayal than did Poland.

It was the plight of the Jews, notably neglected by wartime Hollywood, that was the dramatic center of the last wartime film devoted to Poland, Columbia's *None Shall Escape.*[137] Hastily produced, underfunded, and unremittingly depressing, the film was not well received by critics and probably lost money, though that question remains unresolved. An intriguing work, *None Shall Escape,* though filmed in January 1943 and released the next year, is set in the fictive near future, when a war crimes tribunal is assembled in Warsaw under the auspices of the "United Nations" to judge Nazi outrages. *None Shall Escape* was the first film to address the Holocaust and focus on the massacre of Europe's Jews. Studio head Harry Cohn and producer Samuel Bischof, both Jewish, regarded the film's brutal depiction of the German treatment of the Jews as very controversial, and the project was almost cancelled on more than one occasion.[138] The studio's squeamishness was not alleviated by the directorial notions of idiosyncratic Hungarian émigré André de Toth, a devotee of film noir with a penchant for the macabre.[139] De Toth saw the film as neither investment nor art but rather as a moral statement, a passion shared by its writer Lester Cole, who was, according to Louis B. Mayer, a "Goddamn crazy commie."[140] Both of them wanted to make an ideological film denouncing in stark terms Nazism and its mistreatment of Jews.[141]

Unfortunately, the film was not intelligently conceived, and despite flashes of brilliance, it is not a masterpiece of the director's art. Neither Cole nor de Toth distinguished himself.[142] The film's star, Alexander Knox, later spoke about the film rather sourly, noting its budget of less than one hundred thousand dollars, its shooting schedule of only a few weeks, and its weak script. He was critical of both the director and the studio for such a cheap and hurried effort.[143]

None Shall Escape depicts the career of a singularly revolting German, Wilhelm Grimm, played by Broadway actor Knox, who is the only defendant at the trial. Grimm was a schoolteacher in the fictional village of Litzbark, near Leszno in German Poland, before World War I. After Germany's defeat in 1918, he returned to Litzbark, now in reconstructed Poland, to resume his career. He is, however, so embittered by defeat and his own sacrifices (he has lost a leg) that he is scarcely human. In the next few months, he alienates everyone, is rejected by his fiancée, and rapes one of his students. Driven from the village after being blinded in one eye, he settles in Munich, becomes a Nazi, and shares in the spoils of Hitler's victory after 1933. His conduct toward his own family in Munich is reprehensible: he exploits his own brother, then sends him and his family to a concentration camp. After the German invasion of Poland, Grimm returns to Litzbark as the Nazi civil commissioner for all western Poland. He comes to the village for the sole purpose of revenging himself on the local Poles. The film details Grimm's actions as sadist, murderer, and tyrant, capped by the massacre of the entire local Jewish community in a scene of graphic violence unusual for Hollywood in that era. Grimm's fiendish behavior is its own undoing. His beloved nephew, raised to be a Nazi, revolts against his uncle and his methods. Tearing off his Nazi insignias, the young man kneels to pray over a slain Polish girl; his uncle, predictably, murders him.

Though intended to be a searing indictment of Nazism, this film blunderingly offers instead a portrait of a sociopath who happens to be a Nazi. The only other Nazi presented in the film, the nephew, is at worst a callow adolescent and dies heroically, repentant and redeemed. Thus we are presented not with a corporate inculpation of Nazism but an ad hominem attack on Grimm. Significantly, his campaign of horror begins before he joins the movement, and thus Nazism merely gives him the opportunity to demonstrate his existing malignancy. Moreover, in the typical confusion of Hollywood over whether to blame Germans or Nazism for the war, Grimm is really the only unpleasant German in the film—his family, for example, is saintly and repeatedly mentions that the Nazis are only a small minority. Hence we have neither Nazis nor Germans indicted, suggesting that World War II in Europe is at base the work of a handful of psychopaths like Grimm.

The treatment of the Poles is the most intriguing example of this theme in all Hollywood films of the era. Screenwriter Cole, who had been a member of the Communist Party since 1934 and was a devotee of the Soviet Union throughout his long life, had strong negative feelings about Poland that he admitted in his memoirs.[144] Director de Toth was a leftist, as was the costar Marsha Hunt.[145] Nonetheless the film portrays the Poles, with a few minor exceptions, in a positive light. When Grimm returns from the war, he is greeted with great courtesy by his Polish neighbors and is offered his old job back. His open chauvinism—he repeatedly refers to the Poles as "clowns" and "idiots"—is largely ignored. His Polish fiancée, Maria, is willing to forgive him almost anything; despite his vile behavior, she decides to marry him to dedicate her life to saving his benighted soul. This intention is abandoned only when Grimm's rape of a schoolgirl drives him into exile and the noble Maria into final revulsion.

Polish Jewish-Christian relations are also presented in a most positive manner. The local rabbi is on the best terms with his Christian neighbors. Indeed, the village priest (played with considerable skill by Henry Travers, remembered as the bumbling angel in Frank Capra's *It's a Wonderful Life*) is his closest friend, and the two are virtually inseparable. When the Nazis occupy the village, the Christian Poles try to aid their Jewish fellow townsmen and defend them against Nazi cruelties even at great personal risk. Although the only major revolt is an exclusively Jewish affair, the Christians are supportive; the rabbi dies virtually in the priest's arms.[146]

Motifs from the Polish national anthem are played repeatedly in the background. Although the mayor seeks accommodation with Grimm, he does so from cowardice, not disloyalty, and moreover he is the only morally bankrupt person in the village. When the film ends, with uplifting words about bringing evildoers to justice, a final scene depicts the American, British, Soviet, and Polish flags flying together.[147] This portrayal of the Soviet banner "reflected the Popular Front politics of the times, in that it was pro-Soviet," observed interviewer Glenn Lovell.[148] Obviously the Soviets are coequal members of the coalition of right.

None Shall Escape's depiction of the Poles does not reach the celebratory level of the Norwegian, Czech, and Russian characterizations Hollywood produced. In contrast to the other films depicting European occupation, this film, set in Poland, does not celebrate the existence of a united front of resistance to the invader. In *None Shall Escape,* the only Pole who actively tries to resist the Nazis is a battle-scarred soldier, no longer in his right mind. This is not the united phalanx of heroic opposition attributed, for example, to the Norwegians in *Edge of Darkness,* to the Czechs in *Hangmen Also Die,* or to the Russians in *The North Star.* In fact there is no Polish underground at all, a lack Hollywood repeatedly implied. Although the Poles are not portrayed negatively, they are also not elevated into a nation of heroes.[149] *None Shall Escape* does not attempt to celebrate Polish resistance; no American film did that. It is, however, not an attack on the Poles, as was *In Our Time.* Several of the creators of the film have left recollections, but none have offered any explanation for this rather restrained presentation. Thus we are left to conjecture.

First, the film was designed to be about the Jewish travail; Poland is the backdrop, and not the focus. Hence the positive depiction of the Poles serves only to delineate Grimm's depravity more clearly. The dramatic and moral center of the film is the rabbi's death scene, which is indeed a powerful piece of cinema. Although the film certainly portrays Polish Jewish-Christian amity positively, presenting these relations otherwise would have undermined the film's purposes. The benignity before 1939 makes the horrors of the occupation starker and the role of Nazism as a threat to decent people everywhere the clearer.

Second, we should note that the film is set in western Poland, far from the disputed eastern borders, which would have automatically raised awkward issues vis-à-vis the Russians. Indeed, this is a film that is self-consciously local: a village of normal people who happen to be Polish must deal with a madman.

Finally, we must consider the role of director de Toth. Passionate, physically tough, and adventurous, de Toth had found himself quite unexpectedly in Warsaw in August 1939. He filmed portions of the September campaign in circumstances that are difficult to reconstruct. De Toth was so horrified by what he saw that he did not discuss the matter for half a century. When he finally raised the issue in his 1994 memoirs, he broke off in mid-reflection, unable even then to provide a thorough account of what was, to be sure, an extraordinary event.[150] Shortly before he died, he recalled being forced by the Germans to photograph haunting scenes: "What was so terrible was they lined up the starving people and whipped them like dogs. Then the cameras rolled, with the Nazis shouting, 'Laugh! Smile!' And the people smiled, and they gave the bread. Then they stopped the cameras. 'Enough!' And the soldiers took the bread away. They showed these things all over Germany, all over the world."[151] Was de Toth, who saw the martyrdom of Poland at close range in 1939, unable to preside over a film that disparaged them in 1943? Here we can only wonder.[152]

The BMP regarded *None Shall Escape* as unusually significant and encouraged its production. Originally entitled "Lebensraum" and scheduled for the significant budget of an A picture, the project appeared as a brief outline written by Alfred Neumann and Joseph Than in the spring of 1943.[153] It is an extremely complicated plot, but in substance it reflects the eventual film. The only major differences are that Grimm was originally a rather more significant member of the occupation hierarchy who was given vague but broad responsibilities by Hitler himself regarding Poland. In the original story, there was also a character named Fritz Gruber who acted as Grimm's assistant but eventually appeared in the uniform of the Red Army to offer testimony against Grimm at his postwar trial. Gruber was obviously intended to be an Austrian Communist. He does not appear in the film, a happy deletion, as the character was implausible and politically artless.

The BMP regarded the story as essentially a fictionalized biography of Julius Streicher—not an insightful conclusion[154]—and thought the projected postwar trial for Nazis an intriguing element of the script. The bureau was cautiously supportive of the project. It is noteworthy that for the BMP the film was not about Poland or resistance, but about Nazism.

In the bureau's classification system, it was regarded as IIA, a "Nazi ideology" story, with a "minor" theme of ID1, "peace aims." It was not a IIIA film, the category that included all films about the "United Nations"—in other words, it was not a project devoted to Poland.[155]

Three months later, the script had been reworked by Lester Cole and substantially enlarged. The BMP reevaluated it and gave it a new classification, IIB2, "the enemy," while retaining the secondary categorization, ID. It was still not, in the BMP's view, about Poland. The story was now rather simplified and focused more on Grimm's post-1939 depredations than on his earlier life. It is clear that the writer was at pains to present the Poles and "good" Germans as equal victims of Nazism as epitomized by Grimm. Jewish suffering was still a major theme, as it was in the original version. In the court that judged Grimm, Roosevelt, Churchill, and Stalin all appeared and made portentous speeches about justice. The BMP reacted to this version with extraordinarily lengthy comments. It saw the film as perhaps "the most important [film] produced by Hollywood."[156]

For the BMP, the chief value of the film was to suggest to the public the importance of postwar trials of war criminals. It was unhappy with the manner in which the script handled this preeminent theme. A number of the BMP's observations are most apt. In general it found the characters and their implied motivations "oversimplified." Grimm is a sexual predator and a psychopath, but how is this related to his decision to become a Nazi? The film simply implies that Nazism is the cloaca for all evil impulses, and hence demonstrating that Grimm is a swine would make his attraction to Nazism inevitable.[157] Second, the BMP noted, though only in passing, that the "resistance of the Poles themselves is not represented." This is, obviously, in stark contrast to other films about occupied Europe in which the theme of resistance is central. In a minor but symbolic comment, the BMP found it odd that the script originally called for only the British, American, Chinese, and Russian flags to be shown at the putative postwar court, omitting the Polish flag, among others.[158] The BMP was also perplexed that, although the film obviously intended to "project public thinking to the problems of the post-war period" as "of great importance to the Government's War Information Program," it failed to fulfill its potential and instead was just "another anti-Nazi horror story."[159] What the BMP obviously wanted was not a film that focused on Poland but one that featured postwar trials.

The BMP reviewer provided Columbia with a very lengthy series of suggestions to salvage what it regarded as a squandered potential. First, Grimm's earlier life in prewar Poland was to be reduced and more attention given to German occupation crimes, which the Poles record in a growing indictment. The film should also project a postwar future for Litzbark, the supposedly Polish setting: the citizens, hearing news of German defeat, should "round up" Nazi criminals. The BMP even suggested elaborate changes in plot, characters, and episodes, basically furnishing the outline of a new script.[160] All of these were to make the film a crime story with Poland the setting. Nothing was suggested to make the Poles a less passive element of the film.

By late summer, the BMP was still displeased but hopeful regarding "Lebensraum." At some point, Columbia decided to abandon the project and only recommenced under BMP encouragement.[161] Thus, when the film was released several months later, its evaluation was generally positive. To the BMP, *None Shall Escape,* as the new title indicated, was really not about Poland but about the pledge of the "United Nations" to judge war criminals after hostilities. Thus the film retained its BMP classification as IIB2 with a secondary theme of ID. At no point did the BMP consider or recommend involvement with Polish authorities regarding this film set in Poland, in contrast to its usual practice for films set in other countries. The reason was obvious: it was not intended to be an occupation or "United Nations" film; it was not really about Poland. (And the BMP never consulted Polish authorities in any case.) Even the title change is eloquent: "Lebensraum" evoked German motives for invading Poland; *None Shall Escape* is a hunt for criminals with the war already reduced to a subsidiary role.

Columbia obviously reconceived the film and its purposes in midproduction. In 1943 a number of stories appeared in the press, noting the Polish aspects of the film. Columbia especially noted the presence of Marek Libkow, the Polish producer who had fled Warsaw in 1939, as a technical adviser.[162] In late 1943 Columbia noted that it had also obtained the service of "Fr. J. Jureko, a Polish Catholic" to help with the film. In early 1944, Columbia announced that the "Polish Information Service in Washington" had "found [the script] acceptable" and that some of the scenes, notably the one showing the death of the rabbi, were taken from the recently published *Black Book of Poland.*[163]

However, the Polish emphasis rapidly faded in 1944, probably under

OWI pressure, and the released version of the film was understood by contemporary critics to be about German atrocities (especially but not exclusively against Jews) and the need for punishment. The viewers' attention was thus directed toward the question of postwar trials and away from the specifically Polish issues very much in the news in 1944 because of the Warsaw Rising of August–October 1944. Whereas the trial theme was always present, it now became the overwhelming focus, and the Polish aspects receded into the background.[164]

Although this was the last Hollywood film about Poland made during the war, a fourth was at least contemplated. It is an eloquent testimony to the disregard for Polish sensibilities regnant in Hollywood that in the spring of 1944 Twentieth Century–Fox was considering producing a film based on Franz Werfel's play *Jacobowsky and the Colonel.* The chief characters in this comedy are two Poles, a Jewish refugee in France and an anti-Semitic officer who quarrel, cooperate, and eventually reconcile while dealing with the Germans. The officer is a pompous buffoon quite apart from his anti-Jewish prejudice. He bungles a mission for the Polish government-in-exile because he subordinates his duty to disporting his mistress and generally behaving quite foolishly. The Jewish Jacobowsky has fled Polish anti-Semitism, hardly a positive theme to introduce about one of the "United Nations" in a war against anti-Semitic Nazi Germany.

Appalled by the proposed film, the BMP informed Fox that the "unfavorable portrayal of our Polish allies would doubtless chagrin the State Department as the former would doubtless resent" the film.[165] The studio did not continue the project. However, that such a film was even considered during wartime is significant. To produce a film showing America's Polish ally in so negative a light in 1944, after years of BMP insistence on positive images of Norwegians, Czechs, French, English, and especially Russians, indicates that Hollywood felt no compunction about considering a very negative portrait of Poland. This tasteless project would have been Twentieth Century–Fox's only "Polish" film of the war.

6

Poland: Fleeting, Ambiguous, or Omitted

BEYOND THE THREE FILMS DISCUSSED in the previous chapter, cinematic depictions of Poland were a rarity for Hollywood. Poland and the Poles had minor roles on the margins of a few films, reflecting the margins of the American consciousness to which they were relegated. A comprehensive review of the Polish themes in American cinema of the war years is not a lengthy undertaking.

Hours before the fall of Warsaw in 1939, Columbia began production of the film adaption of the 1928 stage play *Front Page*. Released early in 1940 as *His Girl Friday,* the witty comedy is set in the weeks prior to the invasion of Poland.[1] There are a few scattered references to Poland and Poles in the film, but they are all minor matters. The charming but unscrupulous newspaper editor Walter Burns (Cary Grant) dismisses news about "the Polish Corridor"—a confrontation between Berlin and Warsaw—to pursue a lurid scandal. In an earlier scene, he plots a kidnapping involving an unseen accomplice named Polock Mike. Bickering in an opening scene, Burns and "Hildy" Johnson (Rosalind Russell) refer to a coal mine disaster. Russell ruefully recalls that her honeymoon was interrupted by the story: "I spent two weeks in a coal mine with John Krupski"—instead of her husband. Krupski is not identified as a Pole, but he may be. These are, to be sure, very minor matters—although far more than the usual Hollywood attention to things Polish. *His Girl Friday* is a rather biting satire; municipal administration, reporters, politics, and the justice system are all presented very critically. Nonetheless, it is noteworthy that a film made at the moment Poland was being invaded contains only negative reference to Poland and the Poles: unappetizing miners, petty criminals, and minor political issues.[2] There is no wartime film in which the Russians, Norwegians, or Czechs receive similarly disparaging treatment. The little *His Girl Friday* tells us about Hollywood and Poland during the war is an augury.

In August 1941, Warner Brothers released *International Squadron,* which utilizes the recently completed Battle of Britain as a backdrop.[3] Irresponsible but heroic American Jimmy Grant (Ronald Reagan) discovers the existence of an "international squadron" serving with the RAF. He decides to join after witnessing the effects of the German bombing of London. His behavior is, however, seriously flawed. His undisciplined conduct results in the loss of two other pilots, including his closest friend, a fellow American. Meanwhile he brazenly disports with the girlfriend of a French squadron colleague. Eventually he sees the error of his ways, and he dies in heroic self-sacrifice, showing both intrepidity and belated recognition of his duty to a noble cause.[4]

A poor and derivative film attempting to exploit the public's interest in the Battle of Britain, *International Squadron* also presents a distorted impression of the role of foreigners in the battle.[5] In an early sequence, Grant is introduced to the other members of his squadron: "a Czech, a Pole, a Belgian, and a Frenchman." The Warner Brothers press book released with the film stressed the presence of "fliers from France, Holland, Czechoslovakia, Poland, and Norway"; another advertisement noted aviators from "Czechoslovakia, Poland, Belgium, France, Greece, Norway [and] . . . Holland."[6] Obviously, the film's emphasis was the diversity of the pilots defending England in 1940, thus suggesting humanity's interest in the war, a Warner Brothers preoccupation. However, the film presents this phenomenon in a misleading manner. The RAF officially recognized 510 foreigners in British service during the Battle of Britain, July through October 1940. Of these, only 1 was French, and there were no Norwegians, Greeks, or Dutch at all. There were a large number of Czechs, but by far the largest component was Polish: 139, almost 30 percent of the total number of volunteers. The RAF recognized only 7 Americans among the 510, one-twentieth of the Polish role.[7] Hence a film about international volunteers during the Battle of Britain should have been chiefly devoted to the Poles. Instead, Poles are mentioned only in passing, and it is unclear whether there is even an actor representing a Pole; if there is one, he certainly has no lines. The dialogue and promotional material that suggest that American, Norwegian, Greek, Dutch, and French volunteers are equal if not superior in numbers to the Polish volunteers is preposterous. The large Polish role in the battle was an event of very recent memory and had been widely heralded in the press in Great Britain. Warner Brothers chose to edit the Poles substantially out of one of their major contributions to the war.

A segment of the large-budget RKO production *Once upon a Honeymoon,* featuring such major players as Cary Grant and Ginger Rogers, is set in Warsaw under German occupation.[8] As is often characteristic of films directed by Leo McCarey, all the major roles have Irish names.[9] The only Polish character who appears more than fleetingly in the film is General Borelski, a fatuous miles gloriosus who doltishly falls into the snare of the suave German agent Baron von Luber, played by Walter Slezak.[10] Borelski is played by Albert Bassermann, whose resemblance to General Felicjan Sławoj-Składkowski, a member of the prewar Polish government, is an irony too subtle for RKO to have intended.[11] A brash American journalist, Pat O'Toole (Grant, in perhaps his worst performance), explains that Poland's September defeat was caused by the activities of "fifth columnists," which perhaps was intended as a sympathetic comment, though little more than condescension. As critic Roger Manvell notes, "The film lacks deep feeling for the plight of the betrayed countries."[12] There is a brief scene depicting Polish Jews imprisoned by the Germans in Warsaw, an early, though rather muted, depiction of the initial stage of the Holocaust.[13]

The central Polish figure in the film is Borelski. His role is to be the dupe of von Luber, who tricks him into buying worthless weapons on the eve of the German invasion of Poland, thus undermining the country's defenses. How this outcome is achieved is never explained. Borelski, thanks to O'Toole, discovers von Luber's duplicity at the last moment and tries to warn his government and arrest von Luber. This is foiled when the Germans murder Borelski before he can report his findings. It is this episode that allows O'Toole to make the later claim that Poland fell because it was "betrayed from within." This, of course, reduces the entire September campaign to a minor swindle and allows O'Toole to compare the fall of Poland to the German occupation of Austria, an event marked by no fighting whatsoever.[14] O'Toole repeatedly speaks of "betrayal from within" and "fifth columnists" in Poland, which, of course, suggests that von Luber was aided by Polish traitors. The script's intention to depict Poland as rotten within and ripe for collapse is corroborated by a number of passages later cut from the released version.

When von Luber and Borelski meet to discuss the Polish arms purchase, Borelski laments that he is not confident that Poland will fight if invaded, and hence the weapons are to be distributed to the civilian population: "Put one of these [brandishing weapon] in the hands of each civilian and you could hold out for months, perhaps!"[15] Later the reference to the pusillanimity of the government was cut, and the remark about random distribution of the weapons, now rather puzzling, is left dangling without preamble. Von Luber concludes the scene by incomprehensibly referring to Borelski as "uncle," hinting that key members of the Polish government are related to Nazis.[16] Later Borelski makes fatuous comments about the possibility of preserving peace; the wise O'Toole responds sarcastically, realizing that Borelski's hopes for peace are delusional.[17] Again, Poland is depicted as an appeaser, a government without resolution, unworthy of its population.

A number of early passages flattering to the Poles were cut, leaving the vainglorious Borelski and a waiter as the only Polish characters, except for a maid who is possibly a Pole.[18] For example, a scene in which Katy O'Hara (Rogers) tries to acquaint herself with Poland by reading aloud a description of Józef Piłsudski, "the George Washington of modern Poland," was removed from the final script. References to Ignacy Jan Paderewski, well known to American audiences, were also cut.[19] Borelski's indignant refusal to discuss Poland's surrender of Danzig to German demands and his concluding oath "Poland will fight!" were also cut.[20] The result is an image of Poland on the eve of the war as a helpless country, run by buffoons, duped with ease by the Nazis because its government is honeycombed with Nazi sympathizers.[21]

Similarly, in the 1942 Columbia release *Commandoes Strike at Dawn,* there is a fleeting reference to the German mistreatment of Poles and Jews.[22] The hero, a Norwegian played by Paul Muni, is aghast when his little daughter reports to him that the school under German occupation has taught her a racial hierarchy of European peoples that puts Poles and Jews at the bottom. He is troubled by what the Germans are doing to Norwegian children's good taste. The film, however, is essentially about the plight of the Norwegians.[23]

The most stirring tribute to the Polish underground produced by wartime Hollywood was intended for inclusion in a film originally called "Forced Landing." The film begins with the shadow of a swastika spreading across Poland as the camera moves toward the district of Schneidermuhl, described as being "on the edge of the old [pre-1939] Polish border." The camera gradually focuses on a young Pole crouching in the bushes near a German sentry post. "Suddenly the scene is illuminated with a flash of light, followed by the sound of the explosion. Two more explosions follow in quick order, the light from them showing the young man's exultant satisfaction." Having witnessed the results of his sabotage, he runs off, pursued by the Germans. He reaches a prearranged location in a farmyard where he has hidden a carrier pigeon, to which he attaches a message cylinder. He releases the bird just before he is killed by his pursuers. The bird eventually flies to England. The next scenes indicate the decoding of the message and the hurried assembly of a bomber command, where there are frantic consultations. Squadron leader Clark then briefs the crew: "We received a report that the rail intersection East of Schneidermuhl was dynamited last night by Polish saboteurs," resulting in a massive blockade of German rail traffic and a congestion of munitions trains. Polish agents have thus inflicted a serious blow on the Germans. The aircrew is ordered to attempt a single raid to destroy this conglomeration, which will do "more to advance the cause than ten raids on as many factories."[24] This was how the script's authors intended the film to begin.

However, this elaborate opening showing the daring and intrepidity of the Polish underground did not survive. Within a few days, the Polish aspects of the film had been substantially reduced. By the time it was produced, the Polish scene had been eliminated. The film begins with a plane flying over eastern Germany and making a brief detour across the prewar Polish border. There is no explanation for this route, since the work of the Polish saboteurs has been excised.[25] The fleeting image of Poland on the map is all that remains of the Polish elements of the film.[26]

What resulted is the 1942 Warner Brothers release *Desperate Journey,* a long film of British aviators eluding German capture in a series of implausible episodes that in plot and pacing duplicate typical Hollywood westerns.[27] Errol Flynn is the star, and Ronald Reagan has the supporting role in a story that combines vicious though hopelessly incompetent Nazis with the comic high jinks of heroic Allies who take nothing seriously—repeating the frequent Hollywood portrayal of the insouciant yet indomitable American who effortlessly defeats the Germans at every turn. The only film of the war that tried to suggest that the Polish underground actively opposed the German occupation and rendered real assistance to the war effort was edited to remove the Polish aspects.[28] The result is that the importance of the daring mission is made unclear, and the plot loses much of its urgency.[29]

Polish interests are dealt a more severe blow in Warner Brothers' translation to the screen of a novel by Frederic Prokosch titled *The Conspirators*.[30] It is a complex and convoluted story of political intrigue set contemporaneously in Lisbon. The protagonist is a leader of the Dutch underground, but the cast of characters includes a host of nationalities whose tenuous existence in the Portuguese city underlines the chaos of war and the upheaval in their lives.

Perhaps the most powerful scene in the novel is a meeting among three young exiles, a Serb, a Greek, and a Pole, on a bridge at midnight. All three are homesick, idealistic, and patriotic. All three are filled with remorse about the war yet remain defiant. The conversation turns to the geopolitics of the war. The Pole speaks with contempt for the Czechs and their dependence on artful political maneuver and unwillingness to fight. He presents a ringing defense of his country: "Poland was solid, firm and brave. . . . Poland fought rather than yield. Fought to the end. Fought alone." After a brief pause, he recommences: "We fought to the end! Against hopeless odds. With no foreign troops to help us." When the Serb criticizes the politics of Poland, the huge Pole is enraged; he "seemed to grow three inches." He responds, "Poland has an ancient and distinguished culture. But yours [he addresses the Serb] is a land of bandits! A land of brutes." Though bordering on the fanatical, Prokosch's Pole is a passionate patriot and an imposing physical specimen.[31] In addition to this nameless young patriot, the novel features another Pole, Professor Kazimierski from Galicia, who is a shadowy figure but obviously sophisticated and refined. He moves in elevated circles among the émigrés harboring in Lisbon.

Prokosch's novel evolved in Hollywood. The first several draft screenplays, all by Frederick Faust, eliminated the Polish characters, obfuscated their nationality, or changed them substantially, and for the worse. The key transformation concerns the conversation of the youthful patriots on the bridge. A Czech has now replaced the Serb. This alone shows purposeful Hollywood alterations. Serbs were repugnant people in Hollywood, and the one film featuring their struggles against the Nazis was suppressed.[32] By contrast, the Czechs were favorites of the studios, especially Warner Brothers. Faust notes that the scene depicts the meeting of representatives of the "three most crucified countries," which is a dubious attribute of the Greeks and an absurdity concerning the Czechs, whom the Germans treated quite leniently. Now when the Pole makes the disparaging comment about the Czechs' refusal to fight, he is met with an angry and eloquent rebuttal from the Czech. The Pole is given additional lines that go beyond the patriotic transport in the novel. "Blind with passion and uplifted heart," he says, "the Poles and the Greeks will always fight. Until the last of us is dead. In the mountains, from behind hedges, from the middle of the night. Shall we not always continue?" The Pole's further dialogue suggests that he is emotionally unstable and filled with hatred and, as Faust comments in the text, "reduc[es] everything to dreadful absurdity." Hence, although his defense of Poland has survived from the novel, the speaker is now virtually a madman. Moreover, words are added to the Pole's declaration that Prokosch did not include and that have a clear political meaning: "We were too far off for even promises to reach us or help us."[33] Obviously, this line is designed to make the failure of Great Britain and France to render effective aid to Poland in 1939 appear unavoidable, reasonable even to the aggrieved Pole. This makes Poland a less worthy candidate for sympathy and removes the problem of its abandonment by its allies. At the same time, the nameless Pole is rendered an irrational chauvinist, especially compared to the Czech. The other Polish character, the professor, disappears. However, a new character, Jan Vernaszky, of whom more presently, makes his appearance.[34]

In June, the studio was still unsatisfied with the several versions of the Prokosch novel, and a new treatment by Elliot Paul was submitted. Professor Kazimierski returns, though his role is insignificant. The bridge scene is again recast: the Serb returns, joining the Greek and the Pole, and Faust's Czech is gone. The scene, however, is radically shortened, and the Pole has been transformed. Gone is the indictment of the Czechs, and his defense of his country becomes the rather tepid "Be so kind as to remember that we [Poles] fought, that they're killing us now, one by one." When Poland's reputation is attacked, his defense, which is presented in both the novel and the Faust treatment as perfervid and lengthy, is now abbreviated to a meaningless "You lie!"[35]

Hence the bridge scene shrank as the screenplay evolved at the hands of various writers.[36] Nonetheless, it remained substantially as Paul rendered it until October 18, 1943, when a new screenwriter, Vladimir Pozner, submitted his version. Pozner had impeccable leftist credentials and would later be blacklisted for Communist sympathies.[37] His presence had immediate consequences for the story's Poles. Suddenly, for the first time, the entire scene at the bridge disappears and, with it, the geopolitical discussion of the young patriots, the defense of Poland, and the description of the country's lonely defiance of the invader. The Polish professor is also gone, but Jan Vernaszky, an emotionally unstable denizen of the underworld, now has a rather expanded role. We are told that he is Polish, from Warsaw, and "nervous"—which was to be understood essentially as insane. His behavior is erratic.[38]

It is noteworthy that Polish-Soviet relations deteriorated markedly during 1943 while Warner Brothers was adapting the script. By the time Pozner submitted his version, the Soviets had broken relations with the Polish government-in-exile, and General Sikorski had been killed in a plane crash off Gibraltar. The Soviets had begun a campaign to vilify Poland and denigrate its performance in the war. Pozner's script would accommodate these new realities far better than the original versions, which included a defense of Poland's role in the war.

From October 1943 through February 1944, Pozner's version of the script was substantially maintained. The young Polish patriot and the professor never return, and several scenes feature the unbalanced Pole from Warsaw variously called "Bernazky" and "Bernaszky," all the variant spellings of which are impossible in Polish.[39]

After this protracted evolution of the screenplay, *The Conspirators* was released in 1944, starring an impressive cast led by Paul Henreid, Hedy Lamarr, and Sidney Greenstreet. The only major Polish feature that remains is Bernazsky, played by Peter Lorre in his usual vaguely unsettling manner.[40] There is also a very minor character described as a "Polish man," but his role is virtually invisible. Whether it is a remnant of the professor or the patriot on the bridge is unclear. Thus a novel that contained a declaration of Poland's role in the war, a scene that survived repeated screen adaptations, became a film without any positive Polish elements at all. The new character Bernazsky is hardly designed to reflect well on the Poles. Paul Henreid, who played the indomitable Czech underground leader in *Casablanca,* appears in this film as the heroic leader of the Dutch underground. If there is a Polish underground at all, it is something Hollywood did not care to discuss.[41] Prokosch was appalled at the radical changes to his story and pronounced the final product "nonsense."[42]

Shortly after the invasion of Poland in 1939, the English writer Eric Ambler published a complex novella of intrigue, espionage, and crime set in contemporary Europe, *A Coffin for Dimitrios.*[43] One of the principal characters is Władysław Gródek, a "master spy" who is brilliant, suave, wealthy, and physically imposing. "He is a Pole, and he lives near Geneva" is the way in which we are introduced to Gródek, whose nationality is repeated a number of times. The fact that he corresponds in Polish becomes a minor element in the story.[44] Gródek is an unscrupulous and ruthless criminal, but he is in every way a dominating figure.[45]

Five years later, Warner Brothers brought the Ambler story to the screen as *The Mask of Dimitrios.*[46] Gródek appears, but his nationality is eliminated; neither the line describing him as a Pole nor any of the other references to his origin or his native language appear in the film. Even his first name, the unmistakably Polish Władysław, is omitted from the film, though it does appear, in garbled form, in the credits. The name "Grodek" (without the diacritical mark) is Slavic but not Polish. Hence viewers of the film would not know that Ambler's Gródek was a Pole. Certainly the accent of the Belgian actor Victor Francen (who also played the pro-appeasement Count Orvid of *In Our Time),* who portrays Gródek, is not Polish. The suppression of Gródek's nationality is all the more curious because the film is at pains to dwell on the nationalities of the other characters: Greek, Turk, Dutch, and Danish, among others. To be sure, the original Gródek is not a heroic character, but he is an impressive one, "the most successful professional agent in Europe," Ambler indicates, as well as being a great lover.[47] But in the film Gródek ceases to be identifiably Polish.[48]

Gródek is one of the larger and certainly more impressive Polish roles in the Hollywood films of the war era—and his nationality is kept secret.[49] There are fleeting allusions to Poles in a few other films of the era but no major characters, and the Polish aspects of the role are of no importance. Thus in the 1941 film *So Ends Our Night*—actually released before America's war entry—about refugees escaping the Nazis in 1937, we have a nameless character, "the Pole," whose role is marginal.[50] *Wake Island* (1942) includes a Polish refugee serving in the U.S. Marines. He remarks wistfully about Warsaw to pilot MacDonald Carey, who had thought he was a Russian; the assumption was symbolic. This fleeting Polish appearance is significant because it is sympathetic, albeit extremely brief. With the sloppiness with which Hollywood typically dealt with such issues, this supposed Pole is given a Russian name, Ivan, and acted by an émigré from Odessa, Mikhail Rasumny.[51]

A Pole and references to Poland's wartime fate are featured in the low-budget, sixty-seven-minute *U-Boat Prisoner*, released in August 1944 by Columbia.[52] The film depicts the fate of an American sailor (played by the athletic and dull Bruce Bennett) captured by a German submarine after his ship is sunk. Thanks to a complicated series of plot devices, he succeeds in passing himself off as a German agent. He is introduced into a group of prisoners held in the torpedo room. All of these are distinguished scientists who are being forcibly transported to Germany to help in the production of "secret weapons." These worthies are a Dutchman, a Frenchman, a Briton, and an elderly Pole. The latter is played by the émigré actor Erwin Kalser, who had a long career in German cinema. It is quickly established that, like the American sailor, all are inveterately anti-Nazi, brave, and defiant, save the Frenchman, who is a repulsive sniveler and, as is later revealed, a secret agent of the Germans as well. Nonetheless, Polish misfortune is indeed noted, quite rare for Hollywood, and the Polish character is positive. A brilliant biologist, proud and principled, he immediately makes common causes with the brave American against the Germans (who are all quite disgusting) and the vile Frenchman. The multinational prisoners are sarcastically referred to by their German captors as a "League of Nations," and in this assembly, Poland symbolically occupies a worthy position.

The problem with the Polish aspect of the film is the relationship between the Polish and Dutch captives. Both are supposedly famous scientists, both patriotic. The Dutchman is perhaps the dominating character, and he dies a heroic death, whereas the Pole survives. The Pole, Biencawicz (a typically garbled Hollywood version of a Polish name), is openly bitter about German outrages in Poland, which he remarks on. However, he admits that the Dutchman has equal reasons for grievance, as he is from Rotterdam. This equates the 1940 German bombardment of the Dutch city, in which perhaps eight hundred were killed, with several years of German occupation in Poland, which resulted in millions of casualties.[53] The fact that the film was playing in the United States at the time of the Warsaw Rising (August 1–October 23, 1944) is most unfortunate, as it trivializes Poland's suffering by equating it with Holland's.

Sharp-eyed viewers might have caught an oblique reference to Poland in the cheap 1943 Producers Releasing Corporation film *Submarine Base*.[54] A German submarine, arriving at a secret Caribbean base for new torpedoes, is shown with a series of flags painted on its conning tower representing enemy ships sunk. Two of the flags are American, and one is probably the red and white flag of Poland, indicating the loss of a Polish vessel in the war against the Germans. It is one of the few times Hollywood ever displayed the Polish flag, and here it is fleetingly displayed, small, and obscured by night and mist. Nonetheless it is a tiny reminder to perceptive viewers that Poland fought and sacrificed on the seas.

Viewers of MGM's *Song of Russia* also would have to be alert to catch the Polish aspects of the film. In a particularly striking juxtaposition, Russians are seen listening intently to a radio broadcast of classical music while the Germans, no music lovers, are busily preparing the invasion of the Soviet Union in June 1941. The camera focuses on a border outpost manned by Soviet soldiers whose attention to the concert is shattered by a German bombardment commencing the assault. A Russian émigré, Ayn Rand, later commented on this scene, "Now realize—and that was a great shock to me—that the border that was being shown was the border of Poland. That was the border of an occupied, destroyed, enslaved country which Hitler and Stalin destroyed together. That was the border that was being shown to us—just a happy place with people listening to music."[55]

The critically acclaimed film *The Story of G.I. Joe* (1945) is often cited as an unusually fine production, gritty and realistic, eschewing theatrical heroics to concentrate on the grim world and prosaic courage of the common soldier.[56] It was nominated for four Academy Awards and features a fine performance by Robert Mitchum as the company commander, Captain Bill Walker. The film is also a distortion of the important Italian campaign; it omits the major Polish contribution to the war and assigns the credit to others.

The film is based on correspondent Ernie Pyle's reportage while following an American unit from North Africa through the subsequent Italian campaign. The bulk of the film is devoted to the 1944 effort to break the German Gustav Line south of Rome, which was dominated by the famous monastery of Monte Cassino, though the former is not mentioned and the latter is called only "the Monastery." The film indicates, quite falsely, that it was American troops who captured the heights and thereby opened the way to Rome. It does this by placing the American unit to which Pyle is attached at the base of a hill dominated by what is obviously intended to be Monte Cassino. The company engages in a number of attacks and patrols, all futile, and the soldiers become increasingly demoralized. However, after much suffering, including the emotional breakdown of a key figure in the unit, their stalwart leader rallies them for a last effort, which avenges the ruination of their hapless sergeant, who exits the film in madness. They grimly fix bayonets, and in a series of fast cuts, we see the Americans storming up the hill, reaching the crest, and then, immediately afterward, walking victoriously along a road that is marked by a sign leading to Rome. The viewer is led to believe that American soldiers captured Monte Cassino. A GI greets Pyle immediately after the action by calling out, "Welcome to the other side of Cassino," the only time any reference is made to the battle site. Another says, "We kicked the door open," again suggesting very clearly that it was an American victory with large consequences, clearing the way to Rome.

However, the heights of Monte Cassino were taken not by American troops but by Polish soldiers of General Władysław Anders's Second Corps. The fighting was ferocious, and the Poles endured immense casualties in just a few days. American troops had failed in their assault on the center of Gustav Line—where the film places them—which was an operation conducted under overall British command. When Cassino, and with it the key to the Gustav defenses, fell on May 17, it was a Polish flag that was raised over the field of victory, not an American one.[57] Thus Hollywood made a film that focuses on the Battle of Monte Cassino, one of the most famous and bloodiest Polish victories of the war, but does not mention the Polish presence there. Although omitting reference to the Poles may be excusable in a film that is obviously designed to present the war from the point of view of the typical American infantryman—and eschew larger operational issues—this does not require rewriting history to give the Americans credit for a Polish victory.

The Story of G.I. Joe was made in the last months of 1944, when Poland had just suffered gigantic casualties in the Warsaw Rising and the subsequent occupation of the country by Soviet units. Cassino was one of the few moments of national pride left to the Poles in the midst of much tribulation. As British historian Mathew Parker writes, "The grandest, the most symbolic" cemetery at Monte Cassino is filled with Polish graves. It bears this motto:

> We Polish soldiers
> For Our Freedom and Yours
> Have Given Our Souls to God
> Our Bodies to the Soil of Italy
> And Our Hearts to Poland.

The great majority of the Poles who fought at Monte Cassino, including their commander Anders, had endured protracted Soviet captivity after 1939. At Monte Cassino, 50 percent of the Polish soldiers deployed fell.[58] When the film was released, American audiences were about to resume normal lives; Poles would endure years of Stalinism.

The screenplay was the work of Leopold Atlas, Guy Endore, and Philip Stevenson, all members of the Communist Party.[59] Endore had also written the most blatant Hollywood celebration of the Soviet Union, *Song of Russia.* Stevenson had coauthored, along with John Howard Lawson and two Soviets, the paean to the Russian war effort *Counter Attack* (1945).[60] Both thus had experience in depicting wartime issues in a way convenient for Soviet geopolitical aims. Atlas had no such efforts to his credit; his only previous brush with Polish themes was 1944's *Tomorrow, the World,* in which he names the only Polish character "Dumbrowski." Director Wellman, a staunch anti-Communist who later admitted dislike for the Russians, adored *The Story of G.I. Joe.* The ungenerous treatment of the Poles simply never occurred to him.[61]

Turning from operations to the question of occupation and resistance, we find some strange Polish aspects in Warner Brothers' costly 1943 film *Edge of Darkness,* an "elaborate tribute" to Norwegian resistance.[62] Here, against a large coterie of indomitable Scandinavians, is juxtaposed a contemptible Pole, played by Nancy Coleman.

In the script by Robert Rossen, we meet Katja, "a Polish girl in her twenties brought to Trollness [the mythical Norwegian setting] by and for the German soldiers." She is described as "dark" and again as "dark, small, nervous."[63] She is an actress: "At the time the Germans took my country, I was in Berlin on the stage." But to "prove [her] loyalty" she was required to become a camp follower, which life she has led for two years, and she is now the unhappy mistress of the sadistic German officer commanding the local garrison.[64] She lives at Nazi headquarters, the locus of evil among the good Norwegians, where she alternately boasts of her previous sexual escapades, vulgarly taunts the soldiers, and engages in brutal seductions. Her current services to the Germans, she explains, are necessary if she is to be allowed to resume her acting career. She is a moral bankrupt who craves the approval of her country's despoiler for reasons of personal advancement. The fact that this reprehensible creature is repeatedly identified as a Pole ("Polish sow" at one point) seems at the very least an unkind reference to a people whose occupation was much more ferocious than that being endured by the Norwegians.[65] Katja is a collaborator who conspired with the Germans and sought their favor before the war—a profile that echoes Count Orvid in *In Our Time*. She is, like him, a whore to German interests who only latterly and incompletely realizes their evil. Whereas Gródek's Polish nationality is eliminated from *The Mask of Dimitrios*, Katja's is repeatedly noted—an unfortunate choice for Poland's image in the United States.

Should the viewer not draw the obvious conclusion that the Poles are a nation of moral cretins, Rossen inserted another scene that is not found in the original novel. In this we have an elaborate counterpoint between the "learned" village schoolteacher, Sixtus Andresen, and one of the German soldiers, a particularly thuggish wretch. Andresen dispassionately muses aloud while observing the man, "High receding forehead and flat-topped skull . . . Your ancestors were Slavs, were they not?" To indicate that this anthropological analysis is correct, the script thereafter refers to this solder as "Slav." Incensed that his racial purity is questioned and outraged by the taunts of his fellows, "Slav" shows that psychological depravity accompanies his stereotypical physical grotesqueness by beating and torturing the noble Andresen, who is presented as the soul of dignity.[66] This scene was mercifully cut; it does not appear in the released version.[67]

This episode between Andresen and "Slav" is in many ways quite repulsive. Ironically, it represents exactly the kind of crude racial stereotyping of which the Nazis were guilty. Rossen's attributing such behavior to one of the most honorable of the Norwegians is a blunder, as the film was designed to contrast the baseness of the Germans with the exalted humanity of the Norwegians. Rossen's motives cannot be reconstructed, but the fact that he would go to such lengths to suggest racial degeneracy among the Slavs serving in the German army is unpleasant. There were, of course, many Slavs in the German forces, the great bulk of them drawn from former Polish territories under German occupation. It is more ironic that Andresen, who initiates this racist dialogue with "Slav," was played by Morris Carnovsky, a child of Jewish immigrants from Eastern Europe, the principal targets of German racial prejudice. That this scene was added to a film that already has a Polish degenerate, Katja, makes the whole enterprise an elaborate effort, tinged with race propaganda, to present the most repulsive image possible of the Poles.

Edge of Darkness began as a 1942 novel by William H. Woods but was substantially rewritten for the screen by Rossen, a colorful character who was born in New York City to Russian immigrants named Rosen.[68] Briefly a boxer, Rossen joined the Communist Party because, as he told his son, it was "dedicated to social causes of the sort that we as poor Jews from New York were interested in."[69] According to Sandra Brennan, "His interest and affiliation with the Communist party greatly influenced his writing."[70] A fellow party member described Rossen as "a staunch Communist, very staunch," and a man essentially lacking integrity.[71] These views would scarcely have troubled director Lewis Milestone, himself a leftist who, like Rossen's family, emigrated from Russia. Milestone was active in promoting sympathy for Russia via such organizations as the American Russian Institute, described as a "center for Russian propaganda in Hollywood" and a Communist front organization, and the Russian-American Club.[72] Carnovsky was also a Hollywood Communist.

The BMP saw no problems with *Edge of Darkness* and did not think portraying a Pole as a slattern and collaborator would be in questionable taste. What was important for the BMP was that the film depicted the Norwegians heroically. However, the bureau did note that Katja was (in addition to her other faults) "vacillating," which complicated the efforts of the Norwegians.[73] The MPPDA, however, did object to Katja, not because she symbolically cast the Poles in a bad light but because her behavior "present[ed] the suggestion of illicit sex."[74] Warner Brothers rather offhandedly presented the Katja character to the MPPDA as merely "a rather feather-brained camp flower [sic]" and described her "characterization" as "indifferent" rather than "sympathetic" or "unsympathetic" in its standard schema.[75] Nonetheless, the MPPDA was annoyed by what it described as "loud, angry and anguished cries from Poles as to the handling of the Polish girl in Edge of Darkness," which was its "worst headache . . . right now."[76]

Even the OWI was appalled at one Polish portrayal that Hollywood conjured, this in the unlikely context of a frothy ice-skating film featuring Sonja Henie. Twentieth Century–Fox was musing in late 1942 about a film then titled "Quota Girl," depicting the fate of a Norwegian skater, Nora (Henie), and her uncle stranded in Canada by the German invasion of Norway in the spring of 1940. Unable to return to their occupied homeland, they eventually are allowed to come to New York when, conveniently, she is offered the leading role in an "ice show" there. Her problems quickly melt when she marries an American and both her legal and romantic complications are solved.[77] All of this is quite trivial; the film is little more than a vehicle for Henie to skate about gracefully and be pleasant, the sum and substance of all her films. Here, however, screenwriter Arthur Kober, a Communist Party member, had added an element that made the OWI uncomfortable.[78] Sharing the precarious status of resident alien in Canada with Nora is her friend Katya (again this non-Polish name), a Polish girl whom the OWI reviewer found "unpleasant": "a flighty, self-concerned little creature, who is avidly seeking an American husband so that she can get into the United States from Canada. Although she is Polish, Katya exhibits no concern about the war; the impression is gained that her country's enslavement has had no effect on her whatever, except that she is now stuck in Canada and is extremely annoyed by the fact. When she finally does land an American husband, the implication is quite broad that she is playing him for a sucker."[79]

The OWI found such a portrayal "hardly fair" and was astounded that Twentieth Century–Fox would consider a film in which one of the main characters was so repulsive: "The tragedy of Poland must have had some effect on Katya," the reviewer noted in exasperation at the script; "probably she had friends or relatives there." Could she not be shown "in some small way" to care about her homeland? Perhaps "she can be knitting in her spare time for the Red Cross," the OWI suggested, "or donating blood"? As written, she was "a little cheat" set on a "cold-blooded proposition." Something should be done to make her less unappetizing; perhaps she could "fall in love with the talent scout."[80] Apparently the perplexity of the OWI was enough for producer William LeBaron: "Quota Girl" was radically restructured as a narrative about lighthearted tribulations at a resort in Quebec and released as *Wintertime* without any issues of stranded immigrants and no scheming Polish girl.[81]

These portrayals of foul Poles are minor annoyances compared to the large geopolitical issues considered in *Mission to Moscow*.[82] This cinematic travesty was constructed in close collaboration with the Soviet embassy in Washington.[83] It is ostensibly the film version of the recently published memoirs of Joseph E. Davies, who had served as American ambassador in Moscow in 1937–1938. Davies's long, self-important history of his service sold very well. His avowed purpose in writing the book was to "get better public acceptance for aid to Russia," a goal he explained was "vital to the Christian front."[84] How the volume became transformed into a film is controversial. Shortly after the film's release in 1943, an abbreviated version of Davies's book appeared, complete with film stills. An anonymous foreword claims that Harry Warner had taken the initiative in approaching Davies, who regarded Warner Brothers as the only studio worthy of the effort.[85] However, later Jack Warner admitted that the idea had not originated with his studio but had been more or less forced on it by the Roosevelt administration. President Roosevelt wanted the film made, and Jack Warner, who was a great devotee of FDR, was only too happy to oblige.[86] Jack was so proud of the role this film played in international relations that he sent a letter to the Moscow Conference on American and British Film held in August 1942 boasting that he was going to produce *Mission to Moscow* as a contribution to "Russo-American goodwill."[87]

Mission to Moscow is the most famous film on the list of Hollywood's efforts at the glorification of Russia and the whitewashing of Communism, which have been well discussed in scholarly literature.

The details of this piece of propaganda need not be revisited here, but we should note that the film manages to avoid, among other awkward subjects, any mention of the 1939 Soviet invasion of Poland. The Polish references in the film, though few and minor, are negative. American audiences would receive a version of the war identical to that of the Kremlin, omitting the rather significant fact that the Soviet Union acted as Germany's ally in despoiling Poland and was in occupation of a large portion of its national territory, wherein it was conducting itself in a barbaric manner. Apparently the film originally included no references to Poland at all, but after several months of rewriting, a new screenwriter, Howard Koch, took over and decided to add a number of politically calculated references to Poland.[88]

One of the conditions Koch insisted on before accepting the writing responsibilities was "the right to select his own technical advisor" for the film. His choice was Jay Leyda.[89] Leyda had spent 1933–1936 in the Soviet Union, which he found enchanting. He was a member of the CPUSA and a dedicated Stalinist.[90] His services as technical adviser on *Mission to Moscow* consisted of working closely with Koch to ensure a Stalinist interpretation of recent politics.[91] The Koch-Leyda collaboration on *Mission to Moscow* took place from the late summer through early autumn of 1942. Only a few months later, Koch would start writing *In Our Time.* Whether Leyda also aided Koch in this project is unclear, but the relationship was already well established by the time Koch was working on the Polish film. Koch wrote to Leyda that it was his "fondest wish . . . to have the famous *Mission to Moscow* combination back together" for future films.[92] After the war, when Congress investigated alleged Communist influence in Hollywood, Koch wrote a detailed account of the people and materials he used to write the screenplay. He omitted Leyda.[93]

As Koch conceived it, *Mission to Moscow* would begin with a brief segment in which former ambassador Davies himself would introduce the cinematic version of his embassy to Russia (1937–1938), followed by a montage supposedly suggesting the breakdown of international order in the mid-1930s, the rise of Hitler, and, seemingly as a response, the decision by FDR to send Davies to Moscow—a last desperate gamble by the internationalist Roosevelt to save the peace by building a Russian-American relationship, a chimera the president believed only the intrepid Davies could achieve. Of course all of this was Koch's fancy, as Roosevelt had no such motives and no serious mission could be entrusted to a windy amateur like Davies.

In any event, after this cinematic chicanery, Davies travels to Russia, but, according to Koch, "at the [Polish-Russian] border, an incident occurs which opens [the Davies family's] eyes to the precarious relations between Russia and Poland. A German spy is caught trying to get over the border with forged papers. There is commotion as he is taken into custody. A Russian official apologizes to Davies but says that such incidents are frequent occurrences."[94] This passage is a nasty bit of mischief by Koch. Though it conjures 1936, it was written, let us remember, on the eve of the third anniversary of the invasion of Poland in 1942. To suggest that in the late 1930s Poland was complicit, if even from carelessness, in allowing German spies to enter Russia is a stroke of malign genius by Koch. Because he will later argue that the notorious purge trials were entirely just and uncovered real spies, Koch prefigures this espionage episode, which will dominate the film. The Poles have at least some culpability; at the very least they were not vigilant. German plots against Russia were facilitated by Poland, whose border with Russia thus became a danger for Soviet security. The geopolitical implications of this are obvious. Even Koch was probably embarrassed, and he substantially changed the scene in early September, removing the implications of Polish-Nazi collaboration.[95]

Moreover, Koch fabricated the whole incident. Davies's book *Mission to Moscow,* the ostensible source of the screenplay, makes no mention of any spy incident at the Polish-Russian border. Davies's chauffeur, Charles Ciliberti, who accompanied the ambassador and later published his own memoirs, also said nothing about a spy at the Polish border. Indeed, Ciliberti emphasized how vigilant the frontier guards were. Ciliberti, unlike his credulous employer, harbored no illusions about the Soviet Union. He remarked that he felt "oppression" when traveling in both Nazi Germany and Soviet Russia, a feeling that lifted only during the interval spent crossing Poland.[96]

Koch suggested that the film conclude with a breathless review of 1937–1941. This review features a reference to "England and France . . . holding the bag" by their commitment to defend Poland in 1939; then the invasion of Poland by Germany—with no mention whatever of the Russian attack days later—and then a convenient omission of 1939–1941, the awkward era of the Nazi-Soviet alliance. In this way we are brought rather hurriedly to late 1941 and the heroic defense of Russia. The last words are Stalin's, piously invoking God's aid to FDR.[97]

By the fall of 1942, Koch's screenplay was largely completed. However, several months later, he decided to interpolate a new episode. The scene, which occurs during a billiards game, appears in the released film. Davies—played by a severe Walter Huston, gaunt, taciturn, and crowned with thick wavy hair that the dumpy, windy, and bald Davies lacked—is engaged with three resident diplomats, the Frenchman Robert Coulondre, Great Britain's Viscount Chilston, and Wacław Grzybowski, the ambassador of Poland. Grzybowski is played by John Wengraf, a Viennese émigré who was usually cast as a maniacal Nazi.[98] The fact that Warner Brothers cast as a Polish diplomat an actor usually associated with German arch villains is noteworthy.

The scene opens with Grzybowski's sarcastically noting that the Polish embassy in Moscow is modest, as the Poles are "Stalin's stepchildren."[99] Davies, who is the soul of probity as played by Huston, is instantly suspicious but uncomprehending at this reference. He instinctively senses the duplicity of the slippery European.[100] The arrogant Grzybowski then takes Davies aside and unctuously purrs, "What a pity you weren't assigned to Warsaw, Mr. Davies. You would have enjoyed the social life there much more than here." He smiles repulsively before adding, "We have a saying; a Russian is merely an unfinished Pole." When Grzybowski makes some remark critical of the Soviet government, Davies is incredulous: "I was under the impression that the country is strongly behind the present government!" Grzybowski responds, "Don't be deceived by their propaganda, Mr. Davies. These Russians are experts at dressing their windows for foreign diplomats." The baffled Davies asks, "Do you mean the new five-year plan isn't working out?" The cynical Grzybowski shrugs and sarcastically notes, "Five years—ten—fifteen . . . They will always be the same Russians—full of great plans and small fulfillment." Koch explains the import of this exchange: "Davies surprised by this attitude of hostility looks towards the others [the French and British diplomats] for clarification." Coulondre is noncommittal, while Chilston suggests that Soviet achievements not be belittled. Davies, the virtuous American, is disoriented and shocked: he has fallen in among duplicitous and calculating men. Revolted by the cynicism in the room, he vows to seek the answers to his naive but sincere questions for himself.[101]

The purpose of this scene is obvious.[102] First we are to contrast the open-minded Davies, who vows to find the truth—indeed he is next seen touring the country seeking answers—with the cynical European diplomats who live in isolation, languidly playing billiards and repeating the shopworn prejudice of a time gone by. Though Davies is obviously superior to these three, it is the Pole, Grzybowski, who is the chief villain, the most unlike the American. His corrosive disdain contrasts with the trust and sincerity of Davies. Film audiences should draw the proper conclusion. The Frenchman wearily assents to the Pole's contemptuous assault on the Russians, and Chilston even offers a mild dissent. Grzybowski is the caricature of the Poles as provided by Soviet propaganda: an arrogant aristocrat blind to the realities of the vibrant new Russia, denigrating Soviet achievements, spreading foul rumors, and sowing discord among those who should be allies. The Pole is a troublemaker and a hopeless captive of his own prejudice. Grzybowski is Koch's Uncle Stefan all over again: the corrupt, black-hearted reactionary. He is the epitome of the Soviet representation of the Polish government-in-exile.

As a matter of fact, Chilston was a highly competent and much experienced diplomat near the end of his career; he served competently in Moscow and provided insightful reports to London. Coulondre was one of the most brilliant French diplomats of his generation; his service was exemplary. Grzybowski held a doctorate in philosophy and had lived in the Soviet Union for a considerable period. He knew Russia well. Unlike the plutocrat Davies, he was a political liberal of democratic views. He was also a former cavalry officer with distinguished service during the Polish-Bolshevik War of 1919–1921. Grzybowski was very highly regarded by the diplomatic corps in Moscow as a resourceful and intelligent analyst of Soviet affairs, a reputation confirmed by his incisive reports. By contrast, the neophyte Davies, with his credulousness, was an embarrassment to the resident diplomats. Grzybowski, incidentally, very quickly dismissed him as a man of little ability easily misled by Stalin.[103]

Koch concocted this episode from thin air. It does not appear anywhere in Davies's memoirs.[104] The fact that Koch created this pointed scene in 1943, when the Polish government was desperately attempting to defend its reputation against a Soviet propaganda assault accusing it of the very things Koch attributed to Grzybowski, is perhaps of greater importance. Koch was providing audiences with a Pole who epitomized the very faults the Soviets were attributing to the Poles.

Koch had one more Polish notion for *Mission to Moscow,* but it apparently died aborning. At some point there existed a scene purportedly showing Davies meeting with Paderewski in Warsaw, presumably in 1937 or 1938. There are only scraps to prove the scene existed or to indicate where it was to be inserted in the film—probably near the end. The earliest reference to Paderewski is in a list of film characters from September 1942.[105] In January the Warner Brothers research division was scrambling to find pictures of Paderewski and of the Polish embassy in Paris.[106] Jack Warner was told as late as January that the montage sequence of Davies's tour of European capitals, including Warsaw, where he was to meet Paderewski, was still not filmed.[107] In February, in one of the last scenes shot, Paderewski finally appears.

A stock shot of Warsaw is imposed over the "Polish State Department insignia" to suggest that Paderewski is acting in an official capacity. Of course, Paderewski had not been a member of the Polish government for many years. In voice-over, Davies narrates: "My first visit to the capital of Poland." Next we move to a close-up shot of an actor playing Paderewski, and we hear Davies speaking: "Any information you care to give me, Mr. Paderewski, will be sent confidentially to my President." Paderewski, ensconced, we are told, in his "living room," "after a moment's silence" speaks gravely: "Even confidential cables are tapped these days, Mr. Davies." The latter responds, "I'm aware of that. This will leave by diplomatic courier." Assured, Paderewski continues, "Then you may tell your president that I have positive information that Hitler and Mussolini are meeting to work out an agreement for the partition of Europe. Austria is first on the list." The scene dissolves.[108]

The scene, featuring the German émigré Emil Rameau as Paderewski, was indeed filmed, as at least one still photograph survives.[109] It shows Rameau with Paderewski's characteristic hairdo speaking with Davies in a room dominated by a large piano—in case the viewer needed a visual reminder of who Paderewski was.[110] However, Warner Brothers decided not to include the scene. Paderewski is not listed among the film's characters at the end of February, and in early March the role is among the listed "omitted speaking parts."[111]

The problem with this scene is that the events it depicts did not happen and could not have happened. Paderewski did not reside in Warsaw in the period in question, and he never met Davies. Even Davies, who is probably not to be trusted in any event, does not claim in his turgid memoirs to have met Paderewski.[112] Paderewski's papers, published and unpublished, also do not mention Davies. Koch concocted the whole episode. David Culbert notes that the Paderewski scene was probably included because "the use of this famous Polish pianist . . . was based on the idea that no other Polish leader would be familiar to most viewers."[113] Hence the deceased Paderewski is mischievously employed by Koch for his larger purposes. The references to Paderewski's home or office (the film purposely blurs the two) are part of Koch's effort to suggest that Poland is awash in German spies—or perhaps Polish spies— which he introduced at the border-crossing scene.

After editing in a stock shot of "Polish peasants fleeing in panic" to depict the September campaign of 1939 and a map sequence portraying a fire consuming Poland from the west—but no Russian invasion from the east—what David Culbert calls "polite animation," *Mission to Moscow* was ready for theatrical release.[114] The only reference to Poland is that suggestive yet fleeting depiction of the prewar Polish envoy to Moscow as a blindly anti-Russian reactionary.[115] Koch later insisted that the whole film—including the fictional Paderewski meeting and the nonsensical Grzybowski conversation—was "carefully checked and no political attitudes or events were put in the picture unless they were believed to be true."[116] The film was "in accordance with historical facts" based on a "scrupulous and impartial study of the records."[117] Unfortunately, one of the facts Koch omitted was the remark by a member of the Kremlin security detail to Davies's chauffeur that at some point it would be necessary to shoot Davies because he was a capitalist.[118] Only in 1964 did Koch finally admit that the film was "pro-Soviet."[119]

Though the Warners later tried to distance themselves from the film, when it was released they crowed over its notoriety and ridiculed its detractors.[120] The OWI's overseas propaganda journal, *Letter from America,* exulted on the front page of its May 21, 1943, edition that *Mission to Moscow* "broke all attendance records in its first four days in Hollywood."[121] A few weeks before, it had run an interview with Ambassador Davies noting that he "officially approved" the film.[122] In late June, European readers were told that the most popular film in the Soviet Union was *Mission to Moscow.*[123]

The film was controversial on its release and remains so to this day. The essence of the debate concerns the portrayal of the Soviet Union, not the few references to Poland. However, the Polish aspects of the film also elicited concern from the outset. *Life* magazine correctly noted as soon as the film was released that the depiction of Grzybowski, Chilston, and Coulondre as minor "villains" was strange.[124] John Dewey and Suzanne LaFollette, in a scathing indictment in the *New York Times*, noted that "Hitler's armies are shown invading Poland, but not Stalin's," and that the subsequent partition of the country goes unmentioned. Commenting on the carefully edited concluding portion of the film, they wrote, "By the device of leaping over Stalin's collaboration with Hitler and Churchill's direction of British affairs, it conveys the impression that Stalin's foreign policy has always been democratic and anti-fascist and Britain's one of appeasement. One would never suspect that it was Stalin who enabled Hitler to attack Poland and Chamberlain who came to Poland's defense."[125]

The timing of the film's release is noteworthy. On April 13, 1943, Radio Berlin announced the discovery of the Polish mass graves at Katyń and accused the Soviets of the crime. Two days later, the Kremlin publicly denied the accusation and blamed the Germans. The Polish government was thrown into consternation by the affair and requested an International Red Cross investigation on April 18 without fixing guilt in the interim. On April 25 the Russians issued an outrageous note stating that there was "no doubt that between the Allies enemies, Hitler and the Polish Government, contact and collusion exist." The Russians accused the Poles of acting "to please Hitler's tyranny" and iterated that they were acting in "collusion with the Hitlerite government." With this as a preamble, they announced the severance of relations with the Polish government. The American press generally supported the Russian version of events, placing the Poles in a difficult position.[126] Three days later, *Mission to Moscow* premiered in Washington; it opened the next day in New York before moving quickly to national release. Hence, though Polish themes are marginal to the film, they were in the news when it was released.

Most American critics hailed the film. The *New York Times* regarded it as contributing to a better understanding of Russia.[127] Leftist Jack

McManus praised *Mission to Moscow* to the skies, noting that Hollywood had finally dealt "simply and sanely" with the Russians, which was particularly important as they were the victims of "anti-Soviet attacks" launched by the Poles. The *New York Sun*'s Kate Cameron lamented that it was "too bad" that Davies's efforts to engender a "more sympathetic attitude towards Russia's aims in the war and her aims thereafter" were being jeopardized by the "threatened break with the Polish Government in exile." She noted that the film obviously preached that the United States had to strive to "keep Russia on our side," but it contained no "intimation that the Russians have an obligation towards us or her other allies."[128]

In a conclusion that is particularly apt in summarizing all of Hollywood's wartime portrayal of Poland and the Polish-Soviet relationship, the Dewey-LaFollette commentary rejected Warner Brothers' claims of acting from patriotic motives in promoting American-Soviet amity and described this film and others like it as constituting an assault on simple decency, creating thereby a "moral callousness in our public mind." They concluded, "A few more uncritically accepted films like *Mission to Moscow*—for where thousands read books, millions see motion pictures—and Americans will be deadened to moral values."[129] Quite apart from the motives of Koch and Leyda, the fact that the White House urged the making of the film and then endlessly trumpeted it meant, in the words of Dan Georgakas, that the Roosevelt administration was "party to endorsing an enormous political lie."[130]

In 1995 Koch referred to his authorship of the *Mission to Moscow* script as "the thing I value most in my life."[131] By contrast, Jack Warner later presented himself as a naive victim who had been unable to disclose the fact that he made the film under White House pressure, and moreover only attempting to perform "a service to the American people so they would know more about our then Russian allies." Alas, for his noble service, Warner was pilloried by "Trotskyites everywhere."[132] Davies originally planned additional films about Russia.[133] Mercifully, they were never made.

Another of the several hagiographic Hollywood portrayals of Soviet Russia, RKO's 1943 production *The North Star,* contains one of the characteristic features of the Hollywood Left's treatment of Poland during the war: a rather elaborate and often quite subtle geopolitical code woven into the film.[134] This subtext is sufficiently unobtrusive that the average viewer would be untroubled by it. However, the discerning would note that it constitutes a justification for Soviet political and territorial designs.

The North Star was the work of Lillian Hellman, a Communist Party member since 1938 and a passionate devotee of Stalin's Russia, as illustrated by her anguished cry on learning of Hitler's 1941 invasion of the Soviet Union: "The Motherland has been attacked!" Hellman was a member of innumerable Russian and Soviet friendship organizations during the war and contributed to them generously. Most if not all of them were Communist fronts.[135]

The North Star begins early in the morning of June 20, 1941, the day before the German invasion of the Soviet Union. A radio broadcast reports that German troops are massing along the "Polish border." This is obviously the 1941 border between the German and Russian zones of occupied Poland. The film is set in what is described as a "border village."[136] In August Hellman's script called for a specific reference to "border villages of Kamenets Podolsk District."[137] When the Germans invade the next morning, the village is bombed at once, and the invader is placed at "less than fifty miles away."[138] The fact that some of the village schoolchildren are off on a trip to Kiev, described as a five days' walk distant, suggests that the village is in the west, in former eastern Poland, a territory annexed by the Soviets just fifteen months before, involving deportations, arrests, and executions.

That the film is set in occupied eastern Poland and not farther east, in pre-1939 Ukraine, is confirmed by a very curious declaration made by the village physician, Dr. Kurin (played by a patriarchic Walter Huston), early in the film. Kurin is the moral center of the film and a figure of great gravity and goodness. When the Germans invade, he rallies his countrymen by declaring, "This is our land, our village. We remember we fought another war to make them ours." It is the reference to "another war" that is most peculiar. Kamieniec, the city Hellman apparently intended as the setting, was seized by Russia from Poland at the close of the eighteenth century and remained in Russian control thereafter. Hence the villagers could not have fought "another war" to regain it.[139] However, if the location is intended to be even slightly west of Kamieniec, then the area would logically be in the lands of pre-1939 Poland, and the war fought could only be understood as the 1939 Soviet invasion of Poland undertaken in conjunction with

Nazi Germany, which subsequently joined this area to Ukraine by forcible annexation, later formalized by rigged elections. What other war could these villagers have fought in that resulted in territorial transfer? Hence *The North Star* implies, if ever so subtly, that it is set in occupied eastern Poland. The fact that the Soviets liked the film so much that they imported it speaks for itself.[140]

The importance of the setting is that the villagers are portrayed, without exception, as devoted, passionate Soviet patriots with pictures of Stalin scattered about. They make perfervid declarations of their undying loyalty to the Soviet Union, "our country." In fact, the fanatical and self-sacrificing patriotism of the villagers is the central motif of the film. They need no encouragement to oppose the Germans; they do so instantaneously and unanimously, in contrast to the Polish peasants in *In Our Time,* who run amok with no concern for defense until they are organized by an English girl. But if this geographic reconstruction of the setting is correct, these people have been Soviet citizens only for several months. Such profound emotional devotion is incomprehensible unless, of course, we adduce the argument that this was an area that rightfully belonged to the USSR and was only briefly, and artificially, under foreign—Polish—occupation. In 1941 this village was especially attached to the Soviet motherland because it had spent much of the previous generation languishing under Polish rule, only to know the blessings of Communism for a few short months before the Germans invaded. This was certainly the understanding of the area retailed by the Kremlin after 1939; that it would be implied in an American film is quite extraordinary. Only cognoscenti who accepted the Soviet explanation of its 1939 invasion of Poland and the subsequent occupation of its eastern territories as "liberating" the local population from Polish rule would find this presentation comprehensible and agreeable. For a supporter of Poland, it denigrates prewar Poland while obscuring the Soviet invasion.

Regardless of the exact location of the village, it would be populated not by Russians but by ethnic Ukrainians, hardly a population favorably inclined to Moscow. A few years before the war, a devastating famine, largely ignored if not prompted by the government, had exterminated a huge number, and the invading Germans were largely greeted as liberators from Russian tyranny in 1941. By portraying a Ukrainian village as patriotically Soviet in 1941, Hellman's script achieves a double obfuscation. She retroactively removes the Soviet guilt for mass starvation by presenting the peasants as passionately loyal. Hence the script is a rather elaborate effort to rewrite the recent history of Soviet Russia.

The film's tendency to make oblique negative references to Poland—cinematic winks to the initiated—is demonstrated by a scene added in March 1943. Kurin ridicules the notion of kissing a lady's hand, a practice characteristic of Poles, with this bit of sarcasm: "They'd have done better if they'd used their hands to fight the Fascist, your elegant friends."[141] This version of the September campaign, with Poland's elite described as predatory cowards—unwilling to fight fascists—would later be given its full elaboration in *In Our Time;* here we have only a soupçon.

The North Star's geopolitical arguments would be of no interest to most viewers but would send a clear message to those inclined to support the Kremlin's ideological and geopolitical notions.[142] This is particularly important because MGM's Sam Goldwyn "wanted to make a quality picture for FDR" and spent a fortune on *The North Star,* the largest amount on any film in the studio's history. The film was popular, made money, and garnered six Academy Award nominations.[143] Hence the geopolitical content of the film becomes of greater moment. William Wyler assured his boss, Goldwyn, that the film, though flawed, "fills an enormous and urgent need," which Goldwyn acknowledged.[144] An appalled critic from the *New York Daily News* concluded that *The North Star* was "more Communistic than the Russians."[145]

The OWI was delighted with *The North Star;* Ulric Bell of the Hollywood office even sent a letter to Goldwyn that he had been "privileged" to observe the filming of this "very positive contribution." This sentiment was echoed by BMP reviewer Sally Kaye, who found the film a "tremendous contribution to our understanding of our Russian allies."[146] However, before the film's release, the OWI had had one element of disquiet: if only the film could, somehow, "point up the fact that the invasion" by Germany "was not unexpected," the film would be improved. It was important that the audience be taught that "Russia's whole foreign policy was based on the premise that a conflict with Germany was inevitable."[147] Of course, how the OWI could know the motives of Kremlin policy is not explained, but this comment does coincide with the Kremlin explanation that the Hitler-Stalin pact was not a cynical cooperation but only a desperate effort by the antifascist Soviet Union to gain time. The OWI here echoes the current Communist Party line perfectly and wishes it foisted on the public.

A category apart in Hollywood's depiction of Poland comprises the seven-part documentary series *Why We Fight,* directed by the celebrated Frank Capra. Produced by the U.S. Army and designed for the indoctrination of troops, the series won the 1942 Oscar for best documentary and was released commercially despite opposition from Hollywood, which resented the army's competition for the film audience.[148] Film historians have deemed this series "the most ambitious effort to teach modern history with motion pictures" ever produced.[149] Capra, with his usual combination of self-promotion and bad syntax, insisted that his work "stated . . . in many instances, actually created and nailed down American and world pre-war policy." It was, he crowed in his memoirs, "also accepted as the official policy by our allies."[150] Leaving aside Capra's immodesty, *Why We Fight* was influential and widely seen, and because of its very mounting as a production of the War Department, it seemed to bear the imprimatur of government policy. It was because the War Department was so pleased with the films that it expanded the intended audience to include civilian employees.[151]

The work of Capra and the Russian-born Anatole Litvak, the series was scripted by a group of leftist screenwriters drawn from a list prepared by the Hollywood Writers Mobilization.[152] At least two of the writers (Ben Hecht and Jo Swerling) were CPUSA members. On commencing the project, Capra immediately asked Samuel J. Briskin to join him.[153] Like Litvak, Briskin was Russian born. Capra also acknowledged help from Jay Leyda, though what form that took is unclear.[154] Eric Knight, another writer, was an enthusiastic champion of the Soviet Union. Capra had long been fascinated by Soviet cinema. Thus the creative group behind *Why We Fight* had a considerable nucleus of CPUSA members and Russian expatriates and sympathizers.[155] When Capra saw the initial drafts of the scripts, he was "aghast" and deemed them "Communist propaganda."[156]

Litvak played a large role in the effort, writing at least one of the episodes (*Battle of Russia*) and directing production whenever Capra was absent.[157] Litvak had served with distinction in the Russian army and been wounded during World War I.[158] He became an American citizen in 1940. Arrogant and opinionated, he arrived in Hollywood "telling everyone how great he was."[159] His script for the segment devoted to Russia reflected a profound affection for his homeland.[160]

Why We Fight is a conglomeration of patriotic exhortation, crackpot geopolitical theorizing, and historical mischief making.[161] The series devotes considerable attention to Poland in its second episode, *The Nazis Strike.*[162] The voice-over narrative is virtually the Soviet explanation of the events of 1939. Hence we are told that while Russia was prepared "to back concerted action against Germany," the pusillanimous West was deaf to Moscow's entreaties. Abandoned, Stalin signed the August 23, 1939, pact, which "didn't make any sense" and was at base a ruse by Berlin by which "the Germans hoped they could lull Russia into a false sense of security and the Russians needed time to prepare for the fight they knew was coming."[163]

Here the September campaign is recounted at length, though not with accuracy.[164] "Before the [German] invasion was thirty minutes old, the planes of the Luftwaffe were over Poland wiping out the Polish air force, most of it caught flat-footed on the ground." The pitiful remainder was rapidly "shot out of the sky." Much is made of the Poles' reliance on mounted cavalry. All of this is historically inaccurate as well as calculated to make the Poles appear pathetic rather than heroic. First, the Polish air force was not destroyed on the ground. With considerable forethought, it was moved to prepared camouflaged positions on the eve of the war. It thus avoided losses from the German attack and fought with skill and determination for many days thereafter, inflicting significant losses on the Germans. Only when it ran out of supplies and the front line approached did the Polish air force end its resistance. The cavalry did not engage in frontal assaults against German tanks but, according to prewar tactical plan, approached the point of engagement, where it fought dismounted. Accounts of the cavalry's participation in the fighting report that the mounted units were well employed.

Portraying the Poles as incompetent Quixotes inflicting no damage on their enemies was a Hollywood staple. We have seen this all before, in Paul Henreid's dazed cavalry officer of *In Our Time* and in the introduction to *To Be or Not to Be,* where the September campaign receives a similar recounting.

Finally, there is an odd passage in which the narrator intones that "Local Judases point[ed] out loyal Polish neighbors." This unexplained reference conveys the impression that the Polish population contained a significant percentage of traitors. Although elements of the German minority certainly behaved disloyally in September, the film does not ascribe this behavior to them specifically but implies it was a feature characteristic of the general population. We should remember that a similar comment appears in the film *Once upon a Honeymoon,* released at about the same time. Needless to say, Capra's episode focused on Russia makes no mention of the widespread collaboration of Soviet citizens with the invading Germans in 1941.

Capra presents the September 17, 1939, Soviet invasion of Poland curiously. We are told that within a few days, "Poland was completely destroyed. Completely? Not quite: During the last days of the campaign, the Russian army entered eastern Poland and took up positions along the Bug River. The two strongest armies in Europe faced each other. Hitler could decide now whether to keep on heading east or call it quits. He called it quits. Why did Hitler quit here? He had to. To continue a drive to the east would leave Germany facing the threat he had always sworn to avoid: a two-front war."

Though the campaign was lost, neither the Polish army nor the government capitulated, and the latter quickly removed to Paris and eventually to London, where it functioned throughout the war. The Russian forces did not "enter" Poland to limit the movement of Hitler's forces eastward, but rather invaded as active allies of the Germans. They cooperated in their operations against Polish units, and their intelligence forces collaborated closely in rounding up, incarcerating, and liquidating leading Poles during and after the campaign. The Russians did not "take up" positions along the Bug, which suggests that they were prepared to resist a German advance. Rather they occupied zones determined in the prewar agreement with Hitler. The Germans were dissuaded from farther movement east not by the menace of Russian units but rather because they had reached the limit of their assigned zone of occupation. They had no intentions of moving farther east.

The film's account is not just inaccurate; it is a purposeful effort to present a fraudulent version of the first campaign of the war. It is at pains to suggest that the Soviets were steadfast in their opposition to Hitler and in 1939 reined him in. In fact it was the Soviet-German agreement of August 1939 that allowed Hitler to begin the war, and during the next eighteen months it was Russian raw materials that played a role in allowing Hitler to undertake a series of successful campaigns against the West. This of course omits the simultaneous Soviet aggression against the Baltic states, Romania, and Finland undertaken while Moscow and Berlin were allies between 1939 and 1941. Moreover, it omits the fact that in 1939 the Soviets invaded Poland, with which they had a treaty of nonaggression, and did so while that country was fighting against Germany. That the Soviet invasion was exceptionally brutal is also conveniently omitted from *The Nazis Strike.*

The effort at ex post facto exoneration of the Soviets is elaborated a few minutes later when the September 17 invasion of Poland by Russia is transformed into a seemingly peaceful "occupation" set in the final hours of the war. The viewer would logically conclude that the Soviets committed no aggression and inflicted no casualties. So systematic an effort to present the September campaign in a manner that portrays Poland as a failure and the Soviets as without any guilt for their actions could not possibly be attributed to naive ignorance; it reflects a clear ideological purpose.[165] In the film, the Russians are exculpated.[166]

Episode three, *Divide and Conquer*—devoted substantially to the 1940 German campaign in Western Europe and the fall of France— summarizes the war up to 1940 in a few lines of text at the outset.[167] The events of September 1939 are presented thus: "By September 27, the Germans had wiped out Poland and met the oncoming Russian army. Determined to avoid a two-front war, Germany halted her drive to the east and turned west to first crush Britain and France." This brief summary is quite odd, especially the reference to Poland's being "wiped out." Warsaw did not capitulate until the next day, and the ferocious battle of Modlin nearby raged yet longer. More disturbing is the attempt at misleading the viewer; certainly the words "met the oncoming Russian army" suggest a military confrontation, perhaps even as a result of attempted Soviet assistance to Poland. The reference to the Germans' halting to avoid a "two-front war" is part of an effort to imply that the Russians were intent on engaging the Germans in 1939.

After this introduction, the film again omits the multiple Soviet aggressions of the period from mid-1939 to mid-1940: the Hitler-Stalin pact, the Soviet invasion of Poland, the subsequent political blackmailing of the Baltic republics (October 1939), the invasion of Finland (November 1939), and the seizure of northeastern Romania (June 1940). The film ends with a stirring tribute to France, complete with

"La Marseillaise," French cavalry in full charge, and words of praise. Poland received no such tribute in the segment devoted to it.

Also released in 1943 was the episode titled *The Battle of Britain,* with additional distorted and unkind treatment of Poland's role in the war.[168] The opening sequence exhibits Germany's conquests up to late 1940 by spreading darkness across a map of Europe. Obviously Capra and his team did not know what to do with eastern Poland, which had been invaded and occupied by the Russians, so the map bizarrely leaves almost half of Poland free in 1940. A few minutes later the narrator informs us that "Britain, unlike Poland and the Low Countries, did not make the mistake of bunching its planes on the runways. The planes of the RAF were scattered and hidden." The film thus repeats the false charge about the destruction of the Polish air force on the ground. Later in the film, the significant role of Polish squadrons in protecting London goes completely unremarked. The Poles played a large role in the Battle of Britain, but Capra chose to ignore it. This was the most notable Polish military action since the fall of Poland and was a major contribution to the war. It was widely heralded in Britain at the time.[169] Not mentioning it was both inaccurate and ungenerous.

Rather more significant for Poland was the treatment of Soviet-Polish issues in the next episode, *The Battle of Russia,* which revisits the September campaign in its opening sequence.[170] It is, in sum, a piece of blatant pro-Soviet propaganda posing as factual analysis.[171] Here Capra manages to "skip over the Russo-German Non-aggression pact." This production precisely parallels the version of events as explained by Moscow. It is perhaps no surprise that the series "was studied and greatly admired in the Soviet Union."[172] A critic rhapsodized that *The Battle of Russia* was "the best and most important war film ever assembled in this country."[173] American audiences who learned their geopolitics from *Why We Fight* could never understand any Polish grievance against the Russians.

The Soviets were enchanted by *The Battle of Russia* and devoted a special meeting of the Cinema Section of the American Department of the USSR Society for Cultural Relations with Foreign Countries to discussing it in early 1944. It sent Capra a translated transcript of its meeting. He and Litvak were singled out for paeans of praise that extended over many pages. Along with *Mission to Moscow* and "especially" *The North Star, The Battle of Russia* was particularly popular in Soviet Russia, Capra was assured. It "documents the American attitude towards us." *The Battle of Russia* showed "real knowledge of Russia"; it "breathed good-will towards us"; indeed it was "made with love for us." The film was particularly useful in contradicting the claims of "pro-fascist circles in the West." This was important because Hollywood had earlier produced films like *Ninotchka,* which were "anti-Soviet and slanderous," even "pro-fascist." The Capra-Litvak project was "altogether different."[174]

War Comes to America was one of the last episodes, written by Anthony Veiller, Alan Rivkin, Leonard Spigelgass, and Capra himself.[175] Like the earlier episodes, it begins with a brief summation of the war. However, by now Capra had decided to stop attempting to explain away the Hitler-Stalin pact as an expedient for Russia, allowing them time to face the enemy, and simply eliminated the whole episode from the film—it never happened.[176] The Russian invasion of Poland in September now also is not presented as a defensive advance; it has simply disappeared. This very political editing bothered Darryl F. Zanuck, who worried that such a portrayal of Soviet Russia would invite criticism. He wrote Capra a very delicate letter suggesting inserting "a brief section which admitted the alliance between Germany and Russia," which, he added, could be explained as "sheer necessity." Capra dismissed Zanuck's concerns airily by noting that the issues had been "covered pretty thoroughly in a previous episode."[177] Of course, all the material in the introduction to *War Comes to America* had been discussed in earlier episodes; why eliminate only these portions, which raised awkward questions about Soviet Russia?

Capra sent early drafts of the scripts of the *Why We Fight* series to Eric Knight, one of the series' principal writers, for his evaluation. Knight and Capra were close, and Knight responded with lengthy and blunt comments.[178] Knight stated at the outset that the chief goal of the series was to convince the viewers that Soviet Russia and Great Britain "are our allies, they're damned good allies to have, and anyone who says different is just voicing the crap that Dr. Goebbels is trying to pour out by the manure-cart load." Given this goal, only *The Battle of Russia,* written by the expatriate Litvak, really appealed to Knight. "Watchers feel that Russia is a hell of a swell country to be allied to. That's important." The screenwriter "was believing in something." Knight admitted that it was extraordinarily pro-Russian: "Jesus, they'll say we're pinkos soon, and Russia is the only land we love." But that was necessary because they had to "sell" Russia to a public who had previously heard only that Russians were "bastards."[179]

As for the other episodes, Knight had relatively little to say. "Poland" (apparently the original title for *The Nazis Strike*) worried Knight because it made the Germans appear too powerful. He feared the American conscripts would wonder "how am I going to face" the German war machine if "Poles couldn't—they're husky guys, Poles. I know some polocks." His solution was to reduce German military campaigns to what amounted to a series of mass muggings whose success relied completely on surprise. Hence the United States, forewarned, would not fall victim to Hitler, "a gangster who jumps people when they're not looking."[180] We can only wonder whether this reflected Knight's analysis of the war or he was condescending to create an explanation comprehensible to the hoi polloi.

Originally, the episodes of *Why We Fight* were to be only the first in a number of the Capra team's propaganda films. Capra told the army he would follow with a three-part series titled "Strategic Battles" and a longer group, "Know Your Enemy—Know Your Ally." It is unclear how far these projects advanced, though Capra implied that at least preliminary scripts were produced by autumn 1942.[181]

Capra indicated that the third series would include separate episodes on Great Britain, Russia, China, "Fighting France," Canada, Australia, Brazil, and Mexico, as well as a hodgepodge called "The Unconquered Democracies."[182] This is a very curious list. Mexico and Brazil were scarcely significant allies of the United States in 1942, yet each was to have a separate film. The forces of "Fighting France" were minuscule. The total military contributions of Canada and Australia were also rather minor. There was no significant involvement of Canadian troops on any front until the summer of 1943, and by war's end, the number of Canadians killed was only 45,000. Australian losses were slightly fewer. By comparison, Polish military losses were conservatively estimated at 400,000. In fact, Polish casualties exceeded those of Great Britain and equaled if not surpassed those of the United States. Civilian casualties in Brazil, Mexico, Canada, and Australia were virtually nil; Polish civilian casualties reached into the millions, though the exact figure is still very controversial.[183] By Capra's scheme, however, Poland was not an "ally" worth knowing.

In early 1943, the Polish authorities in the United States hoped that Capra would at least mention Poland in the "Unconquered Democracies" segment and sent him some information regarding Polish military efforts after the September campaign.[184] However, by April 1943, Capra had omitted this segment from the list he sent the War Department of the proposed episodes of enemies and allies.[185] It seems none of these were ever produced.[186]

Why We Fight had limited public release beyond military installations.[187] It was, however, widely heralded. The War Department heaped praise on Capra. General George C. Marshall enjoyed the episodes, finding them "superb."[188] Allen Rivkin, the coordinator of inter-American affairs, was lyrical: he wept at the showing and admitted that he was "fascinatedly educated at the presentation of the Polish campaign."[189] Capra's Hollywood colleagues could not restrain themselves in praising his work: Dore Schary of MGM found *The Nazis Strike* "magnificent" and averred that the impression on him "will last forever."[190] Reports from screenings at various bases reported enthusiastic receptions.[191] Even the minor Polish officials whose reactions are documented first praised the films and only thereafter tried to correct some of the distortions.[192] Given that *Why We Fight* appeared with the imprimatur of the American government, it would have been politically inadvisable, as well as pointless, for the Poles to express open criticism.

Many years later, Capra was still proud of the series, particularly the Russian episode.[193] He admitted that "we had to eliminate things" but justified everything on the basis that the intended audience of "punks" was so immature and ignorant that a more nuanced view of Soviet Russia was quite impossible: all had to be black and white. Since "the immediate thing was the destruction of the [German] war machine," misrepresentation of the Soviets was justified. Indeed, Capra later boasted that he was particularly sensitive to Communist influence in proposed scripts—an influence that he could "smell"—and had rejected any text that reflected the party line.[194] That geopolitics can also "smell" of Communism seems not to have occurred to Capra. If the intended audience of these films was as naive and impressionable as Capra believed, his culpability in filling their heads with propaganda is the greater. Explaining the war in simple terms is one thing; repeating the geopolitical line of the Kremlin is another.[195]

Perhaps the most curious aspect of Hollywood's treatment of Polish issues during wartime is the practice of omitting mention of Poland where simple good sense would require it. Thus the famous *Mrs. Miniver* (for which its star, Greer Garson, won an Academy Award) opens with a touching scene in an English church at which the assembled congregation is shocked and dumbfounded to discover that on that day, September 3, 1939, Great Britain had declared war. Why they were unaware of the fact that the war had actually begun two days earlier, and with the invasion of Poland, is not explained.[196] The effect is to suggest that the invasion of Poland was so insignificant that it could pass completely unnoticed. This, in effect, removes the Polish issue from the war.[197]

The most striking example of the omission of Poland is the celebrated *Casablanca,* a magnificent film despite its many shortcomings, which has become iconic among students of cinema.[198] Apart from its romantic theme, it is an exercise in leftist geopolitics thanks to the screenplay by the Epstein twins and Howard Koch.[199] Koch and the Epsteins were politically kindred spirits, despite later frictions. Julius Epstein later insisted that he was never "ultra-left" and that politics never "affected" his screenwriting. However, when pressed about his claim to have no political motivations in writing *Casablanca,* he admitted that the political views of the film reflected "everybody's attitude then"—a convenient evasion but also doubtless an accurate reflection of the political ambience of Hollywood's screenwriters.[200]

Rick's nightclub is awash with refugees from Central Europe who, rather stupidly, congregate before the suspicious eyes of the Gestapo—and in evening dress, be it noted. We are introduced to Austrians, Germans, Russians, Czechs, Free French, Hollywood's favorite anti-Nazis the ubiquitous Norwegians, and even Bulgarians, but absolutely no Poles, who are conspicuously omitted.[201] Victor László (Paul Henreid, who despite his Hungarian name describes himself as "a Czechoslovakian") leads an amorphous multinational underground peopled liberally by Norwegians. Careful viewers of *Casablanca* will note that László has affiliations not with the Czech government, as one would surmise, but with some extranational body. There was no multinational underground during World War II, save in this film.

In a particularly curious episode, the stoic László is questioned by the serpentine Gestapo officer Major Strasser (Conrad Veidt). The latter recites a long list of European cities with resistance movements—all implicitly linked to László's underground. However, neither Warsaw nor any other Polish city is noted. The clear implication is that there is no resistance movement in Poland.[202] The BMP's reviewer called particular attention to this scene, which she found splendid in enumerating the several underground movements. That Poland's, the largest, was omitted did not trouble her.[203]

If *Casablanca* omits a fictional Pole, the turgid 1944 Twentieth Century–Fox release *Wilson* has far more historically significant omissions.[204] In this endless film, which cost a great deal but returned very little, the Canadian actor Alexander Knox portrays Woodrow Wilson in the most flattering possible light. At a cost of $5 million—considerably more than *Gone with the Wind*—it was the most expensive film yet made, and it was in every way ponderous. The script was begun in late 1942 and was ready one year later. There followed three months in production, including the erection of lavish sets. The film was gigantically promoted: thirty-two thousand billboards erected nationwide, over three thousand radio commercials, innumerable full-page advertisements. The advertising budget alone exceeded $1 million, then a staggering sum.[205] It was released in August 1944 to much fanfare.

Like the better-known *Sergeant York,* this film, though set in the era of the First World War, was designed to rally patriotic sentiment in the Second World War.[206] Moreover, it was designed to encourage an internationalist perspective in the American public.[207] The pet project of producer Darryl F. Zanuck, *Wilson* is more a didactic enterprise than entertainment. It presents the president as a prescient internationalist whose championship of the League of Nations is idealistic and whose wise counsel is scorned by nasty Republicans. Zanuck had vague hopes of using the film as a vehicle for promoting the presidential aspirations of Wendell Wilkie, in whose dedication to internationalism he descried echoes of Wilson.[208]

Although ultimately a financial failure and unpopular in much of the country, *Wilson* was well received by critics and drew large crowds to screenings in major cities; an estimated 10 million saw the film by 1945. It attracted extensive political commentary, which hailed the film's didactic function. The *Philadelphia Record* grandly announced that the film "may conceivably change the history of the world." Bosley Crowther conducted an opinion survey and became convinced *Wilson* had had a profound influence on public attitudes.[209] Thomas J. Knock retrospectively regarded it as being "pregnant with meaning" for American audiences of the time and concurred with Crowther's assessment of the film's impact on American thinking regarding foreign affairs.[210]

Among Wilson's major foreign policy successes was his support for Polish independence, which he endorsed as early as 1917 and later included as the thirteenth of his celebrated Fourteen Points. The restoration of Poland was for Wilson the epitome of the victory of idealism over the cynical practices of the "old diplomacy" and as such characterized American approaches to geopolitical issues as against European practices. Wilson's friendship with Paderewski had been not only advantageous for Poland but valued considerably by Wilson. The Wilson-Paderewski relationship, though often exaggerated as a causative factor in the reestablishment of Poland in 1918, was ritually invoked in the years after 1918 to symbolize American friendship for Poland and the commonality of interests of the two countries. Yet this theme, seemingly so appropriate in 1944, is omitted from *Wilson*. The film was made while Poland was undergoing German occupation and released on the very day the Warsaw Rising commenced, an effort that cost perhaps a quarter million Polish lives. However, there is not one word of Poland in the film: no Paderewski, no thirteenth point, and no American role in the re-creation of an independent state.

The small Polish traces there are in *Wilson* are few, fleeting, and peculiar. In a scene set just after the American war declaration, Wilson is shown visiting soldiers about to embark for Europe. The obvious purpose of the scene, often repeated in Hollywood films and much loved by the OWI, was to show a group of men from different national communities working as Americans. In Lamar Trotti's provisional script, a character called simply "Private" speaks: "Pete heres [*sic*] grandfather was Russian. Me, I'm pure Irish. Joe yonder's folks come from one of those little places nobody can ever remember the name of." The mystery locale is Bratislava, supposedly in Bohemia, we are soon informed, but "that ain't all. We got Swedes and Polocks and Frenchies."[211] Evidently Trotti thought "Frenchies" a bit rude, so he cut the reference, but he left "Polocks." However, as the script evolved, references to the Polish soldiers gradually disappeared, though the Irish soldier remains and the fellow from Bratislava is definitely established as a Czech.[212] In fact Trotti briefly mused over including a maudlin scene between the Czech, who is returning, blinded, from service overseas, and Wilson, who miraculously finds him on Christmas Eve. Overcome with emotion, Wilson exclaims to his wife, "The Bohemian boy we met that day!" Trotti mercifully cut this bit of melodrama.[213]

Later we see Wilson speaking to reporters about his peace program for Europe. He recites, in order, the Fourteen Points, but, after referring to "cooperation with Russia"—a reference not to be found in the Fourteen Points—Wilson, oddly, skips to the fourteenth point, about the League of Nations, omitting point thirteen.[214] Later Trotti cut the obviously loaded reference to Russia but still did not include the independence of Poland in the Fourteen Points.[215]

When Wilson goes on his exhausting speaking tour to promote acceptance of the Versailles treaty, Trotti has the president explain the importance of the League of Nations to dubious midwesterners: "The welfare of a laborer in a Wisconsin mill, or a cotton-grower in Georgia may depend today upon policies in Rumania or Poland."[216] Poland here is used in a reductio ad absurdum to illustrate how even the most exotic and trivial place can affect America. This slighting reference is all we hear of Poland.

Trotti's final evocation of Poland is symbolic of how shadowy Poland became for Hollywood late in World War II. We are introduced to a formal scene in the White House. It is evening. While the president and his wife entertain, Paderewski "is playing his Minuet."[217] In the final version of the script, the scene begins, "Monday November 11, 1918. Semiclose shot of Paderewski at Piano playing." Wilson and his guests listen to the Pole. A close shot of Paderewski while playing follows. Paderewski "finishes number and rises, bowing to applause. Wilson rises. Others rise. Wilson, Edith and others come forward as Paderewski walks to be greeted by them. Wilson says 'marvelous' while Edith adds 'Thank you.' Paderewski departs." He has not spoken a word.[218] Poland has, for the Americans, become silent. Indeed, the film never identifies the pianist, and only someone who has read the script would know that he is intended to be Paderewski.[219]

Extolling Wilson as the architect of reborn Poland would certainly have reflected the film's goal of presenting the president as an idealistic champion of popular rights and good causes. However, by 1944, Hollywood apparently no longer considered Poland a good cause. At a time when Poland was being consigned to Soviet control by the administration of one Democratic president, it was doubtless awkward to note that an earlier one had played a worthy role in helping that country regain its independence. To remind American audiences that Washington once championed Poland would be inconvenient when Washington had no intention of doing so again.

The omission of Poland from *Wilson* may have resulted from simple negligence by Zanuck and Trotti, but it is more likely that it was yet another example of Hollywood's accommodating if not promoting the geopolitical fashions of the day: FDR's foreign policy agenda and the concomitant protection of the public image of the Soviet Union. Indeed, Nelson Poynter, the head of the BMP's Hollywood office, claimed that it was "largely at the suggestion of this office" that the film was made, which obviously suggests administration approval.[220] In any case, it indicates that the linkage between Wilson and Poland had become by 1944 something Hollywood did not wish to mention. The OWI predictably adored the film, and it was critically acclaimed, even winning a number of Oscars, notably for screenwriter Trotti.[221] It is nevertheless relentlessly tedious and portentous; Wilson emerges lifeless and uninteresting. As for Poland, *Wilson* has forgotten it.

The cinematic version of Poland's fate between 1939 and 1945 can be easily limned. A corrupt and reactionary regime cravenly attempting to appease the Nazis (*In Our Time, To Be or Not to Be*) dominates a country composed of backward peasants, venal shopkeepers, and ridiculous aristocrats (again *In Our Time*, and *Once upon a Honeymoon*). The country mistreats its Ukrainian minority so badly that they crave Soviet rule (*The North Star*). In September 1939 Poland is invaded by Germany and is overrun almost instantly (*To Be or Not to Be, None Shall Escape*) because of Poland's reliance on cavalry (*In Our Time, Why We Fight*) and a disloyal population of fifth columnists (*Once upon a Honeymoon, Why We Fight*). The Soviet Union either does not invade or engages in the liberation of eastern Poland; either reading is acceptable (*Why We Fight, The North Star*). There is no organized resistance and no government-in-exile (*To Be or Not to Be*). Any Poles still resisting are really directed by the British (*To Be or Not to Be*). Though the Germans behave badly in Poland, the suffering is only equivalent to that in Holland (*U-Boat Prisoner*). There is no heroic resistance, as there is in Norway or Czechoslovakia (*None Shall Escape*), and Poles are not part of the anti-Nazi struggle throughout Europe (*Casablanca*). Indeed, Polish refugees are either collaborators (*Edge of Darkness*) or conniving cheats (*Quota Girl*) quite unconcerned about their country and its woes. Polish military units, unlike the French, are not to be seen in North Africa (*Sahara*) or Italy (*The Story of G.I. Joe*) in the later stages of the war. Indeed, there are no Polish units fighting in the war, save a handful serving with the RAF. There is no Jewish ghetto rising in 1943 Warsaw, nor is there a general uprising in the capital the next year. A handful of Poles or their descendants serve with American forces, but they are often poorly motivated (*Action in the North Atlantic*) or mentally unstable (*Air Force, Eagle Squadron, The Story of G.I. Joe*). This is to be expected because the Poles in America are a rather pathetic lot (*Pittsburgh, Action in the North Atlantic,* perhaps *Since You Went Away*). This is Hollywood's version of the Poles in World War II.

It is something of a curiosity that Hollywood decided to make not one but two biographies of famous Poles during the war: the 1943 release about Maria Skłodowska, *Madame Curie,* and the 1945 Chopin biography, *A Song to Remember,* which was released after the war in Europe concluded. Both of these films were major studio undertakings with illustrious casts to which extended preparation and considerable cost were devoted. Both were nominated for many awards and enjoyed critical praise, especially *Madame Curie.* Both films treat their Polish subjects with considerable sympathy. Indeed, the viewer is struck by their positive tone regarding Poland in comparison to those devoted to contemporaneous subjects, especially the war. The anomaly is perhaps explained by the fact that both films deal with Polish issues quite irrelevant to the politics of the war era.[222]

Even the Roosevelt administration had been made uncomfortable by the virtual absence of Polish subjects from the screen.[223] These films allowed Hollywood to commemorate Poland from a politically safe distance. However, they were carefully tailored to avoid any issues that might, even by analogy, raise awkward issues about Poland's position in the current war.

Madame Curie features Greer Garson and Walter Pidgeon, who had been successfully teamed in the popular *Mrs. Miniver,* as Maria Skłodowska and Pierre Curie, who married and jointly discovered radium.[224] The film is loosely, indeed idiosyncratically, based on Eve Curie's biography of her mother, published in 1937.[225] The Polish aspects of the film are actually quite brief and incidental. It opens at the Sorbonne, where poor Maria is studying. She faints from hunger during one of her classes. Kindly professor Jean Perot (Albert Bassermann) takes pity on her and provides her a meal, during which the following exchange occurs:

PEROT: You love Poland?
SKŁODOWSKA: Oh, yes, I love Poland.
PEROT: Physics, and Mathematics, and Poland.
SKŁODOWSKA: Yes.

Shortly afterward, she begins to work in the laboratory of young Pierre Curie. She announces that she will return to Warsaw after her impending graduation. Curie urges her to stay in Paris to advance her studies, exalting the importance of dedication to science. As she prepares to respond, the background music changes into the Polish national anthem ("Jeszcze Polska Nie Zginęła," Poland Will Never Die), over which an obviously emotional Maria says, "There are other things that are important too." The anthem ceases. This is a much understated and very moving evocation of Polish patriotism. It is also far too subtle to convey the notion effectively to an American audience. How many American filmgoers could recognize the melody and draw the appropriate conclusion?

The only other Polish aspects in the film are a few passing references to Maria's returning to her aged father in Warsaw and the chance remark by a minor figure that Poland is "an excellent country." These scenes all occur in the first minutes of what is quite a lengthy film. The Polish aspects of the film, quite understated, are then over.

Chronologically, the film is rather odd. Before coming to Paris, Maria was involved in Polish patriotic activities, which the film could profitably have noted. Indeed, the entire first third of the Eve Curie biography is devoted to the Polish years of Maria's life, discussing her family's political adventures, their detestation of tsarist Russia, and Maria's intense Polish loyalties. However, in the film, the fleeting references to her father are the only mentions of Maria's family. Moreover, the film really ends with Pierre's death in 1906, though Maria lived until 1934 and many of her greatest triumphs, including a second Nobel Prize and a professorship at the Sorbonne, occurred after his death.

The film focuses only on the middle third of the book; the final third is also omitted. In that section of the book, we learn that Maria resented bitterly the fact that France boasted of her achievements but avoided mentioning her Polish nationality and refused her, among other honors, membership in the Académie Française. This could never be deduced from the film. Yet Maria's Polish patriotism was, along with science, the passion of her life. Eve Curie reproduces a letter written by Maria to her brother Józef late in 1920, when Poland had just been victorious over Soviet Russia in defense of its newly won independence. Here her attachment to Poland is clear; she never considered herself French:

> So now we, "born in servitude and chained since birth," we have seen the resurrection of our country, which has been our dream. We did not hope to live to this moment ourselves; we thought it might not even be given to our children to see it— and it is here! It is true that our country has paid dear for this happiness, and that it will have to pay again. But can the clouds of the present situation be compared with the bitterness and discouragement that would have crushed us if, after the war, Poland had remained in chains and divided into pieces? Like you I have faith in the future.[226]

Later Madame Curie traveled repeatedly to Poland. In her daughter's view, her greatest dream was to build a cancer treatment center in her beloved Warsaw. The cornerstone of this was laid in 1929, the year she went to the United States "to thank America in the name of Poland" for purchasing radium for the institute in Warsaw.[227]

MGM, however, obviously saw the film as the story of two devoted colleagues in Paris who happened to be happily married, intertwined with a rather detailed exploration of the arduous dedication necessary to achieve scientific progress; everything else was eliminated or reduced to trifles. The film ends oddly with Curie, an old woman, receiving some sort of accolade at the Sorbonne. How much more appropriate it would have been to conclude where her life began, in Warsaw, where she returned in triumph to the free country of which she had long dreamed. Hollywood again failed to exploit the dramatic potential of Poland. Maria Skłodowska was an ardent Polish patriot who was active in a number of Polish causes during her long residence in France and retained an emotional attachment to her native land. Though this is not a significant aspect of the film, it is suggested, and the Polish aspects of Maria's life are not presented unsympathetically. Hence this is probably the most pro-Polish Hollywood production of the war years. It is, however, set in the years before World War I, and the connections between the Poland of that era and the Polish question as it appeared in 1939–1945 were not readily apparent to American film audiences.

MGM had been planning to make the film for a number of years and had commissioned a large number of approaches to the original volume by Eve Curie. Virtually all of these versions devoted considerable space to Poland. The earliest, a commentary by MGM reader Marjorie Thorsen in early 1936, sets the first half of the film in Poland.[228] The first full treatment, by Lynn Riggs in 1937, posits seven main themes of which four are essentially Polish, including Maria's childhood, a meeting with Paderewski in Paris, and a return to a free Poland.[229] Aldous Huxley suggested a different treatment in 1938 in which Maria's father figures prominently and his ardent Polish patriotism is the central element in her life.[230] Other versions devote much space to her joy at the rebirth of Poland's national independence.[231] A 1938 version includes Madame Curie's visit to the United States and a scene in which Poles there welcome her, with the focus on a little girl in national costume, which has a profound effect on her.[232] The 1938 versions also devote extensive attention to Poland.[233]

However, Sidney Franklin's new treatment in September 1939 almost completely omits the story's Polish aspects.[234] Of all the many versions considered by MGM before 1941, only one, a translation from the French, was set almost exclusively in Paris. This was the disposition MGM assumed toward the project in its final phase. The later scripts also eliminate the anti-Russian content of her family's patriotic activities, which had been prominently featured earlier. The scenes from Maria's childhood in Warsaw were originally intended to convey the family's aversion to Russian rule, but by 1942 these scenes were altered to be nothing but nostalgic reminiscences of childhood.[235] By 1943 Poland was a very shadowy presence in MGM's version of Madame Curie's biography.[236] It was this version that eventually became the shooting script. Thus a film project that originally utilized Curie's Polish patriotism as a leitmotif unifying the stages of her life became one in which the Polish aspects were brief, early glimpses without subsequent development.

On November 16, 1943, four members of the BMP's Hollywood

office previewed the film, and two of them collaborated to file an evaluation. It is an eloquent testimonial to how understated the Polish aspects of the film are, and how inconsequential Polish matters were to the BMP, that the evaluation does not contain a single word about Madame Curie's Polish background. It does not mention Poland at all.[237] Either the BMP reviewers missed all the film's Polish references or, having seen them, attached no importance to them. Indeed, the BMP found the film an "important contribution to the government's overseas program by its constructive delineation of the life of the outstanding French scientist." Further, it commended the film for making "several good points on the value of French culture and learning to the world." The film was recommended "for special OWI distribution abroad." The same day, Ulric Bell sent MGM an adulatory letter about the film, noting its "highly affirmative value," whatever that means. Bell also did not mention a single word about Poland or the heroine's nationality.[238] The BMP saw no value for the film whatsoever as a tribute to Poland or its most illustrious daughter.

A Song to Remember is best remembered for the many Chopin pieces it features as recorded by José Iturbi; it is otherwise quite bad.[239] It stars the muscular and athletic Cornel Wilde as the neurasthenic Chopin.[240] A dominatrix-like Merle Oberon plays Georges Sand, and Paul Muni interprets Józef Elsner as a vaudeville character, complete with facial contortions, an elaborate—and often changing—accent, and much gesticulation. Muni, it seems, was so intent on his version of Elsner that he was playing in his own film, in which the other actors were merely props.[241] It is never explained, for example, why Chopin speaks without an accent but Elsner has several.

A Song to Remember had a long and painful gestation. The BMP became aware that Columbia was planning a major biographical study of the Polish composer in the late summer of 1943, when it received an incomplete screenplay by Communist Party member Sidney Buchman. From this draft, it was already apparent that the film was to portray Chopin as a representative of popular forces struggling against tsarist oppression rather than as a Polish patriot responding to Russian occupation. The BMP's Eleanor Berneis happily noted that the Buchman script identified the struggle of the Polish people against tsarist oppression with the struggle of the Russian people against their rulers. She wrote,

A Russian tells the Polish revolutionaries, "We live under the same tyranny. We are brothers in a dungeon—under the whip of the Czar. We seek freedom—as do you. We dearly wish it for ourselves—and for you and for every people on the face of the earth," and he refers to the new nation that has just been born in America, based on the human rights to life, liberty and the pursuit of happiness. This offers an excellent parallel with the struggle against oppression going on today which can strengthen the sense of unity among peoples of the United Nations. This is not a major point in the story, but if this presentation is carried through the rest of the script, it will have great value from the standpoint of this office.

The BMP was eager to receive the complete script, in part because Poland, it admitted, was a "seldom-portrayed member of the United Nations."[242]

Buchman, however, has prostituted both history and Chopin to the goal of presenting the Russian revolutionary movement as both democratic—and hence admiring of the nascent American republic—and supportive of Polish liberation. The rather heavy-handed goal in all of this is to convince the viewer that Poland did not suffer at Russian hands but rather from reactionary tsardom. Early in the film, a Russian lectures a secret meeting of Polish patriots about "life, liberty, and the pursuit of happiness" and evokes visions of Russo-Polish amity. Shortly later, Chopin is informed that "Jan and our Russian friends" have been arrested. Polish patriotic organizations, it seems, included Russians. Indeed, it was the radical tradition in Russia that was the friend of Chopin and the friend of Poland. Since that tradition, in the form of Bolshevism, banished tsardom in 1917 and now ruled Russia, it was, ipso facto, a regime embodying the traditional pro-Polish orientation of Russian radicalism. Thus Chopin is transformed into a symbol of the historical logic of Polish-Soviet friendship. In such a reading of Chopin's biography, Russian radicalism, Polish-Russian relations, and Russian views of Poland in the nineteenth century are presented without historical foundation. Berneis either was unaware of this or was concerned only with propaganda. It is doubtless for this reason that the BMP raised "no objection" to the project, though it was still in a very early stage.

A month later, the script, now in its sixth draft, had doubled in length, and there were some indications of the players to be cast. The BMP again examined it. The role Poland played in the BMP's strategy is clearly presented in a commentary on the new script written by Peg Fenwick of the Hollywood office. The bureau was intrigued that, by raising the "minor theme of Poland's fight for freedom," the film offered "an excellent parallel with the struggle for freedom going on today." This was especially true because "there have been few films on Poland."[243] In other words, Buchman's Chopin would allow Hollywood and the BMP to present a fairy tale of Polish-Russian relations that would provide a historical pedigree for the supposed benevolence of Soviet intentions toward Poland. Moreover, "Poland's fight for freedom" was hardly a "minor theme" for Chopin, but a central passion of his life.

In January 1944, the final script was reviewed by the BMP yet again, a very unusual procedure. Eleanor Berneis again singled out this feature, now noting that "the presentation of the Russian occupation of Poland was particularly well handled, as it establishes that the Russian people suffered under the Czarist tyranny just as the Polish people suffered, and they too were planning revolt."[244] Chopin's support for the Polish November Rising against Russia (of 1830–1831) has been co-opted into a Russo-Polish democratic opposition to tsardom, another bit of manipulative historical mischief.

Eight months later, when the film was finally shot, the project was again considered by the BMP. Writing on August 12, 1944, during the second week of the Warsaw Rising, in which the Russian role was so perfidious, the BMP repeated its satisfaction that the long genealogy of Polish-Russian amity was correctly presented in *A Song to Remember*.[245] Artur Rubinstein, a pianist renowned for his interpretation of Chopin and an ardent Polish patriot, was appalled by the film's inaccuracies and reportedly complained to Harry Cohn of Columbia, who is paraphrased as responding that "few of the American people would know the difference and [besides] he thought that the picture would make money."[246] However, for all its mischievous effort to suggest longstanding Polish-Russian cooperation, the film portrays Chopin as a devoted Polish patriot and presents loyalty to the Polish cause in a most poignant manner.

The OWI later raised a peculiar objection to the film: that the French might react badly to it because, according to the two BMP analysts, "Chopin is as much a 'national hero' in France as he is in Poland." They thought Merle Oberon's Georges Sand and her rather unpleasant behavior toward Chopin would "impress French critics and the public unfavorably." Moreover, the film's emphasis on Chopin's devotion to Poland was troubling because "according to the Encyclopedia Britannica the whole plot as developed in the movie is entirely wrong."[247] Obviously, having consulted an encyclopedia, the BMP was now prepared for a searching evaluation of the historical issues involved, although it had never before troubled itself to verify the historical accuracy of any of the arguments presented in the film.

A Song to Remember had an intriguing creative team. Communist Buchman was a very influential figure in Hollywood. He had been president of the Screen Writers Guild (1941–1942). He was more than a writer at Columbia; he produced a number of films as well, eventually having considerable influence over production and rising to be the studio's vice president. In addition to making this film about the historical cooperation between Polish patriotism and Russian radicalism, he also wrote *Talk of the Town*. Paul Muni, though not a Communist Party member, was well known for leftist views and had in the 1930s expressed indifference as to whether Communism or fascism prevailed in the United States.[248] He had a penchant for playing revolutionaries and champions of the downtrodden, often melodramatically, though his Elsner is unrivalled in idiosyncratic excess. Though born in Poland, he never regarded himself as a Pole.

Pola Negri (1894–1987). Photograph courtesy of Jerry Ohlinger's Movie
Material Store.

Jan Kiepura (1902–1966). Photograph courtesy of Photofest.

Tom Tyler (1903–1954). Photograph courtesy of Jerry Ohlinger's Movie Material Store.

Robert Donat (1905–1958). Photograph courtesy of Jerry Ohlinger's Movie
Material Store.

Carole Landis (1919–1948). Photograph courtesy of Jerry Ohlinger's Movie
Material Store.

(Above) Joe Radek (Paul Muni), a "Polack born and reborn," is carried off by police in *Black Fury*, 1935. Film still courtesy of Jerry Ohlinger's Movie Material Store. *(Below)* Manya Novak (Anna Sten) confronts with horror the prospect of marrying a Pole in *The Wedding Night*, 1935. Her vile father (Sig Ruman) smiles unpleasantly. Film still courtesy of Photofest.

(Above) The Pole as college dolt: Boley Bolenciecwcz (Jack Oakie), arms folded, looks perplexed in *Rise and Shine,* 1941. Film still courtesy of Photofest. *(Below)* Wadislaw Borowsky (Edgar Barrier, second from left) is about to endanger his squadron in *Eagle Squadron,* 1942. Film still courtesy of Photofest.

(Above) The Pole as mock-heroic cuckold: Joseph Tura (Jack Benny, center) in *To Be or Not to Be,* 1942. Film still courtesy of Jerry Ohlinger's Movie Material Store. *(Below)* The Pole as failed sailor: Steve Boleslavski (Edward G. Robinson, right) in *Destroyer,* 1943. Film still courtesy of Jerry Ohlinger's Movie Material Store.

The Pole as a crewman who has to be shamed into doing his duty: Johnnie Pulaski (Dane Clark, center) in *Action in the North Atlantic,* 1943. Film still courtesy of Jerry Ohlinger's Movie Material Store.

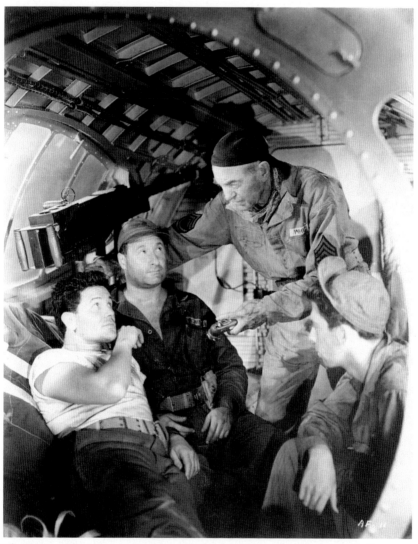

The Pole as obnoxious misfit: Joe Winocki (John Garfield, left) in *Air Force,*
1943. Film still courtesy of Jerry Ohlinger's Movie Material Store.

(Above) The Pole as camp follower: Katja (Nancy Coleman) admires her Nazi paramour's medals in *Edge of Darkness,* 1943. Film still courtesy of Photofest. *(Below)* The Pole as bewildered soldier: Biff Koraski (William Bendix, center) in *Abroad with Two Yanks,* 1944. Film still courtesy of Jerry Ohlinger's Movie Material Store.

(Above) The Polish aristocracy as worthless reactionaries: Janina (Nancy Coleman, left) is a religious fanatic; Stefan is a hen-pecked naif; his mother, Zophiya (Nazimova, right), is frivolous. Only the doughty English shopgirl, Jennifer (Ida Lupino, center), demonstrates both fortitude and good sense in *In Our Time,* 1944. Film still courtesy of Photofest. *(Below)* Marja Pacierkowski (Marsha Hunt) was formerly the fiancée of a fanatical Nazi. The Polish soldier Jan Stys (Trevor Bardette) is the deranged man lurking in the background in *None Shall Escape,* 1944. Film still courtesy of Photofest.

(Above) Polish sergeant Warnicki (Freddie Steele, center) shortly before his breakdown in *The Story of G.I. Joe,* 1945. Film still courtesy of Photofest. *(Below)* The Pole as Czech: John Hodiak in *Lifeboat,* 1944. Film still courtesy of Jerry Ohlinger's Movie Material Store.

A Russian lectures Poles on democracy. A dark-haired Chopin (Cornel Wilde) is seated attentively in the front row in *A Song to Remember,* 1945. Film still courtesy of Jerry Ohlinger's Movie Material Store.

Communist screenwriter John Howard Lawson (1894–1977). Photograph courtesy of Photofest.

Screenwriter Howard Koch (1902–1995). He gave us the Poles in *Mission to Moscow* and *In Our Time*. Photograph courtesy of Photofest.

7

Hollywood and the American Poles during the War

By World War II, Hollywood had a long history of ignoring the Polish population of the United States or presenting them negatively. This, in part, reflected the unenviable position the Poles occupied in American society and consciousness in the decades before the Second World War.

The Poles were among the "new immigrants" from Eastern and Southern Europe who largely displaced the previous flow of arrivals from Western Europe by late in the nineteenth century. Of this group the Poles were a significant number. Exact figures are speculative, but at least 2 million arrived between 1890 and the outbreak of World War I.[1] Among the recent immigrants, only the Italians exceeded the Poles, and not by much. The Poles were far more numerous than any other group from Eastern Europe: many times the number of Czechs, Hungarians, and Balkan Slavs, and far more than the Russians, for example.[2]

Of course, the Polish immigrants were outnumbered by the Irish, German (including German Jews), and British populations, who had been far longer in residence. German Jews had also arrived early in the nineteenth century. After 1880, however, the Jewish arrivals were overwhelmingly from Eastern Europe. By 1914 the Poles probably exceeded the Jewish population in number but were not as well organized. Moreover, Eastern European Jews shared the opprobrium of all Eastern Europeans, including Poles. Polish Jews were in an unusual position. Most joined the American Jewish community and tended not to associate with Christian Poles. This phenomenon had complex roots, but the growing anti-Semitism of certain elements of the Polish population—the "nationalist" movement—certainly was a noteworthy factor.

In general the new immigrants were not well received by American society, which regarded them as inferior to the older stock of Americans. In 1902, Woodrow Wilson described Poles, along with Hungarians and Italians, as "men of the meaner sort" possessing "neither skill nor energy nor any initiative of quick intelligence." They were a "coarse crew," even less desirable than the Chinese.[3] Such views were widespread in American society. John Higham, in a famous work, described them as "conservative racial nativists."[4]

The famous Dillingham Commission, authorized by Congress in 1907, issued a report in 1911 that found the Poles intellectually and psychologically inferior to the resident population. It also concluded that Poles and others from Eastern Europe could not be assimilated, and thus their numbers should be restricted. This report formed one of the bases for the Emergency Quota Act of 1921, which drastically reduced the number of immigrants in general and specifically discriminated against Southern and Eastern Europeans.[5]

Although all of the recent arrivals suffered this burden, Polish immigrants' situation was unusual because of their relatively large numbers. In many ways the Pole was the Eastern European par excellence, probably accounting for the plurality of all the migrants from that part of the world. The Poles were thus in a difficult position: large enough in number to draw attention but too few—and too poor, and too uneducated—to be a powerful presence in their new home. One should add that, with the American government's sanction of their ascribed inferior status, there was little the Poles in America could do to demand equality.

For Hollywood, American Poles were essentially negative characters. In Universal's 1942 *Eagle Squadron,* devoted to the exploits of two American pilots in British service early in the war, we are told one of the two, Wadislaw Borowsky (not a Polish name), was born in Poland but raised in Pennsylvania.[6] Borowsky is emotionally unstable—a common attribute of Poles in Hollywood—and his recklessness results in his betraying the squadron, thus leading to its destruction.[7] The film was regarded as one of the worst releases of 1942.[8]

Although the Hollywood version of the Italian campaign—*The Story of G.I. Joe*—omits Poland's role, as we have noted, it does feature a Polish American, Sergeant Warnicki (played by the obscure ex-pugilist Freddie Steele), who, like the lamentable Borowsky, loses his mind.[9] Indeed, the Pole, or at least the American Pole, as an incompetent misfit is a minor subgenre; Poles seem always on the edge of nervous collapse in Hollywood. The Warnicki role is nonetheless not without moment. The character is sympathetic, even pitiable. Unlike the typical Hollywood Pole, Warnicki has some ethnic substance. Hence, when combat brings him into a church, he reacts with obvious discomfiture, kneels, and begins to pray. He is a Catholic. Though seemingly brave and competent, Warnicki breaks down early in the film when he is unable to withstand a German attack in North Africa; he weeps and has to be consoled by his officer. This is an early sign that the good sergeant is perhaps less sound than he appears. Hence, though he later rallies and performs with courage in the Italian campaign under intense stress, he loses his mind, runs amok, and must be knocked unconscious and led from the field, babbling maniacally. He is the shell of a man. No other soldier is shown to break down in the film; Warnicki does so twice. This was the first, and last, major role for Steele, whose performance is alternatively amateurish and affecting. The film, based on the life of famed war correspondent Ernie Pyle, avoided the mock heroics of most Hollywood treatments of the war for a realistic and poignant perspective of the enlisted man.

The theme of the American Pole as misfit or at best seriously flawed appears with regularity. For example, Warner Brothers' high-budget 1943 film *Air Force* includes a gunner named Joe Winocki, whose ethnicity is so nebulous as to prompt one historian to conjecture that he was "of Native American stock."[10] We may be sure, however, that Winocki was Polish: like Warnicki and Borowsky, he has serious emotional problems that affect his behavior—Hollywood's seeming trope for Polish nationality. John Garfield, already a rising star, portrays Winocki, a featured role.[11]

The film was highly regarded on its release and "mopped up" at the box office, becoming one of 1943's major money-making films.[12] Warner Brothers was inordinately proud of *Air Force,* crowing that the studio had gained the cooperation of General H. H. Arnold, "Chief of the U.S. Air Force," in producing the film, and that it was the first cinematic celebration of this branch of the service since the war had begun.[13] Even before it was commercially released, Jack Warner personally brought a print to Washington to show the War Department.[14] Warner Brothers launched a vigorous promotional campaign for the film that was aided by Boeing, which was gratified to see its aircraft celebrated.[15] It gained, and has held, considerable critical acclaim. It was nominated for several Oscars, including fellow traveler Dudley Nichols's screenplay.[16]

Winocki, embittered after failure in flight school, is a thoroughly unpleasant, self-pitying wretch who must be taught the virtues of duty and maturity by the other members of the crew. Unable to be a pilot, and hence an officer, because he "lacked flying ability," Winocki also endangers his plane and crew by reckless behavior. Later, in a threatening situation, the panicky Winocki has to be knocked unconscious by his own sergeant to save himself from his own folly—just like Warnicki in *The Story of G.I. Joe.* The Irish American pilot who was forced earlier to fail Winocki out of flight training because of his incompetence lectures the Pole on the virtues of duty. Winocki is given a similar scolding by the noble crew chief Sergeant White (Harry Carey). These attempts seem bootless, but the Japanese attack on Pearl Harbor arouses Winocki's indignation, and he becomes motivated and reconciled to military service. He, however, will remain an enlisted man, not the officer he hoped to be, for he is still a man of poor judgment and limited ability, despite his improved disposition.[17] Winocki thus evolves positively but is still an inferior man.[18]

It is instructive to trace the evolution of the Winocki character in the creation of the film and his relationship to the other members of the crew. Dudley Nichols provided the initial outline of the story. The pilot, Kelly Morgan, is described as a "tall, young Irish-American," and the bombardier, McMartin, is probably also intended to be Irish. No other member of the crew has a nationality designated or an obviously "ethnic" name. It is made clear that the pilot is a simply lovable fellow, handsome, affable, competent, the epitome of virtue. By contrast, we have Joe Winocki, a "big, tough faced ex-football tackle from Notre Dame" who is "embittered" because he "lacked natural flying ability" and had "all the ambition but no talent." Nichols comments, in bad prose, that Winocki "has a lesson to learn and he's going to learn it to be the real man he latently is."[19] He soon shows himself to be irritable and bitter, cynical about the claims of patriotism, and dangerously reckless under stress. The crew, quite understandably, dislikes him, and the pilot concludes that he has "no team spirit" and "isn't working out."[20]

When Winocki meets his new crew, he makes it very clear that he is sensitive about the pronunciation of his name and will not brook ridicule. This, by the way, is the only scene in the film, in any of its manifestations, in which some ethnic identity is attributed to Winocki. Unlike the pilot, who is affectionately nicknamed "Irish," Winocki does not have a clear nationality. Only when the production of the film was complete and a version was released in book form, the so-called novelization of the film, was there a reference to a Pole being among the crew. On that slender reference hangs Winocki's nationality.[21]

The revised script in late May was substantially the same. By then a director had been chosen and production had started.[22] Two weeks later, the script was altered to introduce a new character, Weinberg, described as a "former New York taxi driver," who is given a great many lines, especially in the opening sequences of the film. This reflects the standard Warner Brothers practice of including a positive and lovable Jewish character prominently in the military unit. Weinberg is charming and affable, in contrast to the sour and hostile Winocki, who has evolved downward as the script developed. Winocki now no longer defends the correct pronunciation of his name and is considerably more obnoxious, squabbling repeatedly with the crew, speaking contemptuously of the plane (a B-17) and making disrespectful remarks about the pilot with an obvious ethnic edge: "Where's the Irishman?" he asks, only to be corrected, "You mean *Captain* Quincannon," the new name for Kelly Morgan. Now the story introduces the possibility of transferring Winocki because of his foul behavior. In other words, Winocki has deteriorated. He is not just obnoxious and undependable in a crisis; he is also quite stupid. A new line is added reemphasizing Winocki's intellectual shortcomings: "Listen, Winocki, we know you got guts—but you have to use your head, too." There is also a new scene later in the picture, at pilot Quincannon's deathbed. Here Winocki weeps, clearly moved by the noble death of a better man. The script maintains the original physical description of the character: he is "a tough-looking ex-football player from Notre Dame" who at one point intimidates Weinberg by his sheer size.[23]

As the script evolved in June, Winocki's lines and scenes diminished, but the characterization remained substantially the same. Weinberg is still in awe of him; he asks at one point, in obvious admiration, "You played left tackle for Notre Dame?"[24] In July Winocki is given a short lament that only officers have status and a future and that he, as a failure in aerial training, is doomed to insignificance. The defense of his name, previously cut, is not restored.[25] The evolution of Winocki was quite uneven. The references to his college education were cut, but the exchange with Weinberg referring to his playing football for Notre Dame was retained, though Winocki claims that he attended only to be admitted to flying school.[26] As a result, Garfield's Winocki is a very flawed and oddly annoying portrayal. Lawrence Suid perceptively notes that "Garfield plays the character as a rough, unsophisticated man, not a college graduate."[27]

This is virtually the form in which the film was eventually released. Winocki began as an embittered man and became more so as the script evolved. His status as a product of Notre Dame, a college graduate when such was quite rare, was eliminated, making him considerably less impressive and making the suggestions that he is mentally slow seem less incongruous. He no longer defends his name, and hence any suggestion of ethnic pride is removed. As originally conceived, he was clearly inferior to the Irish pilot, but now he also suffers by comparison with the new Jewish character, Weinberg, as well as the ethnically ambiguous remainder of the crew. Winocki the Pole is obviously the least of his fellows. Because Winocki was always described as a huge, powerful man, casting the short and slight John Garfield in the role made little sense. With George Tobias, a massive man, playing Weinberg, the scene in which Winocki intimidates him by sheer size becomes absurd.

The OWI loved the film and was rhapsodic about the ethnic mélange composing the crew. The BMP particularly noted with satisfaction the interrelationship depicted among the various ethnic types as being "first rate," a "good cross-section of America." It was also aware that the Polish character was summarized, according to Warner Brothers' own synopsis of the film issued to the OWI, as "sour," a "malcontent who failed to win his commission."[28] The Roosevelt administration was so pleased with *Air Force* that it presented Warner Brothers with a "victory flag"—the first studio to be so honored.[29]

In conjunction with the release of the film, the novelization of the film by John O. Watson was released. The crew, we are told, consists of "typical Americans," among them "Celts, Poles, and Jews." Winocki's appearance has changed: "He was stocky, beetle-browed, swarthy of face. His eyes, black and cold, shone with a fierce defiance. There was a trace of a sneer about his mouth."[30] This is perhaps a post factum description of John Garfield. It has all the characteristics Hollywood usually employed to describe Poles: dark, swarthy, short.

Garfield, the child of poor Russian immigrants, was a great champion of the Soviet Union who was active in innumerable Communist front organizations during the war—though he later denied his involvement. His wife, a Communist Party activist, guided his political development. Poorly educated and intellectually limited, he was prone to making foolish comments and hence considered unworthy of party membership, which he sought.[31]

Just as *Air Force* was a rousing tribute to that branch of the service, the equally emotional *Action in the North Atlantic,* another 1943 Warner Brothers' release, was meant to pay homage to the merchant marine.[32] A major production starring the celebrated Humphrey Bogart and a dour Raymond Massey, the film presents us with a nautical version of the flawed Winocki in the equally unappetizing Pulaski. As played by Dane Clark, Pulaski cannot understand why he should take any interest in the war, and he has to be shamed and abused by his shipmates into performing his assignments decently.[33] Given that Pulaski, conjuring the Revolutionary War hero, is one of the few Polish names with any resonance among Americans, it is particularly grotesque that this cinematic representation features a scene in which Pulaski is instructed by an Irish American crewman, disgusted by his lack of dutiful patriotism, "Your thinking is cockeyed. . . . Go ask the Poles, the Czechs and the Greeks. . . . The trouble with you, Pulaski, is you think America is just a place to eat and sleep in. You don't know which side your future is buttered on!"[34] Pulaski, the bearer of an iconic Polish name, has to be told about Poland in addition to being reminded of his American responsibilities. He is, like his fellow Poles Borowsky, Warnicki, and Winocki, an unworthy man. Like Winocki, Pulaski has to be scolded and instructed in proper behavior by an Irish American.

Indeed, Warner Brothers seemed to enjoy juxtaposing virtuous Irish and Jewish characters with profoundly flawed Poles. In *Air Force* the unappetizing Winocki is part of a crew led by the indomitable Mike "Irish" Quincannon (John Ridgely) and the lovable and adept Corporal Weinberg (George Tobias). Pulaski's crewmates in *Action in the North Atlantic* are similarly two flawless fellow ethnics, the Irish "Boats

O'Hara" (Alan Hale) and the wise Chips Abrams (Sam Levene).[35] In Hollywood's efforts to emphasize the ethnic variety of America, united in a common patriotism, the Polish character was not equal to his fellow immigrants.

Pulaski is a most curious, albeit minor, character. *Action in the North Atlantic* was adapted from Guy Gilpatric's novel of the same title. It was recast for the screen by John Howard Lawson, a member of the CPUSA since 1934, famous for his doctrinaire domination of the party's Hollywood members: "a commissar, boss of the Commie writers."[36] Lawson's devotion to the Soviet Union and intolerance for any deviation from the party line caused more than one critic to describe him as a "rigid Stalinist."[37]

There is a Polish sailor in the original novel: Mieczysław Stanisławski, a name that is resoundingly Polish but does not have the historic reverberations of Pulaski. But Stanisławski is quite a different fellow. Huge and powerful, unlike the film's Dane Clark, he is a stalwart and worthy member of the crew who is praised by the captain himself for his good service.[38] One sailor questions the value of the war in the novel as well, but the miscreant is an unnamed seaman, not the Pole. Indeed, Stanisławski's role in this episode is to befriend a black steward and invite him to join him after the war in an attempt to break into films. He does this as part of a larger effort to convince the black man that America is a land of opportunity for all.[39]

Hence Gilpatric's Pole seaman is a positive figure, widely respected, a thoroughly decent man whom the readers would find attractive for many reasons. Hollywood—more specifically Lawson—transformed him into a physically insignificant and base fellow who is contemned by his shipmates. The Pole's kindness to the black crew member is also omitted from the film. There is another, albeit minor, alteration regarding Poland in the transformation of the novel to the screen. In a passing reference in the book, Gilpatric notes the presence of Polish naval units as part of the Allied merchant fleet.[40] There are, however, no Polish units in the Lawson film, because, like a good Stalinist, he purged them.

The transmutation of the seaman from the imposing and respected Stanisławski of the novel into the whining Pulaski of the film allows a valuable insight into Warner Brothers' treatment of the Polish type. Originally titled "Heroes without Uniforms," this salute to the merchant marine began in the spring of 1942 as a treatment by Guy Gilpatric.

It featured huge Stanisławski, "a lumpy mixture of Victor Mature and Frankenstein's monster." He has quite a major role, including befriending Jeff Caldwell, the "Negro pantryman." He is patriotic and devoted to his work, an exemplary member of the crew, which, be it noted, contains no Jewish sailor. Again, there is a character who expresses doubts about the war, but he is not named and is definitely not Stanisławski.[41]

Two months later, the Gilpatric treatment had been superseded by a screenplay written by Lawson. Admirable Stanisławski has metamorphosed into obnoxious Johnnie Pulaski, "a wise-cracking child of the NY tenements 19 years old [who] has been a seaman for a year and thinks he knows more than the skipper." The positive Polish figure has disappeared and been replaced by another obnoxious misfit. Joining Pulaski is a new character, Chips McGonigle, a lovable Irishman, and a seaman named Frank Johnson, a "Negro with a magnificent physique," who has replaced the insignificant pantryman. Pulaski has a brother and mother, but neither is significant or appealing.[42]

We are introduced to Lawson's Pulaski onboard an oiler in the North Atlantic. He is frightened and nervous; his obsessive talk about the possibility of being torpedoed demoralizes the crew. His hands "tremble" with fear. He must be calmed by the Irishman. Not just a coward, he is also a fool: Pulaski goes on deck and lights a cigarette. The first mate (Italian American Joe Rossi, who would be played by Humphrey Bogart) violently upbraids him, calls him a "bubble-brain," and threatens to "crack you open like a bed-bug" if he is caught smoking on a ship filled with petroleum again. Pulaski, Lawson notes, has a "bitter dislike" of his superior.[43] Thus we have the Winocki-Quincannon relationship repeated: the stupid and reckless Pole with a dangerously bad attitude has to be lectured and disciplined by another ethnic, the Italian Rossi replacing the Irishman Quincannon. The brave veteran Stanisławski has been replaced by this disruptive coward.

When the ship is soon thereafter torpedoed, Pulaski is the subject of a long series of brief scenes, all showing him to be crazed with fear and astoundingly stupid. His face shows "the agony of fear"; even though everyone is fleeing the doomed ship to go on deck, Pulaski reenters the cabin because "I gotta get my silk shirts . . . genuine silk. I got 'em at a fire sale." The other crewmen have their life vests on, but the fool Pulaski clutches his shirts and, selfishly, gives no aid to those in distress. Later there is a close-up of him with "frenzied terror on his face." While

"Johnnie looks wildly back at the flames," the others manfully attend to their duties. He "looks with horror." He gives "a horrible strangled cry." He is "crying with anger and despair." In short he is a hysteric who behaves with disregard for his ship and its crew. He is, significantly, the only member of the cast who is described as being fearful or acting in a foolish or irrational manner.[44]

Some of the crew, including the wretched Pulaski, scramble aboard a lifeboat. His behavior in this new environment is abominable. He undermines his fellows' morale by bemoaning their fate. He ignobly resents a wounded comrade's having a drink of the scarce supply of water. He carries with him a picture of a "fat blonde," which he stares at "with passionate desire," showing us that he is, among other things, a crude voluptuary. Rossi observes his concupiscence with amused disdain, again emphasizing the moral distance between the two. Pulaski suggests much too earnestly that a shipmate, just deceased, be thrown to the sharks. He is referred to as "you dope" by the others, a rather mild judgment in the circumstances. When rescued, he is boastful and mendacious, and he resents worthier men who behaved better during their common ordeal. But when the reporters turn to him, he is unable to relate his story because he lacks the ability to explain himself with minimal cogency: he is also an ignorant man.[45]

Pulaski returns home to the "steps and entry of an East Side Tenement," where we meet his mother, a common woman of no interest. Their conversation is vulgar. He boasts without shame or honesty; she responds with no particular emotion, save nonchalant incredulity at his nonsense. He tries to harangue locals "and feels the necessity of making himself important." He refuses to dine with his mother, whom, let us remember, he has not seen in some time and who has been understandably grief stricken at his fate. This, however causes no elevated emotions among such a coarse crew as the Pulaskis. He leaves his mother without embrace or farewell and rushes off in search of women. This squalid episode is the more repugnant because Lawson juxtaposes it with the homecoming of Captain Jarvis, which is dignified and touchingly understated.[46] The contrast between the two American types is stark. The Pole is disgusting.[47]

Pulaski sees a woman and is soon "devouring her with his eyes"; Lawson again reminds us that he is a lustful primitive. The woman snubs him in favor of his own brother, who is in an army uniform. There is no word of welcome or affection exchanged between the brothers. Their meeting is that of animals contesting for a conquest. The girl and the brother depart, leaving Pulaski in "a second hand ill-fitting suit donated by the Red Cross." He spends the night in a bar. But Lawson is still not through with him. Pulaski, now drunk, abuses a fellow crewman in the tavern in a most repulsive manner and has to be threatened, again by Rossi, to quiet him.[48] We are dangerously close to seeing another Pole being knocked unconscious for his own good.

When the crew departs on a new voyage, Pulaski continues his foul behavior. He quarrels foolishly with navy personnel assigned to his merchant ship as a gun crew, moved by jealousy. He is later chastised and threatened by a cadet officer, who correctly sees in Pulaski's behavior a threat to the order and discipline of the ship.[49]

Late in the film, the ship is attacked by a German plane, and Pulaski fights with courage and determination. This is the Winocki episode all over again, albeit with a ship replacing the B-17. Pulaski's one positive moment does nothing to exculpate him for a long history of bad judgment, irresponsible behavior, lack of concern for his fellows, and demonstration of limited capacities. Hence, when Lawson adds a scene in which Pulaski muses over the possibility of promotion in the merchant marine and is seemingly advanced by Rossi to "4th mate," the viewer could only be incredulous.[50] That a man as worthless as Pulaski, who has repeatedly jeopardized his ship and his fellows by reckless, cowardly, and foolish behavior, would be selected for greater responsibility is not convincing.

John Howard Lawson's Pulaski is a negative character. Lawson spends many scenes detailing his every shortcoming; there is no failing that Pulaski lacks. The bearer of a name synonymous with heroism is made a poltroon. Other than the Nazis, Pulaski is the only character that is negatively presented in the screenplay. Pulaski, the Pole, is the only unworthy American. The only sin not visited on disgusting Pulaski is attributing to him the antiwar speech originally in the Gilpatric treatment. That, however, will come.[51]

In August, W. R. Burnett joined Lawson for a modest reworking of the script. In typical Warner Brothers style, we now have a Jewish member of the crew, Chips Abrams, who is extraordinary. He is wise, imperturbable, kindly, and the epitome of patriotism. Though well into middle years and financially comfortable, he casts aside his business and family to resume the humble merchant marine duties of his youth. Moreover, he has a son who is stationed in England, in the air force. His sacrifice is thus twofold. Lest it not be obvious, the script informs us that he has returned to the sea "to serve his country." Penciled additions indicate that possible casting options for Chips were already considered: Abrams might have been Lee Cobb or, notably, George Tobias, who already performed the same duties as Weinberg in *Air Force.*[52]

Joining Abrams in the ethnic mélange to replace the McGonigle character from July is Boats O'Hara, who is grotesquely described as "a big solid hunk of Irish manhood." The woeful Pulaski now has a questionable past added to his biography: he "went to sea a year ago to escape from various shady difficulties ashore." The black man with the magnificent physique is gone, as are the meaningless Pulaski family members.[53]

Pulaski remains the same: nervous and panic stricken at the outset. However, Lawson has abbreviated some of the many scenes designed to make us think Pulaski is a fool. Thus the episode of the silk shirts is cut, and the long interlude in the lifeboat is much shortened. His tasteless homecoming is virtually eliminated. His concupiscence is eliminated, and it eventually emerges that he is married. On the film's final voyage, however, he is still a troublemaker and is referred to as "griping as usual"; again he reacts with panic to danger. He is still foolish and irresponsible and has to be told to "shut up" by Chips when his loud behavior threatens to divulge their ship's presence to a German submarine. In a concession to logic, Lawson has altered the scene that mentions Pulaski's promotion, and as now drafted, Rossi only encourages him to dream of eventual elevation.[54]

Lawson adds a bit of "ethnic color" when he briefly notes that Pulaski "crosses himself" at one moment of danger. After all, with his family scene cut, there would be no development of Pulaski's nationality in the film without this suggestion of his Catholicism. There is, however, an ironic evocation of the original Polish member of the crew, Gilpatric's intrepid Stanisławski: when Rossi reads out the names of the dead, one is Bill Stanisławski.[55]

At the end of the film, Russian planes fly over the damaged merchant ship. In what Lawson demands is a "close shot" of "youngsters with smiling faces," Pulaski admiringly and ungrammatically muses,

"They say them Russians is great fliers."[56] Lawson, a devoted Communist, was doubtless concerned that the proper geopolitical references and symbols be employed; the admiration of the Russian flyers is an obvious example.[57] Specifically, it is the Pole Pulaski who speaks in awe of the Russians.

Lawson's emendations became quite petty. In July the script noted that when the ship carrying Pulaski and his fellows arrived at Halifax before crossing the Atlantic, the harbor was crowded with "Norwegian whalers, Free French freighters, former Dutch and Polish luxury liners, English and American ships of every description"—thus presenting both the size and variety of the Allied coalition. However, in August, the arrival at Halifax was slightly altered: now the crew discerns "various ships" and their crews composed of "Norwegian, Russian, French, Dutch, American Negro, Greek, Limey, a Chinaman." There are no Poles; the Russians have suddenly appeared and replaced them.[58]

Lawson, however, had more work for Pulaski. On September 1, 1942, the third anniversary of the invasion of Poland, Lawson submitted a new script. A lengthy scene has been added; it appears in the released film. Pulaski, having returned to New York after a harrowing voyage, is overcome by fear at the prospect of another tour of duty and announces that he will not seek a new berth. His cowardice repulses O'Hara, who tells him that shame will make it impossible for him ever again to gaze on the Statue of Liberty. The virtuous Irishman threatens Pulaski with his fists and pronounces him unworthy of his union membership. Only the intervention of Abrams saves Pulaski from a beating: "You want a safe job? Go ask the Czechs an' Poles an' Greeks that was figgerin' on safe jobs." The Jewish American thus reminds the Polish American of the fate of Poland. O'Hara brutally tears off Pulaski's union button, and the distraught Pulaski crumples in tears and weeps from shame, having been politically emasculated.[59] Hence the original Gilpatric scene in which a nameless seaman questions the need for war service is ultimately visited on Pulaski.

Yet another scene was added to further degrade Pulaski and juxtapose his baseness to the nobility of the other "ethnics." Now, at the start of the film, Pulaski's whining concludes with "A guy's gotta be muscle-bound between the ears to be out here." This cues Abrams to his soliloquy: "You got the wrong angle on it," he explains avuncularly.

He has returned to hazardous duty prompted by his faith "in God, President Roosevelt, an' the Brooklyn Dodgers."[60] The contrast between the former's cowardice and the latter's quiet courage is stark.[61]

Over the fall of 1942, a few minor adjustments were made to Pulaski. He weeps in fear in scenes added in October; later that month he announces that he is transfixed with terror.[62] At the same time, his promotion sequence is further obfuscated. Now he only fingers with melancholy wistfulness the cap of a fallen cadet officer, and Rossi suggests that he too, one day, may aspire to so exalted a status.[63] But Pulaski, the Pole, has a long climb before he is worthy of a position of respect in America.

Lawson's original transformation of the Polish sailor from the Gilpatric outline is striking. The Lawson script obsessively focuses on Pulaski to show him to be cowardly, irresponsible, mean-spirited, and lascivious. To be sure, some of these many digressions were eventually eliminated or shortened; those cuts were more than counterbalanced, however, by an added large scene in which Pulaski fails the test of civic virtue that is exemplified by his colleagues. Though he ultimately has moments of heroism, the very idea that he is a plausible candidate for promotion is preposterous. Rossi knows better than any how flawed and unworthy Pulaski is. Hence his seeming support for the idea is a clumsy deus ex machina from Lawson. Like Winocki, Pulaski finally demonstrates a fighting spirit, but he remains the limited creature he is, the poor relation to his Irish and Jewish colleagues. In other words, the Polish Americans are inferior stock but may have enough value to be salvaged if carefully tended.

The Hollywood office of the BMP much preferred the Lawson reworking to the original Gilpatric treatment, judging it "far superior" and now "excellent in every respect."[64] Poynter was particularly giddy about the film's treatment of Russia, and he endorsed the film personally to Mellett, underscoring this as a "basic propaganda objective" of the OWI.[65] Several members of the BMP thought the Pulaski character was exceptionally good, as it would prove "powerful and heart-warming" to "foreigners" to see him gradually awakened to duty.[66] The industrialist Henry J. Kaiser thought the film would be a "morale booster" and wanted it shown to his workers.[67]

The film was well received by the critics at the time and has retained high regard as a well-made piece of propaganda.[68] It did much to cement the already affectionate relationship between the BMP and Warner Brothers. Pointer wrote an effusive encomium to Jack Warner about how "useful" the film was and congratulated him on the accomplishment. Warner thought Poynter's evaluation "swell," and both agreed that *Action in the North Atlantic* would "aid the war effort."[69] Warner, buoyed by BMP praise, thought so highly of it that he personally urged his hero President Roosevelt to see it.[70]

Whereas Dane Clark's Pulaski is only a secondary character in *Action in the North Atlantic,* Polish Americans are prominently featured in two other films. The first is the rather weak 1943 Columbia production *Destroyer.*[71] Edward G. Robinson is Steve Boleslavski, a decorated veteran of World War I working as a welder in a shipyard.[72] In an implausible series of developments, "Boley" somehow arranges to be reactivated and appointed "leading chief" on a new destroyer. However, he is woefully incapable of discharging his new responsibilities. He alienates the crew and presides over a series of mishaps, leading to his summary court-martial and demotion for "incompetency in leadership." Even the captain, an old and devoted friend, is forced to lament that Boley does not "know what it's all about." Nonetheless, when the ship is in grave danger, Boley performs masterful welding, saves the ship, and regains the love and admiration of the crew.

Boley is touchingly devoted to the ship and capable of inspiring the men by his example, as demonstrated by a patriotic exhortation he delivers on the legacy of John Paul Jones. Nonetheless, he is a martinet, an inept leader, and withal emotionally unbalanced. Boley's concluding heroics partially redeem him, but he is still quite hopeless in a position of responsibility. Like Winocki in *Air Force,* he does not have the temperament or capacity for leadership. He is, like other cinematic Polish Americans, not without courage but badly flawed and thus a rather problematic member of his unit.

Destroyer is a bad film.[73] Robinson, short and squat, wears an ill-fitting uniform and appears too old and too physically clumsy to play the role. Boleslavski is probably intended to be a Pole, though absolutely nothing is done to reinforce that conclusion, and Robinson is an implausible Slav.[74] The only reference to ethnicity in the film is Boleslavski's mention of his Irish wife. Hence the only major film featuring a Polish American character in the main role, and on balance perhaps a positive one, makes the role's ethnicity uncertain; his name is even spelled incorrectly.[75] The film critics, understandably, did not notice that Boleslavski was Polish.[76]

In yet another Hollywood juxtaposition of a positive Irish character and a profoundly flawed Polish one, Boleslavski is contrasted with the Irish Mickey Donohue, played by a very youthful Glenn Ford. Donohue, younger and far more competent—and also much taller and more physically fit—is promoted over Boleslavski when the latter flounders. Again the Polish character suffers by comparison with his fellow ethnics in Hollywood.

The OWI was aware of the significant ethnic elements of *Destroyer.* In general it was pleased that Boley was "presumably a Polish-American." The "chief value of this character," in its opinion, was in the "relationship between his acts and his name," because it demonstrates that "citizens with Polish, Russian, Jewish, Norwegian, or Italian names are just as loyal Americans as those with Anglo-Saxon names."[77]

However, the OWI found the screenwriter's conception of the Boleslavski character hard to understand: "A good deal more could have been made of this character, however, if his Polish origin had been used to more concrete advantage. Boleslavski, of all the characters in the story, would know best, the true meaning of fascism." The analysis deserves to be presented at length because it underscores Hollywood's usual practice of obscuring the Polish ethnicity of a role even when doing so was harmful to the story:

> As Boley is of Polish origin, he could perhaps tell us something of what it means to him to be an American. He could draw some parallel between his life here in a democratic nation and the lives of his countrymen under fascist domination. Undoubtedly Boley would have relatives and friends living in Poland under the Nazi heel. It would be both dramatic and informative if he could cite specific examples of fascist terrorism in the lives of these people he loves. Boley would know what the war is all about. Let him say plainly that he is fighting to free these countrymen and all the oppressed peoples of the world, that he wants these people to enjoy the individual freedom which he enjoys. Drawing this analogy with the people of Poland would make it clear that we are fighting a common enemy, and that we are fighting for a better world.[78]

These are pertinent observations by reviewer Peg Fenwick of the BMP. Why bother to create a Polish character and then fail to exploit the possibilities inherent in that attribution?[79] The only answer would seem to be the screenwriters' unwillingness to raise the Polish issue in a manner certain to arouse the audience's compassion. Otherwise we are forced to conclude that Fenwick's very apt observation simply did not occur to screenwriters Frank Wead, Lewis Meltzer, and Borden Chase, which strains credulity. But here, at least, we cannot blame the radical Left for Boleslavski's shortcomings. Neither director William Seiter nor screenwriter (and author of the original story) Wead was a leftist—indeed, quite the contrary. Only actor Robinson, a fellow traveler who was a major financial supporter of the Communist Party's various front organizations, was part of the radical community in Hollywood.[80]

The second featured role for an American Pole is in the 1941 musical comedy released by Twentieth Century–Fox titled *Rise and Shine*.[81] The plot, based loosely on a story by James Thurber, concerns the tribulations of "Boley" Bolenciecwcz. We are told that this obviously impossible jumble of letters composing his surname is somehow pronounced "Bolenkowitz."[82] "Boley" is a not uncommon American attempt at the Polish Christian name "Bolesław," already utilized in the film *Destroyer*. It is fitting that the possessor of such a name is absurd. A college football player, Boley is so stupid that he is unable to pass his courses and thus continue playing, despite his colleagues' efforts to help him and his instructor's willingness to devise the simplest questions.[83] Jack Oakie, lumpy, and nearly forty, is cast as Boley. Oakie had a long career, usually playing genial clods; his cinema persona is suggested by the names of his various screen roles: Chicken, Whammo, Bilge, Looney, Tap-Tap, Searchlight, Wahoo, Corny, Cake, and of course Slob and Bozo. Boley's utter vacuity and hulking loutishness are underscored by teaming him with a tall, handsome, and clever Irish character, Jimmy McGonagle, played by George Murphy. Jimmy is in every way superior to Boley, even physically a much more plausible football player. Yet again Hollywood juxtaposes a Pole with a fellow ethnic in a manner most unflattering to the former. *Rise and Shine* is one of the very rare Hollywood films with a Polish leading character, and he is a buffoon. *Rise and Shine* is not a serious film, and Boley, unlike his namesake in *Destroyer*, is not intended to be a serious character.

In 1944 Hollywood produced the last wartime film with an American Pole in a featured role, *Abroad with Two Yanks*.[84] The work of Edward Small Productions, this slapdash effort was distributed by United Artists and starred William Bendix as marine corporal Horatio Stanislaus "Biff" Koraski and Dennis O'Keefe as his friend and rival, fellow marine Jeff Reardon. Both are in pursuit of Joyce Stuart (Helen Walker) during a brief furlough in Australia. Neither character is identified specifically by nationality, but Koraski's name plus a reference to his uncle Stanislaus quite obviously suggests he is to be Polish. Lest there be any doubt, Koraski describes his father as a "coalminer"; Bendix's grating accent is explained by a reference to his being from New Jersey, not famous for its coal deposits. Reardon is probably intended to be Irish, given his name and the casting of O'Keefe, who, understandably, usually played Irish roles. This is yet another pairing of the tall, handsome Irishman and the squat, doltish Pole.

The film is badly cast, badly written, badly directed, and very badly acted. O'Keefe, who is asked to feign madness in several scenes, gives an embarrassing performance. Walker seems uncomfortable in a role that gives her nothing to do save look attractive, which she does effortlessly. John Loder, whose character eventually wins Joyce's affection, obviously had only an imperfect command of his lines and must have been ill at ease in a part appropriate for a man a quarter century younger. Bendix is simply absurd.

Koraski is, we are told, a football legend just five years out of college. Belying his jock image, he is also well educated and devoted to music, art, and especially poetry, which he recites from memory. He is also shown to be a man of integrity and decency, in contrast to the seducer Reardon. However, Bendix apparently did not read the script and played the role as a genial lout, constantly befuddled and outsmarted by his Irish friend. Early in the film, he adopts a mannered and precise diction, which he soon inexplicably drops for the Brooklyn slang for which he was known. His limited assortment of vacant expressions and looks of bewilderment quickly becomes tiresome. Though short, dumpy, appearing well into his middle years, and in poor physical condition, he is cast as a professional athlete in his early twenties. He is Jack Oakie in *Rise and Shine* revisited. Just as George Murphy is the impressive Irish contrast to Oakie, here O'Keefe is the tall, handsome counter to the lumpy Bendix. Whereas Oakie is supposed to be stupid, Bendix is supposed to be smart, but that apparently had no effect on him. Viewers are alerted to how to receive Koraski when we are told his name is Horatio. Obviously such a name could adorn only a silly person, and its linking to Stanislaus is thus a joke. It seems that the film could not decide whether Koraski was to be an impressive and sympathetic character or a buffoon, and tried to do both.

Abroad with Two Yanks was cheaply and hurriedly made, an attempt to exploit the old plot device of two squabbling but devoted service buddies. However, it displays poor preparation and inept execution. It does give us a very rare leading character who is Polish, but he is little more than a stereotype: a genial dolt despite the early references to him as a cultured man.

A strange demonstration of Hollywood's obsession with portraying Poles unflatteringly is the casting of the biographer of the songwriter Ernest R. Ball in the 1944 Twentieth Century–Fox release *Irish Eyes Are Smiling*.[85] Among the real people portrayed in this film is the Polish boxer Stanisław Kiecał (better known by the Americanized version of his name, Stanley Ketchel). The real Kiecał was handsome and a physical marvel. He was murdered at twenty-four, thus ending a brilliant career. In the film he is played by "Slapsie Maxie" Rosenbloom, then past forty and far from peak condition, already exhibiting the slightly daffy behavior that was to be his trademark in a number of films. Why the babbling, middle-aged Rosenbloom, homely in his prime, was chosen to portray a handsome man twenty years younger is a good question.

A minor exception to this theme of the Pole as misfit or nincompoop is the 1942 Universal release *Pittsburgh*.[86] Marlene Dietrich is cast as Josie "Hunky" Winters, a hardened escapee from the poverty and degradation of the anthracite region.[87] Though a ruthless social climber and woman of easy virtue, she is an essentially ethical person. Her Polish origins are, however, a major impediment to her advancement, though it is unclear whether it is her class or ethnicity that she seeks to transcend, since they are of a piece.[88] Of course, why someone described as Polish would be nicknamed Hunky is never explained; the distinction between a Pole and a Bohemian (or perhaps Hungarian) apparently was beyond Hollywood.[89] Moreover, Hunky is successful only after she liberates herself from her ethnic degradation by changing her name and delivering an emotive speech on Americanism. Hence this "Polish" character is perhaps no exception at all because she becomes a positive character only by ceasing to be Polish.

However, what is most noteworthy in Hollywood films is not the negative characterization but the lack of Poles. By 1941 perhaps 6 million people of Polish origin resided in the United States, more than 4 percent of the entire population. At least 600,000 Poles served in the American forces, and some estimates are much higher.[90] However, Polish names are almost nonexistent in Hollywood films of the war era, and even among those few, like Boleslavski in *Destroyer* and Winocki in *Air Force,* we have to assume that they are Polish with little to guide us.

In fact, the ethnic representation of the United States in wartime films is most curious. There are almost no blacks or Hispanics, a topic often noted. The majority population of European origin is peculiarly displayed. There are few with German names, an obvious reflection of the realities of the war. There are a few symbolic Jewish characters. The Irish are everywhere. Italians are not uncommon but are usually menials. Poles, as we have seen, are virtually not to be seen. However, there are a handful of exotics whose names are a jumble of consonants obviously designed to represent undifferentiated Eastern Europeans, perhaps even Poles among them. The best examples of this are the pathetic Sergeant Skvoznik in *The Purple Heart* and the well-named Sergeant "Alphabet" Czeidrowski in *Mr. Winkle Goes to War.* These are not nationalities; they are confusion. Neither name makes sense in any language of Eastern Europe; they are just nonsense words. A character whose name is a joke cannot be taken seriously.[91] Studios spent considerable sums on collecting photographs and information for minor adornments to sets and uniforms and yet gave characters preposterous names, which could have been avoided by a simple call or letter or even an interoffice memorandum to one of the many technical advisers on the payroll. This type of disregard of names is not carelessness; it is disdain, perhaps contempt.[92]

A statistical survey of Hollywood films released between 1939 and 1945 provides some fascinating conclusions. Restricting the analysis to films depicting Americans (omitting films set abroad, where American actors are purportedly foreign nationals), I have counted the portrayals representing the Irish, Italian, Jewish, and Polish ethnic communities in the United States.[93] Having analyzed the casts of approximately 400 films, I have made the following determinations: There are perhaps 20 portrayals probably intended to be Polish, 35 Italian, 40 Jewish, and 330 Irish. Even this evidence of Hollywood's disproportionate representation of the ethnic composition of the country is misleading, however. The Jewish, Italian, and Polish characters are almost always minor figures, whereas the Irish character is often one of the film's heroes. There are only a handful of exceptions. An Italian American is the lead in the early *Action in the North Atlantic* (Humphrey Bogart as Joe Rossi) and in *A Bell for Adano* (John Hodiak as Major Joppolo), which was released after V-J day. Polish and Jewish characters rarely if ever have leading roles. Only the failed Boleslavski (*Destroyer*) and the doltish Koraski (*Abroad with Two Yanks*) are major Polish roles, and neither is flattering. By contrast, many films cast not only the heroic lead but also several of the main characters as Irish. In *Guadalcanal Diary, Marine Raiders,* and *Secret Command,* for example, all three of the principal figures are Irish, as is the star of each of the following: *Destination Tokyo, Fighting Seabees, The Sullivans, Blood on the Sun, Back to Bataan, Bombardier, Sailor's Lady, Mystery Sea Raider, Escape to Glory, Top Sergeant Mulligan, Hay Foot, Captains of the Clouds, All through the Night, Two Yanks in Trinidad, Tramp, Tramp, Tramp, Powder Town, Flight Lieutenant, Wake Island, The Navy Comes Through,* and *Air Force.*

For example, the musical extravaganza *This Is the Army,* released by Warner Brothers in 1943, stars Irish George Murphy playing the father of Irish Ronald Reagan who is pursued by a girl with the Irish name Eileen (Joan Leslie). It also features an Irish soldier, Sergeant McGee, played by Irish Alan Hale, and the Irish Mrs. O'Brien, portrayed by Irish Ruth Donnelly. A host of other characters with Irish names are mentioned throughout the film. The only other major role is the Jewish Twardofsky, played by the ubiquitous George Tobias. It is *The Cohens and Kellys* revisited. There are no Poles.[94] In *Pride of the Marines,* released just after the war, a memorable scene depicts marines with a machine gun decorated by a Star of David and a shamrock.[95] It was, of course, produced by Warner Brothers.

Hollywood even altered scripts to change a character into an Irishman from some other nationality. Humphrey Bogart's lovable gambler who thwarts fifth columnists in Manhattan in *All through the Night* was to be an Italian named Gloves Dino, but at the last minute Warner Brothers made him Gloves Donahue, the head of an Irish gang (consisting of Frank McHugh, William Demarest, and Jackie Gleason, with Jewish Phil Silvers in close proximity).[96] Donahue has a running feud with the criminal, but admirably patriotic, Marty Callahan (Barton MacLane), also Irish.[97]

Analysts of Hollywood's portrayal of the ethnic composition of the United States during the war frequently note that a Pole is one of the standard symbolic components of "war films."[98] The evidence from a close study of the films does not support this. Characters clearly distinguished as Polish are, as noted above, quite rare. Even if we assume that every name so peculiar that it cannot be reasonably assigned to any other national community must per force be Polish, it is the very rare squadron, platoon, or crew with a Pole.[99] Although it is difficult to calculate the exact number of "service films" produced—defined as films that substantially deal with units of the military as the principal mise-en-scène—a good guess would be at least two hundred. Because only perhaps ten Poles are depicted by Hollywood in American uniform, the oft-repeated notion that war-era films placed a Pole in every unit is completely without foundation.

Hence there is the phenomenon of the shadowy Polish presence, already indicated by Boleslavski in *Destroyer,* who is Polish and yet seems not to be aware of it. The list of these shadowy presences is fairly long. For example, Pulaski is an American sailor in the obscure, low-budget, and short (only slightly over sixty minutes) 1942 Columbia release titled *Submarine Raider.*[100] Pulaski is flanked by fellow sailors with obviously Jewish (Levy) and Irish (Shannon) names. Forrest Tucker (who had a long though not distinguished career) played Pulaski in one of his first films.[101]

A rather larger role is that of F. X. Matowski, played by Barry Nelson in MGM's 1943 *Bataan,* a film that featured curious ethnic casting: the Irishman, George Murphy, played a WASP named Bentley; the Irish, very non-Semitic character actor Thomas Mitchell was a Jewish soldier named Feingold; and Matowski was played by the Scandinavian Nelson.[102] Nelson's character is quite positive, though he is killed early in the movie. He is a competent soldier and a close friend of a black colleague, a sure sign of special favor in Hollywood.

Unfortunately, Matowski's Polish credentials are rather slim. He does explain that his name is Francis Xavier, which establishes him as a Roman Catholic, already more development of possible Polish ethnicity than the norm. He also is from Pittsburgh, which suggests the kind of grimy proletarian origins expected of Eastern Europeans.

Beyond these scraps, however, the screenwriter thought ascribing odd food culture to Matowski would be sufficient to complete his national stereotype. Hence he delectates over the family's favorite repast of "lima bean soup with vinegar," which reminiscence fills his fellows with understandable disgust. Matowski is shot by a Japanese sniper shortly afterward, though probably not in culinary reprisal.

An even more marginal Polish presence, indeed almost invisible, can be found in the short 1943 RKO release *Gangway for Tomorrow*.[103] Set in an American munitions factory, it is the story of five workers who relate their lives retrospectively, concluding with their enthusiastic determination for service in war production. The film concludes with a paroxysm of gushy patriotism and celebration of unity cobbled from ethnic and social diversity. Not one of these five central players is a Pole, though one is a former "fighter for the French underground," thus reemphasizing Hollywood's celebration of French resistance. There are also Czech and Russian workers in the plant and, of course, a great many Irish.[104] There is also someone referred to in the credits as a "Polish worker" (played by Ludwig Donath, an Austrian émigré). He is perhaps more fortunate than the film's character Sam Kowalski (Al Kunde), probably intended to be a Polish American, who is listed below him in the cast.[105]

It is perhaps as well that the anonymous Polish worker had so small a role. The film originally gave him a larger part. In an extended sequence supposedly transpiring in the imagination of an American laborer, Joe Dunham, the Pole is a poorly motivated worker on the job in Warsaw, "complacent" but unwilling to "concern himself with the troubles of the rest of the world." In the midst of his selfish sloth, the Germans invade Poland. Obviously, the symbolic Pole has brought ruin on his nation's head by his lack of vigilance and sense of duty. By contrast, the film depicts for the viewer a Russian worker, similarly at work, but here the focus is on his response to the German invasion, after which he "left his machine to take up a gun." The OWI objected: "Can we really say it was the complacency and lack of spirit on the part of the Polish, Czech, and French workmen which led to the blitzkrieg of their countries?"[106] Quite apart from whether the OWI wanted war to be explained as conjured by sloth rather than by fascism—its preferred explanation—this juxtaposition of a lazy, selfish Pole and a brave, patriotic Russian is symptomatic of the Hollywood practice of presenting Poland in an unflattering light. This nasty sequence was apparently cut or shortened in the released version, thus reducing Donath's role.

There is another condescending reference to American Poles in the 1943 RKO film *Tender Comrade.*[107] Ginger Rogers portrays Jo Jones, who enterprisingly convinces a group of female colleagues at a defense plant to live together and share expenses. The youngest of the group, Doris White (Kim Hunter), marries a soldier and sheepishly announces the whirlwind courtship to her friends. The following exchange occurs: "What's your new name?" she is asked. "Dumbrowski," she says with obvious embarrassment. "You mean you traded a name like 'White' for 'Dumbrowski'?" she is asked with incredulity by another worker, who stumbles over the name. At this Jo intervenes to inquire censoriously, "What's wrong with 'Dumbrowski?'" The awkward conversation ends. Later, the husband, Mike Dumbrowski (Richard Martin), appears in a brief scene, but he is an awkward nonentity. Both husband and wife are portrayed as hopeless naifs. The scene obviously suggests that a Polish name is a social stigma and that no sensible person would willingly adopt one. That another character objects to expressing society's verdict on the matter indicates only that it is sometimes tasteless to admit certain things publicly, not that they are wrong in the first place. The fact that Hollywood again used the name "Dumbrowski," with its obviously embarrassing spelling, to indicate a Pole suggests disdain.[108]

Beyond this handful of portrayals, there are only scraps. For example, we have the cheap, ludicrous 1942 release *Hitler—Dead or Alive,* which is about mobsters just released from Alcatraz who decide to put their criminal tendencies to patriotic use by murdering Adolf Hitler in return for a million-dollar bounty paid by an even more patriotic wealthy eccentric.[109] The leader of this worthy trio is Steve Maschik, presumably at least a Slav, if not a Pole, played by Ward Bond. Maschik's nationality is not discussed, and his name is given several pronunciations. He and his cronies speak of dealing with Germans in Milwaukee and sing a song about Halsted Street, which implies that they are from heavily Polish Chicago.[110] These are the few wisps the film presents regarding the ethnicity of its main protagonist. It is perhaps as well; this may be the worst film made in the World War II era. Directed ineptly by Nick Grinde from a very bad screenplay by Sam Neuman and Karl Brown, it demonstrates why Bond never became a leading player. The OWI, incomprehensibly, rather liked the film, though it admitted that it was a slapdash production. Was Maschik intended to be a Pole? It is not clear, and the OWI did not raise the issue.[111]

In conjunction with the army, Warner Brothers made a brief, quasi-documentary film lauding the quality of American tanks, titled, appropriately, *The Tanks Are Coming*.[112] The chief character in this piece is a soldier named Malowski—perhaps intended to be Masłowski. The role was given to the stock-player George Tobias, who was Weinberg in *Air Force*. Tobias, large and lumpy with a vacant expression, was often, like Jack Oakie, cast as a genial but cloddish character.[113]

Even the handful of Poles noted here almost invariably have garbled names or names inappropriate for their nationality, such as Katja in *Edge of Darkness* and Ivan in *Wake Island*. One of these is Genya Smetana in the clever and almost forgotten comedy *Hi Diddle Diddle*.[114] Madame Smetana is a Wagnerian soprano. Her nationality is never explained, but the actress has a pronounced Polish accent. In an early scene, she bursts into an angry discourse in Polish, the native tongue of Pola Negri, who came out of retirement to play this small role. It may be the only Polish-language passage in an American film produced during the war. Ironically, listening to her Polish diatribe is Marek Windheim, a fellow Pole, who portrays her accompanist. This may also be the only film of the era featuring two Poles. Neither, however, is identified by nationality: Windheim's character has no name, and "Smetana" is Czech.

Similarly, are Mama Lugovska, Kozzarowski, Granowski, Sinkewicz, Grybinski, and Pianatowski supposed to be Poles? The films in which they appear do nothing to answer this question. But it is only by counting them as Polish characters that we reach the total of about twenty Poles in the American population indicated by Hollywood during the war. Perhaps they are not specifically Polish at all but are simply supposed to be Slavs of some sort, or "Hunyaks," to borrow Warner Brothers' terminology. If we count as Poles only those characters who either are specifically identified as such or for whom there are at least some references to their nationality, the number of Poles in Hollywood films is a very small handful. The rest are simply exotic "foreigners."

The ultimate example of this is the mawkishly sentimental 1944 film aptly titled *An American Romance,* chronicling the rise to wealth and position of the (seemingly) Eastern European Stefan Dangos (Brian Donlevy).[115] The film is awash in quasi–East Central European names, all of them counterfeit: there is someone named "Dubechek," which comes close to the Czech or Slovak "Dubček" but fails. There is a girl called "Katina," a name that does not exist but vaguely suggests a Slavic version of "Katherine." There are also a "Vronsky" and a "Yasha" for flavoring. And, of course, there is the name "Dangos," which hints at a Hungarian origin but is not Hungarian. Dangos is implicitly a Czech character, a conclusion reinforced by the fact that his brother is named "Anton," a Czech name. Early in the film, we are told that the original name was "Dangosbiblichek," which is not Czech, or anything else for that matter. Bosley Crowther described Dangos as "a fumbling, stubborn bohunk," and most reviewers concluded that Dangos was intended to be a Czech.[116]

In this film, everyone speaks in rather elaborately broken English with facial contortions, noisy consonants, and energetic gesticulation—"in the thick style of dialect comedy"[117]—Hollywood's signals for Europeans not from the western fringes of the continent. Any effort to reconstruct Dangos's nationality is impeded by his carrying kroner with him, a Scandinavian currency. It is obvious that Dangos, like many others in the film, is not supposed to be anything in particular; he is merely an Eastern European. Since the Dangos family obviously has no traditional attachments to their native culture—which of course denigrates that culture in the viewers' eyes—they name their children "Theodore Roosevelt," "George Washington," "Thomas Jefferson," and "Abraham Lincoln." However, Dangos, a nationality blur, marries a woman who is clearly identified as Irish.[118]

The Poles often slipped into this Hollywood morass of ethnic nonsense. Why Jews, Italians, and Irish are allowed to be Jewish, Italian, and Irish but Poles, like their regional neighbors, become the "Dangos" nationality is part of the problem the Poles faced in wartime Hollywood. Simply put, there was a tendency to present the people of Eastern and Central Europe as an incomprehensible mélange, without differentiating characteristics. They can have any name as long as it is odd; speak any language as long as it is heavily accented; must show no discernible attachment to the history, traditions, and culture of their ancestors; and above all be cringingly grateful to the United States. They are rendered ethnic raw material, fit only for processing. Hollywood made the America population derived from Eastern Europe into a collective Stepin Fetchit.

In general for wartime Hollywood, the American population consists of two elements: those without any identifiable ethnic or religious characterizations, the Americans *tout court,* and the representative "others": the Irish, who represent all Catholics, and all immigrants. The rest are tokens. For all practical purposes, there are no other inhabitants of the country. Hence, when Poles are presented, they are almost devoid of identifiable characteristics. If they have a religion, it has no outward manifestations. They never speak their native language, even an occasional word, and they seem to have no interest in their ancestral homeland or its woes, like *Destroyer*'s Boleslavski and the nasty conniver in *Quota Girl.* They are, however, it seems, physically clearly differentiable. They are all very dark, swarthy, and short. Edward G. Robinson (five feet, five inches tall), Leo Gorcey (five feet, six inches tall), John Garfield (five feet, seven inches tall), Peter Lorre (five feet, five inches tall) and the tiny Spanish character actor Luis Alberni reflect this notion of what a Pole should look like.[119]

We search in vain for additional American Poles presented by Hollywood during the war, and we find only vague and insignificant hints. For example, one of the East Side Kids led by the Irish Muggs (Leo Gorcey) and Glimpy (Huntz Hall) was named "Stash" and portrayed by Sidney Clements. These were very low-budget, quite bad Monogram films.[120] Stash was probably intended to be Polish, but that is never made clear, and in any event he is a very minor character in the few films in which he appears.[121] Clements also had a small role as Morton Rodakiewicz in the 1943 Columbia comedy *The More the Merrier,* a Jean Arthur vehicle directed by George Stevens that focuses amusingly on the housing shortage in wartime Washington.[122] It is probably because Clements was ethnically Polish that Rodakiewicz may be the only Polish character in a wartime Hollywood film whose name is spelled correctly. In an unkind misspelling, the hapless paperboy in the 1944 United Artists version of the stage play *Tomorrow the World* is named "Stanley Dumbrowski," a less than flattering rendering of a common Polish name, "Dąbrowski." The character is of little moment, but using a name like "Dumbrowski" is an odd touch for a film dedicated to demonstrating the evils of ethnic prejudice.[123]

There are minor Polish traces in the 1942 Columbia effort *The Talk of the Town,* also directed by Stevens and again starring Jean Arthur, this time opposite Cary Grant and Ronald Coleman.[124] Grant's character, oddly named "Leopold Dilg," is an idiosyncratic autodidact worker with anarchistic tendencies who wins the affections and respect of all. The film implies that he is Polish, though it is not explicit, and the hints would be lost on most viewers. Rather more certain is the nationality of Dilg's nemesis, Jan Pulaski, who is obviously intended to be a Pole, a mean conniver.[125] Hence, the Polish character in this film would be for viewers not the charming Dilg but the repulsive Pulaski. Attaching the most beloved name of the Polish American community to a negative character is a particularly nasty gesture.

Another case of a possible Polish role is Victoria Anastasia Wilomirska (Norma Shearer) in the 1942 MGM production *We Were Dancing*.[126] She is probably intended to be Polish, but that is not made clear, and it has no significance for the story. Ostensibly a sophisticated comedy adapted from a play by Noel Coward, the film is unbearable, and its failure probably hastened Shearer's retirement after a brief career.[127] The list of possible Poles who appear fleetingly also includes Mrs. Pulaski, played by the Hungarian expatriate Ferike Boros, in the 1943 Warner Brothers film *Princess O'Rourke*.[128]

Universal's charmingly implausible 1941 musical *Sing Another Chorus* includes the Russian émigré Mischa Auer in a featured role as Stanislaus the janitor.[129] Auer renders his usual fine performance, but is he supposed to be a Pole? Perhaps. However, with both Auer and director Charles R. Lamont having been born in St. Petersburg, Stanislaus was probably intended to be a Russian, not a Pole. Regardless, Universal evidently thought Auer was a superb Stanislaus, so it gave him the same name the next year in a slight comedy titled *Don't Get Personal*.[130] Lest any viewer not realize that people with that name are to be considered ridiculous, the film tells us that his full name is "Stanislaus Noodnick" but he is called "Charlie."

There are a number of cases in which Polish characters that were originally part of the treatment or draft of the screenplay underwent a major evolution. These characters either disappeared or had their nationality changed from Polish to something else or were rendered far less attractive. Curiously, the opposite phenomenon is not to be found. There are no Polish characters originally designated of a different nationality, nor are there those who become positive after initially being presented as negative. Poles in Hollywood only descend or vanish.

In the fall of 1943, *Liberty* magazine began the serialization of a story titled "Destination Tokyo" by Steve Fisher. One of the principal characters is Chief Petty Officer Browski. He is described as massive and quite ugly—"raw meat, a yard wide"—and intellectually ponderous.[131] However, he is a seasoned veteran and both the moral and practical leader of the crew, who have the highest respect for the courage and competence of the "chief-of-the-boat." Browski is also profoundly religious and utterly fearless. He plays a central part in each of the installments of the story, and his role remains in the novel, which collects the serialized parts.[132]

Browski underwent a most peculiar evolution once he traveled to Hollywood. In the first treatment at Warner Brothers, essentially a draft of the story produced on May 1, 1943, the character of the CPO remains, but he is suddenly nameless.[133] A few days later, in the revised treatment, the CPO has disappeared and a new character, Mike Danton, has been created who has many of Browski's features and lines. However, he is without the CPO's physical ugliness.[134] Curiously, Fisher's name is not on this document. The next day, a "revised temporary" version of the story was circulated that added the name of screenwriter Delmer Daves to that of Fisher, now in a subordinate position.[135] In this version, Mike has effectively replaced Browski. This new embodiment survived the evolution of the script in June, and by late that month he emerged as an Irish character. (The film was already in production when a reference was added specifically identifying the character as Irish on June 22.) A new Greek character was also added to the crew to give it greater ethnic diversity.[136] The Polish role, originally central to the story, is gone. By the time *Destination Tokyo* was released in December 1943, it had several additional Irish characters, including Captain Cassidy, played by Cary Grant, complete with English accent, and an Italian, but no Poles at all.[137] It is possible that the disappearance of the Pole was the work of Communist Party member Albert Maltz, who became the third screenwriter. We do know that Maltz was assigned to amend the characterizations and that it was Maltz who invented the Greek character.[138]

Changing Browski the Pole to Mike the Irishman was a minor matter; he was a secondary character, and being Polish was not essential to his function in the story. However, another Polish disappearance is far more significant because it concerned a leading role in the film and weakened the intensity of the story while gaining nothing. This is the well-known 1944 release by Twentieth Century–Fox, *Lifeboat*.[139] Based on an unpublished story by John Steinbeck, *Lifeboat* was rewritten for the screen by Jo Swerling, a Russian émigré of radical leftist views, and directed by the redoubtable Alfred Hitchcock.[140] The story depicts the tribulations of a handful of survivors of a torpedoed ship, an ordeal rendered both practically and morally complicated by the presence of Willy, a German submarine commander (Walter Slezak in a powerful performance), as a fellow survivor.

In Steinbeck's story, the central character is a Polish labor activist whom Steinbeck unfortunately named "Albert Sheinkowitz," a name quite impossible in Polish.[141] Sheinkowitz is an ardent champion of the proletariat, as was his creator Steinbeck. When Hitchcock and his screenwriters recast the story, Steinbeck was horrified by the changes. He particularly objected to the attenuation of the pro-labor sentiments of his protagonist.[142] Steinbeck eventually demanded that his name be removed from the credits; he was embittered by the whole experience. In a letter written in February 1944, he claimed that the changes in his story made the film "dangerous to the American war effort," which suggests Steinbeck had a rather exaggerated notion of what films, even ones written by him, could do.[143]

The most striking changes did concern the Sheinkowitz character. Steinbeck described him in some detail, as he was the central character in the story. He was "a Pole from around Chicago . . . good looking . . . sort of broad . . . a mighty nice looking fellow . . . nice white teeth and curly hair." His "people worked in the stock-yards." The zenith of the film is the rescue of the German from the sea and the survivors' moral perplexity regarding how to deal with him. For Sheinkowitz the choice is clear: "Let's throw the son-of-a-bitch back!" Steinbeck explains his character's motives: "He hadn't forgotten for a minute he was a Pole. Poles, I guess, just don't like Germans any more. Of course, right now nobody likes them, but the Poles just kind of hate them." Soon thereafter Sheinkowitz "gives us a little speech about what the Germans done to the Poles, how they killed so many of them and moved them around and made slaves of them," and "probably the German knows Albert's a Pole too, by the looks." Later Steinbeck's narrator comments, "You know he's a Pole and Poles hate Germans and Albert isn't going to do anything a Pole doesn't do." Even though "Albert's a dumb bastard," he gets the girl in the end.[144]

Swerling changed the character of Sheinkowitz. He remains the son of stockyard workers from Chicago. But his name is changed to

"Kovac," which is a garbled version of the common Hungarian name "Kovacs." Swerling gives him an introductory speech: "Now, me, I'm American, too. I was born right in Chicago. But my people are from Czechoslovakia." Kovac then turns to the German "and almost spits the name in his face." "Did you ever hear of *that* place?"[145] This reference to Czechoslovakia seemed insufficient motive to explain Kovac's maniacal fury and desire to kill the German; hence, in other versions of the script, Swerling has Kovac expatiate, "Czechoslovakia! Prague! And Lidice! Did you ever hear of that place?" Here Lidice rather than Czechoslovakia as a whole becomes "that place."[146]

This alteration is most unfortunate. Sheinkowitz-Kovac was originally described as viscerally anti-German, and his hatred for Willy is enormous. Although this antipathy in the revised version could be in part explained by political motives—Sheinkowitz-Kovac is described as having leftist views and being a champion of the proletariat—the original Steinbeck character has a far more powerful explanation for his reactions. He is a Pole who bitterly resents the German outrages in his ancestral fatherland. This motivation is weakened by changing him into a Czech. Steinbeck's story placed considerable weight on the Polish elements motivating Sheinkowitz. Swerling's character is harder to understand, as the profundity of his antipathy is not adequately explained.[147] It becomes a weak point in the drama. The Czechs simply had far fewer grievances against the Germans than did the Poles, Lidice notwithstanding.[148] For American audiences in 1944, making a union activist come from heavily Polish Chicago was perfectly reasonable. But why make him a Czech? Kovac is an inadequate substitute for Sheinkowitz.[149] Indeed, the character's function in the drama is seriously damaged, and the moral dimension of the story is compromised. In the exchange, nothing is gained. If Steinbeck had a reason to make Sheinkowitz a Pole, why did Swerling transform him into a Czech (and, like Victor László in *Casablanca,* one with a Hungarian name at that), and why did Hitchcock not see the negative consequences of the change? This is yet another example of Hollywood's not making a character Polish when doing so was in its interests. Perhaps a fitting irony is that Kovac is played by John Hodiak, a fine actor of Polish-Ukrainian ancestry. Hodiak was, unfortunately, tall and quite fair, and hence Hollywood could not possibly have cast him as his own nationality.

The BMP did not like *Lifeboat* because its portrayal of Americans was insufficiently positive. Kovac was particularly disappointing for a series of odd reasons. First, though he is described as a veteran of the Spanish Civil War, he is "ineffective," a less dominating figure than the German naval officer. To make matters worse, there is an implication that Kovac cheats at poker, which troubled the BMP greatly. Nationality issues did not occur to the reviewer.[150]

The absence of Poles from the Hollywood serials of the prewar era has already been noted. This practice continued after hostilities commenced, though wartime themes understandably became more common. A thorough search of the complete casts of twenty-nine wartime serials (by Universal, Republic, and Columbia) of four hundred episodes, featuring 1,286 characters, reveals not a single Polish name, even in garbled form. Again, Irish names and characters are very frequently found, as is a sprinkling of Italians (Savini, Taboni, and Tardoni, among others) and Germans, often in rather sinister roles, as well as a few Russians. These cheap films were the major cinema of American youth growing up in the years before and during the war. Adding this sample from the 1939–1945 era to the group from the decade before, we find that Hollywood produced more than twelve hundred of these short films with more than 3,600 characters and never saw fit to depict a single Pole. The invisibility of Poles in this popular genre of American films is astonishing.

Whereas the Poles are rare and overwhelmingly negative in Hollywood's portrayal of American society, the film industry was most solicitous of the Czechs. The depiction of Czechoslovakia as a sympathetic and heroic ally was paralleled by the depiction of Czechs as exemplary immigrants. Sophie, who tearfully recites the poetry inscribed at the base of the Statue of Liberty in *Since You Went Away,* is a Czech; Stefan Dangos, the immigrant success par excellence who names all of his children in honor of American presidents in *An American Romance,* is a Czech; Kovac, the working-class hero of *Lifeboat,* is a Czech. So is Joan Bennett, the suffering and sympathetic wife of a Nazi diplomat in the execrable 1943 film *Margin for Error.*[151] *Lake Placid Serenade* is populated, it seems, exclusively by charming Czechs.[152] Just as the Czechs are the attractive Eastern European allies, their countrymen are the preferred Eastern European immigrants: grateful, quiescent, and obedient.

8

Why Hollywood Was at War with the Poles

HOW MAY WE EXPLAIN THE INATTENTION and hostility with which Hollywood treated wartime Poland? Hollywood's version of the war was a combination of the left-wing, pro-Soviet political sympathies of many of its leading figures and the preference of the U.S. government to present a depiction of the war that supported its policy predilections.

The screenwriters and directors of the films in which Poland is portrayed, most unfavorably, are a virtual gallery of the activist radical Left. John Howard Lawson, Lester Cole, Robert Rossen, Arthur Kober, Jay Leyda, Leopold Atlas, Guy Endore, Philip Stevenson, Lillian Hellman, and Sidney Buchman were members of the Communist Party. Lewis Milestone and Howard Koch were later among the "unfriendly nineteen" of congressional hearing fame. Ellis St. Joseph, Dudley Nichols, Arch Oboler, Vladimir Pozner, and Anatole Litvak, among many others, were fellow travelers well known for their political activism.[1] It is not surprising that several of the names closely associated with Hollywood's treatment of Poland—Koch, Lubitsch, and the Epsteins, among others—appear on the list of "key political activists in Hollywood" assembled by Ceplair and Englund.[2] Even among the actors a pattern emerges: Edward G. Robinson is the Polish American failure who seems to have no relationship with Poland in *Destroyer;* Paul Henreid is the fatuous Polish failure of *In Our Time;* John Garfield is the mentally unstable Polish failure in flight school in *Air Force.* All were among Hollywood's most radical leftists. Similarly, Warner Brothers, the most ardently pro-FDR studio in Hollywood, specializing in "progressive" films, was responsible for the nastily anti-Polish *In Our Time* and *Edge of Darkness,* as well as for the shameless *Mission to Moscow.*[3] As Patrick McGilligan and Paul Buhle note, the "decidedly leftward" atmosphere of wartime Hollywood was the creation not of a handful of Communists but of the far larger number who were "leftists," some of whom were "to the left of the Party," as well as liberals who supported "the same political goals as Party members."[4] The party was *"the* network" in Hollywood for all leftist elements, conclude Buhle and Wagner.[5] It was an ersatz family for transplanted easterners and refugees; it gave meaning and structure to the lives of the Hollywood Left.[6]

The Left dominated Hollywood depictions of the war. Director André de Toth, himself a prominent leftist, noted that in the war era "Hollywoodites went berserk. For a long while the stamp of 'fascist' was a death warrant and 'communist' was the badge of honor."[7] When W. R. Burnett, a key Warner Brothers screenwriter, was asked many years later whether he was aware of the Communist affiliations of colleagues like Lawson and Albert Maltz, he responded, "Are you kidding? We were loaded with card-holders in Hollywood."[8] Lawson, the "commissar," and a few fellow Communists controlled the Screen Writers Guild, which gave them considerable power.[9] Sheridan Gibney, a declared leftist who said "I liked the Communists" in Hollywood, nonetheless admitted that they wanted to "use [the guild] as a weapon in the war."[10] Allen Scott noted that among his fellow writers at RKO, a studio not particularly noted for its leftist sympathies, the prevailing atmosphere was one of "social idealism," which he defined as concern for "Spain, fascism, anti-Semitism, or defending democracy by aiding the allies (as Roosevelt said)."[11] Anne Froelick, a party member, described Paramount as having "left-wing writers . . . all around the lot."[12] Columbia was similarly filled with radical leftist and pro-Russian writers.[13] A memorandum was purportedly circulated at Universal that "being a Communist was no longer sufficient reason to be employed there . . . a bit of work would also be required."[14]

By comparison the political Right in Hollywood was a handful of the isolated and disgruntled, and the middle and Left were ineffective in creating a community apart from party influence: "There was never any organized, articulate, and effective liberal or left-wing opposition to the Communists in Hollywood."[15] Phillip Dunne, a non-Communist but very close to many party members and later one of the principal defenders of the Hollywood Ten, described the writers as "fundamentally left-oriented" activists who considered Russia "sacrosanct."[16]

As a result, as screenwriter Lester Cole noted, films dealing with the war would naturally be assigned to writers of the Left, including Communist Party members such as himself, because "writers were 'cast' for assignments, even as actors and actresses: did they understand the subject; were they familiar with the social forces involved? So when it came to the current vogue of anti-Nazi, anti-fascist films, it was natural that, for example, John Howard Lawson would be 'cast' to write *Sahara* and not a right-winger."[17] Why it was "natural" to have the war explained exclusively by the Left is comprehensible only to someone who understands the "social forces involved."[18] Why Lawson ipso facto could depict combat in North Africa—the content of *Sahara*— more compellingly than a "right-winger" is apparent only to someone for whom ideological and not artistic motivations are paramount.[19] This doubtlessly explains the phenomenon noted by Roy Huggins of writers who would not have worked without the party's influence and connections: "Awful writers . . . but politically smart."[20]

There were Communists in Hollywood, especially among the screenwriters, but their influence has never been satisfactorily evaluated.[21] McGilligan and Buhle reckon the party's membership in wartime Hollywood at "several hundred official members"; it had "widespread appeal" through many related organizations.[22] Communist writer Alvah Bessie remembers a "strong Party organization in Hollywood" with two hundred to three hundred members "in the talent and craft sections alone."[23] The influential Screen Readers Guild (also known as the Story Analysts Guild), which appraised all incoming scripts, was organized by another party member, John Weber. Lillian Bergquist, the chief analyst of the Hollywood BMP—who was very protective of Russian interests in her work—was, conveniently, also vice president of the Screen Readers Guild.[24] Weber also taught at a secret Communist Party school for key Hollywood writers, directors, and producers, yet another avenue of party influence among nonparty screenwriters. In addition, the trade journal *The Screen Writer* was controlled by party member Dalton Trumbo, who gave his daughter, born in 1939, a Russian name in celebration of the socialist motherland.[25] In 1941 the party created the Actors' Laboratory of Hollywood as another means to spread influence and gain adherents. It combined indubitably fine training with radical politics.[26] Hence the party's influence was far greater than even its rather impressive numbers would suggest. Party member Frank Tuttle recalled that during the war, ideological uniformity was created by a sort of unforced consensus of the radical Left, what he called "mental incest": "You see and talk to people for the most part who are either Communist or close to the Communist way of thinking."[27] Lawson, according to his biographer, created a "system" by which party members would bring the scripts they were working on to Party meetings, thus ensuring ideological conformity.[28]

The overwhelming leftist presence, with its dense network of linkages, created an atmosphere in which pro-Soviet versions of the war simply developed naturally; there were virtually no countervailing influences.[29] This inclination was certainly reinforced by the preferences of the BMP, which was dominated by New Deal leftists. Hence, even when a film that mentioned Poland or Poles—such as *Once upon a Honeymoon* or *Destroyer*—was not the product of identifiably leftist screenwriters, it does not deviate from the Hollywood norms.[30] This was a world in which the "Hollywood Bowl was overflowing with members of the community eager to contribute to Russian War Relief."[31] Perhaps more important, as MGM producer Joe Cohn remarked, "People forget that the left-wingers put Russia first. And the moment you disagreed with the Left you were called anti-Semitic."[32] In such an atmosphere, any voice defending Poland could not be heard.

Dan Georgakas notes that, despite a great many specialized studies and many memoirs of participants, it is still unclear whether the "Hollywood Reds" were, "as they have claimed, largely unable to make much of an impact on Hollywood, or if in fact, they succeeded far more than they imagined." Indeed, "extended political and ideological discourse of any kind is conspicuously absent" from the Communist Party members' retrospective accounts.[33] This is extraordinarily important because the Hollywood Communists contributed to as many as fifteen hundred films before 1947.[34] This, Georgakas notes, confirms the House Committee on Un-American Activities' suspicion "of a major CP presence in Hollywood."[35]

The radical Left in Hollywood did not like Poland. To Phillip Dunne, Poland was simply a fascist country, and the Soviet Union was justified in invading it in 1939.[36] For fellow screenwriter Albert Maltz, Poland had invaded the Soviet Union in 1917 and had been planning to invade Czechoslovakia in 1938 as part of a fascist plot. Both assertions were simply untrue. For Maltz the epitome of hardship was being among the opposition in Poland under Piłsudski (1926–1935).[37] Given the existence of Nazi and Soviet regimes, this claim tells us a good deal about the objectivity of his judgment. Robert Rossen's Poles were slatterns and racial degenerates. For Ellis St. Joseph they were fascists, appeasers, and vain frauds. Howard Koch more than once referred to Poland as being fascist. Given that the party and its radical allies saw World War II essentially as a struggle against international fascism, Poland was the enemy. These writers are representative of many.

Ceplair and Englund, despite their sympathy, present a damning portrayal of the ideological fanaticism and moral purblindness of the Hollywood Communists, who, they conclude, were "Stalinists": "Communist screenwriters defended the Stalinist regime . . . and criticized enemies and allies alike with an infuriating self-righteousness, superiority, and selective memory. . . . [They] became apologists for crimes of monstrous dimensions, though they claimed to know nothing about such crimes, and indeed shouted down, or ignored those who did."[38]

But was this ideological disposition determinative for Hollywood as a whole? Certainly the studios' interest in financially successful operations limited the ideological motives of the politically engaged creative elements. Moreover, some studio moguls, like MGM's Louis B. Mayer, were far from leftist in their political views.[39] Even Jack Warner, for all his pro-Soviet apologetics, was an ardent Roosevelt Democrat, not a radical leftist. The geopolitically irresponsible Frank Capra was, for all his populism, a Republican, as was Darryl Zanuck, tsar of Twentieth Century–Fox, though he was far more liberal than Capra.[40] Indeed, even the films of the most relentlessly pro-Soviet studio, Warner Brothers, reflected its passion to produce "punchy, right-out-of the headlines pictures" while promoting the interests of FDR, not to market the notions of the Comintern.[41] For the studio moguls, the motives of the party loyalists were inconsequential; it mattered only that they were congruent with their goals of supporting the Roosevelt administration's definition of the demands of the war effort.

Indeed, the pro-Soviet films were designed by the studios for a temporary wartime goal, not as steps in the Communization of the American public, whatever the hopes of the screenwriters. Hence, films like those in the *Why We Fight* series have been dismissed as "political accidents," temporary ethical lapses to serve a geopolitical end.[42] Even Warner Brothers stopped making war films almost immediately after V-E day. Dalton Trumbo, himself later one of the Hollywood Ten, noted in the *Daily Worker* that he and his fellow travelers' main wartime success was that "they were able to keep the most virulent anti-Communist stories from the screen."[43]

The import of these facts for Poland and its portrayal is weighty indeed. A sympathetic depiction of Poland would raise the most serious questions about the Soviet Union and constitute what we can be sure the Hollywood Left would consider "virulent anti-Communism." For example, Warner Brothers writer Anne Froelick, a protégé of Howard Koch, said years later that during the war she dismissed out of hand any criticism of the Soviet Union or even of Stalin.[44] MGM writer Robert Lees admitted he "bought everything" marketed by the Kremlin until 1956 because he "thought the Party was the only alternative to capitalism and Fascism." Besides, in wartime Hollywood, "everybody decent . . . if they weren't in the Party, they were at least on the left."[45] One of the major organizers of the Screen Actors Guild was Lionel Stander, whose view of politics in wartime Hollywood was that "every person who believed in human decency" was on the Left and the party "took the frontal position" in this phalanx. He was "not disturbed" by the grotesque purge trials or by the cynical Hitler-Stalin pact, and he was dismissive of anti-Stalinist critiques. Even decades later, he rejected anti-Communism.[46] In the face of such fanatical naiveté—or unprincipled pro-Sovietism—the Polish cause in Hollywood was doomed.[47] Columbia writer Paul Jarrico, also a party member, dismissed any problems with the "pro-Russian" sentiment of films of the war era by saying, "Who wasn't?" He summarized the party's position as "What is good for the Soviet Union is good for us," though he admitted that this logic ultimately redounded to his comrades' disadvantage.[48] Years after the war, screenwriter Walter Bernstein concluded that although films like *Song of Russia* and *Mission to Moscow* were nonsense, such nonsense was necessary.[49] Perhaps the bluntest declaration was that of party member Richard Collins, who described "the basic communist positions" as follows: "We have the right to lie, because we are the future—we are the good guys."[50] Unconsciously or otherwise, the Left in Hollywood, in tandem with administration policy, worked against Polish interests. The moguls' political views did not matter.

This raises the superficially appealing argument, frequently claimed by Hollywood leftists after 1945, that the political content of the films they helped create was comprehensible only within the context of the war. The American *raison d'état*—indeed, the cause of freedom in the world—required convincing the public that the Soviets were not repugnant. This was a pressing matter after 1939 because Germany was going from victory to victory, and the collapse of the Soviet Union in the face of the Nazi onslaught in June 1941 would have been an incalculable disaster. Hence presenting a laundered, indeed fraudulent, view of the Soviet Union was motivated by American patriotic necessity: the need to convince a recalcitrant public that the Soviets were worthy of support in order to protect the national interest. Thus the personal political views of a particular screenwriter or director were of no consequence. Indeed, whether the Soviet Union was, on balance, an attractive or repulsive country was irrelevant as well. What mattered was American national interest, the need to present the demands of realpolitik in a manner conducive to public acceptance and support: the Communist as patriot thesis.

This argument, although obviously self-serving, is not without force and deserves consideration. It was given its classical defense by Koch, who was central to Hollywood's depiction of the Soviet-Polish relationship and was probably the most pilloried of the screenwriters after the war because of his work on the most outrageous example of the genre, *Mission to Moscow*. Koch argued in 1947 that Hollywood was seeking films in 1942 "of the character" of *Mission to Moscow* to "aid the war effort" because the "Allied cause was in desperate jeopardy and it was vital that Russia should withstand Hitler's mighty attack." As a result, "the issue was then trembling in the balance" and the Russian defensive efforts were "desperate." Hence Hollywood sought stories—including Davies's memoirs—"to aid the war effort." This had nothing to do with Communism, or even sympathy for Communism, but was prompted by the "necessity to beat Hitler." Hence "it was vital to civilization and to ourselves that Russia should be kept fighting and that anything that could be done to sustain their morale, their courage, and their fighting, was a service to the war effort and deserved support."[51]

This is the best defense Hollywood can offer for its ideologically engaged films of the war era, far surpassing the pathetic excuses offered by a floundering Jack Warner before Congress in 1947. The Koch argument adroitly avoids the need to defend the film's content by stressing what motivated it by pleading obedience to a higher necessity—in essence, by arguing that the end justified the means. By dangling Hitler before our eyes as the ultimate evil, he asks us to accept all actions that might have exorcised him as justifiable, or at least excusable.

Actually, much of this argument must be constructed by inference. We must discard the pathetic remarks about the need to sustain Russians' morale by making pleasant films about them. Obviously, the ability of an American film to affect Russian military efforts directly is zero. Koch was doubtlessly speaking in symbols when he suggests that the Soviets' ability to defend themselves was directly dependent on material support from the United States. This support could conceivably have been curtailed if public opinion were so hostile to the Soviets as to pressure Washington to desist. Hence creating and sustaining a sympathetic disposition toward the Soviet Union among the American public was a necessary precondition for Washington's material support of Stalin, which, in turn, was necessary to prevent a German victory. This theory presumes that the public was, or would have been, anti-Soviet were it not for a concerted attempt to "sell" the Kremlin, an argument that Koch did not offer but that did appear during the war from the American political Left and probably reflected Koch's views as well.

This theory rests on a series of dubious assumptions. The first is that the public was hostile to the Soviets before 1941. American support for the Russian war effort against Germany was, however, as we have seen, overwhelmingly widespread even before Pearl Harbor. The second is that an honest portrayal of the Soviet Union would drive the public into organized mass indignation, which would manifest itself in concerted action to prevent Washington's support for the Soviet war effort. The third is that, in the face of this public pressure, the administration could do nothing to explain the necessity of its policy but would immediately curtail material aid to the Soviets. The fourth is that the Soviets, in the face of diminished American support, would collapse. This calculation of the consequences of American support for the Soviet war effort is exaggerated, and, moreover, it rests on a careless or perhaps purposively misleading use of chronology.[52] The Soviet defense that Koch mentions as so vital to the survival of human freedom occurred in the last half of 1941. *Mission to Moscow* was released in May 1943. *In Our Time,* doubtlessly another misunderstood piece of Koch's patriotic war service, was released in February 1944. By these late dates, the possibility of a Soviet collapse under German blows was implausible, and American support was certainly not necessary to prevent a Russian defeat.

Although pro-Russian films released in 1943 or 1944 could not possibly save Russia and Western civilization in 1941, they could facilitate Soviet Russian imperial ambitions after 1943. It is here that the question of Poland is posed most acutely. Presenting Poland in a bad light could not possibly be covered under the "higher patriotic duty" argument of Koch and company. The Russian war effort was not in any way dependent on Americans' thinking that the pre-1939 Polish government was a band of reactionary friends of fascism or that Polish Americans were an obscure community of misfits and incompetents requiring extended processing before becoming fit company for Irish, Italian, and Jewish Americans.

Inculcating a negative image of the Poles among the American public would be useful only in undermining Polish efforts to defend the nation's sovereignty and territory from Soviet imperialism. By presenting the Poles in America as a phantom presence of no discernible characteristics whose major attributes are bad judgment and limited intellect, Hollywood also weakened the ability of the Polish community in America to present the Polish cause before a public prepared to give it a respectful hearing. If the Koch defense is implausible in exculpating him for producing mendacious propaganda regarding Russia, it is completely unable to explain why he, and so many of his colleagues, wrote such nasty things about the Poles.

Hollywood was only too happy to cooperate with the OWI and its mission to sell Russia, ignoring or denigrating Poland in the process.[53] The powerful influence of left-wing politics in Hollywood at the time made the task far easier, as Washington's policy toward Soviet Russia conveniently matched the ideological predilections of the political Left. The OWI and the Left in Hollywood became natural allies during the war. Indeed, as Saverio Giovacchini notes, the OWI's preferences were virtually identical to the Left's agenda in the 1930s, what he calls the "Hollywood paradigm."[54] The first principle for the OWI was, "Will this picture help win the war," which could be and was easily translated to, Does this film promote the cause of American-Soviet friend-ship?[55] Cooperation between Hollywood and Washington regarding the Russian issue was effortless because the studios, without prompting, decided "not to make anti-Russian films." Probably the first, and cer-tainly the last, Hollywood film to criticize the Soviet Union was the low-budget *Ski Patrol,* released in May 1940, which depicted the brutal Russian invasion of Finland. It was soon withdrawn from distribution. There are no Hollywood depictions of the Russian invasion of Poland, the seizure of the Baltics or Bessarabia, the brutality of Soviet occupa-tion, the wholesale deportation of entire communities, or many other themes difficult to comport with the celluloid celebration of the Soviets. The extraordinary phenomenon of Hollywood's submitting its efforts to the Russian embassy in Washington for approval has been noted ear-lier. Even more significant, as Melvin Small observes, is that Moscow was delighted: "The absence of any major criticism [by the embassy] . . . indicates official Russian approval of the way Hollywood portrayed the Soviet Union." Small notes that Russia was "well served by Hol-lywood," a fact demonstrated by Moscow's desire to award medals to several key Hollywood figures.[56]

James E. and Sara T. Combs summarize the matter well when they write that pro-Soviet films, "made with the tacit encouragement of the wartime government and its propaganda agencies," formed "a coopera-tive government-industry venture."[57] Because Hollywood's goal was to "reinvent the Soviet Union," the Polish issue had to be presented in a way that did not raise awkward questions about the nature and behavior of a regime that Hollywood was busy tarting up for public approval.[58]

Hollywood's unflattering presentation of Poland was further en-hanced by contemporary commentary on the films. The *New York Times'* Bosley Crowther played the key role. Crowther became the *Times'* main film critic in 1940, and he held that position for more than a quarter of a century. He rapidly became very powerful; indeed, Gerald Perry argues that Crowther may have been the most influential film critic in his-tory.[59] Crowther's clumsily written and intellectually puerile film judg-ments were distinctly leftist and pro-Soviet Russia. His most damning criticism was reserved for films that were, in style or content, what he regarded as old-fashioned. To his discredit, Crowther was delighted by the OWI's intrusiveness into Hollywood films, as he thought the war justified more government direction of the industry: free speech (a "not

particularly valid" question relative to films, Crowther noted) was subordinated to what he saw as an opportunity to cease "making mistakes
which arise from a way of thinking that belongs to another world."[60]

Crowther's reviews are instructive. He did not like *To Be or Not
to Be,* finding it tasteless, which may well be true.[61] But concerning
the portrayal of Polish or Jewish characters or the political implications of the film, he had nothing to say. As for the somewhat later *In
Our Time,* Crowther's views were more complex. The film was slow,
verbose, and—horror of horrors—old-fashioned. These criticisms were
exclusively directed at matters of technique and narration. The performances were also not to his liking. As for the content of the story, there
was nothing wrong with the film's politics; it was just boring because it
was about Poland, which was "stale."[62] That the film was an indictment
of the Polish government at a critical moment in the war went unnoted
by Crowther. Of course, the film's characterization of Poland as "medieval" and filled with bloviating aristocrats was a standard canard of the
pro-Soviet Left. The British government was much more conspicuously
staffed with titled aristocrats, yet class differences in British society,
when mentioned at all by Hollywood, where dismissed as a minor remnant of the past of no real importance, a sort of charming anachronism.
Here we may mention *Mrs. Miniver* or the 1941 Twentieth Century–
Fox production *A Yank in the R.A.F.* as examples.[63] Polish aristocrats are
social exploiters; English aristocrats are delightful ornaments.

Although Crowther did not find it necessary to say anything
about the Poles' sacrifices or military contributions in reviewing films
on Polish subjects, this was not a binding aesthetic restraint. When
his attention turned to films about Russia, the critic's judgment was
informed—indeed, overwhelmed—by political considerations. Hence
Mission to Moscow was "the most outspoken picture on a political subject that an American studio has ever made." The film's presentation of
the Moscow trials, in which the accused, all quite innocent, are made
to appear cunning traitors, was fine for Crowther, who noted sarcastically that "so-called Trotskyites" might object. Crowther praised this
embarrassing paean to Stalin as constituting "a valuable influence to
more clear-eyed and searching thought," as it exhibited "boldness" in
"understanding Russia's point of view."[64]

This was not the worst. *Song of Russia,* described by Bernard F.
Dick as "Russomania. . . . a Stalinist tract written by Communist writers

Paul Jarrico and Richard Collins, with propaganda taking precedence even over the plight of a besieged nation," was introduced to American audiences by a giddy Crowther this way: "Prepare yourself for a surprise folks—an exciting surprise." It was "a honey of a . . . film full of rare good humor, and vitality, and a proper respect for the Russians' fight in this war."[65] However, a Russian émigré, reacting to this portrayal of the Soviet regime, remarked, "It made me sick."[66]

Politics became everything when Crowther turned to the wretched *The North Star,* the film written by Lillian Hellman that begins like a frothy operetta, complete with happy peasants singing lustily, only later to descend into bathos when passionately patriotic Soviets defy all odds in resisting the Germans. Crowther does not notice that the film is set in Ukraine, where Soviet rule brought great misery and uncountable deaths. Crowther blithely described this grossly dishonest portrayal of Soviet Russia as "without any political pondering [*sic*] at all." He noted with satisfaction that it premiered simultaneously at two theaters—"an honor accorded to only a few previous films"—but this was only proper, as it was a tribute to those "resisting the Fascist hordes" and hence was "a heroic picture." After having written so much nonsense, Crowther concluded, with perhaps a trace of bad conscience (along with odd syntax), "*The North Star* has so much in it that is moving and triumphant that its sometimes departures from reality may be generally overlooked."[67]

Capra's *Why We Fight* episode devoted to Russia, *The Battle of Russia,* moved Crowther to rhapsodies of praise; that it was mendacious and manipulative was of no consequence.[68] Crowther praised films about Russia for depicting the Russians positively, even if they stoop to distortion and misrepresentation in the effort. Films about Poland, by contrast, need not portray the Poles in any way at all, even when they resisted "Fascist hordes." Whatever ill use Poland received from Hollywood was exacerbated by Crowther's engagé ruminations.

Crowther's opinions were damaging to Polish interests in the United States, especially because there was no countervailing voice in the major papers. In general, film critics had little or nothing to say about the Polish aspects of films because the issue almost never arose. Regarding the few films that do focus on Poland, the overwhelming majority of reviews found the negative impression of Poland either accurate or unremarkable. I have been unable to find a single major review that criticized any wartime Hollywood film for portraying Poland or the Poles harshly.

Quite apart from Washington's predilections and the complimentary pro-Soviet Hollywood radicalism abetted by such cheerleaders as Crowther, there was no serious impediment in Hollywood to a negative portrayal of Poland.[69] No prominent director, screenwriter, or producer was Polish; there were no major stars of Polish descent. The absence of actors of Polish origin from the films we have noted reflects this dearth of Polish talent available in Hollywood.

Many of the creative forces behind the films we have noted were Jewish émigrés from Eastern Europe.[70] Given the prominent Jewish role in wartime Hollywood, this is a factor of moment, and this theme has been the subject of a number of important studies.[71] The screenwriter Julius Epstein noted that the Jewish presence was so powerful that even gentiles in Hollywood were "Jewish" in thought.[72]

Given the increasing anti-Semitism in Polish life after the late nineteenth century, especially in the years after 1919, it is more than understandable that these Jewish refugees from anti-Semitism would not have much cause for sympathy toward Poland. A number of studies note the linkage among Jewish filmmakers between profound American patriotism and rejection of their European origins. Alan Spiegel describes the complex interplay of attachment to Jewishness, scorn for their Eastern European past, and gratitude to the United States: Studio moguls "never ignored their Judaism, [but] hastened to underscore their allegiance to national ideals in preference to immigrant roots. This they did both as a gesture of gratitude . . . and as a strategy for outflanking their numerous anti-Semitic critics." They knew how to "smother Jew-baiters in a conciliatory bearhug of appreciation, loyalty, and frantic flag-waving."[73]

It is quite obvious that, long before the Second World War, Jewish Americans, many of Polish origin, regarded their ancestral homeland as particularly anti-Semitic. Neal Gabler notes that, for the Eastern Europeans of Jewish origin in Hollywood, "what united them in deep spiritual kinship was their utter and absolute rejection of their pasts."[74] Screenwriter Albert Maltz was convinced that it was characteristic of the children of Jewish émigrés like him to know absolutely nothing of their family's Polish past.[75] Fellow screenwriter and Communist Walter Bernstein, who also traced his origins to Eastern Europe, had no idea where his family came from: "No one was exactly sure."[76] John Howard

Lawson's autobiography notes that his grandparents "escaped from a Polish ghetto" and nothing more.[77] Jack and Harry Warner could not or would not disclose their original family name even to their children.[78] Hal Wallis, the producer, "did not wish his past known" and also did not admit his original name. His family was from historical northeastern Poland, but he, like many others, had "purged the past."[79] Phillip Roth has named this phenomenon "willful amnesia."[80] Anzia Yezierska speaks of the Polish Jews as having "uprooted themselves" on leaving Poland and the old world "dead behind us."[81]

Almost all of the major Hollywood studios during World War II were headed by Jewish immigrants to America or their children, the single exception being Darryl F. Zanuck at Twentieth Century–Fox. The degree to which these studio bosses were responsible for the content of their films varied, but in all cases it was significant. Of the several films that feature Polish issues, only a few were directed by Jewish émigrés. However, the writing staff responsible for the stories was heavily Jewish: the Epstein twins, Hellman, Lawson, Kober, Rossen, Swerling, Litvak, Cole, Lubitsch, St. Joseph, and Mayer, among others. This is of moment because Poland and the Poles enjoyed very low esteem in Jewish eyes in the years preceding World War II.

The origins of this unfortunate situation are complex, and it is striking that the story of Polish-Jewish relations in America has not yet been told. The Polish state, which reappeared on the map in 1918, was immediately surrounded by controversy over the status of its very large Jewish population. Poland was engaged in a series of military encounters in its first years, of which the most important was the Polish-Bolshevik War of 1919–1921, a major encounter. During hostilities, reports were widely circulated in the West of pogroms erupting near the front lines. These accounts disturbed American Jewry, which became convinced that Poland was overwhelmingly hostile to its Jewish population. Although these reports were later proven to be greatly exaggerated, it was too late to undo the damage. Relations between the Polish and Jewish communities in the United States were infrequent and generally unpleasant. For Poles the reborn homeland was a source of pride; for many Jewish Americans, especially those of Polish origin, it was a place of unpleasant memories, which, once restored, had proven unfriendly to its minorities, including over 3 million Jews. Hence the two communities were driven even further apart, and the mistrust has proven lasting. For Christian Poles, Jews were all Communists; for Jews, Christian Poles were all anti-Semites. This is not a relationship; it is a disaster. The ghastly developments of World War II exacerbated this already unfortunate situation.

In general, American public opinion cared little for Poland in the interwar era. Far away, exotic, and relatively insignificant in international diplomacy, Poland failed to become a major market for American products or locus of investment. The international Left despised the Poles as the enemy of Soviet Russia that had defeated Communist expansion at the gates of Warsaw in 1920. Not surprisingly, Moscow regarded Poland as an implacable reactionary presence, at least a nuisance, if not a threat. Contrariwise, Germany, both before and after Hitler came to power, was inveterately anti-Polish, as it saw that country as unfairly occupying historically German lands. Hence there were powerful forces arrayed against the creation of a good image for Poland. Other than the Polish community in the United States, which was poor and relatively powerless, there were few sources of support for Poland here. The Catholic Church in general was well inclined toward heavily Catholic Poland, but in the United States, the church was dominated by the Irish, who regarded the Poles as, at worst, rivals for domination of the hierarchy and, at best, naive recent arrivals to be manipulated in both urban politics and church affairs. It is little wonder that American Poles felt themselves under enormous pressure to Americanize. The consequences of this, of course, were to weaken still more what little resources Poland could marshal in the United States.

The Christian Poles in America came to see their Jewish fellow citizens as enemies, dedicated to denigrating Poland on the international scene and maligning them domestically. Hollywood, where Jewish executives and writers were influential, was thus profoundly mistrusted. Conversely, the relative indifference of the major studios to Polish aggravations is quite understandable. First, the Poles were not sufficiently powerful to make their complaints meaningful. Second, the great bulk of the American people almost certainly did not understand, let alone share, Polish complaints. Third, and perhaps most important for many of the Hollywood Jewish community, Polish complaints merely indicated that they were anti-Semites, and hence their grievances were unworthy of consideration. Maja Trochimczyk's recent study finds that Polish Jews in Hollywood, even those completely assimilated to Polish culture and accustomed to describing themselves as Poles, largely dropped their Polish attachments after a period in Hollywood and emphasized their Jewish origins, even when they had previously largely ignored them. Being Polish in Hollywood was simply not convenient.[82]

In the midst of the Holocaust, Jewish Americans were understandably sensitive to anti-Semitism. Director de Toth recalled that the first time he met Columbia's Harry Cohn, the only question he was asked was, "Are you a Nazi?"—a memorable introduction almost certainly provoked by the fact that de Toth was Hungarian.[83] Given Poles' foul reputation regarding Jewish issues, it is reasonable to assume that Jews instinctively were suspicious of and disinclined toward Poles. Increasing anti-Semitism in certain political factions in Poland in the years before the war doubtlessly exacerbated this disposition. Here, however, direct evidence is virtually nonexistent. There were few Poles in Hollywood to record their impressions, and it is unreasonable to assume that a studio head would admit his private disquiet in writing. Besides, a dislike of Poland was not, ultimately, a policy; it was a feeling, a disposition, something too vague to be expressed in a few words. Many of the Hollywood figures of Jewish origin were understandably temperamentally disinclined toward Poland.

The powerful presence of Jewish Americans in Hollywood did not ipso facto make films anti-Polish; indeed, the very fact that there were so few films about Poland indicates quite clearly that they were not obsessed with the Poles. More, despite recent works that emphasize the uniformity of the Jewish community in the film industry, there was no "Jewish opinion" that operated as normative.[84] They were as variegated as any other ethnic minority in the country, perhaps more so. However, that Poland enjoyed very low esteem among the Jews of America seems beyond dispute. For Jewish Americans, the late 1930s meant the rise of fascism and the threat of militant state-sponsored anti-Semitism. By comparison Poland was a minor and derivative issue. Certainly there was no conspiracy against Poland or the Poles. Rather, what we notice is the creation of a climate of opinion, created by several mutually reinforcing factors.

The political Left was traditionally hostile to Poland. The war, which made the Soviet Union perforce an American ally, made the traditional geopolitical predilections of the Left temporarily powerful. This was especially true because the Roosevelt administration's foreign policy shared the same view of the realities of international politics after 1941. Hence, Jewish aversion to Poland would be encouraged by powerful political forces. The Hollywood mentality was singularly disinclined to defend Polish interests. Hence the films reflected an atmosphere in which the Poles were regarded as at best inconsequential and at worst an enemy of both progressive forces and the Jewish people.

Ironically, the sensitivity of executives and writers of Jewish origin in the Hollywood world to any discussion of the Holocaust indirectly but significantly damaged the Polish cause in the United States. The annihilation of Europe's Jewry, one of the great dramas of modern history, was virtually ignored by the film industry. This was the result of enormous pressure from the Roosevelt administration, particularly the OWI, which did not want the issue of anti-Semitism emphasized in any discussion of the war. Moreover, for most of those of Jewish origin in Hollywood, this was a difficult issue, as they were reluctant to do anything to make the war seem an attempt to protect the Jews.[85] Joseph I. Breen of the Production Code office reminded studios that anti-Semitism was popular in the United States as a hint that Jewish themes in films not be emphasized.[86] As Antony Polonsky reveals, repeated polls between 1938 and 1940 showed "60 per cent [of Americans] . . . thought that Jews had objectionable qualities." Indeed "in 1938 20 per cent wanted to 'drive the Jews out of the United States.' In 1939, 31.9 per cent thought Jews had excessive power in the business world and that 'something should be done about this'; 10.1 per cent thought Jews should be deported. In 1940–1, 17 to 20 per cent of the population saw the Jews as a menace to the United States. . . . 12 to 15 per cent were ready to support a general anti-Semitic campaign. . . . Antisemitism in America actually increased during the war."[87] A bill in Congress designed to admit Jewish refugees in 1938 proved most unpopular and died aborning.[88] In 1946 only 5 percent of Americans supported admitting Holocaust survivors into the country; the great majority wished to curtail if not terminate the Jewish immigration to the United States.[89] Moreover, American anti-Semitism had characteristically attacked Hollywood as a favorite target in denouncing Jewish power in the country.[90]

These facts explain the trepidation that Harry Cohn and Samuel Bischoff of Columbia had about *None Shall Escape,* which was, essentially, a proto-Holocaust film presenting a microscopic mise-en-scène of the annihilation.[91] Any depiction of Poland during the war could not avoid mentioning the systematic destruction of its Jewish population. Even the few Polish films Hollywood did produce have only muted references to the Holocaust. The suffering of Greenberg in *To Be or Not to Be* is a symbolic reminder of the Jewish plight; the haunting scene of incarcerated Warsaw Jews in the otherwise insignificant *Once upon a Honeymoon* evokes the first stages of the segregation of the Jews preceding extermination. To speak of occupied Poland is to speak of the Holocaust. Hollywood's Jewish community understood this, as did the Roosevelt administration.[92] In 1943 a survey of studio heads found that they did not wish to make films specifically about Jewish suffering. It would constitute "making *rishis*" and would raise the specter of the public's regarding the struggle as a "Jewish war."[93]

Ignoring or minimizing Poland was thus a shared goal of a number of overlapping interest groups. The Roosevelt administration's OWI did not want Poland mentioned because it raised the issue of Soviet behavior during the war and its expansionist foreign policy, which made Washington's support for the Soviets an awkward public issue. The political Left had regarded Poland as a topic best forgotten ever since the 1939 Hitler-Stalin pact. For many in the Hollywood Jewish community a film about Poland inevitably implied some discussion of German anti-Semitism, which it was under considerable pressure to avoid. Jewish leftists supportive of FDR thus had many, mutually reinforcing motives that explain their reluctance to raise Polish issues. If Poland could absolutely not be avoided, it was to be presented in a manner calculated to garner the least public sympathy. Poland was a dangerous topic for many powerful interests in wartime Hollywood.[94]

Who ultimately would be served by a sympathetic treatment of Poland? The Polish government-in-exile was, after 1943, virtually abandoned by Washington. By 1944 Poland itself was substantially under Soviet occupation. Raising issues that suggested Poland was a good cause would make the Soviet Union's status ambiguous, whereas most Americans preferred to regard it as an unalloyed good. It was only after the war that doubts as to the virtues of the Soviets became widely expressed. By that time, however, Poland was a "captive nation," deserving only inefficacious pity.

The most relentless source of anti-Polish propaganda in wartime Hollywood was the Warner Brothers studio. It was Warner Brothers that was responsible for the vicious *In Our Time;* it was Warner Brothers that presented the Polish misfits Pulaski in *Action in the North Atlantic* and Winocki in *Air Force* and the slatternly Nazi camp follower Katja in *Edge of Darkness,* which also included a racial degenerate "Slav" serving in the German army. This is to say nothing of the studio's execrable *Mission to Moscow.*

The Warners were of Polish origin; Krasnosielc, their native village, is perhaps fifty miles north of Warsaw in the region of Mazowsze in Russian Poland.[95] The area is predominantly agricultural but heavily forested and known for its natural beauty. Krasnosielc is even today quite small and remote, enjoying an isolated existence, as it did when the Warners' ancestors lived there late in the nineteenth century. At that time the partition frontier, where German territory met the Russian empire, was nearby, only a few miles north of Krasnosielc. Records of the town's population are few and fragmentary, but it is clear that there was a substantial Jewish presence locally, perhaps two-thirds of the population of approximately one thousand by the late nineteenth century.

The family's original name was almost certainly not "Warner," but beyond that little is known. In 1937 *Forbes* magazine described the head of the family as "a Polish farmer who emigrated in 1883 in search of religious freedom," a most unhelpful summary.[96] Ben, apparently a cobbler and not a farmer, and wife Pearl (née Eichelbaum) Warner migrated first to London, Ontario, where their most famous child, Jack, was born before settling in Youngstown, Ohio. Jack Warner later recalled that what his father told him of Poland, "while not entirely secretive, could not be called informative or enthusiastic." Jack's memoirs describe a scene of poverty and primitiveness where his father was "barred by the Russians from going to school because he was a Jew." The Jews in Krasnosielc, he continued, lived in a "ghetto" and were forced to learn of Judaism surreptitiously, hiding in cemeteries and running great risks, under perpetual threat from the police. When Ben Warner came to America, he "closed the door on Krasnashiltz [Krasnosielc], and never went back," Jack noted meaningfully.[97]

Jack seems to have had a rather ambiguous attitude regarding his Polish origins. His paternal recollections are all negative and fanciful. The only Poles mentioned in Jack's memoirs are a "nitwit" who lied to his father, "a big muscle-bound Polock named Herman Nowitzky," and the owner of an unspeakably foul restaurant. But Jack also writes about Poland as a "proud old country" and quotes someone as referring to "Polocks like you" when addressing him.[98]

Other Warners do not seem to have cultivated positive feelings regarding their ancestral homeland. Indeed, they speak of suffering repeated "pogroms" before departing for America. Harry's daughter, for example, noted recently that her father "loved being in America, away from the frequent pogroms against Jews in his native Poland."[99] Biographies speak of "Polish police" preventing the Warner family from even studying the Torah.[100] There were, however, no "ghettos" in late-nineteenth-century Russian Poland. Moreover, the tsarist state was certainly unpleasant to its Jewish citizens, but it lacked the ability or devotion necessary to prevent the huge population of historical Poland from reading scripture. The reference to Polish police is disturbing, as no Poland then existed; the police were agents of the Russian, not Polish, government. Hence this would seem to represent less a memory than a subsequent reconstruction. In addition, although ethnic and religious antagonism in the western borderlands of the tsarist state was common in the late nineteenth century, to suggest frequent "pogroms" is inaccurate. Regardless of the details of these putative episodes, the fact that the family would recall them in this manner makes it clear that they regarded their life in Poland as dangerous and unhappy. Significantly, it is the Poles, co-victims of Russian oppression, who are seemingly blamed for the unhappy lot of the family, rather than the Russians. Poland became for the Warners a foul place in which the Poles denied Jews religious freedom and subjected them to constant persecution.

Harry, Jack's older brother, born in Krasnosielc, supposedly never mentioned his childhood in Europe, and the whole issue was regarded as a family taboo.[101] Jack later claimed that he later met other "people who were born in Poland and later made their name—Nijinsky, Sholem Asch, Paderewski, Marie Curie, David Ben-Gurion, Artur Rubinstein," but when he met "these Polish immortals . . . I never spoke to them of our past or theirs. . . . I did not want to know."[102] During the war, Harry christened a ship bearing his father's name. In the interest of Allied unity, he might well have mentioned that his family came from Poland. Instead, Harry's only mention of his family's origin was a reference to "oppression."[103]

Harry told the Census Bureau in 1930 that his father and mother were both born in Poland and that the language at home in his childhood was Polish. Younger brother Jack, however, told the Census Bureau in 1920 that his parents' first language was German (he probably meant Yiddish) and that their place of birth was Russia. Older brother Harry at least acknowledged that his parents were Jewish immigrants from Poland; Jack, it seems, tried to erase that reality.[104]

Harry was devout and observant; by contrast, his youngest brother Jack was impatient with religious instruction and was a dedicated assimilationist, even marrying a gentile.[105] Both, however, generously supported Wilshire Boulevard Temple in Los Angeles, as well as Jewish charities. Their support for these grew markedly after Hitler's rise to power.[106] Jack may have been casual about religious observation, but he was serious about loyalty to what his son called "tribal memories." He was very active in Jewish causes.[107] Alvah Bessie recalled an extraordinary story about Jack's insistence that all his Jewish employees donate a percentage of their income to the United Jewish Welfare Fund:

> During a fund-raising drive, he would call them into the studio commissary.
>
> When we were all assembled . . . Warner marched in and—to our astonishment—brandished a rubber truncheon, which had probably been a prop for one of the anti-Nazi pictures we were making. He stood behind his table and smashed the length of rubber hose on the wood, and then he smiled and said, "I've been looking at the results of the Jewish Appeal drive, and believe you me, it ain't good." Here he paused for effect and said, "Everybody's gonna double his contribution here and now—or else!" The rubber truncheon crashed on the table again as everybody present . . . reached for our checkbooks.[108]

The Warners also were at pains to produce films that dramatized Jewish triumphs over prejudice and adversity, such as *Disraeli* (1929); the indirect account of the Dreyfus Affair, *The Life of Emile Zola* (1937); *Dr. Ehrlich's Magic Bullet* (1940); and *A Dispatch from Reuters* (1940). Just before the war, Warner Brothers produced a short film biography of the Polish Jew Haym Solomon, born in Leszno, who was an important financier of the American Revolution. The film manages to avoid any

mention of either Kościuszko or Pułaski, two of Solomon's countrymen who served the American cause at the same time and belonged to
the same circle.[109] Some argue that Solomon is to be understood as a
symbol for Harry Warner.[110] Later Warner Brothers films devoted to the
war feature attractive Jewish characters such as George Tobias's Weinberg in *Air Force,* Sam Levene's Abrams in *Action in the North Atlantic,* and S. Z. Sakall's Karl, the lovable head waiter, in *Casablanca.*
Ethan Mordden deems Warner Brothers "the only studio with a Jewish
identity."[111]

Despite his seeming indifference to traditional Judaism, Jack was
obviously intent on defending and promoting the Jewish image in the
United States. This reached, on occasion, rather extreme lengths. He
even pressured Twentieth Century–Fox's Darryl F. Zanuck to include
some reference to the putative Jewish ancestry of the Roman Catholic and ethnically Irish brothers whose death in action is portrayed in
The Fighting Sullivans. Zanuck was appalled and refused to insert such
awkward references, which he deemed "crude propaganda." He lectured his erstwhile boss about manufactured Jewish characters' being
inserted at random in films.[112]

Although the Warners are often portrayed as ardent supporters of
FDR during the war, their involvement in politics was erratic. Certainly
their early interest in issues of social justice would associate them with
the progressive Left. However, until at least 1928, the Warners seemed
to be rather conventional Republicans.[113] In 1932, however, for reasons
that are not quite clear, Harry suddenly decided to champion Roosevelt
and virtually ordered Jack to follow his lead.[114] This was a whirlwind
courtship. Harry was invited to the White House in 1933 in gratitude
for the brothers' campaign support in the presidential election, and he
reciprocated by making generous financial donations to Roosevelt's
Warm Springs Foundation.[115] Jack even asserted that FDR offered him
a diplomatic post which, typically, Jack summarized as his becoming
"the first Jewish ambassador to Ireland."[116]

This shift to the Democrats was rather short-lived, however. In
1934–1935, Harry was indicted for violation of the Sherman Antitrust
Act. He appealed to Roosevelt, assuming he would be able to use his
support in the election to induce presidential intervention. When that did
not happen, he bitterly denounced FDR for faithlessness and became,
in his daughter's words, "a staunch Republican."[117] Harry's reversion to

the GOP, or at least absence from politics, lasted until 1940, when his indictment was quashed.[118] Whether Jack followed Harry into this brief revolt is unclear. By 1940, however, the Warners were again solidly backing FDR, a disposition that lasted throughout the war and became steadily more intimate.

Jack had followed Harry's lead and indeed seemed to pursue a personal relationship with Roosevelt with vigor. By 1940, he presumed to sign birthday missives to FDR "your friends . . . Ann and Jack Warner."[119] He peppered the president with cards and telegrams on holidays and congratulated him effusively on various successes. Jack was duly invited to the 1941 inauguration, which Harry took to be an invitation to the studio to proffer strategic advice concerning the war in Europe.[120] Hence, in July 1941, Harry suggested the United States should "man the island," by which he meant Great Britain—a gambit he modestly admitted was "only a suggestion."[121]

Jack was a guest at the White House repeatedly over the war years and frequently asked for meetings with Roosevelt, as did Harry in mid-1942 to discuss the "greater utilization" of films in the war effort.[122] Jack explained the production of *Mission to Moscow* and *Air Force* as "morale and inspirational" films, which constituted Warner Brothers' direct contribution to the war effort. Jack specifically urged Roosevelt to see *Action in the North Atlantic* and *Mission to Moscow,* though he warned Roosevelt that "Trotskyites" disliked the latter, as though Jack would know a Trotskyite from a stalactite.[123] Whether Roosevelt ever viewed the films is unknown, but the tone of the correspondence was certainly most warm, with FDR addressing Warner as "dear Jack."[124] Jack later boasted, "I had a personal friendship with [FDR] any man would envy."[125]

Harry, obviously the more serious student of public affairs, made the studio's decisions regarding politics, both international and domestic. Jack's political views were unsophisticated at best. He was legendarily vulgar and ignorant—some sources insist that he was only marginally literate.[126] A 1942 anecdote is most revealing. Warner was asked to hire Bessie, then a Communist Party member, but refused because Bessie was "a red." However, when he was lectured by a friend of Bessie's that "those goddamn reds are saving your fucking moving-picture business on the Stalingrad front tonight," Warner hired Bessie for triple what he was asking and brought him to Hollywood.[127]

Perhaps the most valuable insight into Jack Warner's political credo can be gained from the virtually incoherent testimony he made on October 20, 1947, before the House Committee on Un-American Activities. Obviously frightened—a longtime employee described him as "cowardly"[128]—Warner, "windy, stuttering, obsequious," began with a ringing peroration pledging his support in ferreting out Communists in the country.[129] He then dismissed as "fantasy" the accusation that the White House had pressured his studio to make *Mission to Moscow* in 1942, a charge he specifically admitted later. However, it is in his responses to committee investigator Robert Stripling that Warner's explanations for the ideological content of his studio's wartime films become incomprehensible:

STRIPLING: Now, when the picture *Mission to Moscow* was made, were you aware that there were certain historical events which were erroneously portrayed in the picture?

WARNER: I told you, I don't know if it was all correct or not. . . .

STRIPLING: Here is a picture, however, which portrayed Russia and the Government of Russia in an entirely different light from what it actually was?

WARNER: I don't know if you can prove it, or that I can prove that it was . . .

STRIPLING: Well, is it your opinion now, Mr. Warner, that *Mission to Moscow* was a factually correct picture, and that you made it as such?

WARNER: I can't remember.

STRIPLING: Would you consider it a propaganda picture?

WARNER: A propaganda picture—

STRIPLING: Yes.

WARNER: In what sense?

STRIPLING: In the sense that it portrayed Russia and communism in an entirely different light from what it actually was?

WARNER: I am on record about 40 times or more that I have never been in Russia. I don't know what Russia was like in 1937 or 1944 or 1947, so how can I tell you if it was right or wrong?

STRIPLING: Don't you think you were on dangerous ground to produce as a factually correct picture one which portrayed Russia—

WARNER: No; we were not on dangerous ground in 1942, when we
    produced it. There was a war on. The world was at stake . . .
STRIPLING: Well, do you suppose that your picture influenced the
    people who saw it in this country, the millions of people who
    saw it in this country?
WARNER: In my opinion, I can't see how it would influence
    anyone.[130]

Essentially, Warner said that he had no idea what the ideological content
and historical accuracy of his films were, but, if they were propaganda,
it would be forgivable because of wartime necessity, and, ultimately,
what difference did it make because no one cared anyway. Although
this colloquy referred specifically to *Mission to Moscow,* by extension
it applies to all Warner Brothers' wartime films: We had no idea what
we were doing; what we were doing was motivated by patriotism, and
it ultimately did not matter; hence all is excusable.[131]

    Yet these arguments specifically contradict the Warner Brothers stu-
dio policy well established before the war. Harry, as we have seen, consciously employed the studio to further ideological ends and regarded
cinema as an unusually efficacious means for public education. In a
statement before the Senate in late September 1941, Harry had boasted
that Warner Brothers had been "producing pictures on current affairs for
over 20 years" and that all such films were "carefully researched" and
"accurate" and that they "show the world as it is." Moreover, in contrast
to Jack's claim that the contents of the pictures were irrelevant because
they were without influence, Harry noted that his films were designed
to present the American public with "the truth" concerning "what is
happening in the world."[132] In other words, Harry said the studio was in
the business of influencing taste and opinion, made studied efforts to do
so, and stood by its results.[133] Michael Birdwell, a sympathetic student
of Warner Brothers, concludes that the studio consciously attempted to
"influence foreign policy."[134] Accepting Jack's 1947 statement would
require us to conclude that the studio discarded its 1941 policy immediately after Harry enunciated it and began the capricious production of
films regarding "current affairs" without concern for research or accuracy. Harry stood by his films in 1941; Jack ran from them in altered
circumstances in 1947.

    Indeed, only a few months before his testimony, Jack had expatiated on the function of film to address important themes and not just entertain; now that notion was inconvenient.[135] Simply put, Harry's policy statement made Warner Brothers' wartime films very awkward for Jack in 1947, as he would have to admit that the studio either knowingly produced pro-Soviet propaganda or recklessly distributed films without due care for their content or effect on the public. Communist Ring Lardner Jr. was absolutely correct when he reflected many years later that the Warners, like other studio heads, "deliberately . . . made movies favorable to the Soviet Union [and after 1945] they were trying to disclaim them."[136]

The Warners had a long history of bad relations with Poland. There seems little doubt that Harry regarded Poland as simply a foul memory. During the 1930s the studio was famous for the production of films of social realism, exposing the less attractive side of contemporary urban America: crime, the penal system, delinquency, poverty. These films often featured criminals and other unsavory characters. In one of these films, *The Life of Jimmy Dolan,* a foul character is named Puławski. In another, *How Many More Knights?* a "gangster and murderer" is named Kościuszko.[137] Warsaw was particularly incensed by the latter film because, at a time when Polish-German relations were quite bad, the Warner Brothers film depicted "the man who rescues Kościuszko's victim [as] a German." The *New York Times* quoted the Polish Ministry of the Interior: "The names Puławski and Kościuszko . . . are dear to every Pole, and the American producers ought to have been aware of this. Since apparently they were not, the Polish government has decided to prohibit not only the two films, but any" other films produced by Warner Brothers and two other companies. As far as Warsaw was concerned, Warner Brothers was guilty of perpetrating a "slur" against the Polish nation and conducting "anti-Polish propaganda."[138]

Although it may appear that Warsaw was overreacting to an insignificant provocation, we must bear in mind that Berlin had been conducting a veritable campaign against Poland for some years, portraying the Poles darkly. It was important to Warsaw, and to the Poles in the United States, that the image of Poland be protected, a cause most Poles regarded as depressingly difficult given the meager resources available.

Studio head Harry Warner reacted by describing the Polish government as "anti-Semitic."[139] Despite this counter, Warner Brothers refilmed portions of the film and later apologized to the Polish government.[140] Harry seems to have been obsessed by anti-Semitism; he kept files on people and organizations he suspected of the sentiment.[141] To give a character a Polish name is quite reasonable, be he positive or negative, but "Pułaski" and "Kościuszko" are not names; they are symbols. They are not references, like "Nowak" or "Kowalski," that would indicate Polish nationality; rather, they represent Poland *tout court,* especially in the United States, where little was known of Poland and few Polish names had any resonance. It would be as though films produced in, say, Nazi Germany in the 1930s had villains named "Lincoln" and "Washington" and the studio claimed that nothing was intended by the references. The government of Poland, in a grave geopolitical situation, needed American support desperately and would understandably be outraged by this needless nastiness by Warner Brothers. To describe such indignation as constituting anti-Semitism discloses the ill will of Warner in his effort to inculpate his accuser. The fact that Warner Brothers would later call another negative character "Pulaski," in 1943's *Action in the North Atlantic,* rather than use the name "Stanisławski" employed in the original text, suggests a willfulness on Warner Brothers' part.

Conclusion

HOLLYWOOD IN WORLD WAR II DISPLAYED a perfect combination for the woeful depiction of Poland. An administration bent on selling Russia found ready allies in a politically left-wing community that tended to regard Poland as a reactionary obstacle to Soviet-American cooperation and the celebration of their ideological convictions. Ceplair and Englund describe the Communist Party screenwriters as forming "an anti-fascist, pro-Russian army."[1] The implications of this are significant: since, to the radical Left, Poland was fascist and opposed Russian designs on its territory and sovereignty by definition, the writers were effectively soldiers campaigning against Poland in Hollywood.

Poland, overrun earlier in the war, with its government living out of suitcases in London, was not in a position to defend robustly its national interests in the United States. Before the war, Warsaw had often lamented the poor image Poland enjoyed in America. After 1939 that sorry heritage became a disaster, as the Poles could offer only the feeblest and most ineffective defense of their own vital interests. The only potential ally of Poland in wartime America was American Polonia, and that proved a very weak reed. The Polish community, though large, was quite poor and still occupied a modest position in American society. Under great pressure to assimilate in the decades before 1939, the Poles in America had conspicuously abandoned the loyalty to the Polish cause that had distinguished their parents' generation. The fact that absolutely no one publicly known as Polish existed in wartime Hollywood discloses both the defensiveness of the Poles in America and their insignificance. American Poles deserve considerable blame for their failure to defend their nationality's reputation more devotedly.

By 1939, it was a tradition in American film to ignore Poland and to treat the Poles in America with disdain or inattention. The brief Hollywood interest in the ethnic mosaic of America was rapidly fading by 1939, and thereafter, national unity in the face of external threat prevented the emergence of a renewed interest in ethnic heterogeneity. The Poles had become diffused into "Eastern Europeans," "Slavs," or "Hunyaks": nothing specific, merely foreign. The Irish had become the only "other" group in America for Hollywood, and only decades later would that situation change with the rise of Italian, Jewish, black, and Hispanic films.

Finally, we must consider the presence of a large and powerful Jewish community in Hollywood for whom Poland was either a blurry memory freighted with familial disapprobation, powerful though inchoate, or an object of resentment. Fascist, reactionary, and later anti-Semitic would be the principal tropes for Poland and the Poles in Hollywood.

There was no conspiracy against Poland in wartime America, in part because none was needed. America, in general, was not concerned with Poland. The Poles in America were insignificant. Hollywood—for whatever reason—had never shown any interest in depicting the Poles. The radical Left in Hollywood saw Poland as an obstacle to selling Russia, as did the Roosevelt administration. The studios had no reason to champion the Poles, whom they either did not know or did not like. Given these facts, it is hard to imagine what could have enlarged or improved Hollywood's portrayal of Poland and the Poles. Poland was simply a theme that had no friends and many enemies. We do not need to find specific evidence of motives to say nasty things or alter scenes; all we need is to remember that there was a powerful anti-Polish disposition and enormous inertia in place to maintain it. And underlying all this tangle of motives was a simple reality: Americans insisted that the war be one in which "the good guys were firmly distinguishable from the bad guys."[2] To make the Russians good, the Poles had to be bad, because if the Russians were bad, the simple moral clarity of the war disappeared. This combination of factors resulted in an episode in American motion picture history that has the dubious distinction of contributing to the American public's rapid abandonment of Poland by maligning a cause that deserved far better.[3]

Notes

Preface

1. The war allowed Communist screenwriter Walter Bernstein to "believe in both Stalin and Roosevelt"—doubtless a grace for an atheist. Walter Bernstein, *Inside Out: A Memoir of the Blacklist* (New York: DaCapo), 1996), 60.

2. Peter Novick, *The Holocaust in American Life* (Boston: Houghton Mifflin, 1999), 85.

Introduction

1. John Whiteclay Chambers II and David Culbert, introduction to *World War II, Film, and History,* ed. John Whiteclay Chambers II and David Culbert (New York: Oxford University Press, 1996), 4. Robert Fyne observed, "Putting aside a few cynics, wags, or eggheads, most viewers readily accepted as gospel what flitted before them on the silver screen." Robert Fyne, *The Hollywood Propaganda of World War II* (Lanham, MD: Scarecrow, 1997), 8. Obviously, it is impossible to prove this assertion.

2. Robert Sklar, *Movie-Made America: A Cultural History of American Movies,* rev. ed. (New York: Vintage, 1994), 269–70. Melvin Small's earlier study estimates that 50 percent of Americans saw a movie monthly during World War II, and about 33 percent attended the cinema weekly. Melvin Small, "Buffoons and Brave Hearts: Hollywood Portrays the Russians, 1939–1944," *California Historical Quarterly* 52, no. 4 (1973): 326.

3. *International Motion Picture Almanac, 1942–43* (New York: Quigley, 1942), 825.

4. Few viewers, Fyne notes, were probably aware that they were being manipulated. This doubtlessly increased the magnitude of the achievement. Fyne, *Hollywood Propaganda,* 11–12.

5. Small, "Buffoons," 326.

6. Ken D. Jones and Arthur F. McClure, *Hollywood at War: The American Motion Picture and World War II* (New York: Castle), 123.

7. Sandburg quoted in Nancy Snow, "Confessions of a Hollywood Propagandist: Harry Warner, FDR and Celluloid Persuasion," in *Warners' War: Politics, Pop Culture, and Propaganda in Wartime Hollywood,* ed. Martin Kaplan and Johanna Blakley (Los Angeles: Norman Lear Center, 2004), 70.

8. A Roper poll indicated that in the wake of the German invasion of Poland, only 2.5 percent of Americans favored war against the Germans in support of Poland, England, and France. See Robert L. McLaughlin and Sally E. Parry, *We'll Always Have the Movies: American Cinema during World War II* (Lexington: University Press of Kentucky, 2006), 27.

9. Richard C. Lukas, *The Strange Allies: The United States and Poland, 1941–1945* (Knoxville: University of Tennessee Press, 1978), 105.

10. Ibid., 91–95.

11. See Larry Ceplair and Steven Englund, *The Inquisition in Hollywood: Politics in the Film Community, 1930–1960* (Garden City, NY: Anchor/Doubleday, 1980), 174–75.

12. See, for example, Melvin Small, "How We Learned to Love the Russians: American Media and the Soviet Union during World War II," *Historian* 36 (1974).

13. Thomas J. Knock, "'History with Lightning': The Forgotten Film *Wilson,*" *American Quarterly* 28, no. 5 (1976): 539. Cf. David Culbert, "Our Awkward Ally: *Mission to Moscow*" in *American History/American Film: Interpreting the Hollywood Image,* ed. John E. O'Connor and Martin A. Jackson (New York: Ungar, 1979), 143–44.

14. Small, "Buffoons," 335.

15. David G. Januszewski, "The Case for the Polish Exile Government in the American Press, 1939–1945," *Polish American Studies* 43, no. 1 (1986).

16. Jones and McClure estimate that 500 of the 1,700 U.S. films made between 1942 and 1945 were "war movies." Jones and McClure, *Hollywood at War,* 124. Only slightly more than 1 percent of American films were related to the war in 1939; that percentage increased greatly in 1942 only to decline rapidly by 1944. Russell Earl Shein, *An Analysis of Motion Pictures about War Released by the American Film Industry, 1930–1970* (New York: Arno, 1970), 31.

17. Kathryn Kane, *Visions of War: Hollywood Combat Films of World War II* (Ann Arbor, MI: UMI Research Press, 1976), 120.

18. This omits the 1942 release by Republic titled *Suicide Squadron,* a

film about a Polish pilot who, incidentally, also happens to be a concert pianist. Although shown in the United States, it was a British film, originally called *Dangerous Moonlight* (1941). It is a slapdash production featuring the Viennese expatriate actor Anton Walbrook playing a Pole who, inexplicably, bears a Czech name (Radetzky) that most people would associate with Austria (i.e., the famous Radetzky March named in honor of the field marshal of the Napoleonic era). The other supposed Poles in the film are an unnamed bomber pilot played by an émigré actor from Hamburg, Frederic Valk, and the pilot Kapulski, a very youthful Michael Rennie. There were, it seems, no Poles involved in any aspect of the film, and it shows. For all of its weaknesses, however, this was the most pro-Polish film shown in the United States and the only one that mentions the extraordinary Polish participation in the Battle of Britain. The *New York Times,* May 14, 1942, dismissed the film in a caustic review as a "sentimental fable" and "hackneyed fiction."

19. Regarding the Norway themes, see Fyne, *Hollywood Propaganda,* 84. Films devoted to Norway include Warner Brothers' *Edge of Darkness* (1943) and *The Moon Is Down* (1943); Columbia's *Commandos Strike at Dawn* (1942) and *First Comes Courage* (1943); and PRC's *They Raid by Night* (1942) and *Avengers* (1942; also known as *The Day Will Dawn*), a British production released by Paramount. McLaughlin and Parry argue that Norway was a popular topic for American films because of the spirited resistance of the Norwegians to the German invasion. McLaughlin and Parry, *We'll Always Have,* 175. This thesis is unconvincing.

20. Bernard F. Dick, The *Star-Spangled Screen: The American World War II Film* (Lexington: University Press of Kentucky, 1985), 150.

21. French resistance was celebrated in these major studio releases: RKO's *This Land Is Mine* (1943) and *Joan of Paris* (1942); Twentieth Century–Fox's *The Pied Piper* (1942), *Tonight We Raid Calais* (1943), *Diplomatic Courier* (1943), and *Paris after Dark* (1943); MGM's *The Cross of Lorraine* (1942), *Assignment in Brittany* (1943), and *Reunion in France* (1942); Warner Brothers' *Uncertain Glory* (1944); Universal's *The Impostor* (1944) and *Paris Calling* (1941); and United Artists' *Paris Underground* (1945). Republic also released the British import *At Dawn We Die* in 1943.

22. Films based in Czechoslovakia, all quite laudatory, include Twentieth Century–Fox's *Four Sons* (1940), MGM's *Hitler's Madman* (1943), United Artists' *Hangmen Also Die* (1943), Paramount's *Hostages* (1943), and PRC's *A Voice in the Wind* (1944). There are also the 1943 MGM release of a British production from Gainsborough Studios known variously as *Tartu* and *Sabotage Agent* and Paramount Productions' fifteen-

minute 1942 short devoted to the Lidice massacre titled *We Refuse to Die,* which was nominated for an Oscar in the documentary category. The use of Czechs to suggest positive and trustworthy characters was tropic: in the cheap 1942 PRC production *A Yank in Libya,* the evil Nazi agent trying to rouse the Arabs against the British poses as a Czech to win the confidence of the Allies in North Africa. Badly directed but well acted, this is a fascinating, largely forgotten film. In *Hangmen Also Die,* a Czech tells a Nazi official, "Our peasants and workers are . . . sympathetic to the Russians." See "Hangmen Also Die: Shooting Script," October 28, 1942, screenplay by John Wexley, 1, folder "Hangmen Also Die," box 9, John Wexley Papers, Wisconsin Center for Film and Theater Research, Wisconsin Historical Society, Madison.

23. Vojtech Mastny, *The Czechs under Nazi Rule: The Failure of National Resistance, 1939–1942* (New York: Columbia University Press, 1971).

24. I am omitting, of course, the entire category of films focusing on Britain, which were innumerable and unfailingly laudatory.

25. *Since You Went Away* (1944), a virtual *Mrs. Miniver* set in America, depicting idealized family life and race relations, features a refugee named Sophie Koslowska who is mawkishly devoted to the United States. Despite her clearly (though slightly misspelled) Polish name, she is specifically identified as a Czech. See Michael Paris, "Lessons for Democracy: American Cinema, 1942–1945," *European Review of History* 5, no. 1 (1998), Northern Light Special Collection document BM19981102020053500. The OWI, which adored presentations of American minority groups as cringingly grateful to the United States, thought this "Czech woman" was excellent. See Ulric Bell to David Selznick, October 14, 1943, file "Since You Went Away," box 3525, RG 208, National Archives, College Park, MD. The main scene involving Sophie features Anne (Claudette Colbert) explaining to her husband that she has met a woman whose Slavic origins would have excluded her from membership in their club but is nonetheless groveling in her gratitude to the United States, which she deems a "fairyland." A conservative film historian has labeled this repulsive degradation of a Czech woman the "best scene of the American idea" in cinematic history. Spencer Warren, "The 100 Best Conservative Movies," *National Review,* October 24, 1994, http://findarticles.com/p/articles/mi_m1282/is_n20_v46/ai_15905983/. Sophie was and is thought to be a Pole by many viewers. See, for example, American Film Institute, "History through a Filmmaker's Lens," session 4, http://www.fathom.com/course/21701723/session4.html.

26. See, for example, the memorandum by Eleanor Berneis of the

Bureau of Motion Pictures, October 7, 1943, and that of her colleague Peg Fenwick, November 30, 1943, both in file "Song to Remember," box 3526, RG 208, National Archives.

27. Paul Buhle and Dave Wagner, *Radical Hollywood: The Untold Story behind America's Favorite Movies* (New York: New Press, 2002), xvii.

28. Victor S. Navasky, *Naming Names* (New York: Viking, 1980), 80. Gerald Horne displays similar sarcasm regarding the hearings in *The Final Victim of the Blacklist: John Howard Lawson, Dean of the Hollywood Ten* (Berkeley: University of California Press, 2006), vii.

29. Anthony Lewis quoted in Phillip Dunne, *Take Two: A Life in Movies and Politics* (New York: McGraw-Hill, 1980), 2. Horne similarly finds the idea of John Howard Lawson and the other members of the Hollywood Ten "smuggling Red views into movies" to be "laughable." Horne, *Final Victim,* 88.

30. William Triplett, "Busting Heads and Blaming Reds: How Movie Producers Used the Blacklist to Crack Down on Hollywood Unions," *Salon,* January 11, 2000, http://archive.salon.com/ent/movies/feature/2000/01/11/blacklist/print.html. Cf. the dismissive comments by Ring Lardner Jr. in *I'd Hate Myself in the Morning: A Memoir* (New York: Thunder's Mouth/Nation, 2000), 5, about how limited was the ability of party members to influence films.

31. Albert Maltz, "The Citizen Writer in Retrospect," interviews by Joel Gardiner, 1983, 2:656–57, Albert Maltz Collection, Howard Gotlieb Archival Research Center, Boston University, Boston.

32. Foster quoted in Navasky, *Naming Names,* 78.

33. Triplett, "Busting Heads," 9.

34. Navasky insists that party members in Hollywood realized that screenwriters had no chance of "influencing the content of movies." Navasky, *Naming Names,* 78.

35. As far back as 1920, the Second Comintern Conference had obliged every party to give "unconditional support to any Soviet republic in its struggle against counter-revolutionary forces." Since in 1939–1945 Soviet Russia was really the Soviet republic and counterrevolutionary forces were, by definition, anything opposing it, the Communist Party of the United States of America was logically required to defend the foreign policy of Moscow unconditionally. For the text, see Robert V. Daniels, *A Documentary History of Communism* (New York: Random House, 1960), 99. Art Eckstein notes that the party in Hollywood (as elsewhere) had as "its central function . . . to further the interests and policies of a foreign country and great power—namely the Soviet Union." Art Eckstein, "The

Hollywood Left Revealed," *Front Page,* June 8, 2005, http://www.front-pagemag.com/articles/Read.aspx?GUID=B76A6172-16C9-419D-86C7-F4885925691D.

36. Ceplair and Englund, *Inquisition in Hollywood,* 48.

37. Stalin quoted in "Poland," *Time,* March 28, 1955, http://www.time.com/time/magazine/article/0,9171,937139-2,00.html.

38. Dan Georgakas, "The Hollywood Reds: 50 Years Later," *American Communist History* 2, no. 1 (2003): 72.

39. Lardner recalls, "Being a communist was time-consuming. I attended events of one sort or another four or five nights a week." These included Russian relief events. Lardner, *I'd Hate Myself,* 98.

40. "We are not just 'the people of the book,'" Novick writes, "but the people of the Hollywood film and the television mini-series." Novick, *Holocaust,* 11–12.

41. Roosevelt's OWI opposed any film that emphasized anti-Semitism. See K. R. M. Short, "Hollywood Fights Anti-Semitism, 1940–1945," in *Film and Radio Propaganda in World War II,* ed. K. R. M. Short (Knoxville: University of Tennessee Press, 1983), 160, 169.

42. Siegfried Kracauer, "National Types as Hollywood Presents Them," *Public Opinion Quarterly* 13, no. 1 (1949): 72, 56.

1. The Polish Presence in American Cinema before 1939

1. "Stars," as Ian C. Jarvie points out, were usually "Americans" with no ethnic coloration. Ian C. Jarvie, "Stars and Ethnicity: Hollywood and the United States, 1932–1951," in *Unspeakable Images: Ethnicity and the American Cinema,* ed. Lester D. Friedman (Urbana: University of Illinois Press, 1991), 82–111.

2. Apolonia Chałupiec was born in Lipno, in Russian Poland. Her mother was Polish; her father was a Slovak of at least partial Roma origin. He immigrated to Poland and became involved in patriotic antitsarist political activity, for which he was arrested and imprisoned in the infamous Pawiak Prison in Warsaw.

3. See "Pola Negri," *Gazeta Wyborcza,* April 20, 2001, and Roman Solecki, "Pola Negri," *Prominent Poles,* http://www.angelfire.com/scifi2/rsolecki/pola_negri.html.

4. Negri served in the Polish Red Cross during World War II. Her ardent patriotism is displayed in her memoirs, where, among other things, she admits sobbing uncontrollably at a funeral service for Poland's national hero Marshal Piłsudski in 1935. See Pola Negri, *Memoirs of a Star* (Garden City, NY: Doubleday, 1970), 16, 143, 376, 391.

5. "Gilda Gray, Shimmy Dancer of 20s, Dead," *Stevens Point (WI) Daily Journal,* December 23, 1959, 23; "Gilda Gray, 'Ex-Shimmy' Queen, Dies in Obscurity," *Sheboygan (WI) Press,* December 23, 1959, 10. Jan-Christopher Horak regards Negri as a very important figure in Hollywood; however, he seems unaware of her nationality and suggests she was German. Jan-Christopher Horak, "Sauerkraut and Sausages with a Little Goulash: Germans in Hollywood, 1927," *Film History* 17, nos. 2–3 (2005): 245.

6. The *Wikipedia* entry for Roberti directs readers to Kirk Crivello, *Fallen Angels: The Lives and Untimely Deaths of Fourteen Hollywood Beauties* (Secaucus, NJ: Citadel, 1988), 270.

7. Material concerning Korjus is scarce. "Miliza Korjus, sopraan," is a helpful Dutch-language source; it is available online at http://www.avro. nl/web/avro_klassiek/luisterkamer/keel/korjus.aspx.

8. Korjus's daughter served as American ambassador to Estonia and publicly emphasized her Estonian origins.

9. Landis was a Roman Catholic, though it is unclear whether she spoke Polish. She referred to herself as half Norwegian and half Polish, but whether she was involved in any way with the Polish community of America is unknown. Eric Gans to author, October 5, 2005. Known for her striking beauty, Landis was also very intelligent. She wrote the book on which her film *Four Jills in a Jeep* was based. There is an uneven biography of her by E. J. Fleming, *Carole Landis: A Tragic Life in Hollywood* (Jefferson, NC: McFarland, 2005).

10. Among her other misfortunes, Landis was married to a man named Horace Schmidlapp. The chief Internet site regarding her is titled *Carole Landis, Norwegian American.*

11. There is some useful information about Parker on both *IMDb* and *Wikipedia.*

12. Jan Kiepura was born in Sosnowiec, in Russian Poland, in 1902. Many of his films were made in Germany. This probably explains why he was occasionally, and unfairly, accused of pro-Nazi sympathies. In reality, Kiepura was an intensely patriotic Pole (whose mother, incidentally, was Jewish) who fought against the Germans in 1919 in defense of Polish claims to Upper Silesia though he was only a boy. During World War II he tried to join the Polish army in exile but was urged to raise funds instead and personally contributed one hundred thousand dollars. Though he died in New York in 1966, at his wish he was buried in Warsaw. The Parliament of Poland proclaimed 2002 Jan Kiepura Year on the centennial of his birth. See Estelle von Wachtel-Torres, "Unforgettable Jan Kiepura," *Bimonthly Newsletter of the Polish American Arts Association of Washington DC,* September–October 2002, 1.

13. *Give Us This Night,* directed by Alexander Hall, screenplay by Edwin Justus Mayer and Lynn Starling, starring Jan Kiepura and Gladys Swarthout (Paramount, 1936). Ironically, Mayer later wrote 1942's *To Be or Not to Be,* one of the few "Polish" films of the war.

14. Markowski was born in the tiny hamlet of Port Henry, very near the Witherbee, New York, birthplace of the famous baseball star Johnny Podres, who, like Tom Tyler, was a Pole whose ethnic origins are not widely known. A useful brief study of Tyler with a complete filmography is Buck Rainey's quaintly tilted "Tom Tyler: Like a Whiff of Honeysuckle across a Cow-Dung Pasture," in *Heroes of the Range: Yesteryear's Matinee Movie Cowboys* (Waynesville, NC: World of Yesterday, 1987), 14–160.

15. "Ex–Film Star Tom Tyler Dies," *Redlands (CA) Daily Facts,* May 3, 1954.

16. The only possible exception is the role of Gus Banshek in the 1938 Paramount release *King of Alcatraz.* This is really of no significance because Tyler's part was so small that it was listed after two unnamed characters ("radio operator" and "officer") in the credits. No nationality is indicated for Gus in any event. Tyler was, however, the eponymous Irishman in the serial *Clancy of the Mounted* (1933). See Rainey, "Whiff of Honeysuckle," 140–41.

17. "Markowski" is a Polish, not Lithuanian, name. The few biographical fragments we have of Tyler all suggest that he was a child of Polish immigrants from historical northeastern Poland. Some of his obituaries garbled his last name as "Marko," further obscuring his obviously Polish surname.

18. For an evaluation of both his talent and his fragility, see *King Vidor on Film Making* (New York: McKay, 1972), 54–55, 60.

19. There is much irony here. In the original Buchan novel (published in 1915), the hero resides at Portland Place, a real address correctly situated in London. This address is also used in the later film and stage adaptations. Only in the 1935 version featuring the Polish Donat does the nonexistent Poland Place appear, though why and by whose emendation is not known. In a final twist, the Polish embassy is now located precisely on Portland Place, though there was no embassy in 1915 when Buchan wrote the novel, and when the first film adaptation was released, in 1935, it was located elsewhere.

20. In reality Tone was of French and Irish descent. The name Stanislas was frequently used by his family, ultimately from Lorraine, because of their high regard for the eighteenth-century Duke of Lorraine, Stanisław Leszczyński, erstwhile king of Poland and son-in-law of Louis XV. Tone may have had Polonophile traditions, but he was not a Pole. Lisa Burks to

author, June 26, 2006. Burks's major study of Tone, a gifted actor who has not received the attention he deserves, is forthcoming.

21. See Roman Solecki, "Ryszard Bolesławski Known as Richard Boleslawski, Real Name Bolesław Ryszard Śrzednicki," *Prominent Poles,* http://www.angelfire.com/scifi2/rsolecki/ryszard_boleslawski.html. Bolesławski's only child, Janek, tragically died in his twenties. Cf. Lardner, *I'd Hate Myself,* 77–78.

22. See Joseph A. Herter, "Stojowski—the Polish Patriot," *Polish Music Newsletter,* January 2002, 14.

23. Scott Eyman, *Ernst Lubitsch: Laughter in Paradise* (New York: Simon and Schuster, 1993), 19.

24. Jolson was born in about 1885 in Średniki, not far from Kowno, in the northeastern Polish *kresy.* The small town is now in Lithuania and known as Seredzius. Jolson is often referred to as a Russian in biographies. This is correct only in the sense that this territory was under Russian occupation in 1885, having been gained from Poland in the partitions a century earlier.

Cass, a dapper, thin, little man, often played dignified characters far older than his real age, for example the French official in *Submarine Base* (Producers Releasing Corporation, 1943). Cass portrayed every national type and apparently once played a probable Pole, Professor Bowilowicz, in the cheap musical *Youth on Parade* (Republic, 1942), a film of which very little is known. The role was so small that Cass was uncredited and may not have had any dialogue, a fate he endured in many of the more than one hundred films he made in a long career.

Very short, dark, and bald, Katch (whose original name was Isser Kac) specialized in exotic roles, often quite unpleasant ones. He was, for example, a cunning Nazi in *Watch on the Rhine* and an idiosyncratic Turkish policeman in *Mask of Dimitrios.*

Warner Brothers cast Windheim in a very large number of films during the war, eight in 1943 alone, often playing Frenchmen. He was tiny and elfin.

Granach, whose original first name is usually given as Jessaja, had a brief career in German and Russian films before coming to Hollywood, where he often played Nazis or other unpleasantly foreign people—he is perhaps best remembered for the Gestapo officer Alois Gruber in *Hangmen Also Die.* He died in 1945, barely into his fifties.

The others were minor players: Lumet may have made only one film; Rich (whose real name could not possibly have been Freddie Rich) was basically a band leader and played that role in a few films. Camille Astor made more than thirty films, apparently all silent. Anna Held was better known for being the paramour of Flo Ziegfeld than for her short film career.

25. Muni, however, was briefly involved in efforts to raise money for Polish relief in the autumn of 1939. The Polish press in the United States, which reported this, noted prominently that he was "born in Lwów." "Aktorzy Amerykańscy dla Polskich Ofiar Wojny," *Ameryka-Echo* (Toledo, OH), November 26, 1939, 3.

26. These were preceded by a series of films of the World War I era that often featured Cossacks, usually portrayed unflatteringly. See Oksana Bulgakowa, "The 'Russian Vogue' in Europe and Hollywood: The Transformation of Russian Stereotypes through the 1920s," *Russian Review* 64, no. 2 (2005): 228–30.

27. Regarding Nazimova, a Russian Jewish émigré who was both bizarre and pathetic, see Gavin Lambert, *Nazimova: A Biography* (New York: Knopf, 1997).

28. Olga Matich, "The White Emigration Goes Hollywood," *Russian Review* 64, no. 2 (2005): 189.

29. Quoted in ibid., 203. Other films include *When a Girl Loves* (1924), *The Eagle* (1925), *Into Her Kingdom* (1926), *Forbidden Paradise* (1924), *The Volga Boatman* (1926), *Resurrection* (1927), *Love* (1927), *Mockery* (1927), *Last Command* (1928), *The Mysterious Lady* (1928), *Red Dance* (1928), *Clothes Make the Woman* (1928), *The Patriot* (1928), *Song of Flame* (1930), *Rasputin and the Empress* (1932), *The Red Dawn* (1932), *The World and the Flesh* (1932), *The Scarlet Empress* (1934), *Anna Karenina* (1936), *Tovarich* (1939), *Balalaika* (1939), *Ninotchka* (1939), and *Comrade X* (1940).

30. See Jeff Peck, "The Heroic Soviet on the American Screen," *Film and History* 9 (September 1979).

31. Matich, "White Emigration," 203.

32. For comments on many of these performers, see Beth Holmgren, "Cossack Cowboys, Mad Russians: The Émigré Actor in Studio-Era Hollywood," *Russian Review* 64, no. 2 (2005).

33. Hans J. Wollstein, *Vixens, Floozies and Molls: 28 Actresses of Late 1920s and 1930s Hollywood* (Jefferson, NC: McFarland, 1999), 9, 17. Baclanova was to be the new Pola Negri, a goal she did not reach.

34. See Matich, "White Emigration," 187.

35. Peck, "Heroic Soviet," 56–57.

36. Brian D. Harvey, "Soviet-American 'Cinematic Diplomacy' in the 1930s: Could the Russians Have Infiltrated Hollywood?" *Screen* 46, no. 4 (2005): 489–98.

37. Peck, "Heroic Soviet," 58.

38. Charles Marowitz, *The Other Chekhov: A Biography of Michael Chekhov, the Legendary Actor, Director, and Theorist* (New York: Applause Theatre and Cinema Books, 2004), 203–4.

39. See, for example, Maltz, "Citizen Writer," 1:436. Cf. Nancy Lynn Schwartz, *The Hollywood Writers' Wars* (New York: Knopf, 1982), 147–48.

40. Novick, *Holocaust,* 92.

41. Peck's conclusion that "heroic Russians had long been seen on the American screen" before World War II is worth noting. Peck, "Heroic Soviet," 54.

42. "Production Notes," "Publicity—Misc.," folder 683, *In Our Time* Collection, Warner Bros. Archives, Cinematic Arts Library, University of Southern California, Los Angeles.

43. Stuart Samuels, "The Evolutionary Image of the Jew in American Film," in *Ethnic Images in American Film and Television,* ed. Randall M. Miller (Philadelphia: Balch Institute, 1978), 25.

44. Stephen J. Whitfield, "Our American Jewish Heritage: The Hollywood Version," *American Jewish History* 75 (1986): 325.

45. Dennis Clark and William Lynch argue that in many films the Irish were portrayed stereotypically, which is certainly true; however, the important fact is the number of films depicting the Irish. Clark and Lynch, for example, discern seven genres of films with substantial Irish content. See Dennis Clark and William J. Lynch, "Hollywood and Hibernia: The Irish in the Movies," in *The Kaleidoscopic Lens: How Hollywood Views Ethnic Groups,* ed. Randall M. Miller (Englewood, NJ: Ozer, 1980), 98–113.

46. See Charles Musser, "Ethnicity, Role-Playing, and American Film Comedy: From *Chinese Laundry* to *Whoopee* (1894–1930)," in Friedman, *Unspeakable Images,* 50.

47. Clark and Lynch, "Hollywood and Hibernia," 107; Leonard J. Leff and Jerold L. Simmons, *The Dame in the Kimono: Hollywood, Censorship, and the Production Code from the 1920s to the 1960s* (New York: Grove Weidenfeld, 1990), 9–10, 283–92; Thomas Doherty, *Projections of War: Hollywood, American Culture, and World War II,* rev. ed. (New York: Columbia University Press, 1999), 37. Regarding Breen's dislike of Jews, see Steven Carr, *Hollywood and Anti-Semitism: A Cultural History up to World War II* (Cambridge: Cambridge University Press, 2001), 130–31.

48. See Francis R. Walsh, "*The Callahans and the Murphys* (MGM, 1927): A Case of Irish-American and Catholic Church Censorship," *Historical Journal of Film, Radio and Television* 10 (1990). Also see Francis G. Couvares, "Hollywood, Main Street, and the Church: Trying to Censor the Movies before the Production Code," *American Quarterly* 44, no. 4

(1992): 602–3, where the author notes that the initial impetus and sustaining energy for the effort were of Irish origin and not broadly Catholic.

49. Carr, *Hollywood and Anti-Semitism,* 76–78.

50. Clark and Lynch refer to this, in passing, as an "Irish-Catholic opinion bloc." Clark and Lynch, "Hollywood and Hibernia," 109.

51. Michael Freedland, *The Warner Brothers* (New York: St. Martin's, 1983), 125.

52. A striking example is from 1947, when RKO was considering producing a film about anti-Semitism. According to an internal studio memorandum, the film's "spokesman" was to be an Irish policeman because "he understands anti-semitism because he's Irish and a Catholic. He understands it more clearly than other people because his grandfather . . . was murdered in a riot against the Irish people." Evidently, for Hollywood, only the Irish had ever suffered discrimination before the appearance of anti-Semitism. See Ceplair and Englund, *Inquisition in Hollywood,* appendix 5, 443. As a matter of fact, as Richard Jensen demonstrates, the story of anti-Irish persecution in the United States is substantially a "myth of victimization." See Richard Jensen, "'No Irish Need Apply': A Myth of Victimization," *Journal of Social History* 36, no. 2 (2002): 405–29.

53. Lester D. Friedman, *Hollywood's Image of the Jew* (New York: Ungar, 1982), 29.

54. Gina Marchetti, "Ethnicity, the Cinema, and Cultural Studies," in Friedman, *Unspeakable Images,* 305.

55. Ana M. Lopez, "Are All Latins from Manhattan? Hollywood, Ethnography, and Cultural Colonialism," in Friedman, *Unspeakable Images,* 406.

56. Friedman notes the same phenomenon, which he deems "assimilationist films par excellence." Friedman, *Image of the Jew,* 29.

57. See the comments of David Desser regarding Irish-Jewish films in "The Cinematic Melting Pot: Ethnicity, Jews, and Psychoanalysis," in Friedman, *Unspeakable Images.*

58. The only film that, we may conjecture, was a Polish-Jewish reconciliation production was the 1913 *The Bleeding Hearts, or Jewish Freedom under King Casimir of Poland,* of which, save the title, I know nothing.

59. See Dave Wagner and Paul Buhle, *Blacklisted: The Film-Lover's Guide to the Hollywood Blacklist* (New York: Palgrave Macmillan, 2003), 214.

60. Samuels, "Evolutionary Image," 25.

61. Patricia Erens, "Between Two Worlds: Jewish Images in American Film," in Miller, *Kaleidoscopic Lens,* 120. For the silent era, see ibid., 117–19.

62. A very thorough examination is Patricia Erens, *The Jew in American Cinema* (Bloomington: Indiana University Press, 1984), 125–27, 146, 423–24.

63. Karen Majewski, *Traitors and True Poles: Narrating a Polish-American Identity, 1880–1939* (Athens: Ohio University Press, 2003).

64. McClean quoted in Musser, "Ethnicity," 49.

65. Peter Bondanella, *Hollywood Italians: Dagos, Palookas, Romeos, Wise Guys, and Sopranos* (New York: Continuum, 2004), 21–24.

66. Carlos E. Cortés, "Italian-Americans in Film: From Immigrants to Icons," *MELUS* 14, nos. 3–4 (1987): 108–9.

67. Alberni was at various times cast as Jewish, Greek, Mexican, Spanish, French, Russian, and Roma, among others. Once he was seemingly even a Pole, Stanislaus Pysinski—in a 1939 college musical by Warner Brothers titled *Naughty but Nice.*

68. A few of Alberni's Italian roles were in British films, though these were also released in the United States.

69. The 1930s films in which Naish is incontrovertibly an Italian are *The Mouthpiece* (1932), *No Other Woman* (1933), *Upperworld* (1934), *Girl in Danger* (1934), *The Return of Jimmy Valentine* (1936), *Song of the City* (1937), and *We Who Are About to Die* (1937).

70. The Italians enjoyed an image of "romantic domesticity" before the wave of crime films. Edward G. Robinson may have been a vicious killer in *Little Caesar,* but before that he was an Italian charmer in 1930's *A Lady to Love.* See Daniel Golden, "The Fate of La Famiglia: Italian Images in American Film," in Miller, *Kaleidoscopic Lens,* 77.

71. These include an anarchist in 1919's *Dangerous Hours* and an unpleasant character in 1924's *Manhandled.* See Cortés, "Italian-Americans," 109.

72. See Bondanella, *Hollywood Italians,* 99, 100–101. Warner Brothers cast John Garfield and William Lundigan as Italian brothers in *East of the River,* not a wise decision.

73. The film's priest is, of course, Irish, played by the Irish William Gargan, who usually played Irish characters in his long career.

74. Bondanella, *Hollywood Italians,* 172–73.

75. Cortés, "Italian-Americans," 111.

76. Probably the earliest gangster film was the 1912 Biograph release by D. W. Griffith, *The Musketeers of Pig Alley.* The gangs it portrays are almost exclusively Irish. See John McCarty, *Hollywood Gangland: The Movies' Love Affair with the Mob* (New York: St. Martin's, 1993), 3.

77. In reality the Capone mob had Polish members, but not in Hollywood's version. See McCarty, *Hollywood Gangland,* 62.

78. Winokur notes that Hollywood has traditionally employed an "extremely disproportionate" number of "new immigrants." Mark Winokur, "Improbable Ethnic Hero: William Powell and the Transformation of Ethnic Hollywood," *Cinema Journal* 27, no. 1 (1987): 5.

79. Whitfield observes that "in the 1930s . . . Jews were disappearing from the screen." Whitfield, "Our American Jewish Heritage," 327.

80. Kracauer, "National Types," 67–68. In *Ninotchka*, Hedy Lamarr comments, "I kissed a Polish lancer, too—before he died." See Bosley Crowther, *The Great Films: Fifty Golden Years of Motion Pictures* (New York: Putnam, 1967), 128.

81. Jerzy Bossak, "Ostrożnie—temat polski!" *Srebrny ekran,* nos. 13–14 (1938): 12–13 (my translation). I am indebted to Sheila Skaff of the University of Texas at El Paso for providing me a copy of this essay.

82. Lester D. Friedman argues that Hollywood presents a "bland conception of Americanness" in which "all ethnic groups are seen as substantially identical." Lester D. Friedman, "Celluloid Palimpsests: An Overview of Ethnicity in the American Film," in Friedman, *Unspeakable Images,* 24, 26.

83. Ella Shohat, "Ethnicities-in-Relation: Toward a Multicultural Reading of American Cinema," in Friedman, *Unspeakable Images,* 227.

84. *Isn't Life Wonderful,* directed by D. W. Griffith, screenplay by D. W. Griffith, starring Carol Dempster, Neil Hamilton, and Erville Anderson (D. W. Griffith Productions, 1924).

85. The *IMDb* synopsis describes the protagonists as "Polish refugees," but "refugees from Poland" would be more accurate.

86. *Palooka,* directed by Benjamin Stoloff, screenplay by Jack Jevne, Arthur Kober, and Gertrude Purcell, starring Stuart Erwin, Jimmy Durante, and Lupe Velez (Reliance Pictures, 1934).

87. "Palooka" is "a term widely considered a slur on blue-collar Polish-Americans." Wagner and Buhle, *Blacklisted,* 170.

88. The comic strip began in 1930, but Fisher conceived the character of the "amiable but dim-witted pugilist" in 1921. Indeed, the use of "palooka" to designate a "boxer without ability, a nobody" was already common in 1926, if not earlier. Regarding the term, see Michael Quinion, "Palooka," *World Wide Words,* http://www.worldwidewords.org/qa/qa-pal1.htm. Regarding the origins of the Fisher character, see T. Wayne Waters, "Joe Palooka Goes to War," *American History,* December 2002, 48–54.

89. In 1940 the comic strip character Palooka joined the army. He was the first character in the funny papers to join the armed forces, and he thus became a model of patriotism and civic-mindedness. There were a series

of Palooka films from 1946 to 1951 with an entirely different cast. All were very low-budget productions, unlike the 1934 release.

90. *Black Fury,* directed by Michael Curtiz, screenplay by Abem Finkel and Carl Erickson, starring Paul Muni, Karen Marley, John Qualen, and J. Carrol Naish (Warner Brothers, 1935).

91. Harry R. Irving, *Bohunk: A Melodramatic Comedy,* 1932, copy in folder 5, box 33, Warner Brothers Scripts, series 1.3, United Artists Corporation, Wisconsin Center for Film and Theater Research.

92. Ibid., I-13. There is also a Polish character named Sam Anzok. Ibid., I-21.

93. Ibid., I-6, I-34, I-36.

94. M. A. Musmanno, "Joe Volkanik," n.d., folder 6, box 33, Warner Brothers Scripts. The words "Black Hell" are written in black crayon across the front.

95. Ibid., 7.

96. Abem Finkel, "Black Hell," first draft, April 28, 1934, folder 7, box 33, Warner Brothers Scripts. This treatment specifically acknowledges the Irving and Musmanno manuscripts as its sources.

97. Ibid., 5.

98. Abem Finkel, "Black Hell," revised treatment, June 1, 1934, folder 8; Abem Finkel, "Black Hell," final revised treatment, June 13, 1934, folder 9, both in box 33, Warner Brothers Scripts.

99. Finkel, "Black Hell," final revised treatment, 132.

100. Abem Finkel and Carl Erickson, "Black Hell," temporary, 2, September 4, 1934, folder 1, box 34, Warner Brothers Scripts.

101. Abem Finkel and Carl Erickson, "Black Hell," final, October 8, 1934, 11, folder 2, box 34, Warner Brothers Scripts.

102. Deborah L. Johnson, "Black Fury," *Turner Classic Movies,* http://www.tcm.com/thismonth/article/?cid=18773.

103. Muni referred to himself as an Austrian Jew. See "Glancing Backward," *Esquire,* December 1934, and "Der Film: Bei Paul Muni," *Neues Wiener Tagblatt,* December 24, 1937. Muni left Poland when he was very young and did not learn the language; Yiddish was his native tongue. Michael B. Druxman, *Paul Muni: His Life and His Films* (South Brunswick, NJ: Barnes, 1974), 34, 39, 41–42. He traveled to Poland in 1934 and spoke very highly of Polish theater but did not identify himself as being of Polish origin, and the Polish press in Warsaw did not claim him as a Pole. See J. Migowa, "Teatr polski ma w Ameryce opinję najlepszego w świecie- powiada Paweł Muni, znakomity aktor amerykański," *Kronika Warszawy,* January 24, 1934. Muni was ardently Jewish and traveled before the war to Palestine, where he was very popular reciting the works of Sholem

Aleichem in Yiddish. He was an ardent supporter of Israel and other Jewish causes. See Druxman, *Paul Muni,* 76–83, and the clippings in box 3, series 2, Paul Muni Papers, Billy Rose Theatre Collection, New York Public Library for the Performing Arts, New York.

104. Muni quoted in Johnson, "Black Fury."

105. Druxman, *Paul Muni,* 26.

106. Cossacks were used as armed detachments by the tsarist authorities in Russian Poland and enjoyed a reputation for brutality among Poles. Czechs and Slovaks who lived under Austrian rule had no experience with Cossacks. Hence for Radek, in a moment of passion, to denounce a brutal murderer as a Cossack constitutes a sign, however esoteric and fleeting, that he is a Pole.

107. *The Racial Slur Database,* http://www.rsdb.org, insists that "Hunyak" is "a contraction of Hungarian and Polock" but neither offers provenience nor indicates when the term came into use. The very existence of a hybrid Hungarian-Pole requiring American ridicule strains credulity. Most likely Warner Brothers simply used the term to indicate opprobrium directed at recent immigrants.

108. The following later works conclude that Radek is a Pole: Tino Balio, *Grand Design: Hollywood as a Modern Business Enterprise, 1930–1939* (Berkeley: University of California Press, 1993), 259; Caroline Goląb, "Stellaaaaaa . . . . . . !!!!!! The Slavic Stereotype in American Film," in Miller, *Kaleidoscopic Lens,* 139, 146; and Nick Roddick, *A New Deal in Entertainment: Warner Brothers in the 1930s* (London: British Film Institute, 1983), 171–74. This view reflects the contemporary conclusion of Meyer Levin in "The Candid Cameraman," *Esquire,* June 1935. *Variety,* April 17, 1935, complained that Muni's "Polish brogue [was] too thick." However, Louella Parsons thought him to be a "smiling bohunk." Louella Parsons, "Curtiz Scores Greatest Hit in 'Black Fury,'" *Los Angeles Times,* May 24, 1935. Harrison Carroll, writing in the *Los Angeles Evening Herald,* May 24, 1935, deemed Radek a "big Slovak," as did the *Hollywood Citizen,* May 24, 1935. All clippings in "Scrapbook, 1929–1935," box 5, series 3, Muni Papers. Most of the clippings in this collection either make Radek a Slovak or are noncommittal; virtually none designate him a Pole.

109. See *Slovenské Noviny,* March 21, 1935, which describes the film as showing the "lives of Slovak miners" (života slovenských baníkov), and *Nědelní Svorost,* March 23, 1935, which describes Muni as depicting the life of a "Slovak coalminer" (slovenského uhlokopa).

110. *Hollywood Reporter,* May 25, 1935, clipping in "Scrapbook, 1929–1935."

111. *As the Earth Turns,* directed by Alfred E. Green, screenplay by

Ernest Pascal, starring Jean Muir and Donald Woods (Warner Brothers, 1934).

112. Carroll explained in 1934 that her goal was to show Maine in effect digesting the foreigners and not changing in the process. Stanislaus A. Blejwas, "Puritans and Poles: The New England Literary Image of the Polish Peasant Immigrant," *Polish American Studies* 42, no. 2 (1985): 29.

113. See the correspondence between Carroll and Walter Zebrowski quoted extensively in Walter Zebrowski, "Poles in Gladys Hasty Carroll's *As the Earth Turns,*" *Polish American Studies* 20, no. 1 (1963): 18–21. Zebrowski's conclusion that the Poles are "inauthentic" is generous.

114. The name "Marian" is a common male name in Polish. "Marion" does not exist, and Poles would not adopt it for a female.

115. Regarding Janowski's experience in the needle trade, see Gladys Hasty Carroll, *As the Earth Turns* (New York: Macmillan, 1942), 190.

116. Ibid., 190, 253.

117. Ibid., 15, 25. Reading the novel, we learn such useful items as "you can't kill a Polack without a gun" and that Poles may be willing to live in barns, unlike Anglo-Saxons. The locals "doubted if even a Polish woman could live in a barn." Ibid., 25, 60, 99.

118. Jen assumes that the Poles have no means to treat illness: "There was no telling what Polocks might or might not have ready." Ibid., 97.

119. Keele must be watched constantly because he cheats his customers. He refers "sadly" to the Janowskis as being "the right kind of Polish," unlike him, because they are farmers, whereas he is a peddler. He is, he tells a Yankee, "not that kind Polish." The meaning of all of this is not clear, but, given Carroll's obvious ignorance of things Polish, it probably means nothing. Ibid., 44, 43. Keele's loyalty to his fellow Poles is noted in ibid., 314–15.

120. Ibid., 38.

121. Ibid., 314.

122. Ibid., 244, 306.

123. Jacob Wilk to Gladys Hasty Carroll, March 1, 1934, box 7, Gladys Hasty Carroll Collection, Gotlieb Archival Research Center. Warner Brothers tried to send Carroll to New York to help promote the picture and had earlier sent her to Hollywood. Its publicity campaign repeated the story that she had carefully monitored the film to assure its accuracy, a claim she indignantly rejected. See Sidney Davidson to Gladys Hasty Carroll, telegram, March 16, 1934, and Hal Wallis to Gladys Hasty Carroll, April 20, 1934, both in box 7, Carroll Collection.

124. See S. Charles Einfield (Warner Brothers), news release, March 19, 1934, box 7, Carroll Collection.

125. See "As the Earth Turns Storms Dallas Following Unique Realism vs. Hokum Campaign," scrapbook 1a, box 18, Carroll Collection. This sheet reproduces many articles about the film, none of which mention the Polish characters.

126. Gladys Hasty Carroll to Hal Wallis, April 10, 1934, box 7, Carroll Collection.

127. Many cast members presented Carroll with signed photographs. These, along with a large number of stills from the film, are in scrapbook 1a, box 18, Carroll Collection. These are important, as few if any intact copies of the film exist. The UCLA Film and Television Archive has only an incomplete version.

128. The actress portraying Mrs. Janowski, who had earlier played "a Negro mammy" and "an Eskimo," lamented that her latest role also required her to dress unattractively; she wanted a chance to wear "swell clothes." *Detroit Free Press,* December 4, 1933, clipping in scrapbook 2, box 18, Carroll Collection.

129. See scrapbook 2, box 18, and the clipping collection in box 20, Carroll Collection. The lengthy review in the *New York Times,* rather lukewarm, never mentioned that the Janowskis were Polish, referring to them only as "foreigners." "The Call of the Soil," *New York Times,* April 12, 1934.

130. *The Wedding Night,* directed by King Vidor, screenplay by Edith Fitzgerald, starring Gary Cooper and Anna Sten (United Artists, 1935).

131. Helen Vinson's Dora has been well regarded. See Wollstein, *Vixens, Floozies and Molls,* 235–36. Cf. Robert A. Juran, *Old Familiar Faces: The Great Character Actors and Actresses of Hollywood's Golden Age* (Sarasota, FL: Movie Memories, 1995), 278.

132. Larry Swindell, *The Last Hero: A Biography of Gary Cooper* (Garden City, NY: Doubleday, 1980), 179. Cf. James Robert Parish and William T. Leonard, *Hollywood Players: The Thirties* (New Rochelle, NY: Arlington House, 1976), 493.

133. Goldwyn quoted in Parish and Leonard, *Hollywood Players,* 491.

134. Raymond Durgnat and Scott Simmon, *King Vidor, American* (Berkeley: University of California Press, 1988), 168.

135. Vidor is described in the FBI files as a "fellow traveler who follows the Communist Party line ardently." Pt. 1, 104, 108, file 100-138754, Communist Infiltration—Motion Picture Industry, Federal Bureau of Investigation, Washington, DC (hereafter cited as COMPIC).

136. Swindell refers to her as "Russian and blonde," which is half right. Swindell, *Gary Cooper,* 177. Parish and Leonard give her name as Anjuschka Stenski Sujakevitch and describe her as of Ukrainian-Swedish descent. Parish and Leonard, *Hollywood Players,* 488.

137. Sten lived in Kiev when the Polish army arrived in 1920. She later recalled "the gaunt Polish warrior singing wild songs of victory." Sten quoted in Parish and Leonard, *Hollywood Players,* 490.

138. Manya chooses "consent" over "descent," to use Sollors's terms as quoted in Vivian Sobchack, "Postmodern Modes of Ethnicity," in Friedman, *Unspeakable Images,* 331–32.

139. Durgnat and Simmon note that the film would have been better if Tony had showed any respect for Manya's "roots." Durgnat and Simmon, *King Vidor,* 168.

140. It is depressing that Jeffrey Meyers, in his biography of Cooper, opines that the film has the virtue of conveying "some idea of Polish life in rural New England." Jeffrey Meyers, *Gary Cooper: American Hero* (New York: Cooper Square, 1998), 112.

141. *The Emperor's Candlesticks,* directed by George Fitzmaurice, screenplay by Harold Goldman and Monckton Hoffe, starring William Powell, Luise Rainer, Robert Young, Maureen O'Sullivan, and Frank Morgan (MGM, 1937).

142. Some sense of the complexity of the plot can be gleaned from the summary in Sanderson Beck, "*The Emperor's Candlesticks,*" *Movie Mirrors,* http://www.san.beck.org/MM/1937/Emperor'sCandlesticks.html.

143. *Conquest,* directed by Clarence Brown, screenplay by S. N. Behrman, starring Greta Garbo and Charles Boyer (MGM, 1937).

144. Boyer's portrayal of Napoleon was criticized as too sympathetic, and the casting of the role was long delayed. See Larry Swindell, *Charles Boyer: The Reluctant Lover* (New York: Doubleday, 1983), 98–102.

145. Bossak, "Ostrożnie—temat polski," 13.

146. First National alone released *The Stolen Bride* and *The Whip Woman* in 1927, *Yellow Lily* in 1928, and *The Squall* in 1929. Universal produced 1931's *Dracula* and 1934's *The Black Cat.* MGM was responsible for the large-budget film *The Shop around the Corner* in 1940. All were set in Hungary. Additionally, though MGM's *I Married an Angel* was released in 1942, it was set in the prewar era.

147. Judith E. Doneson. *The Holocaust in American Film,* 2nd ed. (Syracuse, NY: Syracuse University Press, 2002) 16, 30. There are far harsher critics of Hollywood's silence about German persecution of the Jews. See, for example, Nancy DeWolf Smith, "When Hollywood Went Silent," *Wall Street Journal,* April 1, 2005.

148. Jack R. Fischel, "Reds and Radicals in Hollywood," *Virginia Quarterly Review,* Winter 2003, http://www.vqronline.org/articles/2003/winter/fischel-reds-radicals-hollywood/.

149. Jack Warner stresses this factor in his memoirs. Jack L. Warner

with Dean Jennings, *My First Hundred Years in Hollywood* (New York: Random House, 1965), 261–64.

150. Harry Warner's early devotion to the anti-Nazi cause is discussed in detail and with great sympathy in Michael E. Birdwell, *Celluloid Soldiers: The Warner Bros. Campaign against Nazism* (New York: New York University Press, 1999).

151. See Roddick, *New Deal,* esp. 73–98.

152. Christine Ann Colgan, "Warner Brothers' Crusade against the Third Reich: A Study of Anti-Nazi Activism and Film Production, 1933 to 1941" (PhD diss., University of Southern California, 1985), 25–26, 41–43.

153. *Confessions of a Nazi Spy* was distributed in Poland just before the war and was very popular despite German efforts to have it banned. Exhibitors were later executed by the Germans. Ibid., 486–88.

154. *Black Legion,* directed by Archie Mayo, screenplay by Abem Finkel, starring Humphrey Bogart, Dick Foran, and Ann Sheridan (Warner Brothers, 1937). The film was inspired by actual events. See Colgan, "Warner Brothers Crusade," 101–3. Originally Edward G. Robinson was considered for the lead role, but he was rejected as too "foreign" in appearance. Birdwell, *Celluloid Soldiers,* 47–48.

155. See Robert Lord, "Black Legion Story," June 8, 1936, folder 3, box 34, Warner Brothers Scripts.

156. Abem Finkel and Robert Lord, "Treatment Black Legion," July 8, 1936, folder 4, box 34, Warner Brothers Scripts. The character's father, "old man Dombrowski," also appears in this version. See the comments in Colgan, "Warner Brothers' Crusade," 115–17. Carr argues persuasively that the Jewish character was changed at the insistence of Breen of the Production Code office, who argued that the story would broach an "inflammatory subject," racial prejudice, were the protagonist to remain Jewish. Hence he was changed to a Pole. Carr, *Hollywood and Anti-Semitism,* 157–58. However, although the character's name may have been changed, nothing was done to create a Polish persona for him, leaving some to speculate that the character remained Jewish despite the change of name.

157. Finkel and Lord, "Treatment Black Legion," 1–2, 7, 8, 13–14.

158. Ibid., 8, 16. Birdwell simply declares him a Pole but does not explain why. He suggests that the character is referred to as a "Polock" in the film, but there is no such reference. Birdwell, *Celluloid Soldiers,* 49, 51.

159. Abem Finkel and Robert Lord, "Black Legion: Part I, Temporary," July 20, 1936, 4, 66, folder 5, box 34, Warner Brothers Scripts.

160. Abem Finkel and William Wister Haines (screenplay) and Robert

Lord (story), "Black Legion," November 22, 1936, 46, folder 6, box 34, Warner Brothers Scripts.

161. Colgan considers the character to be Polish. Colgan, "Warner Brothers' Crusade," 104.

162. In the Warner Brothers press book, the character is only described as "foreign-born." Quoted in Colgan, "Warner Brothers' Crusade," 803.

163. See Roddick, *New Deal,* 157–59. This is an intriguing thesis, though Roddick offers precious little evidence from the script. The fact that the elder Dombrowski was played by a Jewish actor, Egon Brecher, is not of moment: Warner Brothers regularly used Jewish actors to portray Poles.

164. That the Warner family, most born in Poland, would know nothing about Poles is, of course, absurd on the face. Hence the blurry presentations of Polish characters must reflect purposeful obfuscation, not ignorance.

165. The obscure Soubier had few film roles in a rather long career.

166. Dombrowski is referred to, for example, as a "hard-working Slav" by one observer; the character is simply too nebulous for a closer identification. Wyn Craig Wade, *The Fiery Cross: The Ku Klux Klan in America* (New York: Simon and Schuster, 1987), 262.

167. Some notion of the type Brandon was thought by Hollywood to represent is suggested by a few of his roles over a long career: Fu Manchu, Hassan, Malik, Genghis Khan's son Juchi, and the unforgettable Wapato the medicine man. John Ford delighted in casting him as an Indian chief.

168. *Girl in Danger* was a very "ethnic" film, with several Italian and Irish characters as well as Wynkoski. Needless to say, Hollywood cast in every role an actor who was not of the nationality he portrayed.

169. I have omitted the character Yoroslaff, who had a minor role in the 1937 Columbia serial *The Mysterious Pilot.* Although "Yoroslaff" could be regarded as a garbled spelling of the Polish Christian name "Jaroslaw," it is most unlikely that the script had this intention. Yoroslaff is played by Frank Lachteen, a Lebanese who portrayed Levantines of various sorts; doubtless that is what was intended here as well.

2. Poland in the Second World War

1."Secret Additional Protocol" in *Documents on Polish-Soviet Relations, 1939–1945* (London: Heinemann, 1961), 1:40.

2. Steven Zaloga and Victor Madej, *The Polish Campaign, 1939* (New York: Hippocrene, 1991), 152–53, 191–92. Cf. Ryszard Szałowski, "The Polish-Soviet War of September, 1939," 31, in *The Takeover of the Polish Eastern Provinces, 1939–41,* ed. Keith Sword (New York: St. Martin's,

1991). Andrzej Ajnenkiel reckons the initial Russian invasion as counting about five hundred thousand and growing to eventually triple that figure. Andrzej Ajnenkiel, "Z Problematyki polskiego czynu zbrojnego," in *Naczelni wodzowie i wyżsi dowódcy Polskich Sił Zbrojnych na zachodzie,* ed. Stefan Zwoliński (Warsaw: Wojskowy Instytut Historyczny, 1995), 18.

3. See Szałowski, "Polish-Soviet War," 33–43. The Soviets admitted to three thousand casualties. See John Erickson, "The Red Army's March into Poland, September, 1939," in Sword, *Takeover,* 21–22.

4. See Keith Sword, introduction to Sword, *Takeover,* xvi–xvii.

5. Regarding Polish reaction to the Soviet invasion, see Ambassador Wacław Grzybowski's note of September 17, 1939, and the Polish government's communiqué of the same date. The Soviet justification for the invasion is presented in Molotov's statement of the same date. For all three documents, see *Documents on Polish-Soviet Relations,* 1:47–48. The Soviets' defense of their behavior toward Poland, from the signing of the accord with Hitler through the invasion of September 17, is a concoction of falsehoods, distortions, and nonsense. It was, however, accepted as axiomatic by Communist Party members and much of the nonparty Left for decades. For a demolition of the traditional Soviet apologia, see Erickson, "Red Army's March," 1–23.

6. Ajnenkiel, "Z Problematyki," 19.

7. Ewa M. Thompson, "Nationalist Propaganda in the Soviet Russian Press, 1939–1941," *Slavic Review* 50, no. 2 (1991): 388–89.

8. Georgi Dimitrov, *The War and the Working Class* (1939), reprinted in *A Documentary History of the Communist Party of the United States,* ed. Bernard K. Johnpoll (Westport, CT: Greenwood, 1994), 6:129–30, 140.

9. Thompson, "Nationalist Propaganda," 390–91.

10. See the comments in Cajus Bekker, *Luftwaffe War Diaries* (New York: Doubleday, 1969), 19–59. I am indebted to Michael Alfred Peszke for this information.

11. This is the central theme of *In Our Time,* and it also appears as a motif in the opening portion of *To Be or Not to Be.* The OWI, as we will see, specifically insisted that references to appeasement on the part of London or Paris be removed from films. It made no such demand regarding Warsaw.

12. This is presented specifically as a cause of Poland's 1939 defeat in *Once upon a Honeymoon* and suggested in *To Be or Not to Be.*

13. Norway's population at the time of the German invasion was fewer than 3 million. The indigenous version of the Nazi Party, Nasjonal Samling (National Union), attracted about 60,000 members, and there were perhaps 2,000 Norwegian volunteers for the SS. After the war, 90,000 Nor-

wegians were investigated for collaboration; more than half were found guilty, and 18,000 were imprisoned. See Stephen M. Cullen, "Collaboration," in *World War II in Europe: An Encyclopedia,* ed. David T. Zabecki (New York: Garland), 1:37–39.

14. Andrzej Toczewski, "Cooperation between the Soviet Union and the Third Reich in Exchanges of Polish Population and Prisoners of War in the Years 1939–1941," *Polish Review* 37, no. 2 (1992): 209–15.

15. Thompson, "Nationalist Propaganda," 390–92.

16. Recent estimates conclude that almost 2 million Polish citizens were placed in "extreme psychological and physical" conditions by the Soviets, including arrest and deportation. Toczewski, "Cooperation," 210.

17. Keith Sword, *Deportation and Exile: Poles in the Soviet Union, 1939–48* (London: St Martin's, 1994), 3–4.

18. See "To nie był mord polityczny," *Rzeczpospolita,* March 4, 2006.

19. Sword, *Deportation and Exile,* 6–10, 15–27.

20. About half of the Polish casualties resulted from the fall of France in 1940, when large numbers of soldiers were abandoned to the enemy. An additional four hundred thousand Poles served on the eastern front under Soviet command. Ajnenkiel, "Z Problematyki," 25–26.

21. These conclusions were reached by a joint British-Polish research group whose results were published in 2004. See Dominika Pszczołkowska, "Gdyby nie polski wywiad," *Gazeta Wyborcza,* August 31, 2005.

22. Ajnenkiel, "Z Problematyki," 24.

23. Ajnenkiel reckons Polish military casualties at over 1 million. American war losses were perhaps 350,000, drawn, of course, from a much larger population base. Ibid., 27.

3. Radical Hollywood and Poland

1. The FBI later argued that this 1925 commentary should be "considered as a directive to the American Communists." "Digest: Communism in the Motion Picture Industry," October 2, 1947, pt. 6, 1, COMPIC. An expanded version of this analysis is "Summary on the Communist Infiltration into the Motion Picture Industry," October 2, 1947, pt. 7, 1–3, COMPIC.

2. "Summary on the Communist Infiltration," 9.

3. John Bright, interview by Patrick McGilligan and Ken Mate, in Patrick McGilligan and Paul Buhle, *Tender Comrades: A Backstory of the Hollywood Blacklist* (New York: St. Martin's, 1997), 145.

4. Ceplair and Englund, *Inquisition in Hollywood,* 58. Jerome was

born in 1896 in Stryków, near Łódź in central Poland. He immigrated to England as a boy in about 1903. Jerome later wrote extensively in Yiddish but tried to learn Polish only later in life. In 1952 he published a semiautobiographical novel, *A Lantern for Jeremy,* which refers to his childhood in Poland. There is brief biographical material in "Biographical Notes—V. J. Jerome," by his wife Alice Jerome, and in the anonymous "A Biographical Sketch of Victor Jeremy Jerome," both in folder 557, box 38, Victor Jeremy Jerome Papers, Sterling Memorial Library, Yale University, New Haven, CT. For his efforts to learn Polish, see Victory Jeremy Jerome, interview, *Świat,* July 19, 1959, clipping in folder 563, box 38, Jerome Papers. Albert Maltz noted that Jerome wrote essays concerning Poland, but I have not been able to unearth any. Maltz, "Citizen Writer," 1:339. Cf. Horne, *Final Victim,* 117–18, 160. Cf. John Howard Lawson, "Life and Death of a Magazine," 454A, folder 3, box 99, John Howard Lawson Papers, Special Collections, Morris Library, Southern Illinois University, Carbondale.

    5. Howard Rushmore, testimony, May 15, 1947, House Committee on Un-American Activities, *Hearings Regarding the Communist Infiltration of the Motion Picture Industry* (Washington, DC: GPO, 1947), 12–17. Regarding Jerome's organizing efforts, see Ronald Radosh and Allis Radosh, *Red Star over Hollywood: The Film Colony's Long Romance with the Left* (San Francisco: Encounter, 2005), 30–32. He was especially concerned with agitprop. See Victor Jeremy Jerome, "The National Agit-Prop Conference Plan of Preparation," December 1934, folder 52, box 20, Jerome Papers.

    6. "Communist Infiltration of the Motion Picture Industry," February 18, 1943, pt. 1, 5–7, COMPIC.

    7. Bright, interview, 145; Horne, *Final Victim,* 14. Horne writes of Lawson's father, Simeon Levy, leaving Poland in the "1840s" due to "an outburst of anti-Semitism." Horne, *Final Victim,* 14. For Lawson's account of his initial activities, see John Howard Lawson, "The First American Writers' Conference," [1968], 394, folder 1; John Howard Lawson, untitled section of autobiography, 853, folder 4; and John Howard Lawson, "Concerning the Soul," 853–54, folder 5, all in box 99, Lawson Papers.

    8. "Summary on the Communist," 11.

    9. Pt. 1, 61, COMPIC. Cf. "Communist Infiltration of Labor Groups," April 27, 1947, pt. 3, 6, COMPIC. The guild was famous in its early years for interminable and constant meetings, leading one writer to conclude that only a Communist could endure such endless discussion. "Summary on the Communist Infiltration," 80. The guild was reorganized in 1937 virtually under party auspices. See Radosh and Radosh, *Red Star,* 44.

    10. Pt. 1, 74, COMPIC; Kenneth Lloyd Billingsley, *Hollywood Party:*

How Communism Seduced the American Film Industry in the 1930s and 1940s (Rocklin, CA: Prima, 1998), 64.

11. Lawson, "First American Writers' Conference," 394–394A.

12. Lawson quoted in Schwartz, *Hollywood Writers' Wars,* 59.

13. Billingsley, *Hollywood Party,* 54. Stephen Koch refers to Lawson as having as his "life's work . . . organizing Stalinist opinion in the American entertainment industry." Stephen Koch, *Double Lives: Stalin, Willi Münzenburg, and the Seduction of the Intellectuals,* rev. ed. (New York: Enigma, 2004*),* 245. Cf. Radosh and Radosh, *Red Star,* 25–28. After the war, Lawson equated participating in films like *The Desert Fox,* which was sympathetic to Rommel, to working for the Nazis. John Howard Lawson, *Film in the Battle of Ideas* (New York: Masses and Mainstream, 1953), 107. In that case, his participation in films that were sympathetic to Stalin was the equivalent of working for the Soviet Union. Lawson's self-righteousness is thoroughly displayed in this small book.

14. Jeffrey Lawson quoted in Horne, *Final Victim,* 3.

15. Maltz, "Citizen Writer," 1:364–65, 514–15. Edward Dmytryk, one of the Hollywood Ten, recalls a "summons" from "Gauleiter" Lawson to demand changes in the ideological content of a film in 1945. Edward Dmytryk, *Odd Man Out: A Memoir of the Hollywood Ten* (Carbondale: Southern Illinois University Press, 1996), 20–21. One of Lawson's ideological devotees was stunned to find that Lawson visited a dentist: "He seemed to be beyond the frailties of humankind." Quoted in Schwartz, *Hollywood Writers' Wars,* 153. Party discipline was such that a writer had to seek permission in advance to write a book. Schwartz, *Hollywood Writers' Wars,* 155. Lawson admitted later, "I began to have more authority than is healthy or proper." Lawson, "Concerning the Soul," 854.

16. This observation, recorded by Edward Dmytryk, is quoted in Radosh and Radosh, *Red Star,* 152–53.

17. Billingsley, *Hollywood Party,* 91. Buhle and Wagner note that Lawson strove to "uphold the Party line on all questions aesthetic, political, and above all international." Buhle and Wagner, *Radical Hollywood,* 42.

18. Lawson quoted in Robert Mayhew, *Ayn Rand and* Song of Russia*: Communism and Anti-Communism in 1940s Hollywood* (Lanham, MD: Scarecrow, 2005), 175.

19. Koch, *Double Lives,* 90. It is possible that Katz made earlier trips to Hollywood, but these have not been reconstructed. The 1935 events are well known. Billingsley gives Jerome principal credit for founding the league. Billingsley, *Hollywood Party,* 69.

20. The FBI noted that the "majority of officers and many prominent members" were "identified with Communist activity." See FBI, Los

Angeles, file 65-796, February 1, 1941, 1, 34–38, file 100-6633, Holly-wood Anti-Nazi League, Federal Bureau of Investigation (hereafter cited as HANL). Among the initial activists were many who were not Jewish and even prominent Republicans like actress Ginger Rogers. See ibid., 10.

21. Radosh and Radosh, *Red Star,* 51.

22. The Comintern officially described Poland as "fascist" in 1935. See "The Tasks of the Communist International in Connection with the Preparations of the Imperialists for a New World War" and "Resolutions on the Report by M. Ercoli [Palmiro Togliatti], Adopted August 20, 1935 by the Seventh Congress of the Communist International," both in Johnpoll, *Documentary History,* 4:44.

23. Phillip Dunne, who was very sympathetic to the Hollywood Left, later noted, "It may well have been that all of [the Hollywood Popular Front organizations] really had been founded by Communists." They were "the ones who knew how to pull things together." Phillip Dunne, interview by Douglas Bell, 1991, 49–50, Oral History Collection, Margaret Herrick Library, Academy of Motion Picture Arts and Sciences, Los Angeles.

24. Irving Howe and Lewis Coser, *The American Communist Party: A Critical History, 1919–1957* (Boston: Beacon, 1957), 386.

25. Here we should consider the very intriguing arguments regard-ing both the degree to which Hollywood reflected the emergence of a "left national popular culture" in the 1930 and the simultaneity of the "golden age of the American left and of American cinema in the 1930s." See Kath-leen Moran and Michael Rogin, "'What's the Matter with Capra?' Sulli-van's Travels and the Popular Front," *Representations* 71 (Summer 2000): 100–102.

26. A great many details of Hollywood party members' efforts to oppose war and armed preparedness are found in FBI, Los Angeles, file 65-796, 36–38.

27. John Howard Lawson, "The Hitler-Stalin Pact," 859, folder 7, box 99, Lawson Papers. After initially denying its existence, Lawson was still defending the Hitler-Stalin pact in the 1960s. See ibid., 853–54.

28. Maurice Isserman, *Which Side Were You On? The American Com-munist Party during the Second World War* (Urbana: University of Illinois Press, 1993), 32–36.

29. See ibid., 33.

30. "The Meaning of the Non-aggression Pact," *Soviet Russia Today,* September 1939.

31. Harvey Klehr, John Earl Haynes, and Kyrill M. Anderson, *The Soviet World of American Communism* (New Haven, CT: Yale University Press, 1998), 73–78.

32. See Isserman, *Which Side,* 33.

33. Considerable evidence of this about-face is in pt. 1, 120–36, COM-PIC.

34. This summary of CPUSA positions in September 1939 is based substantially on Howe and Coser, *American Communist Party,* 388–89. The rapid pace of developments was most embarrassing. The *New Masses* called on the Roosevelt administration to give economic assistance to Poland in the edition appearing on September 19, two days after the Soviet invasion. See Isserman, *Which Side,* 39.

35. "National Committee Communist Party of the United States of America: Keep America out of the Imperialist War!" (October 1939) in Johnpoll, *Documentary History,* 6:169–72. This document contained the resolutions of the September meeting in Chicago.

36. Earl Browder, *Unity for Peace and Democracy* (1939), reprinted in Johnpoll, *Documentary History,* 6:46–50.

37. Quoted in Thompson, "Nationalist Propaganda," 389.

38. Document 15 in Klehr, Haynes, and Anderson, *Soviet World,* 81–83.

39. Political Committee of the CPUSA, "America and the International Situation," reprinted in Johnpoll, *Documentary History,* 6:159.

40. Howe and Coser, *American Communist Party,* 402. American Zionists, to their credit, attacked the Jewish section's analysis as "loathsome." See ibid.

41. Schwartz, *Hollywood Writers' Wars,* 149, 87.

42. Isserman, *Which Side,* 43.

43. Lardner, *I'd Hate Myself,* 101.

44. See Lawson, "Hitler-Stalin Pact."

45. Robert Minor (CPUSA official) quoted in Klehr, Haynes, and Anderson, *Soviet World,* 77–78.

46. A Hollywood journalist compared the Hitler-Stalin pact to the introduction of sound in films in the magnitude of the perturbation it caused in Hollywood, an analogy that tells us much about the parochial mentality of Hollywood. See Billingsley, *Hollywood Party,* 77.

47. Klehr, Haynes, and Anderson, *Soviet World,* 72.

48. *Hollywood Now* (then issued by the Hollywood League for Democratic Action), August 1940, clipping in FBI, Los Angeles, file 65-796, 12.

49. See FBI, Los Angeles, file 65-796, 4.

50. See ibid., 7.

51. Ibid., 73.

52. Executive Board, "Statement of the Hollywood League for Democratic Action," August 1940, in ibid., 15–17.

53. See FBI, Los Angeles, file 65-796, 68.
54. Koch, *Double Lives,* 252.
55. Howe and Coser, *American Communist Party,* 395.
56. Koestler quoted in Billingsley, *Hollywood Party,* 205.
57. Stewart quoted in Radosh and Radosh, *Red Star,* 80.
58. Stewart quoted in Schwartz, *Hollywood Writers' Wars,* 173–74.
59. Billingsley, *Hollywood Party,* 86.
60. Moran and Rogin, "'What's the Matter with Capra,'" 110.

4. The Roosevelt Administration and Film during the War

1. This was the conclusion of the congressional committee investigating the Katyń Massacre after the testimony of Ambassador Averill Harriman and Under Secretary of State Sumner Welles regarding American policy toward Poland and Russia. See "Final Report" in *Reprinting of House Report No. 2505, 82nd Congress, Concerning the Katyn Forest Massacre* (Washington, DC: GPO, 1988), 4–6.

2. Piotr S. Wandycz, *The United States and Poland* (Cambridge, MA: Harvard University Press, 1980), 250–51.

3. Roosevelt quoted in Anna M. Cienciala, "Polityka mocarstw zachodnich wobec Polski i Powstania Warszawskiego," *Białostockie Teki Historyczne* 3 (2005): 273.

4. Roosevelt quoted in ibid., 278.

5. "Final Report," *House Report No. 2505,* 9–11.

6. Cienciala, "Polityka," 274. The remark was made to Harry Hopkins in March 1943. The rather cavalier disdain with which Roosevelt treated Polish issues is evinced by his intention of appointing the Irish political hack James Curley (the "Irish Mussolini," who had been jailed twice for corruption) ambassador to Warsaw in 1938.

7. Jan Ciechanowski quoted in William Larsh, "W. Averell Harriman and the Polish Question, December 1943–August 1944," *East European Politics and Society* 7, no. 3 (1993): 552.

8. Roosevelt quoted in Cienciala, "Polityka," 279. The remark was made in May 1944.

9. Richard C. Lukas, *Bitter Legacy: Polish-American Relations in the Wake of World War II* (Lexington: University Press of Kentucky, 1982), 129.

10. Roosevelt's Justice Department had charged the movie industry with complex antitrust violations in 1938. When the studios became cooperative, the case was dropped after obvious White House intervention in 1940. Hence Hollywood was both beholden to and cowed by FDR. See

Richard W. Steele, "The Great Debate: Roosevelt, the Media, and the Coming of the War, 1940–1941," *Journal of American History* 71, no. 1 (1984): 70–73.

11. K. R. M. Short, "Hollywood: An Essential War Industry," *Historical Journal of Film, Radio and Television* 5 (March 1985).

12. This sketch of the OWI relies substantially on two excellent studies: Clayton R. Koppes and Gregory D. Black, "What to Show the World: The Office of War Information and Hollywood, 1942–1945," *Journal of American History* 64, no. 1 (1977), and Clayton R. Koppes and Gregory D. Black, "Blacks, Loyalty, and Motion-Picture Propaganda in World War II," *Journal of American History* 73, no. 2 (1986): 384–86.

13. Koppes and Black, "What to Show," 87.

14. Culbert, "Our Awkward Ally," 137.

15. Koppes and Black describe the OWI as "left-liberal." Clayton R. Koppes and Gregory D. Black, *Hollywood Goes to War: How Politics, Profits, and Propaganda Shaped World War II Movies* (Berkeley: University of California Press, 1990), 111.

16. Davis quoted in ibid., 88.

17. Steele, "Great Debate," 70.

18. Leo C. Rosten to Elmer Davis, August 1942, quoted in Gregory D. Black and Clayton R. Koppes, "OWI Goes to the Movies: The Bureau of Intelligence's Criticism of Hollywood, 1942–1943," *Prologue* 6, no. 1 (1974): 48.

19. Memorandum, April 30, 1941, box 324, Sherwood Collection: OWI, Harry L. Hopkins Papers, Franklin D. Roosevelt Presidential Library, Hyde Park, NY.

20. Harry L. Hopkins to Stephen Early, September 3, 1941, box 324, Sherwood Collection: OWI.

21. Office of Emergency Management to Harry L. Hopkins, March 9, 1942, enclosing Cornelius DuBois, "Survey of Intelligence Materials No. 12 for Office of Facts and Figures, Bureau of Intelligence," box 324, Sherwood Collection: OWI. See esp. p. 5.

22. See John Earl Haynes and Harvey Klehr, *Venona: Decoding Soviet Espionage in America* (New Haven, CT: Yale University Press, 1999), 196–98.

23. See Schwartz, *Hollywood Writers' Wars,* 295n199.

24. For Dunne, the Russians were "historically threatened," and their desire to dominate Poland was understandable. See Dunne, interview, 120, 264.

25. See Louis Robert Coatney, "The Katyn Massacre: An Assessment of Its Significance as a Public and Historical Issue in the United States and

Great Britain, 1940–1993" (master's thesis, Western Illinois University, 1993). A deputy director of the Overseas Branch admitted, very delicately, that the OWI had been criticized for the content of its "overseas work" regarding Poland's frontiers. See Joseph Barnes, "Fighting with Information: OWI Overseas," *Public Opinion Quarterly* 7, no. 1 (1943): 37. Dunne dismisses as nonsense the idea that there were Communists in the OWI. He refers to the OWI, alive with partisan politics, as a "no-politics organization." He also explains that he worked with party members because "they seemed so sincere." Dunne, *Take Two,* 110, 160–61, 165.

26. Regarding Bergquist's party membership, see the FBI's "Communist Infiltration of the Motion Picture Industry," July 8, 1947, pt. 5, 6, COMPIC, where her last name is misspelled as "Birquist." Her party membership was confirmed in a subsequent FBI report. "The Communist Infiltration into the Motion Picture Industry," July 15, 1949, pt. 8, 24, COMPIC.

27. The manual is reprinted in K. R. M. Short, ed., "Washington's Information Manual for Hollywood," *Historical Journal of Film, Radio and Television* 3 (October 1986). It was technically issued not by the OWI but by one of its predecessors, the Hollywood Branch of the Office of the Coordinator of Government Films, part of the Office of Government Reports. Cf. Short, "Washington's Information Manual," 171. Even the leftist Buhle acknowledges the radical nature of the manual. See Buhle and Wagner, *Radical Hollywood,* 204.

28. Short, "Washington's Information Manual," 176–77.

29. Memorandum, n.d., folder 2, box 9, Lawson Papers

30. Short, "Hollywood Fights Anti-Semitism"; Doneson, *Holocaust in American Film,* 44–46.

31. Fyne, *Hollywood Propaganda,* 10.

32. "Motion Pictures Go to War," *Letter from America,* August 27, 1943, 4, clipping in container 212, John Winant Papers, Roosevelt Presidential Library.

33. "Disney Finishes Film for Russia," *Letter from America,* December 31, 1943, 4, clipping in container 212, Winant Papers. It should be noted that *Letter from America* also ran "Critics Praise 'Madame Curie'" (January 28, 1944, clipping in container 212, Winant Papers), which, like the film, notes in passing that she was a Pole but does not discuss Poland.

34. "Rough Draft: Resume of Activities of Hollywood Office, Bureau of Motion Pictures, OWI, during the First Year of Operation (May, 1942 to April 1943 inclusive)," 6, file "Nelson Poynter from 4/13/43–6/16/45," box 1442, RG 208, National Archives.

35. Ralph Ingersoll to Nelson Poynter, September 15, 1935, folder "Poynter, Nelson," box 16, Lowell Mellett Papers, Roosevelt Presidential Library.

36. Mayhew, *Ayn Rand,* 21.

37. Walter Wanger, "OWI and Motion Pictures," *Public Opinion Quarterly* 7, no. 1 (1943): 100, 103, 104.

38. Ulric Bell to Nelson Poynter, May 19, 1943; Nelson Poynter to Lowell Mellet, April 29, 1943, both in folder "Poynter, Nelson."

39. See Wanger, "OWI and Motion Pictures," 103–4.

40. "War Information Manual" enclosed in Warren Pierce to Lowell Mellett, April 19, 1943, 1, 3, file "Nelson Poynter from 4/13/43–6/16/45."

41. Nelson Poynter, "We Can Do Business with Russia," October 10, 1942, file "Nelson Poynter from 8/1/42 thru 11/30/42," box 1443, RG 208, National Archives. In May 1943, Poynter told Mellett that there was a huge number of new Russian films under way—biographies of Stalin, celebrations of battlefield heroics, and so forth—from virtually every studio. Only one film from the list he provided was ever completed. See Nelson Poynter, "Motion Pictures Dealing with the Soviet Union," May 8, 1943, folder "Poynter, Nelson."

42. Poynter, "We Can Do Business."

43. Quoted in Mayhew, *Ayn Rand,* 34.

44. Ibid., 22.

45. Paul Jarrico, interview by Patrick McGilligan, in McGilligan and Buhle, *Tender Comrades,* 339.

46. See John Wexley, interview by Patrick McGilligan and Ken Mate, in McGilligan and Buhle, *Tender Comrades,* 715. Cf. Mayhew, *Ayn Rand,* 13–14. *Song of Russia* did not protect Mayer from the scorn of John Howard Lawson, who dismissed him as unable to grasp the essence of the "antifascist struggle." Lawson, *Film in the Battle,* 35–36.

47. Mayhew, *Ayn Rand,* 31.

48. "Summary on the Communist Infiltration," 113. The Hollywood Writers Mobilization, a quintessential party front, was begun in 1942 and was dominated by party members. Its chairman was Robert Rossen, and prominent members included John Howard Lawson, Ring Lardner Jr., Richard Collins, John Weber, Abraham Polonsky, Jay Gorney, and Herbert Biberman. Howard Koch was also a member. Ibid.

49. Nelson Poynter to Robert Buckner, December 3, 1942, folder "Poynter, Nelson."

50. See Jack L. Hammersmith, "The U.S. Office of War Information (OWI) and the Polish Question, 1943–1945," *Polish Review* 19, no. 1 (1974). The 1940 MGM film *Comrade X,* a comedy that portrayed the

Soviet Union unsympathetically, was reedited after the German invasion of Soviet Russia in 1941. An "explanatory forward" was added, "asserting that any spoofing of the Russians . . . was intended only as good, clean fun between comrades-in-arms." Fyne, *Hollywood Propaganda,* 27, 103.

51. Regarding Beneš's determination to propitiate Moscow, see, e.g., Larsh, "Harriman," 514–15.

52. That Victor László was a Czech was not lost on reviewers. Bosley Crowther managed to mention the fact four times in a brief review. *New York Times,* November 27, 1942.

53. Ethan Mordden, *The Hollywood Studios: House Style in the Golden Age of the Movies* (New York: Simon and Schuster, 1988), 230.

54. Lowell Mellett to Harry Warner, November 7, 1940, file "Warner Brothers," box 1448, RG 208, National Archives. For Jack Warner's offer, see Steele, "Great Debate," 74.

55. Charles Einfeld to Lowell Mellett, December 26, 1941, file "Einfield, Chas.—Warner Brothers," box 1433, RG 208, National Archives.

56. Lowell Mellett to Harry Warner, January 10, 1942, file "Warner Brothers," National Archives

57. Charles Einfeld to Frank Capra, April 24, 1942, folder "1942 Mar.–Apr.," box 6A, Frank Capra Collection, Wesleyan Cinema Archives, Wesleyan University, Middletown, CT.

58. Snow, "Confessions," 61.

59. This was Poynter's reaction to Jack Warner when discussing his film *Edge of Darkness:* "I would have to trot out every superlative to tell you what a truly fine and penetrating picture" it is. Nelson Poynter to Jack Warner, March 11, 1943, file "Edge of Darkness," box 3515, RG 208, National Archives.

60. See M. Thorsen, "Script Review," November 28, 1942, file "Mission to Moscow," box 3521, RG 208, National Archives. The OWI was impatient for the film's release and urged the broadest possible screening. OWI, memorandum, April 29, 1943, file "Mission to Moscow," National Archives.

61. Nelson Poynter to Howard Koch, June 1, 1943; Nelson Poynter to Charles Einfeld, June 1, 1943, both in file "Mission to Moscow," National Archives.

62. Ulric Bell to NN, April 29, 1943, file "Mission to Moscow," National Archives.

63. Nelson Poynter to Lowell Mellett, "Trends in Hollywood Pictures," May 24, 1943, file "Nelson Poynter from 4/13/43–6/16/45."

64. Opinion polls, compiled 1943, file "Mission to Moscow," National Archives.

65. BMP, memorandum, December 28, 1942, file "Song of Russia," box 3526, RG 208, National Archives.

66. Lowell Mellett to Warren Pierce, January 9, 1943, file "Song of Russia," National Archives; Warren Pierce to Maurice Revners (MGM), January 11, 1943, file "Song of Russia," National Archives; Lowell Mellett to Vladimir Bazykin, January 5, 1943, file "Bazykin, Vladimir I," box 1432, RG 208, National Archives. In the inserted dialogue, the character who suggests that the Hitler-Stalin pact revealed cooperation between the Soviets and the Germans is shown to be wrong and embarrassed by his fatuity. See Paul Jarrico and Richard Collins, "Russia," October 30, 1942, 20, file "Maurice Reves—MGM," box 1445, RG 208, National Archives.

67. See Lillian Bergquist, report, December 31, 1942, file "Boy from Stalingrad," box 3512, RG 208, National Archives.

68. For example, see the enthusiastic comments about 1945's *Counterattack* in J. Bercovici and M. Gyorgy, report, May 24, 1945, and similar praise for 1944's *Days of Glory* written by Dorothy B. Jones, April 1, 1944, both in box 3514, RG 208, National Archives. *Boy from Stalingrad* (1942) was criticized only because it did not make the Russians "heroic" enough by spending more time on the importance of the Battle of Stalingrad. Bergquist, report, December 31, 1942. *Mission to Moscow* was "remarkable" and "a very great contribution," M. Thorsen raved (review, November 28, 1942, file "Mission to Moscow," National Archives); *Song of Russia* was greeted with enthusiasm (memorandum, December 28, 1942, file "Song of Russia," National Archives); and *The North Star* was "tremendous" and a "privilege" to review, its only flaw being an insufficiently explicit defense of Moscow's policy during the years of Soviet-Nazi collaboration (Sally Kaye, review, May 12, 1943; Ulric Bell to Sam Goldwyn, September 24, 1943, both in file "The North Star," box 3522, RG 208, National Archives). No film was ever criticized for showing the Soviet Union or Communism too positively.

69. Review, September 21, 1942, file "Appointment in Berlin," box 3511, RG 208, National Archives.

70. Review, September 21, 1942, file "Counter Espionage," box 3514, RG 208, National Archives.

71. Review, n.d., file "Diplomatic Courier," box 3517, RG 208, National Archives.

72. Review, April 14, 1943, file "American Cavalcade," box 3511, RG 208, National Archives.

73. Reviews, n.d., files "Block Busters" and "Blonde Fever," box 3512, RG 208, National Archives.

74. Review, September 18, 1942, file "Assignment in Brittany," box 3511, RG 208, National Archives.

75. Review, n.d., file "Secrets of the Underground," box 3525, RG 208, National Archives.

76. Memorandum, January 27, 1943, file "Hitler's Madmen," box 3518, RG 208, National Archives.

77. Memorandum, December 22, 1942, file "Hangmen Also Die," box 3517, RG 208, National Archives.

78. Review, October 16, 1942, file "Avengers," box 3511, RG 208, National Archives.

79. Review, March 15, 1943, file "Background to Danger," box 3511; review, December 15, 1942, file "Bomber's Moon," box 3512, both in RG 208, National Archives.

80. M. B. Gratz, feature review, September 14, 1942, file "Miss V from Moscow," box 3521, RG 208, National Archives.

81. Peg Fenwick, review, July 29, 1943, file "Destroyer," box 3515, RG 208, National Archives.

82. Before shooting himself in 1962, Brennan wrote a number of scripts, none noteworthy, most featuring Irish characters.

83. Sandy Roth, feature script review, March 22, 1943, file "Memo to a Firing Squad," box 3521, RG 208, National Archives.

84. The studios were very sensitive to issues of ethnicity. For example, Warner Brothers was concerned that a negative character in *Casablanca* might have been understood to have a Spanish-sounding name. He had to be clearly Italian, hence from an Axis power, or the name would be changed. Warner Brothers apparently had no such concerns about offending Poles. See Stephen D. Youngkin, *The Lost One: A Life of Peter Lorre* (Lexington: University Press of Kentucky, 2005), 204.

85. Regarding Ireland, see Warren H. Pierce to John Mock (Columbia Pictures), June 16, 1943, file "Motion Picture, Bureau of—Hollywood Office," box 1438, RG 208, National Archives.

86. Kracauer, "National Types," 64.

87. See McLaughlin and Parry, *We'll Always Have,* 118.

88. Lopez, "Are All Latins," 405.

89. BMP, "The White Cliffs," memorandum, March 1, 1943, folder "Poynter, Nelson."

90. See files for *Edge of Darkness, North Star, Tomorrow the World,* and *Desperate Journey,* Clipping Files, Herrick Library.

91. See folder 247, "Air Force," Motion Picture Association of America Production Code Administration Records, Herrick Library (hereafter cited as MPAA-PCA).

5. Hollywood's Version of the War: The Polish Films

1. In early 1943 Warner Brothers briefly considered making a film about a Polish aviator based on a radio broadcast written by Robert St. John. Apparently, this project was dropped, and certain elements may have been incorporated into the film *In Our Time.* The evidence is fragmentary. See James J. Geller to R. J. Obringer, January 4, 1943; contract, signed by Robert St. John, January 13, 1943; and W. G. Wallace to R. J. Obringer, February 17, 1943, all in story file 2792, *In Our Time* Collection, Warner Bros. Archives.

2. *To Be or Not To Be,* directed by Ernest Lubitsch, screenplay by Edwin Justus Mayer, starring Jack Benny, Carole Lombard, and Robert Stack (United Artists, 1942).

3. See the contemporary reviews by John T. McManus in *PM* and Herb Sterne in Rob Wagner's *Script,* both reprinted in Anthony Slide, *Selected Film Criticism, 1941–1950* (Metuchen, NJ: Scarecrow, 1983), 236–38. Benny's discussion of the film in his autobiography is disappointingly superficial. See *Sunday Nights at Seven: The Jack Benny Story* (New York: Time Warner, 1990), 149–51.

4. Joseph Boskin, writing in 1999, described the film as "a classic of very high rank." Joseph Boskin, "Jack Benny," in *American National Biography,* ed. John A. Garraty and Mark C. Carnes (New York: Oxford University Press, 1999), 2:600–602. Lubitsch had been regarded by the FBI as a fellow traveler before *Ninotchka.* However, he was so attacked by Hollywood Communists for this satire of the Soviet Union that they reconsidered that characterization. See pt. 1, 69, COMPIC. A positive and intelligent reading of the film is in Eyman, *Ernst Lubitsch,* 289–305.

5. Colin Shindler, *Hollywood Goes to War: Films and American Society, 1939–1952* (London: Routledge and Paul, 1979), 46–47. Reviewing the film in 1942, the *New York Times'* Bosley Crowther noted that it opened "under delicate circumstances at best," because of Lombard's recent death in a plane crash as well as the sensitive topic. Crowther condemned the film: "To say it is callous and macabre is understating the case." *New York Times,* March 7, 1942, reprinted in *The New York Times Film Reviews, 1913–1968* (New York: New York Times Books, 1970) 3:1851–52. Cf. William Paul, *Ernst Lubitsch's American Comedy* (New York: Columbia University Press, 1983), 225–27.

6. Ruman was, let us remember, a Pole in 1935's *The Wedding Night,* though he was then billed as Siegfried Rumann. Ruman's performance in *To Be or Not to Be* has been highly praised. See Juran, *Old Familiar Faces,* 251.

7. See John Russell Taylor, *Strangers in Paradise: The Hollywood Émigrés, 1933–1950* (New York: Holt, Rinehart and Winston, 1983), 178–79, and Paul, *Ernst Lubitsch's American Comedy,* 225–49. There were a few positive contemporary evaluations. The *Hollywood Reporter,* February 18, 1942, pronounced the film "a farce of far deeper significance than ordinary," and the *Motion Picture Herald,* February 28, 1942, called it a "thrilling patriotic melodrama" but cautioned that Poles might not appreciate it. Clippings in *To Be or Not to Be* files, Clipping Files, Herrick Library.

8. Bosley Crowther, "Against a Sea of Troubles: In 'To Be or Not to Be,' Ernst Lubitsch Has Opposed Real Tragedy with an Incongruous Comedy Plot," *New York Times,* March 22, 1942.

9. Theodore Strauss, "Again the Ten Worst," *New York Times,* December 27, 1942.

10. "Survey of War Pictures," *Communiqué,* August 22, 1942, 7, copy in file "Nelson Poynter from 8/1/42 thru 11/30/42."

11. Irving Hoffman summarized many critical evaluations in his "Lombard, Benny Performance Hailed by Gotham Critics," *Hollywood Reporter,* February 18, 1942. The *Philadelphia Inquirer* (clipping, n.d.) pronounced the film "tasteless." *Film Music Notes,* March 1942, found the humor "weird." Robert Stack later recalled that the film was "lambasted" for being "in terrible taste." See his letter to the *Los Angeles Times,* April 13, 1997. Clippings in *To Be or Not to Be* files, Clipping Files, Herrick Library. Reports of people refusing to work on the film and one woman—who had recently been in Poland—fainting on the set added to the controversy. See Eyman, *Ernst Lubitsch,* 295.

12. Fyne argues that the propaganda value of the film was limited because the Germans were all "buffoons or incompetents" and the joking about the war lacked "propriety or sensitivity." Fyne, *Hollywood Propaganda,* 215.

13. Lubitsch quoted in Eyman, *Ernst Lubitsch,* 302. The exact date of this statement is unclear; it was probably late 1943 or 1944. Reports that Polish American film audiences liked the film suggest that any portrayal of Poland was appreciated by a population whose homeland was usually ignored.

14. Shindler, *Hollywood Goes to War,* 46–47.

15. "The Poles are brave, nationalistic, and contemptuous of their Nazi rulers" is the conclusion of James E. Combs and Sara T. Combs in *Film Propaganda and American Politics* (New York: Garland, 1994), 60. Doneson remarks that the Poles are shown as able to "foil the Nazis." Doneson, *Holocaust in American Film,* 46.

16. As Leland A. Poague notes, "to understand" the film, the viewer has

to appreciate Tura's "devotion to the cause of Poland." Leland A. Poague, *The Cinema of Ernst Lubitsch* (South Brunswick, NJ: Barnes, 1978), 90. Calvin MacPherson, however, noted that the Poles, save Greenberg, were "untouched by grief," a feature he found disturbing. Calvin MacPherson, "Nazis Not So Fearful as Funny," *St. Louis Post-Dispatch,* March 22, 1942, clipping in *To Be or Not to Be* files, Clipping Files, Herrick Library.

17. Roger Manvell emphasizes that both director Lubitsch and producer Korda were Jewish and concludes that "some of the key comic characters involved were rather sentimentalized Polish-Jewish types." Roger Manvell, "To Be or Not to Be," in *The International Dictionary of Films and Filmmakers,* 1st ed., vol. 1, *Films,* ed. Christopher Lyon (Chicago: St. James, 1984), 478. This is a serious misreading of the film; only Greenberg is definitely Jewish, and thus his repeated rendering of Shylock's Rialto soliloquy is peculiarly appropriate and moving. This is true regardless of whether he is referring specifically to the Nazis' mistreatment of Poland's Jews or to the trial of the entire population of Poland; both interpretations are possible in what was probably an intended ambiguity.

18. Lubitsch was aware of the criticism that his film made the Poles appear ridiculous. His response was that it was actors, not Poles, who were figures of ridicule in the film. See Paul, *Ernst Lubitsch's American Comedy,* 249. Cf. Toronto Film Society, "Film B of Series A," March 13, 1998, clipping in *To Be or Not to Be* files, Herrick Library. In his defense, Lubitsch claimed that the brief scenes of destroyed Warsaw made his view of the war obvious. See Sam Ho, "To Be or Not to Be," in *Cinema Texas: Program Notes,* March 21, 1983, 17–23, clipping in *To Be or Not to Be* files, Herrick Library.

19. To be sure, the Polish forces stationed in Great Britain worked closely with the British authorities, but a Polish airman would report to his own, Polish, commanders first.

20. See Eyman, *Ernst Lubitsch,* 297–98. Eyman regards Lubitsch's proposal as insincere, but that is only speculation.

21. This raises, of course, the tangential matter of Hollywood's glowing portrayal of the British during the war.

22. Lubitsch remarked, "Never have I said in a picture anything derogative about Poland or the Poles. On the contrary. I have portrayed them as a gallant people who do not cry on other people's shoulders in their misery but even in the darkest day never lose courage and ingenuity or their sense of humour." Lubitsch quoted in Taylor, *Strangers in Paradise,* 179.

23. Lengyel—a name that ironically means "Pole" in Hungarian—was born Menyhert Lebovics in 1880. Variously a journalist and playwright, he was long associated with Lubitsch. The Jewish Lengyel left Europe

268 Notes to Pages 87–88

for America in 1935. He is best known as the author of the screenplay *Ninotchka*. He was also the librettist for Béla Bartók's *The Miraculous Mandarin*. Regarding his politics and attitudes toward Poland, nothing is known. See André de Toth, *Fragments: Portraits from the Inside* (London: Faber and Faber, 1994), 126n2. Mayer was described by the FBI as a "follower of the Communist Party line." See pt. 1, 115, COMPIC. Cf. "Hungarian Dramatist Dies at 94," *Los Angeles Herald-Examiner,* October 29, 1974, clipping in Melchior Lengyel files, Clipping Files, Herrick Library. The original story came largely from Lubitsch. Eyman, *Ernst Lubitsch,* 290.

24. Dick, *Star-Spangled Screen,* 161–63.

25. Bruce Eder, "Alexander Korda: Biography," *AllMovie,* http://all-movie.com/artist/alexander-korda-97893/bio.

26. See Taylor, *Strangers in Paradise,* 130–33. Cf. de Toth, *Fragments,* 281.

27. The chief villain, Professor Siletsky, a Nazi posing as a Pole, does, however, have a misspelled name.

28. The Jewish Benny had family ties to Poland. He was born Benjamin Kubelsky in 1894 in Chicago (though he always joked about being from Waukegan). Benny's father was born in Russian Poland; his mother was the daughter of immigrants from historical Lithuania. See Boskin, "Jack Benny," 2:600–602. In his autobiography, Benny refers to his father as coming from "a ghetto village near the Polish border"; what, precisely, that means is difficult to determine. Benny, *Sunday Nights at Seven,* 8.

29. *In Our Time,* directed by Vincent Sherman, screenplay by Ellis St. Joseph and Howard Koch, starring Ida Lupino and Paul Henreid (Warner Brothers, 1944). The film is described as "forgettable" and "negligible" by a student of the Warner Brothers oeuvre. Ted Sennett, *Warner Brothers Presents: The Most Exciting Years—from* The Jazz Singer *to* White Heat (New Rochelle, NY: Arlington House, 1971), 43–44, 313.

30. See Howard Koch, *As Time Goes By: Memoirs of a Writer* (New York: Harcourt Brace Jovanovich, 1979), 93–95.

31. See Ellis St. Joseph's brief memoir in *Forties Film Talk: Oral Histories of Hollywood, with 120 Lobby Posters,* ed. Doug McClelland (Jefferson, NC: McFarland, 1992), 162–64. Director William Wellman later described Warner as "one of the most despicable men I've ever known in my life. . . . I hate him." William Wellman, interview by Patrick McGilligan, in Patrick McGilligan, *Film Crazy: Interviews with Hollywood Legends* (New York: St. Martin's, 2000), 242.

32. In 1947 Jack Warner mentioned Koch "among others as a writer he had fired for his political leanings." Though Koch subsequently defended himself, he was "graylisted" thereafter. Warner's motives in denouncing

Koch have been questioned. See Charles L. P. Silet, "Howard Koch," in *International Dictionary of Films and Filmmakers*, 2nd ed., vol. 4, *Writers and Production Artists*, ed. Samantha Cook (Detroit: St. James, 1993), 424–27. Cf. Bethany Neubauer, "Jack Leonard Warner," in Garraty and Carnes, *American National Biography*, 22:693.

33. Koch, *As Time Goes By*, 98. A sympathetic biographer describes Koch as "left but not a communist." Gerald Horne, *Class Struggle in Hollywood, 1930–1950: Moguls, Mobsters, Stars, Reds and Trade Unionists* (Austin: University of Texas Press, 2001), 134. Ceplair and Englund, in their study of Hollywood politics in the era, describe Koch, along with Lillian Hellman and Dalton Trumbo, as "Communists in everything but name," an overly indulgent conclusion because Hellman had been a Communist and Koch was a Stalinist even if not formally a party member. See Ceplair and Englund, *Inquisition in Hollywood*, 132. Koch's correspondence is replete with references to contemporary politics, which he followed avidly. It is liberally sprinkled with references to "reactionaries and fascists." See, for example, Howard Koch to Jay Leyda, February 20, 1944, January 14, [1945], folder "Koch, Howard & Anne," box 5, Jay and Silan Chen Leyda Papers, Tamiment Library and Robert F. Wagner Labor Archives, Elmer Holmes Bobst Library, New York University, New York. A 1943 FBI report described Hellman as "a fanatical follower of the C.P. line." Pt. 1, 35, COMPIC. The FBI regarded Koch as a probable Communist. "Summary on the Communist Infiltration," 158. Koch once said that though he was not a Communist, "I was doing the same things that they were doing." Koch quoted in Aljean Harmetz, *The Making of Casablanca: Bogart, Bergman and World War II* (New York: Hyperion, 2002), 52.

34. See Eliot Stein, "Howard Koch, Julius Epstein, Frank Miller Interview," May 1995, http://www.vincasa.com/indexkoch.html. Cf. James Fisher, "Phillip G. Epstein," in Garraty and Carnes, *American National Biography*, 7:547, where it is noted that Koch "strengthened [*Casablanca*'s] political tone." In 1942 Koch described his role as creating a "serious melodrama of present-day significance." Howard Koch to Hal Wallis, May 11, 1942, in *Inside Warner Bros. (1935–1951)*, ed. Rudy Behlmer (New York: Viking, 1985), 205. The authorship of the script is a most controversial question. Julius Epstein plausibly maintains that he and his brother were the principal authors. "Julius J. Epstein: A King of Comedy," interview by Pat McGilligan, in *Backstory: Interviews with Screenwriters of Hollywood's Golden Age*, ed. Pat McGilligan (Berkeley: University of California Press, 1986), 185–86. Cf. Dick, *Star-Spangled Screen*, 273n17. Koch, who obviously disliked the Epsteins, rejected their claim to authorship and argued, curiously, that "no one authored Casablanca," an original

hypothesis to be sure. Howard Koch to Jay Leyda, April 12, [?], folder "Koch, Howard & Anne."

35. Dick, *Star-Spangled Screen,* 275n6.

36. Koch quoted in Rudy Behlmer, *America's Favorite Movies* (New York: Ungar, 1982), 169.

37. Koppes and Black, *Hollywood Goes to War,* 216. Even Koch admitted that the film was bad, though this was due, it seems, to the adulteration of his work. Howard Koch to Jay Leyda, February 28, 1944, folder "Koch, Howard & Anne."

38. Radosh and Radosh, *Red Star,* 98. In his memoirs, Koch describes Lawson as someone who "believed in people." He notes, "If politics had been a religion, he would have made sainthood." This tells us much more about Koch than it does about Lawson. Koch, *As Time Goes By,* 89.

39. Radosh and Radosh, *Red Star,* 98.

40. See the FBI's "Communist Infiltration of the Motion Picture Industry," July 8, 1947, 12, where she is listed as "Green, Anna, aka Ann Koch."

41. Dick, *Star-Spangled Screen,* 113. Cf. Ceplair and Englund, *Inquisition in Hollywood,* 437–38. Norma Barzman was introduced to Henreid as one of "the Hollywood Progressive Community," many of whom were later suspected of being Communists. Norma Barzman, *The Red and the Blacklist: The Intimate Memoir of a Hollywood Expatriate* (New York: Thunder's Mouth/Nation, 2003), 7. Koch admitted membership (though he was "not a very active participant") in his lengthy political defense, "To Whom It May Concern," [after 1947], 5, folder 15, box 3, Howard E. Koch Papers, Wisconsin Center for Film and Theater Research.

42. See pt. 1, 78, COMPIC. Lupino's biographer notes that leftism was a "political bond" between Lupino and Henreid. William Donati, *Ida Lupino: A Biography* (Lexington: University Press of Kentucky, 1996), 108, 184.

43. Michael was the nephew of writer Anton Chekhov. St. Joseph later lectured at Michael Chekhov's acting school. *Hollywood Reporter,* September 17, 1993, clipping in Ellis St. Joseph files, Clipping Files, Herrick Library.

44. Sherman quoted in Marowitz, *Other Chekhov,* 233–34. Sherman cast Nazimova and Chekhov as ridiculous Poles. They had given him a part years before, during difficult times, and he repaid them with employment in the picture. See Donati, *Ida Lupino,* 108.

45. Henreid's knowledge of Poland came principally from an affair he had with a Polish girl when he was a teenager. See his appropriately titled *Ladies Man: An Autobiography* (New York: St. Martin's, 1984), 3–4.

46. Bosley Crowther, "In Our Time," *New York Times,* February 12, 1944, reprinted in *New York Times Film Reviews,* 3:1984.

47. Crowther, who had no political objections to the film, found the performances uniformly bad. Ibid., 1984–85.

48. See St. Joseph's recollections in McClelland, *Forties Film Talk,* 163.

49. Wojciech Roszkowski, *Landowners in Poland, 1918–1939* (New York: Columbia University Press, 1991), 133.

50. Windheim had never before played a Pole in his long career. Warner Brothers, with unconscious irony, publicized the strange fact that Poles were never cast as Poles in American films in a press release titled "A Pole Cast as a Pole? In Hollywood, Yes!" See "Your Warner's Press Book," "Publicity—Press Books," folder 683, *In Our Time* Collection, Warner Bros. Archives. Warner Brothers thought it amusing that the studio really had no idea what Poles looked like and had to consider the matter carefully in the film's crowd scenes to cast the right "types." See "Production Notes," "Publicity—Misc.," folder 683, *In Our Time* Collection, Warner Bros. Archives.

51. Quoted in Horne, *Class Struggle,* 79.

52. Henreid, *Ladies Man,* 158.

53. Ellis St. Joseph, "Story Outline: In Our Time," folder 4, box 195, Warner Brothers Scripts.

54. The last king of Poland, Stanisław August Poniatowski, left the throne in 1795, which would make anyone of "royal birth" at least 144 years old in 1939.

55. St. Joseph, "Story Outline: In Our Time," 7.

56. Ibid., 8, 10, 11.

57. Quoted in Donati, *Ida Lupino,* 109.

58. St. Joseph, "Story Outline: In Our Time," 12.

59. Sherman insisted that he never joined the party, though he admitted to being invited on several occasions. "Vincent Sherman: Actor Turned Writer Turned Director," interview by Ronald L. Davis, 1981, in *Just Making Movies: Company Directors on the Studio System* (Jackson: University Press of Mississippi, 2005), 83, 99. After World War II, Warner Brothers fired Sherman without explanation because of accusations that he was a Communist. See "Hollywood Director Sherman Dies at 99," *New York Times,* June 20, 2006.

60. Ellis St. Joseph, "Treatment #2," April 22, 1943, 1–2, folder 5, box 195, Warner Brothers Scripts.

61. Ibid.

62. Ibid., 1, 4.

63. Ibid., 8, 13.

64. Ellis St. Joseph, "Temporary," April 28, 1943, 38, folder 6, box 195, Warner Brothers Scripts.

65. Ibid., 48, 55.

66. Ibid., 65.

67. Ibid., 67, 71.

68. Ellis St. Joseph, "Final," May 20, 1943, folder 7, box 195, Warner Brothers Scripts. In October producer Wald suggested this be replaced by these words to begin the film: "Lest we forget—a small but brave country Poland where our story begins." See Jerry Wald to Steve Trilling, October 1, 1943, folder 1998, *In Our Time* Collection, Warner Bros. Archives. The words suggest that, to Wald, Poland and the September campaign were already lost in the mists of time.

69. St. Joseph, "Final," 35, 51–53.

70. Ellis St. Joseph, "Revised Final," May 29, 1943, 87, 82–83, 124, folder 8, box 195, Warner Brothers Scripts.

71. Ibid., 128, 129.

72. Ibid., 132–33.

73. Ibid., 138.

74. Starzyński quoted in Marian Marek Drozdowski, *Moja droga do III Rzeczypospolitej* (Warsaw: Typografika, 1999), 108.

75. The circumstances of Starzyński's death in German captivity have never been elucidated, but the most likely date is 1943. Contrary to the nonsense suggested by the script for *In Our Time,* Starzyński directed Warsaw in uniform (he was a reserve officer) to show his solidarity with the army and government of Poland. To suggest that he epitomized a populist reaction to the Polish government is a contradiction of reality. See Marian Marek Drozdowski, *Stefan Starzyński, prezydent Warszawy* (Warsaw: PWN, 1976), esp. 172–74 and, regarding his death, 321–22.

76. Maltz's additions, dated June 28, 1943, are in folder "Scenario," folder 1998, *In Our Time* Collection, Warner Bros. Archives. The July 5, 1943, addition of the speech about a "people's Poland" is in folder "Story—Proposed Outlines, Acts II and III," folder 1998, *In Our Time* Collection, Warner Bros. Archives. It is not signed by Maltz, but it corresponds to the period when he was involved with the film; hence I have attributed it to him.

77. Maillison to T. C. Wright, July 20, 1943, July 22, 1943, August 11, 1943, August 28, 1943, folder 1487, "Production Daily Progress Report 10f2"; Jack Warner to Vincent Sherman, July 3, 1943, folder 1998, all in *In Our Time* Collection, Warner Bros. Archives.

78. See "In Our Time" with the words "By Ellis St. Joseph, Howard

Koch" added in Koch's handwriting, May 29, 1943, folder 6, box 1, Koch Papers, Wisconsin Center for Film and Theater Research. This script also contains the insertions made by Koch in July and August. The arrogant Koch added to the script that Łazienki Palace in Warsaw was the work of the architect Bacciarelli. Bacciarelli was, of course, a painter, not an architect; the palace was the work of Merlini.

79. Ibid., 53, 55.

80. Howard Koch, "In Our Time Treatment #3," 2, October 22, 1943, folder 3, box 195, Warner Brothers Scripts.

81. "In Our Time Story Outline—Part II to End," October 22, 1943 (stapled to ibid. but separately paginated), 6–7, folder 3, box 195, Warner Brothers Scripts.

82. Koch's comments on the way the Polish farmers are to be depicted is instructive: they are "superstitious, inept, and disinterested." Koch, "In Our Time Treatment #3," 2. Koch would soon write *Mission to Moscow,* in which Russian peasants are portrayed as alert and eager.

83. "In Our Time Story Outline," 5–6.

84. Koch, "In Our Time Treatment #3," 4.

85. Ibid.

86. Ibid., 6.

87. Ibid., 8–9, 11–12.

88. Drozdowski, *Stefan Starzyński,* 300; Edward Henzel, "Stefan Starzyński, niezłomny Prezydent Warszawy," *Zwoje* 7, no. 11 (1998), http://www.zwoje-scrolls.com/zwoje11/text11.htm.

89. Koch apparently told his wife, Anne, when the picture was done, that whereas the "first two thirds" of the film were "splendid," he and St. Joseph then "went off" and the "last [third] fell to pieces." In a cryptic note, she wrote that St. Joseph and Koch had "run [the film] off for the overseas censors." Anne Koch to Jay Leyda, [1944], folder "Koch, Howard & Anne."

90. Koch, *As Time Goes By,* 94.

91. There was a radical Right movement in prewar Poland, but fascism was rare and certainly could not correctly be used to describe anyone in the 1939 government. Perhaps in Koch's mind, since Finland and Poland both fought against Soviet aggression, they were fascist.

92. See "Production Notes: In Our Time," 1, "Publicity—Miscellaneous," folder 683, *In Our Time* Collection, Warner Bros. Archives. Cf. Donati, *Ida Lupino,* 108.

93. See "Your Warner's Press Book," 1.

94. This suggests that the scope of St. Joseph's story was still very unclear and that the Robert St. John story about a Polish aviator may well

274 Notes to Pages 103–104

have been still under consideration. See Herman Lissauer, "Chronology of World War II from the Invasion of Poland to October 7, 1940," March 19, 1943, "Research," folder 104, *In Our Time* Collection, Warner Bros. Archives.

95. See ibid., 11–13.

96. Herman Lissauer to Jerry Wald, "Further Research Notes," March 27, 1943, "Research," folder 104. This information was repeatedly conveyed by Lissauer's research division. Note the entry for May 21, 1943, in "Research Record," "Research," folder 104.

97. See Herman Lissauer, memoranda, February 27, 1943, March 3, 1943, and April 2, 1943, and his letter to Jerry Wald, May 1, 1943 (which contains a passing reference to work by Barasch), all in "Research," folder 104.

98. Herman Lissauer, "A Chronicle of the Leading Political and Military Events in Europe, 1933–39," "Research," folder 104.

99. Herman Lissauer to T. Strzelecki, April 13, 1943, "Research," folder 104. Warner Brothers also apparently had some rather nebulous dealings with the Polish émigré film producer Marek Libkow. Libkow was in Los Angeles, ostensibly as the "Motion Picture representative of the Polish Information Center, Hollywood." The very status of this agency is unclear. Libkow was providing Warner Brothers, perhaps via Barasch, with technical assistance for the film, but Warner Brothers became convinced that he was simply trying "to soak us." The whole issue is very murky. See Marek Libkow to Jerry Wald, June 18, 1943, "Story—Memos and Correspondence," and Jerry Wald to Lee Anthony, July 16, 1943, both in folder 1998, *In Our Time* Collection, Warner Bros. Archives.

100. Herman Lissauer to T. Strzelecki, March 25, 1943; T. Strzelecki to Herman Lissauer, March 30, 1943; Herman Lissauer to T. Strzelecki, April 7, 1943, all in "Research," folder 1014, *In Our Time* Collection, Warner Bros. Archives.

101. Regarding *Edge of Darkness,* which was released on March 23, 1943, see chap. 4.

102. T. Strzelecki to Herman Lissauer, April 13, 1943, "Research," folder 1014.

103. Herman Lissauer to Jerry Wald, April 19, 1943, "Research," folder 1014.

104. As Lissauer noted, there was no validity to the eye-gouging reference in any event. See Herman Lissauer to Ellis St. Joseph, April 29, 1943, and Herman Lissauer to Jerry Wald (with copies to Ellis St. Joseph and Vincent Sherman), May 6, 1943, both in "Research," folder 1014.

105. T. Strzelecki to Herman Lissauer, May 3, 1943; Lech Niemo-

Niemojowski to Jack Warner, May 20, 1943, both in "Story—Memos and Correspondence."

106. John J. Olejniczak (president, Polish Roman Catholic Union of America) and Stephen S. Grabowski (secretary general, Polish Roman Catholic Union of America) to Warner Brothers, November 8, 1943, folder 1998, *In Our Time* Collection, Warner Bros. Archives.

107. Stefan Ostrowski (president, Polish Refugee Association) to Warner Brothers, November 3, 1943, folder 1998, *In Our Time* Collection, Warner Bros. Archives.

108. Walter Kuman (secretary, Alliance of Polish Clubs) to Warner Brothers, November 10, 1943, folder 1998, *In Our Time* Collection, Warner Bros. Archives. Kuman addressed his protest in the name of "several hundred thousand Polish Jews as well as 5 million Poles in the US."

109. Smith to Jack Warner, "Monday" (form letter by Charles Einfeld with pencil marginalia by Warner), n.d.; Charles Einfeld to Jack Warner, December 2, 1943, both in folder 1998, *In Our Time* Collection, Warner Bros. Archives.

110. Regarding the passion with which Einfeld served Warner Brothers, see Harmetz, *Making of* Casablanca, 270.

111. Form letter commencing with "In answer to your letter," n.d., folder 1998, *In Our Time* Collection, Warner Bros. Archives.

112. Regarding Jack Warner's intervention over minor details, see Jack L. Warner to Steve Trilling and Jerry Wald, September 8, 1943, and Jack L. Warner to Jerry Wald, October 7, 1943, both in folder 1998, *In Our Time* Collection, Warner Bros. Archives.

113. Eleanor Berneis, feature review, January 6, 1944, file "In Our Time," box 3519, RG 208, National Archives. Joseph Breen also reviewed the script and, with its characteristic combination of prudery and political obtuseness, sent a letter to Jack Warner expressing worries about drinking and sex in the film. It was utterly oblivious of the film's political implications. Joseph Breen to Jack Warner, May 25, 1943, "Story—Memos and Correspondence."

114. Berneis, feature review, file "In Our Time," National Archives.

115. "Production Notes: In Our Time," "Publicity—Miscellaneous," folder 683, *In Our Time* Collection, Warner Bros. Archives.

116. Berneis, feature review, file "In Our Time," National Archives.

117. Donati, *Ida Lupino,* 108.

118. The OWI supplied Warner Brothers with material regarding the September campaign for use in the film. Unfortunately, no trace of this can be found. See Mary Elliot (Jerry Wald's secretary) to OWI, n.d., "Story—Memos and Correspondence."

119. Ulric Bell to Steve Trilling (copies to Jerry Wald, Jack Warner, Charles Einfeld, and James Geller), January 8, 1944, file "In Our Time." National Archives. The radical screenwriter Phillip Dunne described both Bell and Poynter as leftists and ardent supporters of FDR. Dunne, interview, 103–4.

120. William S. Cunningham to Steve Trilling, January 10, 1944, file "In Our Time." National Archives.

121. Howard Koch to Jay Leyda, [January–February 1944], folder "Koch, Howard & Anne."

122. Koch to Leyda, February 20, 1944.

123. Marowitz, *Other Chekhov,* 234; Henreid, *Ladies Man,* 158; Sherman quoted in Marowitz, *Other Chekhov,* 233.

124. Little information about the political inclinations of the rest of the film's cast can be ascertained. As noted above, at least three of the featured players were ethnic Russians.

125. Virginia Wright, unidentified clipping, n.d., folder 15, box 1, Koch Papers.

126. Edwin Schallert, "Ida Lupino, Henreid Duo of Quality," *Los Angeles Times,* February 19, 1944, clipping in *In Our Time* files, Clipping Files, Herrick Library.

127. "The Current Cinema: The Polish Question," *New Yorker,* February 12, 1944, clipping in *In Our Time* files, Clipping Files, Herrick Library.

128. Lowell E. Redelings, "In Our Time," *Citizen News,* February 19, 1944, clipping in *In Our Time* files, Clipping Files, Herrick Library.

129. Otis L. Guernsey Jr., "On the Screen," *New York Herald-Tribune,* February 12, 1944.

130. Crowther, "In Our Time," 3:1984.

131. Walter Winchell, "On Broadway," *Zanesville (OH) Signal,* February 15, 1944.

132. Mary Beth Crain, "Henreid Lights Up and Lets Fly," *Los Angeles Times,* August 21, 1977, clipping in Paul Henreid files, Clipping Files, Herrick Library.

133. John T. McManus, "Cinderella Plots a Better Poland," *PM,* February 13, 1944, clipping in *In Our Time* files, Clipping Files, Herrick Library.

134. Buhle and Wagner, *Radical Hollywood,* 253.

135. *Joan of Paris,* directed by Robert Stevenson, screenplay by Jacques Thery, George Kessel, and Ellis St. Joseph, starring Paul Henreid, Michelle Morgan, and Thomas Mitchell (RKO, 1942).

136. Dick, *Star-Spangled Screen,* 150.

137. *None Shall Escape,* directed by André de Toth, screenplay by

Lester Cole, starring Marsha Hunt, Alexander Knox, and Henry Travers (Columbia, 1944). *None Shall Escape* has rarely if ever been broadcast on television and has never been reproduced in VHS or DVD format; only a few prints survive. I was fortunate to arrange a private screening of a 16mm version from the collection of the film archives of the George Eastman House in Rochester, New York. I should like to thank the staff of the archives for their generous cooperation.

138. Jewish producers were very chary about films that too openly raised the issue of anti-Semitism. As Neal Gabler notes, Hollywood was aware of opinion surveys that showed the American public to be distrustful of Jews. Neal Gabler, *An Empire of Their Own: How the Jews Invented Hollywood* (New York: Random House, 1998), 344–45.

139. Long neglected, de Toth's cinematic oeuvre is now being rediscovered. See Fred Camper, "Harsh Master: Films by Andre de Toth," *Chicago Reader,* http://www.chicagoreader.com/movies/archives/1097/10037.html.

140. Mayer quoted in Gabler, *Empire of Their Own,* 368. Cf. Buhle and Wagner, *Radical Hollywood,* 156. Mayer, a Republican, was known for tolerating Communists if they were talented. See Jules Dassin, interview by Patrick McGilligan, in McGilligan and Buhle, *Tender Comrades,* 204.

141. Schwartz correctly and laconically describes Cole's screenplay as "expos[ing] Nazi brutality to the Jews." Schwartz, *Hollywood Writers' Wars,* 274. Cf. Bernard F. Dick, *Radical Innocence: A Critical Study of the Hollywood Ten* (Lexington: University Press of Kentucky 1989), 39.

142. De Toth later argued that Cole "wanted to advocate revenge" in the film, and the two had fundamental disagreements. Unfortunately, de Toth did not elaborate. See *De Toth on de Toth: Putting the Drama in Front of the Camera; A Conversation with Anthony Slide,* ed. Anthony Slide (London: Faber and Faber, 1996), 47.

143. Alexander Knox, "None Shall Escape" (presentation before the Actors' Laboratory of Hollywood, [late 1945–early 1946]), transcript, 1–4, folder "Lectures on Films." Recently an effort has been made to reevaluate the film more positively, but the effort fails. Sylvie Pierre, "A Propos of *None Shall Escape,*" trans. Hilary Radner and Alistair Fox, *Senses of Cinema,* http://archive.sensesofcinema.com/contents/03/26/none_shall_escape.html.

144. See *Hollywood Red: The Autobiography of Lester Cole* (Palo Alto, CA: Ramparts, 1981).

145. Hunt, an admitted political activist, was effectively blacklisted after 1947 for alleged Communist ties, which she denied. See Marsha Hunt, interview by Glenn Lovell, in McGilligan and Buhle, *Tender Comrades,* 305–24. When asked if the film was pro-Soviet many years later,

Hunt's only reaction was to say, with breathless innocence, "Goodness, in those days we were allies." Ibid., 310.

146. See Novick, *Holocaust,* 27.

147. Grimm's final words are "We [Nazis] will rise again and again," and a concluding voice-over intones that "Nazis are all Wilhelm Grimms." These are rather clumsy efforts to suggest that the film has depicted something it has not. This is neither an exposé of the corrupting influence of Nazism nor a critique of the German people; it is a study of a foul human being. Neither the writer nor the director wished to produce such a film, and the final seconds are, it seems, a desperate effort to save it from the consequences of their own folly.

148. McGilligan and Buhle, *Tender Comrades,* 310.

149. There are a few less than flattering aspects. The war is repeatedly referred to as being over "in three weeks"; in reality, fighting lasted from September 1 to October 6. The heroine's daughter carries on a romance with a young Nazi despite the fact that her father has just been killed by the Germans, widowing her heroic mother. This implausibility along with a few other gaffes should be attributed to the obviously hasty preparation and flawed writing.

150. See de Toth, *Fragments,* 251–53, 445.

151. Quoted in Patrick Francis, "Wise Guys: A Virtual Roundtable with Three American Filmmakers of an Extremely Rare Vintage," *LA Weekly,* May 2, 2002, http://www.laweekly.com/2002-05-02/film-tv/wise-guys.

152. This possibility is prompted by a remark de Toth recalled making to Harry Cohn: "*None Shall Escape . . .* should be felt, thought, lived [as] . . . I lived through it." De Toth, *Fragments,* 315. De Toth, however, made it clear that he had no special affection for the Poles. Ibid., 259. Cf. Rick Lyman, "Andre de Toth, the Director of Noted 3-D Film, Is Dead," *New York Times,* November 1, 2002, where it is noted that he was "assigned to make Nazi propaganda films and chronicled the German invasion of Poland in 1939."

153. Than was born in Vienna of Czech Jewish parents; Neumann may have been a Jewish refugee from Germany, though that is not certain.

154. Streicher was a Bavarian; Grimm was from western Poland. Streicher was a journalist; Grimm was a schoolteacher. Streicher had nothing to do with Poles and Poland and never served as a civil administrator in occupied Poland, which is the essence of Grimm's biography. The only similarities Streicher shared with Grimm were that both were Nazis and thoroughly unpleasant.

155. See Sally Kaye, feature script review, March 31, 1943, file "None Shall Escape," box 3522, RG 208, National Archives.

156. Warren H. Pierce to John Mock (Columbia Pictures), June 29, 1943, file "Motion Picture, Bureau of—Hollywood Office," box 1438, RG 208, National Archives. Pierce noted the BMP evaluation was "the most complete and detailed review and comment" the office had ever made.

157. Knox argued that he was criticized for making Grimm too sympathetic, an odd comment, as the character is repulsive. Knox, "None Shall Escape," 1.

158. The final version of the film does show all the flags, as the BMP suggested.

159. Eleanor Berneis, feature script review, June 23, 1943, file "None Shall Escape," National Archives.

160. Ibid., separate pages labeled "Suggestions."

161. Warren Pierce to John Mock, August 11, 1943; Lillian Bergquist, feature viewing, December 24, 1943; Gene Kern (BMP) to John Mock, December 27, 1943, all in file "None Shall Escape," National Archives.

162. Libkow's involvement with the film cannot be reconstructed in any detail, though he was said to have contributed materials and made specific recommendations. See "Studio Avoids Using Tongue Twisters in Film Laid in Poland," October 20, 1943, and "Film Expert Owns Only Historic Map of Poland's Boundaries," November 2, 1943, both clippings in *None Shall Escape* files, Clipping Files, Herrick Library. See also the intriguing article "Geitner Will Show 'None Shall Escape,'" *Dunkirk (NY) Evening Observer,* April 1, 1944, which suggests that some of the scenes in the film were based on Libkow's reminiscences.

163. "The Screen Anticipates Nazis at Bar," *New York Herald-Tribune,* October 10, 1943; "Promised Trials of Nazi Chiefs Form a Basis for New Picture," April 2, 1944, clipping in *None Shall Escape* files, Clipping Files, Herrick Library. *The Black Book of Poland,* a detailed compilation of German outrages in Poland, was issued by the Polish Ministry of Information in London. It was published in the United States in 1942 by G. P. Putnam's Sons in New York.

164. See Sara Hamilton, "None Shall Escape Tells Nazi Intrigue," *Los Angeles Examiner,* April 12, 1944; Virginia Wright, "Picturized Review," *Los Angeles Daily News,* April 12, 1944; Phillip K. Scheuer, "One War Criminal Faces Trial in Grim Photoplay," *Los Angeles Times,* April 12, 1944; and Kassy Thompson, "Grim Touch to Film at Egyptian," *Hollywood Citizen,* April 12, 1944, all clippings in *None Shall Escape* files, Clipping Files, Herrick Library.

165. Marion Michelle, report, April 3, 1944 (regarding a 291-page script for "Jacobowsky and the Colonel"); William S. Cunningham (OWI) to Jason Joy (Twentieth Century–Fox), April 7, 1944, both in file "Jacobowsky and the Colonel," box 3519, RG 208, National Archives.

6. Poland: Fleeting, Ambiguous, or Omitted

1. *His Girl Friday,* directed by Howard Hawks, screenplay by Charles Lederer, starring Cary Grant and Rosalind Russell (Columbia, 1940).

2. I should also note that no Poles appear on screen. By comparison, there are four Irish characters (Murphy, McCue, Cooley, and Molly Malloy): three reporters and one sympathetic denizen of the lower orders.

3. *International Squadron,* directed by Lothar Mendes, screenplay by Barry Trivers, starring Ronald Reagan, James Stephenson, and Julie Bishop (Warner Brothers, 1941).

4. Colgan correctly observes that the film is really more about Grant's "shenanigans" than about the international squadron. Colgan, "Warner Brothers' Crusade," 628–31. Cf. *New York Times,* November 14, 1941.

5. See Colgan, "Warner Brothers' Crusade," 628–31, 812–13.

6. Ibid., 629, 631–32.

7. This excludes the Eagle Squadron, which only became operational in February 1941 and was American in composition. Its pilots had, in large part, come to Europe to aid Finland in its war against Soviet Russia, a theme hardly likely to be mentioned in an American film. Moreover, the Eagle Squadron—or squadrons; there were eventually three—was not an exceptional military formation; it lost more pilots than it shot down in battles with the Germans. By comparison, the Polish Kościuszko Squadron destroyed 126 German planes by itself, almost double the total of all three American squadrons put together, and lost only eighteen men, fewer than 25 percent of the American losses. They were the real eagles.

8. *Once upon a Honeymoon,* directed by Leo McCarey, screenplay by Sheridan Gibney, starring Cary Grant, Ginger Rogers, and Walter Slezak (RKO, 1942). The technical adviser, who was probably responsible for, among other things, the Polish aspects of the film, was Eugene Sharin, of whom nothing is known. See Leo McCarey to Walter Daniels, May 26, 1942, folder B372, box P-129, Production Files, RKO Collection, Performing Arts Special Collections, Charles E. Young Research Library, University of California, Los Angeles.

9. Hence Cary Grant is named O'Toole, Ginger Rogers is O'Hara, etc. McCarey also is responsible for the cloying incarnations of Irish Catholicism featuring Bing Crosby as Father O'Malley (*The Bells of St. Mary's,* 1944, and *Going My Way,* 1945). McCarey was a rarity in contemporary Hollywood, a Catholic and an anti-Communist. He was part of the "Irish crowd" in Hollywood, regarded by party members as "anti-Semitic" and virtually fascist. See Bright, interview, 143–44.

10. The Polish character was originally named Boranski; why the

name was changed is unclear. See "Budget of Production Cost," June 4, 1942, folder B372, box P-129, Production Files, RKO Collection.

11. Although the scenes with Borelski were gradually diminished as the film developed, it was always a minor part. Grant and Rogers were shooting the film for over two months; Basserman, for forty-eight hours. "Name of Cast and Number," June 8, 1942, folder B372, box P-129, Production Files, RKO Collection. RKO was sensitive to the Polish aspects of the film; extras with "good moustaches" were sought for scenes in Warsaw. "Daily Talent Requisition," June 29, 1942, folder B372, box P-120, Production Files, RKO Collection.

12. Roger Manvell, *Films and the Second World War* (New York: Dell, 1976), 121.

13. The OWI understood the scene to depict the plight of Jews, not Polish Jews, a distinction worth noting. See Lillian Bergquist, review, October 30, 1942, file "Once upon a Honeymoon," box 3523, RG 208, National Archives. This film has its defenders, especially those who think McCarey has been unjustly ignored by film scholars. See Paul Harrill, "Leo McCarey," *Senses of Cinema,* http://archive.sensesofcinema.com/contents/directors/02/mccarey.html.

14. O'Toole's exact words in the released film, in a radio broadcast from Warsaw under bombardment, are "Poland, like Austria, has been betrayed from within."

15. "First Draft Continuity," May 14, 1942, 40, 41, folder S912, box P-129, Production Files, RKO Collection. Borelski explains, in relation to the Polish government's propensity to fight, "I don't know if they can or not." Ibid., 40.

16. "Cutting Continuity," November 10, 1942, 34, folder S912, box P-129, Production Files, RKO Collection.

17. See ibid., 40.

18. A major event in the story is Katie's rescue of her Jewish maid from Nazi clutches by providing her with a false passport. The character of the maid was repeatedly rewritten. Originally she was shown carrying a Polish passport that described her as a Jew. Later this was altered, making her a German citizen. Polish passports did not indicate ethnic or religious background. For her original status as a bearer of a Polish passport, see "Final," June 6, 1942, folder S912, box P-129, Production Files, RKO Collection. It was later changed to a German passport. Ibid. The maid also originally had a Polish Jewish name, Rachel Polanski. See file "International Honeymoon," box P-129, Production Files, RKO Collection. By the time the film was released, her name had been altered. She is shown reading and understanding Polish, but she speaks to her children only in German.

19. See "First Draft Continuity," 48.

20. Borelski's melodramatic utterance appears in "Final," 45–46.

21. The screenplay was the work of Sheridan Gibney with some contributions by McCarey. Gibney later claimed that McCarey wrote nothing and was a "terrible drunk," a "cheat," and a "crook." Sheridan Gibney, interview by Patrick McGilligan, in McGilligan, *Film Crazy,* 157–62. Gibney was later accused by Jack Warner of being a Communist and was "graylisted." Gibney, however, was never a party member, though he was known for his leftist sympathies. See Jack Warner, testimony, October 20, 1947, House Committee on Un-American Activities, *Hearings,* 12–17. On its release, the film was billed as "Leo McCarey's Most Exciting Romantic Hit." "Trailer Continuity," November 28, 1942, folder S912, box P-129, Production Files, RKO Collection. This is a dubious description of a film that shows the invasion of Poland and the beginning of the Holocaust and has references to involuntary sterilization. The film has perhaps the most cloying scene of the era: an endless exchange between Ginger Rogers's and Albert Dekker's characters, who convince each other of their American patriotism by a series of dialect jokes, rhapsodize over the Brooklyn Dodgers, and then jointly recite the Pledge of Allegiance. The scene verges on self-parody.

22. *Commandoes Strike at Dawn,* directed by John Farrow, screenplay by Irwin Shaw, starring Paul Muni, Anna Lee, Lillian Gish, and Cedric Hardwicke (Columbia, 1942).

23. The BMP was particularly happy about this scene in a film it found superb. See file "Commandoes Strike at Dawn," box 3513, RG 208, National Archives. Why the scene did not suggest to the OWI that the Poles and Jews were more deserving of cinematic attention than the Norwegians is an intriguing question.

24. See Robert Rossen and Arthur Horman, "Desperate Journey: Treatment," January 16, 1942, folder 7, box 95, Warner Brothers Scripts.

25. See Arthur T. Horman, "Forced Landing: Original Treatment," December 1, 1941, folder 6; "Forced Landing" ("Desperate Journey" added in pencil), n.d., folder 8; and Arthur T. Horman, "Desperate Journey: Original Screenplay," n.d., folder 9, all in box 95, Warner Brothers Scripts.

26. The BMP reviewer of the film had no idea after these elisions that the film was about a bombing mission over occupied Poland and assumed, quite understandably, that it was set in Germany. M. B. Gratz, review, August 11, 1942, box 3514, RG 208, National Archives. *Variety,* August 19, 1942, at least caught the quick reference to a target over Poland. One of the trailers used to promote the film showed—very briefly—a map of Ger-

many. The other showed no map. See file 149, "Desperate Journey," Marty Weiser Papers, Special Collections, Herrick Library.

27. *Desperate Journey,* directed by Raoul Walsh, screenplay by Arthur T. Horman, starring Errol Flynn, Ronald Reagan, Nancy Coleman, and Raymond Massey (Warner Brothers, 1942).

28. The film contains no Polish characters. However, no fewer than five Irish actors appear in featured roles. This perhaps reflects the preferences of Walsh, nicknamed "Irish," who cast fellow Irishmen in his films because "the Irish have to stick together." Raoul Walsh, interview by Patrick McGilligan, in McGilligan, *Film Crazy,* 43.

29. It is noteworthy that even in this film the Polish underground reports not to its own government-in-exile, in London, but directly to the English. Again, as was the case with *To Be or Not to Be,* the Poles apparently have no government, and their underground effort, though heroic and valuable, is essentially superintended by the British. American audiences would learn by implication that Poland did not exist as a legal entity.

30. *The Conspirators,* directed by Jean Negulesco, screenplay by Vladimir Pozner, starring Hedy Lamarr, Paul Henreid, Sydney Greenstreet, and Peter Lorre (Warner Brothers, 1944).

31. Frederic Prokosch, *The Conspirators* (New York: Harper, 1943), 206–16. A copy is filed in folder 7, box 74, Warner Brothers Scripts.

32. The film was Twentieth Century–Fox's 1943 release *Chetniks,* directed by Louis King from a screenplay by Jack Andrews. It featured the typically taciturn Dutchman Philip Dorn as Colonel Draja Mihailovitch and the uninteresting Anna Sten in the female lead. The OWI excoriated the film at length. See file "Chetniks," box 3513, RG 208, National Archives. Similarly, the radical Left denounced the film as "doing harm." See the front-page editorial in *People's World Daily,* March 27, 1943.

33. Frederick Faust, "The Conspirators: Screenplay," April 30, 1943, 95, 96, folder 10, box 74, Warner Brothers Scripts.

34. See Frederick Faust, "The Conspirators: Temporary," n.d., 1, folder 2, box 75, Warner Brothers Scripts. Compare the bridge scene here (113–16) with the April 30 version, also by Faust; it is almost identical.

35. Elliot Paul, "The Conspirators: Treatment," n.d., 101, folder 1, box 75, Warner Brothers Scripts.

36. See Frank Gruber, "The Conspirators," September 11, 1943, 98–101, folder 3, box 75, Warner Brothers Scripts. The bridge scene here remains substantially as Paul had shortened it.

37. Party member John Weber of the William Morris Agency represented Pozner. He described him as a "left-wing writer." John Weber, interview by Paul Buhle, in McGilligan and Buhle, *Tender Comrades,* 693.

Self-described Communist Norma Barzman described Pozner as part of her "Communist milieu" in Paris after World War II. Norma Barzman, interview by Larry Ceplair, in McGilligan and Buhle, *Tender Comrades,* 15. Pozner published an essay after the war titled "I Am a Communist." See Barzman, *Red and the Blacklist,* 168–72, 346. Pozner was a regular correspondent of Jay Leyda. See, for example, Vladimir Pozner to Jay Leyda, October 12, 1942, folder "Chronological Correspondence, 1942,"and Vladimir Pozner to Jay Leyda, March 23, 1943, folder "Chronological Correspondence, 1943," both in box 9, Leyda Papers. Pozner was also close to Lillian Hellman, a fact that attracted FBI attention in 1944. See Lillian Hellman, 197, file 100-28760, Federal Bureau of Investigation.

38. Vladimir Pozner, "The Conspirators: Screenplay," October 18, 1943, folder 4, box 75, Warner Brothers Scripts. Regarding "Vernaszky," see ibid., 47.

39. See Valdimir Pozner, "The Conspirators: Revised Temporary," November 16, 1943, folder 5, box 75, Warner Brothers Scripts. In the "cast of characters," the repugnant Jan Vernaszky is the only Pole. Cf. "The Conspirators: Final," November 27, 1943, folder 6, and Jack Moffitt, "The Conspirators," February 12, 1944, folder 7 (where the name becomes "Bernazky"), both in box 75, Warner Brothers Scripts.

40. "The Conspirators: Revised Final," February 22, 1944, folder 1, box 76, Warner Brothers Scripts. Here the only Polish character mentioned is Bernaszky. Hollywood had a strange notion of the physical appearance of the typical Pole. John Garfield, Edward G. Robinson, and Peter Lorre, all of whom were cast as Poles, were very short and very swarthy.

41. It is intriguing that Jay Leyda and Howard Koch were exchanging remarks about their mutual friend Pozner and the film at this time. Koch thought Pozner had "done everything that could be done with The Conspirators" and that his work made "an excellent impression." One can only speculate what aspects of the film they had in mind. See Koch to Leyda, February 20, 1944.

42. Prokosch quoted in Youngkin, *Peter Lorre,* 221.

43. *A Coffin for Dimitrios* is reprinted in Eric Ambler, *Intrigue: Four Great Spy Novels* (New York: Knopf, 1960), 146–294.

44. See ibid., 207.

45. Ambler, an ardent leftist, was enamored of the USSR and often made Soviet agents the heroes of his novels. That he would make the sinister Gródek a Pole is hence not surprising. In *A Coffin for Dimitrios,* he also identifies a group of prostitutes as Poles. In fact, there are no positive Poles in Ambler's oeuvre.

46. *The Mask of Dimitrios,* directed by Jean Negulesco, screenplay by

Frank Gruber, starring Zachary Scott, Peter Lorre, and Sydney Greenstreet (Warner Brothers, 1944). Unpopular when first released, this film has subsequently gained critical acclaim. It boasts a literate script, based on the Ambler story, and uniformly quality performances. Lorre is particularly noteworthy in the lead playing, uncharacteristically, an essentially positive role.

47. Ambler, *Coffin for Dimitrios*, 209, 215.

48. It is curious that the role of Colonel Haki, the Turkish police official in this film, was played by Kurt Katch (real name Isser Kac), a Polish Jew from Grodno who had been in Yiddish and German films in the 1920s. Katch specialized in playing sinister characters of exotic and often ambiguous ethnicity.

49. The OWI was concerned about the propriety of overseas distribution for the film given the number of "shady European characters" in the temporary script it reviewed. Among these was "Władysław Gródek, a Pole, a master spy who takes money from all comers." Only that character's nationality was omitted in the released version of the film. See Eleanor Berneis, review, October 26, 1943, file "The Mask of Dimitrios," box 3521, RG 208, National Archives.

50. *So Ends Our Night,* directed by John Cromwell, screenplay by Talbot Jennings, starring Frederic March, Glenn Ford, Margaret Sullivan, Erich von Stroheim, Anna Sten, and Leonid Kinskey (United Artists, 1941). The minor role is played by Alexander Granach, a Polish Jew.

51. To add insult to injury, the credits list Ivan's last name as Probenzky, an impossible name in Polish.

52. *U-Boat Prisoner,* directed by Lew Landers, screenplay by Aubrey Wisberg, starring Bruce Bennett and Erik Rolf (Columbia, 1944).

53. The German bombing and shelling of Rotterdam in May 1940 resulted in slightly over eight hundred fatalities, a figure gigantically exaggerated during the war. The siege of Warsaw several months earlier inflicted perhaps fifty thousand Polish casualties. The film, however, equates Rotterdam with all of Poland, in which the casualties ran into the millions. The Rotterdam bombing was endlessly exploited by Hollywood. For example, Capra's *Divide and Conquer* (episode three of *Why We Fight*) devotes considerable time to the matter, claiming "thirty thousand were killed in ninety minutes" in the city. In a subsequent episode, *Battle of Britain,* Capra twice equates Rotterdam with Warsaw. Even the small Polish city of Wieluń lost far more people to aerial bombardment on September 1, 1939, than huge Rotterdam had lost. No one in the United States was made aware of Wieluń.

54. *Submarine Base,* directed by Albert H. Kelley, screenplay by

George H. Kelley and Arthur St. Claire, starring John Litel and Alan Baxter (Producers Releasing Corporation, 1943).

55. Rand quoted in Mayhew, *Ayn Rand,* 124. It is a grim irony, as Mayhew notes, that the fictional village of Tschaikovskoye, where this film is set, is located near the real village of Katyń, where the Russians had murdered several thousand Polish officers a few months before the events depicted in the film.

56. *The Story of G.I. Joe,* directed by William Wellman, screenplay by Leopold Atlas, Guy Endore, and Philip Stevenson, starring Burgess Meredith, Robert Mitchum, and Freddie Steele (United Artists, 1945). See Lawrence H. Suid, *Guts and Glory: Great American War Movies* (Reading, MA: Addison-Wesley, 1978), 67.

57. There were three assaults on the heights in 1944—January 17–25, February 15–18, and March 15–25—involving U.S. and British troops as well as units from India, Canada, South Africa, Australia, and New Zealand. They sustained large casualties but failed to take the position. On May 11–19, a Polish assault was victorious, and the "Hejnał" bugle call was played at Monte Cassino. The unfurling of the Polish flag there is comparable to the American flag's being raised at Iwo Jima in its status in national military lore and pride; hence its omission is very offensive as well as being historically inaccurate.

58. Matthew Parker, *Monte Cassino: The Hardest-Fought Battle of World War II* (New York: Doubleday, 2004), 289, 352. The Polish victory elicited enormous praise for Anders and his men but was almost immediately forgotten, to the Poles' great bitterness. See ibid., 342–43.

59. Atlas apparently wrote the great bulk of the script. However, he had a reputation for party indiscipline; hence, when Communist "stalwarts" Endore and Stevenson demanded equal billing, the party arranged it. Billingsley, *Hollywood Party,* 96.

60. Gerald Horne specifically denies that Lawson ever produced "cinematic paeans to Moscow." Horne, *Final Victim,* xviii.

61. Wellman, interview, 251, 254.

62. *Edge of Darkness,* directed by Lewis Milestone, screenplay by Robert Rossen, starring Errol Flynn, Ann Sheridan, and Nancy Coleman (Warner Brothers, 1943); Fyne, *Hollywood Propaganda,* 180.

63. Robert Rossen, "Edge of Darkness," May 16, 1942, 8, folder 4, and "Edge of Darkness: Part I, Temporary," June 9, 1942, folder 5, both in box 111, Warner Brothers Scripts.

64. "Edge of Darkness: Final," July 24, 1942, insert, September 11, 1942, 89–90, folder 6, box 111, Warner Brothers Scripts. The scene in which she recounts this history is retained substantially in the film.

65. The character of Katja (not a Polish name) is rather more significant in the original version of the story and even more repulsive. See William Woods, *Edge of Darkness* (Philadelphia: Lippincott, 1942), 45–48,
62, 299–304.

66. "Edge of Darkness: Part I, Temporary," 90, 96, 104.

67. See the inserted material in "Edge of Darkness: Final," on blue
pages, in which the racial discussion is eliminated from the script.

68. Regarding the reworking of the text, see Stephanie Thames, "Edge
of Darkness," *Turner Classic Movies,* http://www.tcm.com/thismonth/
article/?cid=318.

69. Stephen Rossen quoted in Navasky, *Naming Names,* 348.

70. Sandra Brennan, "Robert Rossen: Biography," *AllMovie,* http://
www.allmovie.com/artist/robert-rossen-109015/bio.

71. Walter Bernstein, interview by Paul Buhle, in McGilligan and
Buhle, *Tender Comrades,* 46.

72. Milestone's original name was Lev Milstein. The FBI regarded
him as pro-Soviet, possibly even a party member. See pt. 1, 20, 72, 109,
COMPIC. Regarding the American Russian Institute, see the FBI's "Com-
munist Infiltration of the Motion Picture Industry," July 8, 1947, 52, 58–62.
Regarding the Russian-American Club, see "Summary on the Communist
Infiltration," 147.

73. Peg Fenwick, memorandum, March 18, 1943; unsigned memorandum, March 18, 1943, both in file "Edge of Darkness," National Archives.

74. Joseph I. Breen to Jack Warner, July 30, 1942, file "Edge of Dark-
ness," National Archives; Joseph I. Breen to Jack Warner, August 4, 1942,
August 21, 1942, MPAA-PCA. The Breen office specifically objected to
Katja's being referred to as "you Polish sow," but the line was not altered.

75. Alex Evelove, "Analysis of Edge of Darkness," n.d.; "Analysis
Chart," January 11, 1943, both in MPAA-PCA.

76. Walter Trumbull to Geoffrey Shurlock, April 26, 1943, MPAA-
PCA. Warner Brothers was well aware of the protests over the film, but
it is unclear whether it made any attempt to respond. See Smith to Jack
Warner, May 3, 1943, folder 1998, *In Our Time* Collection, Warner Bros.
Archives.

77. See Arthur Kober, "Quota Girl (20th), First Draft Cont.," December 7, 1942, 1, box 1435, RG 208, National Archives.

78. Kober, a Polish Jew from Brody (in Austrian Galicia), was a radical leftist once married to Lillian Hellman (she left him for Dashiell Ham-
mett). For his membership in the party, see pt. 1, 103, COMPIC.

79. Kober, "Quota Girl (20th)," 1. Kober's offensive portrayal of
Katya is nothing compared to the dialogue he provided for the 1933 Fox

film *It's Great to Be Alive,* in which a chorus chants, "We are the women of Czechoslovakia. We are strong and how we can sockya!"

80. Kober, "Quota Girl (20th)," 2; Lillian Bergquist, "Film Analysis Section: Quota Girl," December 10, 1942, 1, box 1435, RG 208, National Archives.

81. *Wintertime,* directed by John Brahm, screenplay by Jack Jevne and Arthur Kober, starring Sonja Henie, Jack Oakie, and S. Z. Sakall (Twentieth Century–Fox, 1943).

82. *Mission to Moscow,* directed by Michael Curtiz, screenplay by Howard Koch, starring Walter Huston, Ann Harding, and Oskar Homolka (Warner Brothers, 1943).

83. Culbert, "Our Awkward Ally," 133.

84. Joseph E. Davies to Lowell Mellett, December 31, 1941, folder "Davies, Joseph E.," box 11, Mellett Papers. Whether Stalin knew he was recruited to the "Christian front" is unclear.

85. Foreword to Joseph E. Davies, *Mission to Moscow* (Garden City, NY: Garden City, 1943), vii.

86. Regarding Roosevelt's interest in *Mission to Moscow,* see Phillip L. Gianos, *Politics and Politicians in American Film* (Westport, CT: Praeger, 1998), 124, and Shein, *Analysis of Motion Pictures,* 67. Poynter, of the BMP, claims *Mission* was one of several films "developed either at the suggestion or with the encouragement of the Hollywood Office" of the BMP. See "Rough Draft: Resume of Activities of Hollywood Office," 6. Screenwriter Koch later repeated the claim that FDR had asked Warner to make the film. Howard Koch to the editor, *Los Angeles Times,* June 5, 1977, clipping in Howard Koch files, Clipping Files, Herrick Library. Cf. Warner, *My First Hundred Years,* 290–91. Davies contended in 1947 that the whole thing was his idea. Joseph E. Davies to Representative Thomas, June 10, 1947, folder 13, box 3, Koch Papers, Wisconsin Center for Film and Theater Research. Roosevelt regarded Warner Brothers as "a good Democratic studio." See Bright, interview, 153. Douglas Gomery notes that Harry Warner "alone on Hollywood's executive row enthusiastically supported FDR's progressive policies." Douglas Gomery, "Harry Morris Warner," in Garraty and Carnes, *American National Biography,* 22:691. The characterization is appropriate for the other Warners as well. *Time* magazine captured this with inimitable crudity in 1943: "Warner Bros. continued public rumbleseating with the President of the United States. It is still any gossip's guess whether the engagement is official or whether they like each other very, very much." *Time,* August 16, 1943, 94. After the war, in a demonstration of his perfervid Americanism, Jack Warner offered to pay to send pro-Communists to Russia. Radosh and Radosh, *Red Star,* 150.

87. *Moscow Conference on American and British Cinema, August 21–22, 1942* (Washington, DC: Embassy of the USSR, [1942]), 40–41. Koch later said that Warner had told him that Roosevelt wanted the film made because the Soviet Union "was the object of many years of prejudiced reporting in our press and was, therefore, misunderstood." Howard Koch, "Files on 'Mission to Moscow,'" January 1964, folder 8, box 2, Koch Papers, Wisconsin Center for Film and Theater Research.

88. The Polish scene does not exist in Erskine Caldwell's "Treatment 1" of *Mission to Moscow,* dated August 4, 1942, or his revised draft of August 21 ("Treatment 1-A"), or in the undated screenplay, also by Caldwell, probably prepared shortly thereafter. See folders 5–7, box 263, Warner Brothers Scripts.

89. Leyda received $150 weekly plus round-trip expenses for himself and his wife. See Nick Napoli to Jay Leyda, July 9, 1941, and the associated documents regarding his contract, folder "Mission to Moscow Correspondence," box 20, Leyda Papers. Cf. Steve Trilling to R. J. Obringer, September 24, 1942, October 8, 1942, picture file 2808, and Leyda's six-week contract, folder 12628, *Mission to Moscow* Collection, Warner Brothers Archives.

90. In 1943 the FBI described Leyda as having "a long record of Communist activity" and being an "ardent" member of the party. See pt. 1, 71, 102, COMPIC.

91. Radosh and Radosh, *Red Star,* 98–104. The significance of Leyda's involvement in the production was noted by contemporaries. The *New Leader* publicly cautioned the OWI about the possibility of *Mission to Moscow*'s bearing "the grotesque pattern of Communist propaganda," specifically noting that "the technical advisor on this vicious fabrication . . . was Jay Leyda, well-known Kremlin cultural agent." "Ask OWI Watch 'Mission' Film," *New Leader,* December 26, 1942, 1, clipping in file "Nelson Poynter from 12/1/42–4/12/42." Arnold, a friend of Leyda's, wrote him on June 30, 1943, congratulating him for the "political contribution" he made to *Mission to Moscow.* Judging by his references, Arnold was a Hollywood insider. Arnold to Jay Leyda, June 30, 1943, folder "Chronological Correspondence, 1943." For the many pages of changes Leyda suggested for the script, see folder "Film Script: Mission to Moscow—Jay Leyda Revisions To," box 19, Leyda Papers. With doubtlessly unintended irony, Leyda complained that he had difficulty working with the film's director, Michael Curtiz, who he said acted "as if I had some ulterior motive" in providing script changes. Jay Leyda to Robert Buckner, [n.d.], folder "Mission to Moscow Correspondence."

92. Koch to Leyda, [January–February 1944]. Koch later worked

closely with Leyda to convince Frank Capra to make a film about the postwar "world unity" based on "the utterances of United Nations leaders." Elmer Davis of the OWI was apparently interested in the project, as was Capra's collaborator Litvak. See ibid. and Howard Koch to Jay Leyda, January 7, [1945?], February 28, 1945, both in folder "Koch, Howard & Anne." The film, "World Unity," was designed to "disarm present-day critics of international action." "World Unity" (signed by Howard Koch), folder "Film Script," box 24, Leyda Papers. Koch also made herculean efforts to have Capra hire Leyda for his films in conjunction with the War Department. See Irving Lerner (OWI) to Jay Leyda, January 16, 1944, folder "Chronological Correspondence, 1944," box 9, Leyda Papers. Failing these efforts, Leyda was to be sent to the OSS. See NN to Jay Leyda, February 13, 1944, "Chronological Correspondence, 1944." Capra was also trying to arrange Leyda's transfer to a more congenial military assignment. Frank Capra to Lt. Col. Emanuel Cohen, March 1944, folder "1944 Mar. 21–31," box 8A, Capra Collection.

93. Koch, "To Whom It May Concern," 9. Warner Brothers had strange notions as to who would be appropriate advisers for the film. It hired Ivy Litvinov, wife of the Soviet ambassador to Washington, but she demanded more money than Warner Brothers was willing to pay. See Ivy Litvinoff [*sic*] to Jack Warner, October 20, 1942, folder 2785, *Mission to Moscow* Collection, Warner Bros. Archives. In pouring over other candidates for technical adviser, Lissauer and Buckner agreed not to hire Russian émigrés because they would not be "sympathetic" to the Soviets. They settled on an employee of the local Soviet consulate. Herman Lissauer to Robert Buckner, August 28, 1942, folder 1015, *Mission to Moscow* Collection, Warner Bros. Archives.

94. Howard Koch, "Mission to Moscow: Suggested Treatment," August 28, 1942, 5, folder 8, box 263, Warner Brothers Scripts.

95. "Mission to Moscow: Story Outline," September 6, 1942, box 263, folder 9, Warner Brothers Scripts.

96. Joseph E. Davies, *Mission to Moscow* (New York: Simon and Schuster, 1941), 11–12; Charles Ciliberti, *Backstairs Mission in Moscow* (New York: Booktab, 1946), 10–12, 50–51, 58. Ciliberti did, however, report observing Russians suspiciously attempting to enter Poland. Ciliberti, *Backstairs Mission,* 96–97.

97. Koch, "Mission to Moscow: Suggested Treatment," 16–18.

98. He was, for example, the fanatical Gestapo official in *U-Boat Prisoner.* He had many similar parts; he was essentially typecast as a very bad man.

99. Howard Koch, "Mission to Moscow: Screenplay," October 15,

1942, added pages 51a–51c, January 28, 1943, folder 1, box 264, Warner Brothers Scripts.

100. It is instructive to compare Davies's self-serving memoirs (or their yet less impressive cinematic version) with Grzybowski's far briefer summary account of his ambassadorial tenure in Moscow. Not only is the latter far more insightful and accurate, but it fails to so much as mention Davies. Wacław Grzybowski, "Final Report," *Documents on Polish-Soviet Relations,* 1:71–91. Whereas the intellectually limited Davies was ignorant of the country to which he was accredited, Grzybowski, a man of unusual intelligence and discerning judgment, was a professional diplomat of aristocratic origin who knew Russia well. The film, among its other shortcomings, does a disservice to Grzybowski.

101. Koch, "Mission to Moscow: Screenplay," 51c.

102. In the "Continuity Outline" of January 15, 1943 (folder 2085, *Mission to Moscow* Collection, Warner Bros. Archives), it is described as "foreign diplomats" demonstrating their "prejudice and distrust."

103. See the important study by Marek Kornat, "Ambasador Wacław Grzybowski i jego misja w Związku Sowieckim (1936–1939)," *Zeszyty Historyczne* 142 (2002): 5–80.

104. The only mention of Grzybowski in Davies's memoirs does not involve any conversation between the two and has nothing to do with this arch mise-en-scène. Davies, *Mission to Moscow* (1941), 336.

105. See "Temporary Script," September 29, 1942, folder 1015, *Mission to Moscow* Collection, Warner Bros. Archives.

106. "Research Record," January 29, 1943, 21–22, folder 1015, *Mission to Moscow* Collection, Warner Bros. Archives.

107. Robert Buckner to Jack Warner, January 21, 1943, folder 2085, *Mission to Moscow* Collection, Warner Bros. Archives.

108. See "Changes to Mission to Moscow," January 28, 1943, folder PP17, *Mission to Moscow* Collection, Warner Bros. Archives. However, the "Daily Production Progress Report" (folder 14816, *Mission to Moscow* Collection, Warner Bros. Archives) indicates that the scene was not shot until February 11, 1943.

109. Rameau's role is uncredited in the film. Warner Brothers appreciated Rameau's performance in this small part and considered him for other roles, though it regarded him as "not very easy to work with." E. D. Dupont to Don Siegal, May 25, 1943, folder 1998, *In Our Time* Collection, Warner Bros. Archives.

110. See the still photograph of the Paderewski scene in Joseph E Davies, *Mission to Moscow,* ed. David Culbert (Madison: University of Wisconsin Press, 1980), 49.

111. Herman Lissauer to Miss Orbison, February 24, 1943; Jay Leyda to Miss Orbison, March 3, 1943, both in folder 1015, *Mission to Moscow* Collection, Warner Bros. Archives. In May Rameau was not listed in the cast, but he appeared at the very last in the press book issued to accompany the film's release. See the untitled document from the publicity department, May 10, 1943, folder "Legal, 12722," and "Joseph E. Davies' Mission to Moscow: Your Warners Press Book," folder 684, both in *Mission to Moscow* Collection, Warner Bros. Archives.

112. The only mention of Paderewski in the volume is that on July 16, 1937, while stationed in Moscow, Davies saw the film *Moonlight Sonata,* in which Paderewski appeared. Davies, *Mission to Moscow* (1941), 175–76.

113. Davies, *Mission to Moscow* (1980), 238n59.

114. Koch, "Mission to Moscow: Screenplay," 146; Davies, *Mission to Moscow* (1980), 50 (photograph), 239n68.

115. See Bosley Crowther, "'Mission to Moscow,' Based on Ex-Ambassador Davies's Book, Stars Walter Huston, Ann Harding at Hollywood," *New York Times,* April 30, 1943, reprinted in *New York Times Film Reviews,* 3:1933–34. Cf. Fyne, *Hollywood Propaganda,* 107.

116. Koch, "To Whom It May Concern," 9.

117. Howard Koch to Joseph E. Davies, September 25, 1947, folder 13, box 3, Koch Papers, Wisconsin Center for Film and Theater Research.

118. Ciliberti, *Backstairs Mission,* 124.

119. Koch, "Files on 'Mission to Moscow.'"

120. See Jack Warner to Nelson Poynter, May 19, 1943, file "Action in the North Atlantic," box 3511, RG 208, National Archives, in which Warner boasts that *Mission to Moscow* is "the talk of the town."

121. This Week in America, *Letter from America,* May 21, 1943, 1, clipping in container 212, Winant Papers.

122. This Week in America, *Letter from America,* May 7, 1943, 1, clipping in container 212, Winant Papers.

123. This Week in America, *Letter from America,* June 23, 1944, 4, clipping in container 212, Winant Papers.

124. "'Mission to Moscow': Davies Movie Whitewashes Russia," *Life,* [1943], 39, clipping in folder 3, box 2, Koch Papers, Wisconsin Center for Film and Theater Research.

125. John Dewey and Suzanne LaFollette, "Several Faults Are Found in 'Mission to Moscow' Film," *New York Times,* May 9, 1943. Dewey acknowledged that LaFollette wrote this letter, which he hoped would turn public opinion against the film. John Dewey to Robby, May 11, 1943, folder 6, box 13, John Dewey Papers, Special Collections, Morris Library.

126. Januszewski, "Case for the Polish."

127. Crowther, "'Mission to Moscow.'"

128. These critical evaluations are drawn from the summary in Irving Hoffman, "On 'Moscow' and Warners," *Hollywood Reporter,* May 3, 1943, 8.

129. Dewey and Suzanne LaFollette, "Several Faults Are Found."

130. Georgakas, "Hollywood Reds," 70. Not surprisingly, the *Daily Worker* labeled all criticism of the film part of a "Nazi-dominated fifth column," and John Howard Lawson denounced critics as "traitorous." See the clippings from July 1943 in folder 3, box 9, Lawson Papers.

131. Koch quoted in Mayhew, *Ayn Rand,* 151. Koch never admitted that his film was propaganda, or even a misrepresentation of people and events, but insisted long after that it was merely intended to address the critical image of Soviet Russia then dominant in the United States by casting it in "a more favorable light." See Howard Koch, "Truth on Trotsky," *Los Angeles Times,* July 24, 1977, and Howard Koch to the editor, *Los Angeles Times,* June 5, 1977, both clippings in Koch files, Clipping Files, Herrick Library.

132. Warner, *My First Hundred Years,* 292–93.

133. Joseph E. Davies to Lowell Mellett, April 19, 1943, folder "Davies, Joseph E."

134. *The North Star,* directed by Lewis Milestone, screenplay by Lillian Hellman, starring Anne Baxter, Dana Andrews, Walter Huston, and Walter Brennan (RKO, 1943).

Bernard F. Dick argues in his sympathetic discussion of the film that FDR's adviser Harry Hopkins was personally responsible for the film's being made. Bernard F. Dick, *Hellman in Hollywood* (East Brunswick, NJ: Farleigh Dickinson University Press, 1982), 97–107.

135. Hellman quoted in William Wright, *Lillian Hellman: The Image, the Woman* (New York: Simon and Schuster, 1986), 131. Hellman was one of 150 signatories of a published statement in 1938 that supported the Stalinist position on the guilt of those accused in the show trials of the 1930s. She also campaigned against Finland in its struggle against the Soviet invasion of 1939 and heaped abuse on the Finns, much of it nonsensical or dishonest. In 1942 Hellman urged the United States to declare war on Finland. See "Lillian Hellman," June 15, 1941, February 4, 1944, December 9, 1948, Hellman, file 100-28760. As late as 1969, Hellman was still defending the Soviet Union from criticism by dissidents. See Billingsley, *Hollywood Party,* 267–68.

Jay Leyda tried to arrange to be technical adviser to this film by writing to director Lewis Milestone that he knew Ukraine well; whether he was successful in his efforts is unclear. Jay Leyda to Lewis Milestone, November 27, 1942, folder "Chronological Correspondence, 1942."

136. Hellman apparently could not decide where she wanted the film to be set. In her initial correspondence about the film, she wrote of a "village between Smolensk and Moscow," but the locale migrated southward, and by late summer of 1942 it was "near the Soviet border." See the Lillian Hellman–Lowell Mellett correspondence in file "Hellman, Lillian," box 1433B, RG 208, National Archives, especially Lillian Hellman to Lowell Mellett, July 15, 1942, and [Lillian Hellman], "Russian Story," August 26, 1942. While developing her script, Hellman maintained a close relationship with Soviet ambassador Maxim Litvinov and MGM's William Wyler. See William Wyler to [Mrs.] Maxim Litvinov, July 15, 1942, folder 781, William Wyler Papers, Special Collections, Herrick Library.

137. See [Hellman], "Russian Story," 68.

138. The August script mentioned "Germans . . . pouring through the Bessarabian corridor . . . not more than 35 miles away." Ibid., 75.

139. During the Polish-Bolshevik War of 1919–1921, Kamieniec and its environs briefly came into Polish possession, but the city reverted to Russia in the March 1921 Treaty of Riga. There was no war over the territory.

140. "Obviously pleased with Hollywood's films, the Soviets imported several of them. *North Star,* for example, played to 50,000 people over a three-week period in a theater in Siberia." Lukas, *Strange Allies,* 105. Soviet audiences were duly appreciative. See "Hellman's *Watch on Rhine* Acclaimed in Moscow," *People's World,* September 5, 1945. In late 1944 Hellman paid a very lengthy visit to the Soviet Union at Moscow's invitation and expense. She was even allowed to tour the battlefront in Poland. She returned aglow with praise for the Russians. See memorandum to FBI director, August 30, 1955, Hellman, file 100-28760, and "Russia Acclaimed by Miss Hellman," *New York Times,* March 2, 1945.

141. This is scene 38, added in March 4, 1943. It was later apparently cut; it does not appear in the released version. See "The North Star, Revised Final, February 16, 1943," 15, unlabeled folder, Lewis Milestone Papers, Special Collections, Herrick Library. The author was probably Lillian Hellman, though her initials do not appear on the added scene.

142. For the MPPDA, it was a "Russian village" on the border of "Bessarabia"; hence for the geographically naive American analyst, the film had achieved its purpose of assimilating the territory to Soviet Russia. L. Greenhouse, analysis, September 22, 1943, file "The Northern Star," MPAA-PCA.

143. Georgakas, "Hollywood Reds," 70. The film was a "Box Office Champion" and gained Goldwyn and Milestone praise from other studios, notably Warner Brothers. Goldwyn was delighted at the popularity of and critical praise for the film. See Irving Rapper to Lewis Milestone, April 5,

1943, folder 8; Red Kann to Lewis Milestone, November 29, 1944, folder 29; Joseph Steele to Lewis Milestone, November 17, 1943, folder 29 ; and Samuel Goldwyn to William Herbert, n.d., folder 29, all in Milestone Papers.

144. William Wyler to Samuel Goldwyn, November 18, 1943; Samuel Goldwyn to William Wyler, November 20, 1943, both in folder 781, Wyler Papers. Wyler also assured Goldwyn that William Randolph Hearst's dislike of the film was a "tribute," as Hearst was "evil." Cf. Louis Pizzitola, *Hearst over Hollywood: Power, Passion, and Propaganda in the Movies* (New York: Columbia University Press, 2002), 408–9.

145. Quoted in Kracauer, "National Types," 68.

146. Bell to Goldwyn, September 24, 1943; Kaye, review, May 12, 1943.

147. Memorandum, January 2, 1943, file "The North Star," National Archives.

148. See Koppes and Black, *Hollywood Goes to War,* 122–25. Capra's militantly self-righteous version can be found in Frank Capra, *The Name above the Title: An Autobiography* (New York: Macmillan, 1971), 325–26. Cf. F. H. Osborn to Frank Capra, November 26, 1942, folder "1942 Nov. 25–30," box 6A, Capra Collection.

149. William Thomas Murphy, "The Method of *Why We Fight,*" *Journal of Popular Film* 1, no. 3 (1972): 185.

150. Capra, *Name above the Title,* 336–37.

151. See Maj. General A. D. Surles to Lowell Mellett, March 10, 1943, file "Prelude to War," box 1439, RG 208, National Archives. Five of the seven episodes of the series were released in 1943; the sixth, *The Battle of China,* appeared in 1944; and the final, *War Comes to America,* focusing on the home front, appeared in 1945.

152. Joseph McBride, *Frank Capra: The Catastrophe of Success* (New York: St. Martin's Griffin, 2000), 459. The exceptions were the Epstein twins, whom Capra procured independently. The attorney general's office accused the mobilization in 1947 of being a Communist front organization. Ibid., 461.

153. See "A Biography of Samuel J. Briskin" in *Biographies: Liberty Films,* an undated twelve-page pamphlet in folder 11, box 1, William Hornbeck Collection, Wesleyan Cinema Archives.

154. Frank Capra to Jay Leyda, July 10, 1942, folder "1942 Jul.," box 6A, Capra Collection.

155. The Capra team behind *Why We Fight* apparently became quite close; after the war several of them joined to create the ill-fated Liberty Films. See William Hornbeck, interview by Kristin Thompson and David Bordwell, July 9, 1980, folder 15, box 6, Hornbeck Collection.

156. Capra quoted in McBride, *Frank Capra,* 459.

157. Frank Capra to Lt. Col. Paul Sloane, [April 11, 1943], folder "1943 Ap. 11–13," box 7A, Capra Collection. Litvak and Capra wee apparently very close. Capra referred to him by his Russian nickname of "Tola." Litvak was enthusiastic about his service with *Why We Fight.* See Anatole Litvak to Frank Capra, April 1, 1942, folder "1942 Mar.–Apr.," box 6A, Capra Collection.

158. Litvak, who was born in Kiev, was a second lieutenant in the Russian army. In 1943, Senator Ralph O. Brewster inquired about Litvak to the War Department; apparently the good senator was concerned that Litvak owed his position with the army signal corps as part of Capra's team to the influence of his wife, actress Miriam Hopkins. The War Department informed Brewster that Litvak and Hopkins were divorced. Julius H. Amberg (special assistant to the secretary of war) to Sen. Ralph O. Brewster, April 5, 1943, folder "1943 Aug.–Sept.," box 7A, Capra Collection.

159. Swindell, *Charles Boyer,* 103.

160. Capra claims that he "outlined the scope and thrust" of each segment of *Why We Fight* and that he and Anthony Veiller did "most of the script writing." Capra, *Name above the Title,* 338.

161. Leif Fuhrammar and Folke Isaksson describe the series, restrainedly, as enjoying "a not entirely deserved reputation for objectivity." They characterize the initial segments as "pretty blatant pieces of demagoguery." Leif Fuhrammar and Folke Isaksson, *Politics and Film* (New York: Praeger, 1971), 64. Capra credits the scripts to his collaboration with Anatole Litvak, Anthony Veiller, Robert Heller, and Leonard Spigelgass. Capra, *Name above the Title,* 335. Litvak was associated with left-wing causes in Hollywood, as was Veiller; Spiegelgass was a "moderate liberal"; and Heller's political views are unknown. Ceplair and Englund, *Inquisition in Hollywood,* 275–76, 422, 435–36; Taylor, *Strangers in Paradise,* 69; Combs and Combs, *Film Propaganda,* 72; de Toth, *Fragments,* 316n8.

162. *The Nazis Strike* (War Department Special Service Division information film 2, 1943). *The Nazis Strike* presents the Germans as racially consumed by a lust for conquest, a biological propensity that, the film explains, somehow did not affect German Americans. Cinematographic legerdemain links the Third Reich to Genghis Khan, both being directed by "geopolitics," a very bad word, reflecting a simplified version of the views of Herbert Mackinder, who, of course, was neither Mongol nor German. Bernard F. Dick has some intriguing comments on Capra's interpretation of the war in *Star-Spangled Screen,* 2–9.

163. Screenwriting credit for the released version of this episode was

given to Knight and Veiller. See the copy of the script in folder "The Nazis Strike," box 10, Capra Collection. The program notes for *The Nazis Strike* also credit the narrative to Veiller and Knight. "Program Notes: Nazis Strike," folder "Program Notes," box 7A, Capra Collection.

164. According to the narration of the film, the Poles had 600 "nondescript" tanks to face 5,000 German ones, and "less than" 1,000 planes to challenge 6,000 German aircraft. See the copy of the script in folder "The Nazis Strike," Capra Collection. In reality, the figures were quite different: the Germans had perhaps 2,700 tanks and 1,300 planes versus 800 tanks and 400 planes for the Poles. The size of German forces is always wildly exaggerated in *Why We Fight*.

165. Even key members of the Capra team knew that this version of the Soviet invasion of September 17, 1939, was nonsense. William Hornbeck, a longtime associate of Capra's and the editor of the entire *Why We Fight* series, wrote in his diary (folder 7, box 1, Hornbeck Collection) on September 17, "Russia invades Poland on Eastern borders." On September 29, he added, "Russia & Germany come to agreement over division of Poland." He later made reference to Finland's being "threatened by Russia." In his memoirs, Capra, in his vulgar style, refers to September 17 this way: "Soviet Russia raced into Poland to claim its half of the carcass." Capra, *Name above the Title,* 288.

166. No Polish figure is praised in the film, though Czechoslovakia's wily and elastic Eduard Beneš is introduced as "incorruptible." Hollywood is probably the only place where that adjective would have been attached to his name.

167. *Divide and Conquer* (War Department Special Service Division information film 3, 1943).

168. *The Battle of Britain* (War Department Special Service Division information film 4, 1943).

169. The rise—and fall—of British appreciation of the Poles' role in the aerial defense of Great Britain is well covered in Lynne Olson and Stanley Cloud, *A Question of Honor: The Kościuszko Squadron: Forgotten Heroes of World War II* (New York: Knopf, 2004).

170. *The Battle of Russia* (War Department Special Service Division information film 5, 1943). The program notes list Veiller as the writer and Litvak as the producer. See folder "Program Notes." However, the script makes Veiller and Litvak coauthors. See the copy of the script in folder "Battle of Russia," box 10, Capra Collection.

171. In addition to being laudatory, *The Battle of Russia* was very long, almost double the running time of any other segment in the *Why We Fight* series. See Richard Barsam, "Why We Fight," in *Frank Capra: The Man*

and His Films, ed. Richard Glatzer and John Raeburn (Ann Arbor: University of Michigan Press, 1975), 153.

172. Murphy, "Method of *Why We Fight,*" 194, 193.

173. Quoted in Lukas, *Strange Allies,* 105. The fact that it was likened in this review to *The Birth of a Nation* was surely an unintended irony.

174. Ryessa D. Liberson to Frank Capra, April 26, 1944, enclosing "Stenographic Report: Meeting of the Cinema Section to Discuss the Film 'The Battle for Russia,'" March 5, 1944, folder "1944 March," box 8A, Capra Collection. See also "Soviet Writers Greet Hollywood," *Communiqué,* December 1, 1944, copy in folder 1, box 8, Lawson Papers.

175. *War Comes to America* (War Department Special Service Division information film 7, 1945).

176. See the copy of the script in folder "War Comes to America," box 10, Capra Collection.

177. Darryl Zanuck to Frank Capra, April 21, 1945; Frank Capra to Darryl Zanuck, April 23, 1945, both in folder "1945 Ap.," box 9A, Capra Collection.

178. Capra, *Name above the Title,* 331.

179. Eric Knight to Frank Capra, April 15, 1942, folder "1942 Apr. 15," box 6A, Capra Collection.

180. Ibid.

181. F. H. Osborn to George Marshall, October 24, 1942, folder "1942 Oct.," box 6A, Capra Collection. Litvak was slated to produce the segment on Russia. It was not completed. See Robert Stevenson, interview by Patrick McGilligan, in McGilligan, *Film Crazy,* 214.

182. Osborn to Marshall, October 24, 1942.

183. As late as the summer of 2006, total Polish casualties for World War II were estimated at between 4.5 million and 7.5 million. The government announced a major national effort to establish a more precise figure and compile a list of all Polish losses, obviously a huge and lengthy research effort. See "Ile polskich ofiar pochłonęła okupacja" and "Ustala, ilu Polaków poległo za Ojczyznę," *Rzeczpospolita,* September 2, 2006.

184. Aniela Mieczysławska (Polish Information Center, New York) to George J. Janacek, March 29, 1943, folder "1943 March 24–31," box 7A, Capra Collection.

185. Frank Capra, memorandum to General Harrison, [April 7, 1943], folder "1943 Ap. 7–10," box 7A, Capra Collection.

186. The army apparently still anticipated at least some of these films in the autumn of 1943. See F. H. Osborn, memorandum, [October–November 1943], folder "1943 Oct.–Nov.," box 8A, Capra Collection.

187. Doherty, *Projections of War,* 79.

188. F. H. Osborn to Frank Capra, October 23, 1942, folder "1942 Oct."; George C. Marshall to F. H. Osborn, October 25, 1942, folder "1942 Oct."; F. H. Osborn to Frank Capra, November 26, 1942, folder "1942 Nov. 25–30," all in box 6A, Capra Collection.

189. Allen Rivkin to Frank Capra, February 10, 1943, folder "1943 Feb 9–12," box 7A, Capra Collection.

190. Dore Schary to Frank Capra, February 26, 1943, folder "1943 Feb. 25–28," box 7A, Capra Collection. Schary was a principal producer at MGM whose leftist political views clashed with those of Republican studio head Mayer. It is an example of the myriad connections in the Hollywood community that Schary was the producer of *Lassie Come Home,* a popular film based on a story by Capra's confidant Eric Knight. Thus Knight was working with MGM at the time of his service with Capra.

191. See the considerable correspondence in folders "1943 Ap. 11–13" and "1943 May–July" in box 7A, Capra Collection.

192. For example, Mieczysławska of the Polish Information Center pronounced each of the first two episodes "really splendid" and certain to "serve its purposes." For *The Nazis Strike,* she also included a series of politely worded corrections regarding the duration of Polish resistance, the fact that the Polish forces were not fully mobilized because of Allied pressure, and the claim that Poland had rejected German blandishments to join in a campaign against Soviet Russia. The letter concluded with a lengthy quotation from General Sikorski, the Polish premier. Mieczysławska to Janacek, March 29, 1943. Frank Babirecki from the "Polish Film Council" in London—the official status of which is uncertain—told the OWI that he "enjoyed" the films and nothing more. Frank Babirecki to Joyce Weiner, March 23, 1944, folder "1944 Mar 21–31," box 8A, Capra Collection.

193. It was, Capra noted in 1975, "one of the best episodes and a true one." Frank Capra, "Why We (Should Not) Fight," interview by George Bailey, 1975, in *Frank Capra: Interviews,* ed. Leland Poague (Jackson: University Press of Mississippi, 2004), 125.

194. Ibid., 124–27.

195. In 1944 Jay Leyda, with Howard Koch's help, was trying to induce Capra to produce his own film, "A Century of Friendship," about the putative tradition of American-Russian comity. The treatment includes a number of significant touches: a history of the war that omits the Soviet invasion of Poland, a representation of the liberation of various European capitals in which Warsaw is shown with a Soviet flag flying over it, and a fade-out with an actor playing Truman standing in front of Soviet and American flags. See folder "Film on Russian-American Friendship," box 24, Leyda Papers. Earlier Leyda urged Capra to provide him a regular column in the

journal *Army-Navy Screen Magazine* for "Fighting Together," in which
Leyda would discuss armies fighting as a "common front." "Project to Col.
Frank Capra," [1942], folder "Proposal to Capra," box 27, Leyda Papers.

196. Indeed, early in the film, a character refers to the invasion of Poland
as having brought war. His interlocutor dismisses such reasoning as "silly."
Quoted in McLaughlin and Parry, *We'll Always Have,* 137.

197. The passionately patriotic English novelist Evelyn Waugh, writing
at about the time *Mrs. Miniver* was being filmed, recalled that the week
preceding the invasion of Poland was one of "surmise and apprehension
which cannot, without irony, be called the last days of 'peace.'" Evelyn
Waugh, *Put Out More Flags* (Boston: Back Bay, 2002), 3.

198. *Casablanca,* directed by Michael Curtiz, screenplay by Julius J.
Epstein, Phillip G. Epstein, and Howard Koch, starring Humphrey Bogart, Ingrid Bergman, Paul Henreid, and Claude Rains (Warner Brothers,
1942). Jack Nachbar suggests a role for *Casablanca* in helping Americans
to understand "why they were fighting." Jack Nachbar, "Doing the Thinking for All of Us: *Casablanca* and the Home Front," *Journal of Popular
Film and Television* 27, no. 4 (2000), 5. Whereas France, Norway, Russia,
and Czechoslovakia are all sympathetically represented in this film, Poland
is omitted. Hence the war *Casablanca* helped justify to Americans was one
without a Polish cause.

199. Richard Corliss refers to the hero, Rick (Humphrey Bogart), as a
"socialist adventurer." Richard Corliss, "Analysis of the Film," in Casablanca*: Script and Legend,* comp. Howard Koch (Woodstock, NY: Overlook, 1973), 187.

200. "Epstein: A King of Comedy," 189. Jack Warner claimed the brothers were "probable Communists." Warner quoted in ibid., 171. Warner's
post-1945 denunciations, however, should not be taken seriously. Party
member Allen Boretz, a writer, considered the Epsteins not Communists
but mere "Social Democrats" and rather "lackadaisical and spoiled" at that.
Allen Boretz, interview by Patrick McGilligan and Ken Mate, in McGilligan and Buhle, *Tender Comrades,* 118.

201. Even analyses specifically focused on the geopolitics of *Casablanca* have not remarked the odd omission of Poles in this plethora of
nationalities. See Craig R. Smith, "Internationalism in Casablanca," in
Reelpolitik: Political Ideologies in '30s and '40s Films, ed. Beverly Merrill Kelley, John J. Pitney Jr., Craig R. Smith, and Herbert E. Gooch III
(Westport, CT: Praeger, 1998), 77–94.

202. A possible alternative reading is that Poland is not part of the film's
powerful yet mysterious underground. This raises the possibility that the
underground was supposed to be a Comintern network with which Poland

was not involved, but that assumes far too much subtlety on the writers' part. A more reasonable conclusion is that Poland is not part of the underground because the latter is a collection of progressive elements. Poland, in leftist circles, is unredeemably reactionary and hence cannot be joined in such worthy company.

203. Lillian Bergquist, review, October 28, 1942, file "Casablanca," box 3515, RG 208, National Archives. In obvious expiation for a war film without an Irish lead character, Warner Brothers cast "Dooley" Wilson as the black piano player. Wilson gained his nickname by playing Irish characters in "whiteface." Harmetz, *Making of* Casablanca, 142–45.

204. *Wilson,* directed by Henry King, screenplay by Lamar Trotti, starring Alexander Knox, Geraldine Fitzgerald, Cedric Hardwicke, and Charles Coburn (Twentieth Century–Fox, 1944).

205. Knock, "'History with Lightning,'" 529, 538–41; Koppes and Black, *Hollywood Goes to War,* 319–20.

206. For the use of World War I motifs in World War II films, see Dick, *Star-Spangled Screen,* 263.

207. See Thomas J. Knock's useful though perhaps insufficiently critical essay "'History with Lightning.'"

208. Ibid., 525, 536–37.

209. Reviews quoted in ibid., 536.

210. Ibid., 524.

211. Lamar Trotti, "Woodrow Wilson Story," temporary script, January 5, 1943, 98–99, folder 1, Twentieth Century–Fox Collection, Performing Arts Archives, Cinematic Arts Library.

212. Lamar Trotti, "Woodrow Wilson," revised temporary, March 15, 1943, folder 1, Twentieth Century–Fox Collection. Here the fellow from Bratislava (which of course is in Slovakia, not Bohemia) is now named Anton—the beginning of his rapid expansion in the script. There are still "Polocks." By July, however, the Polish soldier is only an anonymous part of a vague crowd scene. Lamar Trotti, "Woodrow Wilson," revised final, July 13, 1943, 110, folder 2, Twentieth Century–Fox Collection.

213. The blind Bohemian scene first appears in Trotti, "Woodrow Wilson," revised temporary, 116. The scene seems to have vanished by July. See Trotti, "Woodrow Wilson," revised final.

214. Trotti, "Woodrow Wilson Story," temporary script, 100–101.

215. Trotti, "Woodrow Wilson," revised temporary, 109–10.

216. Trotti, "Woodrow Wilson," revised final, 133. This scene seems to have disappeared by August. See Trotti, "Woodrow Wilson," second revised final, August 24, 1943, folder 3, Twentieth Century–Fox Collection.

217. See Trotti, "Woodrow Wilson," revised final, 115. Paderewski is still playing his minuet in the August version. Trotti, "Woodrow Wilson," second revised final, 126.

218. "Wilson: Continuity and Dialogue Taken from the Screen," September 11, 1944, p. R13 P14, folder 5, Twentieth Century–Fox Collection. Paderewski did not play at the White House on November 11, 1918. To add irony to the scene, Armistice Day for the Americans is, for the Poles, Independence Day.

219. The actor is not well cast: he is too tall and thin, and his hair is the wrong color. But since the pianist is never identified, what does it matter?

220. "Rough Draft: Resume of Activities of Hollywood Office," 6.

221. Trotti also received an award from the party's cultural journal, *New Masses,* for the film. "Communist Infiltration of Labor Groups," 23.

222. Hollywood had also produced a series of "scientist biographies" (including biographies of Pasteur and Bell and two of Edison) starting in the last 1930s, which category neatly accommodates the Curie film. See Michael Troyan, *A Rose for Mrs. Miniver* (Lexington: University Press of Kentucky, 1999), 158.

223. For its concern about the lack of attention to Poland in general, see Hopkins to Early, September 3, 1941, Sherwood Collection: OWI. For the concern that Poland was "seldom-portrayed" in films, see Eleanor Berneis, feature script review, October 6, 1943, file "Song to Remember," National Archives.

224. *Madame Curie,* directed by Mervyn LeRoy, screenplay by Paul Osborn, starring Greer Garson and Walter Pidgeon (MGM, 1943). Garson claimed that she "read everything" about Curie for her role, even having material translated from Polish. It is, indeed, a most sympathetic portrayal. See Troyan, *Rose for Mrs. Miniver,* 160.

225. Eve Curie, *Madame Curie: A Biography* (Garden City, NY: Doubleday, Doran, 1938).

226. Ibid., 305. The letter quotes Adam Mickiewicz's patriotic masterpiece, *Pan Tadeusz.*

227. Curie, *Madame Curie,* 343.

228. Marjorie Thorsen, "Marie Curie," April 17, 1936, folder 1, "Madame Curie," MGM Collection, Performing Arts Archives, Cinematic Arts Library. A heavy Polish emphasis is also apparent in the script outline by EC, March 2, 1936, folder 1, "Madame Curie," MGM Collection.

229. Lynn Riggs, "The Essential Dramatic Line," October 26, 1937, folder 2, "Madame Curie," MGM Collection.

230. Aldous Huxley, "Treatment," August 26, 1938, folder 2, "Madame Curie," MGM Collection.

231. For example, see Rada Doone, "Madam [*sic*] Curie," September 6, 1938, folder 1, "Madame Curie," MGM Collection.

232. Bruno Frank, "Treatment," October 25, 1938, folder 3, "Madame Curie," MGM Collection. This version emphasizes the family's violent dislike of the Russians.

233. For example, see Lazlo Vadani, "Dialogue Continuity," December 12, 1938, folder 3, "Madame Curie," MGM Collection.

234. Sidney Franklin, "Treatment," September 9, 1939, folder 4, "Madame Curie," MGM Collection. As early as 1937, Riggs had proffered an alternative version that emphasized Pierre at the expense of Poland. Lynn Riggs, "Alternative," November 12, 1937, folder 2, "Madame Curie," MGM Collection. This reflects the French "outline" by Jacques Thery of May 24, 1939 (folder 4, "Madame Curie," MGM Collection), which was translated by MGM.

235. Paul Osborn had included a long childhood Polish episode, which Sidney Franklin later altered to remove its political implications. Compare Paul Osborn, "Composite Script," February 11, 1941, folder 5, with Sidney Franklin, "Treatment," December 9, 1942, folder 6, and Hans Rameau and Paul Osborn, script with notation "okayed by Sidney Franklin," folder 7, all in "Madame Curie," MGM Collection.

236. See the evaluation by Elene Aristi of the screenplay by Paul Osborn and Paul H. Rameau, October 5, 1943, folder 1, "Madame Curie," MGM Collection.

237. Peg Fenwick and Dorothy B. Jones, feature viewing, November 29, 1943, file "Madame Curie," box 3521, RG 208, National Archives.

238. Ulric Bell to Maurice Revnes (MGM), November 16, 1943, file "Madame Curie," National Archives.

239. *A Song to Remember,* directed by Charles Vidor, screenplay by Sidney Buchman, starring Paul Muni, Merle Oberson, and Cornel Wilde (Columbia, 1945).

240. Wilde, an American-born Hungarian and Roman Catholic, was married for many years to a Pole (Jean Wallace), close for World War II Hollywood to casting a Pole as a Pole.

241. Charles P. Mitchell has correctly described the film as "deceptive and misleading." He notes, "For some bizarre reason, the focus . . . is not really Chopin, but his teacher . . . Elsner." Charles P. Mitchell, *The Great Composers Portrayed on Film, 1913 through 2003* (Jefferson, NC: McFarland, 2004), 51. The answer is simple: Muni was an established star, and Cornel Wilde, a neo-phyte. Besides, Muni was a ham. Cf. Druxman, *Paul Muni,* 76–78, 202–3.

242. Berneis, feature script review, file "Song to Remember," National Archives

243. Peg Fenwick, "Frederic Chopin," November 30, 1943, file "Song to Remember," National Archives

244. Eleanor Berneis, second review, January 11, 1944, file "Song to Remember," National Archives.

245. Joseph Johnston, feature viewing, August 12, 1944, file "Song to Remember," National Archives.

246. See "Summary on the Communist Infiltration," 158.

247. Jack Norman and Margit Gyorgy, review, March 9, 1945, file "Song to Remember," National Archives.

248. The FBI considered Muni a "fellow traveler." See pt. 1, 119, COM-PIC. Regarding his prewar political views, see a 1935 interview in which he said he was "not concerned with the depression, or with communism or capitalism. . . . If communism comes along, swell! If fascism, it's all right by me." "A Word with Paul Muni," *New York Times,* January 27, 1935.

7. Hollywood and the American Poles during the War

1. See Helena Znaniecki Lopata, "Polish Immigration to the United States of America: Problems of Estimation and Parameters," *Polish Review* 21, no. 4 (1976): 85–107.

2. Here we except the Jews, who outnumber the Poles only if country of origin is omitted.

3. Woodrow Wilson, *A History of the American People* (New York: Harper, 1902), 5:212–13.

4. John Higham, *Strangers in the Land: Patterns of American Nativism, 1860–1925* (New Brunswick, NJ: Rutgers University Press, 1955), 139.

5. Regarding the Dillingham report, see James S. Pula, "American Immigration Policy and the Dillingham Commission," *Polish American Studies* 37, no. 1 (1980): 5–31.

6. *Eagle Squadron,* directed by Arthur Lubin, screenplay by Norman Reilly Raine, starring Robert Stack, Diana Barrymore, and Jon Hall (Universal, 1942).

7. Kane, *Visions of War,* 159–60. Regarding *Eagle Squadron,* see Jones and McClure, *Hollywood at War,* 89.

8. Strauss, "Again the Ten Worst."

9. Kane, *Visions of War,* 164. Steele, whose acting credits were few, had been middleweight boxing champion of the world between 1936 and 1938. Perhaps this explains his mental difficulties.

10. *Air Force,* directed by Howard Hawks, screenplay by Dudley Nichols, starring John Ridgely, Harry Carey, and John Garfield (Warner

Brothers, 1943); Paris, "Lessons for Democracy." *Air Force,* done in pseu-
dodocumentary style, makes embarrassing viewing, indulging in race-
based anti-Japanese propaganda. See Koppes and Black, *Hollywood Goes
to War,* 78–80.

11. Party member Ring Lardner Jr. regarded Garfield as one of "our
comrades in or close to the Party." Ring Lardner Jr., interview by Patrick
McGilligan, in McGilligan and Buhle, *Tender Comrades,* 412.

12. Lawrence Howard Suid, ed., *Air Force* (Madison, WI: University
of Wisconsin Press, 1983), 32–33. The *Hollywood Reporter,* February 3,
1943, pronounced the film "magnificent," and similar praise came from the
Motion Picture Daily, February 3, 1943. See clipping collection in file "Air
Force," MPAA-PCA.

13. Max Miller (managing director, Warner Brothers in London) to
Ambassador John Winant, April 5, 1943, folder "Warner Brothers Pictures," box 226, Winant Papers.

14. Jack Warner to Lowell Mellett, November 12, 1942, folder "Warner Brothers," box 18, Mellett Papers.

15. See files 9, 10, and 11, "Air Force," Weiser Papers. Garfield was
prominently featured in the publicity campaign.

16. Suid, *Air Force,* 33. Nichol's status as a fellow traveler is confirmed in pt. 1, 33, COMPIC.

17. Winocki is never expressly identified as Polish, though "ethnic"
roles abound in the film. The heroic and much beloved flight commander
Quincannon is identified as Irish; another stalwart fellow is the obviously
Jewish New York cabbie Weinberg.

18. Though Winocki "hates Quincannon" initially, the fact that they
later "find they like each other" caused the MPPDA to classify Winocki
as "sympathetic." C. R. Metzger, report, October 8, 1942; Beverly Jones,
"Analysis Chart," November 10, 1942, both in file "Air Force," MPAA-
PCA.

19. Dudley Nichols, "Air Force: Part I, Temporary," April 24, 1942,
1–4, folder 3, box 9, Warner Brothers Scripts. In the extended analysis of
the film by Suid, Winocki is described as "an embittered, washed-out pilot
about to leave the service." Suid, *Air Force,* 25.

20. Nichols, "Air Force: Part I, Temporary," 58, 78, 91, 94, 95–96,
136, 183.

21. John O. Watson, from the screenplay by Dudley Nichols, *Air Force*
(New York: Grosset and Dunlop, 1943), 5. A copy is in folder 10, box
10, Warner Brothers Scripts. Reviewers often did not notice that Winocki
was supposed to be Polish. The *Washington Evening Star,* for example,
described the crew as "the Jewish corporal from Brooklyn" and "the bitter

disillusioned, grousing tail gunner played by Garfield." Jay Carmody, "Air Force: Gripping Tale of Aerial War at Best," *Washington Evening Star,* n.d., clipping in folder 688, *Air Force* Collection, Warner Bros. Archives.

22. "Revised Temporary," May 29, 1942, folder 4, box 9, Warner Brothers Scripts.

23. "2nd Revised Temporary," June 12, 1942, 1–6, 7, 15–16, 30–34, 149, 6, 104, folder 5, box 9, Warner Brothers Scripts.

24. "Final," June 18, 1942, scene 167, folder 6, box 9, Warner Brothers Scripts.

25. Dudley Nichols, "Revised Final," July 3, 1942, 23, folder 1, box 10, Warner Brothers Scripts.

26. See scene 167 in Suid, *Air Force,* 128–29.

27. Ibid., 220n2.

28. See the BMP analysis of the revised final script, October 2, 1942; Nelson Poynter to Lowell Mellett, October 30, 1942; Larry Williams, analysis, February 2, 1943; Warner Brothers, "Synopsis," n.d., all in file "Air Force," box 3511, RG 208, National Archives. Cf. Poynter to Mellett, "Trends in Hollywood Pictures," and Ulric Bell to Jack Warner, February 6, 1943, *Air Force* Collection, Warner Bros. Archives.

29. "The First Victory Flag Awarded to a Motion Picture Co.," *Hollywood Reporter,* June 3, 1943, 6–7.

30. Watson, *Air Force,* 13.

31. Pt. 1, 72, COMPIC. Cf. Radosh and Radosh, *Red Star,* 190–200, and Buhle and Wagner, *Radical Hollywood,* 114 and esp. 310n15.

32. *Action in the North Atlantic,* directed by Lloyd Bacon, screenplay by John Howard Lawson, starring Humphrey Bogart, Raymond Massey, and Alan Hale (Warner Brothers, 1943). See Dick, *Radical Innocence,* 237–39.

33. There is an excellent brief discussion of *Action in the North Atlantic* in Koppes and Black, *Hollywood Goes to War,* 114–19.

34. Quoted in ibid., 117.

35. Later we are introduced to the ship's gun crew: Goldberg and Ahearn. John Howard Lawson, "Action in the North Atlantic," August 7, 1942, folder 2, box 76, Lawson Papers.

36. "W. R. Burnett: The Outsider," interview by Ken Mate and Pat McGilligan, in McGilligan, *Backstory,* 73. Fellow Communist Leonardo Bercovici also refers to Lawson by that title. Leonardo Bercovici, interview by Paul Buhle, in McGilligan and Buhle, *Tender Comrades,* 37. Even fellow Communists regarded Lawson as doctrinaire and narrow minded. See Lardner, interview by McGilligan, 407.

37. See, for example, Art Eckstein, "The Truth about the 'Hollywood

Ten,'" *FrontPage,* April 18, 2005, http://www.frontpagemag.com/readArticle.aspx?ARTID=8914. In the 1960s Lawson still was undecided about the Stalinist purge trials of the 1930s. See John Howard Lawson, untitled section of autobiography, 799A–805, folder 5, box 99, Lawson Papers.

38. Guy Gilpatric, *Action in the North Atlantic* (New York: Dutton, 1943), 19. The captain greets the Pole on their new ship thus: "Oh! Why, hello there Stanisławski! Glad to have you with me again!" Ibid., 83.

39. Ibid., 122–26.

40. Ibid., 108.

41. Guy Gilpatric, "Heroes without Uniforms: Original Treatment, Part I," May 25, 1942, 1, 12–54, 66, 97–98, 99–101, 130, folder 1, box 2, Warner Brothers Scripts. By this time a producer had been selected, Jerry Wald, though the final portions of the story existed only in brief outline.

42. J. H. Lawson (screenplay) and Guy Gilpatric (treatment), "Action in the North Atlantic: Part I, Temporary," July 1942, n.p., folder 3, box 2, Warner Brothers Scripts.

43. Ibid., 4–8.

44. Ibid., 12, 15, 17, 20, 23, 24, 25.

45. Ibid., 33–34, 36, 40–41, 47, 55, 60, 62.

46. Ibid., 64–68.

47. In 1943 Lawson wrote a screenplay that was never produced titled "Women at War." It features a Mrs. Pleznik, who is a sympathetic character but coarse and illiterate: at one point she hands the heroine a slab of raw meat as a token of esteem. John Howard Lawson, "Women at War," June 11, 1943, folder 2, box 77, Lawson Papers.

48. Lawson and Gilpatric, "Action in the North Atlantic: Part I, Temporary," 70–75.

49. Ibid., 112–13, 117–18.

50. Ibid., 129.

51. Lawson was content in July with altering that scene so that the malcontent sailor directs his principal attack against the black sailor. This allows Lawson to make the Rossi character a champion of racial equality when he violently rebukes the offender. See ibid., 116.

52. John Howard Lawson and W. R. Burnett (screenplay) and Guy Gilpatric (treatment), "Action in the North Atlantic: Part I, Final," August 7, 1942, 1, folder 4, box 2, Warner Brothers Scripts.

53. Ibid., 1, 2.

54. Ibid., 10–15, 20, 25, 26, 34–40, 100, 123, 128, 132, 150, 170.

55. Ibid., 167, 173.

56. Ibid., 189. In his famous 1947 testimony before Congress, Jack Warner specifically accused Lawson of inserting Communist propaganda

in *Action in the North Atlantic.* Lawson, he said, "tried to swing a lot of things in there." Warner, testimony, 15. See also Maltz, "Citizen Writer," 2:545.

57. Bernard Dick characterizes Lawson as a "Russophile" and "Stalinist." Dick, *Radical Innocence,* 55, 57.

58. Compare Lawson and Gilpatric, "Action in the North Atlantic: Part I, Temporary," 114, with Lawson, Burnett, and Gilpatric, "Action in the North Atlantic: Part I, Final," 83.

59. John Howard Lawson and W. R. Burnett (screenplay) and Guy Gilpatric (treatment), "Action in the North Atlantic: Part I, Revised Final," September 1, 1942, 57–61, folder 5, box 2, Warner Brothers Scripts. This scene was added on September 30, according to internal evidence.

60. Ibid., 1–14. This scene was added on September 18, according to internal evidence.

61. Pulaski now is married and expects a child. Abrams again surpasses him: he has three children. As Dave Wagner and Paul Buhle note, this scene is set in the merchant marine hall, a "Popular Front hotbed," emphasizing the leftist credentials of Abrams and his fellows. Wagner and Buhle, *Blacklisted,* 4.

62. Ibid., 25 (material added October 21, 1942), 131 (material added October 28, 1942).

63. Ibid., n.p. (material added October 21, 1942).

64. Script review, September 8, 1942, file "Action in the North Atlantic," National Archives.

65. Nelson Poynter to Lowell Mellett, May 12, 1942, file "Action in the North Atlantic," National Archives.

66. "Comment," May 19, 1943; Lillian Bergquist, memorandum, May 19, 1943, both in file "Action in the North Atlantic," National Archives.

67. Kaiser quoted in Nelson Poynter to Lowell Mellett, May 18, 1943, file "Action in the North Atlantic," National Archives.

68. Wagner and Buhle, *Blacklisted,* 4.

69. Nelson Poynter to Jack Warner, May 18, 1943; Jack Warner to Nelson Poynter, May 19, 1943, both in file "Action in the North Atlantic," National Archives.

70. Jack Warner to Marvin McIntyre (Roosevelt's secretary), November 10, 1942, file 1050, President's Personal File, Roosevelt Library.

71. *Destroyer,* directed by William A. Seiter, screenplay by Frank Wead, Borden Chase, and Lewis Meltzer, starring Edward G. Robinson, Glenn Ford, and Marguerite Chapman (Columbia, 1943).

72. Robinson was a major financial supporter of party front organizations and was considered by the FBI to be a "Communist sympathizer." See

pt. 1, 20, COMPIC. His memoirs tell us nothing about the film. See Edward G. Robinson with Leonard Spigelgass, *All My Yesterdays: An Autobiography* (New York: Hawthorn Books, 1973).

73. The *New Yorker* described Robinson as "swamped in nonsense," but most reviews were positive. See "It's the Same Old Story," *New Yorker,* September 11, 1943, and other clippings in *Destroyer* files, Clipping Files, Herrick Library.

74. Leo Gorcey has a minor role in *Destroyer* as Sarecky, another character possibly intended to be Polish, but with a garbled Slavic name. Gorcey, like Robinson, was very short and swarthy.

75. In Polish the name would be "Bolesławski," not "Boleslavski." In Columbia's "Synopsis," released on May 12, 1943, by the studio's director of publicity (*Destroyer* files, Clipping Files, Herrick Library), the character's name is doubly misspelled as "Boleslavsky." Also note that, when Boley's daughter marries, she does so before a justice of the peace, whereas a priest would have been a rather obvious choice for an overwhelmingly Roman Catholic nationality.

76. In the large collection of contemporary reviews of *Destoyer* in the Herrick Library, not one mentions that the Robinson character is Polish or that his nationality has any significance.

77. See Fenwick, review, file "Destroyer," National Archives.

78. Ibid.

79. Of course, a Polish patriot familiar with his national history would be unlikely to sing the praises of John Paul Jones. Leaving aside whatever service he may have performed for the fledgling American navy, Jones was later a mercenary in the service of Catherine II of Russia, a principal architect in the destruction of Poland at the close of the eighteenth century, and hence Jones could hardly represent a positive figure for Poles.

80. See pt. 1, 20, COMPIC.

81. *Rise and Shine,* directed by Allan Dwan, screenplay by Herman J. Mankiewicz, starring Jack Oakie, George Murphy, and Linda Darnell (Twentieth Century–Fox, 1941).

82. Screenwriter Mankiewicz was the American-born son of Jewish immigrants from Germany. The Mankiewicz family was of Polish origin, and it seems inconceivable that a Mankiewicz would not realize that "Bolenciecwcz" is neither spelled logically nor pronounced "Bolenkowitz."

83. Robert Juran restrainedly describes the Oakie character as "dumb." Juran, *Old Familiar Faces,* 202.

84. *Abroad with Two Yanks,* directed by Allan Dwan, screenplay by Fred Guiol, starring William Bendix, Helen Walker, and Dennis O'Keefe (Edward Small Productions, 1944).

---

85. *Irish Eyes Are Smiling,* directed by Gregory Ratoff, screenplay by Earl Baldwin and John Tucker Battle, starring Monty Woolley, June Haver, and Dick Haymes (Twentieth Century–Fox, 1944).

86. *Pittsburgh,* directed by Lewis Seiler, screenplay by Kenneth Garnet, starring Marlene Dietrich, Randolph Scott, and John Wayne (Universal, 1942).

87. Dietrich was very critical of the film and of costar John Wayne's performance. See Donald Spoto, *Blue Angel: The Life of Marlene Dietrich* (New York: Doubleday, 1992), 178.

88. She describes herself as being of Polish noble ancestry in the film.

89. In reviewing this film for the BMP, Bergquist illogically noted, "People call Josie Hunky because she's Polish." Lillian Bergquist, review, November 30, 1942, file "Pittsburgh," box 3523, RG 208, National Archives. The BMP, by the way, was very pleased with the film.

90. The size of the Polish population in the United States in the war era has not been definitively established. The Polish American Congress (formed in 1944) always claimed to speak for a community of 6 million—probably a generous reckoning. The OSS estimated only 4 million Poles in the United States—certainly too low. Robert Szymczak of Pennsylvania State University, a leading authority on wartime Polonia, recommends the number of 5.5 million as reasonable. Robert Szymczak to author, February 17, 2005.

91. The BMP, which was horrified when a Russian American character was presented as comic, had no objections to presenting a Polish American whose name was a joke. See Sally Kaye's analysis of *Mr. Winkle Goes to War,* April 2, 1943, file "Reviews and Activities Reports—3/1/43–4/15/43," box 1439, RG 208, National Archives. According to Kaye, Sergeant "Czeideskrowski"—yet a different spelling—was a "forthright" character. The sergeant with the impossible name was played by Richard Lane, who appeared in a great many films, always in minor roles, and later became famous for his emotive commentary on roller derby and wrestling on local television in Los Angeles.

92. Mark Winokur argues that Hollywood was characterized by the "absence of direct, proportional representation of the immigrant as complex character and lead player, and the substitution instead of ethnic stereotypes"—a paradox, he notes, given that "the medium is to a great extent dominated by immigrants and children of immigrants." Winokur, "Improbable Ethnic Hero," 5. His observation is valid but obscures the fact that certain immigrant groups (the Irish) were well represented, others (Jews and Italians) less well, with the Poles being virtually invisible. In other words,

the lack of "proportionate representation" varies gigantically. Here we may consider Lester D. Friedman's argument that Hollywood purposely sought to "cast off 'foreignisms,'" including names. Friedman, "Celluloid Palimpsests," 30. Similarly, Ella Shohat remarks, "Generally, the ethnic characters lack even the most basic marker of identity—a name." Shohat, "Ethnicities-in-Relation," 226. However, Irish, Jewish, and Italian characters in film were far more identifiable than Polish ones.

93. In order to avoid the problem of a prejudicial selection, I utilized a preexisting sample, the approximately 400 films in Jones and McClure's *Hollywood at War.* From the cast list therein I isolated characters with names obviously characteristic of the several ethnic groups. Thereafter I attempted to find as many of the films and scripts as possible to look for additional indicators of intended ethnicity. Obviously, this method is hardly flawless, but it is reasonably accurate. Because I assumed that Polish names would be rare before beginning the survey, I adopted the following procedure: All names probably intended to be Polish I assumed to be Polish even without additional evidence. Hence I counted characters named Kozzarowski, Sinkewicz, Savitski, and Madame Lugovska (among others) as Polish. I was more demanding for deeming someone an Irish character, which, I presumed, would be a far larger sampling.

94. It is typical that, although Alvin York specifically mentioned serving with Poles in public addresses during World War II—see Birdwell, *Celluloid Soldiers,* 127—the famous Warner Brothers film biography of the Tennessean, *Sergeant York,* has no Polish characters, though there are Irish and Jewish ones.

95. Doherty, *Projections of War,* 141.

96. See the evolution of the scripts for *All through the Night* from March, 19, 1941, through a last-minute "Revised Final" of July 31, 1941, in folders 3–7, box 13, Warner Brothers Scripts.

97. As is discussed later in this chapter, the Polish chief petty officer in *Destination Tokyo* was also transformed at the final moment into an Irish character.

98. Versions of this theory abound: "Every combat team included its quota of integrated Jewish, Polish and even Hispanic Americans." Paris, "Lessons for Democracy."

99. Indeed, the service films with no Poles at all are the great majority; this hardly exhaustive list illustrates this clearly. In 1940 appeared *Sailor's Lady* about the navy, *Flight Command* about naval aviation, and *Buck Privates* about the army. The next year saw *I Wanted Wings* about the army air force; *Rookies on Parade, Caught in the Draft, Parachute Battalion, Top Sergeant Mulligan, You're in the Army Now,* and *The Bugle Sounds*

about the army; *Sailors on Leave, Navy Blues,* and *In the Navy* about the navy; and *Dive Bomber* about naval aviation. In 1942 films devoted to the navy included *The Fleet's In, The Navy Comes Through,* and *Stand By for Action;* army films were *True to the Army* and *Private Buckaroo,* with *Flight Lieutenant* concerning the army air force; and *To the Shores of Tripoli* was about the marines. In 1943 the army was the topic of *It Ain't Hay, Corregidor,* and *Sahara;* the army air corps was the focus of *Bombardier* and *A Guy Named Joe;* the navy had *Crash Dive, Hi Ya, Sailor,* and *Destination Tokyo;* and the marines were featured in *So Proudly We Hail, The Marines Come Through,* and *Guadalcanal Diary.* The next year devoted *The Sullivans* to the navy and *Wing and a Prayer* to naval aviation, while *Winged Victory* dealt with the army air force and the marines were the topic of *Marine Raiders* and *Hail the Conquering Hero.* Finally, 1945 gave us *This Man's Navy, Anchors Aweigh,* and *They Were Expendable* regarding the navy and *Back to Bataan* and *Operation, Burma* for the army. In this sample of over forty films, with scores of roles featured, there is not a single Polish name. There are, however, over one hundred Irish characters in the films.

100. *Submarine Raider,* directed by Lew Landers, screenplay by Aubrey Wisberg, starring John Howard, Marguerite Chapman, and Bruce Bennett (Columbia, 1942).

101. See Jones and McClure, *Hollywood at War,* 90–91, which contains a photograph of the youthful Tucker as Pulaski. Tucker, curiously, was again seemingly cast as a Pole in the immediate postwar release by Warner Brothers titled *Never Say Goodbye,* a 1946 film rather better than its obscurity would suggest. Tucker played the cloddish but sympathetic marine corporal Fenwick Lonkowski, a name obviously intended to make him ridiculous.

102. *Bataan,* directed by Tay Garnett, screenplay by Robert Hardy Andrews, starring Robert Taylor, George Murphy, Thomas Mitchell, Lloyd Nolan, Lee Bowman, Robert Wagner, and Desi Arnaz (MGM, 1943). The OWI was predictably pleased by the multiethnic aspect of the movie, especially the appearance of a black soldier. That these various ethnic groups were symbols without content was not of moment. See file "Bataan," box 3511, RG 208, National Archives. Paris is sure Matowski is Polish. Paris, "Lessons for Democracy."

103. *Gangway for Tomorrow,* directed by John H. Auer, screenplay by Aladar László and Arch Oboler, starring Margo, Robert Ryan, and John Carradine (RKO, 1943).

104. We have a Dunham, a Nolan, and two Burkes, all with featured roles in the film.

105. See "Full Credits for *Gangway for Tomorrow* (1943)," *TCM Movie Database,* http://www.tcm.com/tcmdb/title.jsp?stid=75985&category=Full Credits. The same fate befell Dickie Meyers, who portrayed Norwaski, presumably a Pole, in a microscopic role in the mercifully forgotten film *Good Luck, Mr. Yates* (Columbia, 1943).

106. See Sandy Roth, analysis, June 22, 1943, and the unsigned comments of June 15, 1943, in file "Gangway for Tomorrow," box 3516, RG 208, National Archives.

107. *Tender Comrade,* directed by Edward Dmytryk, screenplay by Dalton Trumbo, starring Ginger Rogers, Robert Ryan, and Ruth Hussey (RKO, 1942).

108. The Rogers character is both the leader of the group and their *custos morum.* At one point she delivers a perfervid lecture on patriotism and civic responsibility. The Polish characters are by comparison both minor and silly.

109. *Hitler—Dead or Alive,* directed by Nick Grinde, screenplay by Karl Brown and Sam Neuman, starring Ward Bond, Dorothy Tree, Warren Hymer, and Paul Fix (Ben Judell, 1942).

110. Halsted, however, which runs for quite a distance in the city, in the 1930s was not a symbolically Polish street in Chicago. In the south it skirted rather than traversed a Polish neighborhood and would actually have been more a symbolically Irish street in the Bridgeport neighborhood. In the north it ran east of Polonia and would have been closer to an old German settlement.

111. See BMP, memorandum, September 9, 1942, file "Hitler—Dead or Alive," box 3518, RG 208, National Archives.

112. *The Tanks Are Coming,* directed by B. Reeves Eason, screenplay by Owen Crump, starring George Tobais and Gig Young (Warner Brothers, 1941).

113. The names of Tobias's various screen roles indicate the persona Warner Brothers had in mind for him: Lug, Gabby, Blimp, Pinky, Sloppy Joe, Rosie, Slug McNutt, and Panhandle. He was always slightly ridiculous.

114. *Hi Diddle Diddle,* directed by Andrew L. Stone, screenplay by Frederick J. Jackson, starring Adolphe Menjou and Pola Negri (United Artists, 1943).

115. *An American Romance,* directed by King Vidor, screenplay by King Vidor and Herbert Dalmas, starring Brian Donlevy, Ann Richards, and Walter Abel (MGM, 1944). Bosley Crowther described the film—which was an expensive box office disaster—as "banal and tedious . . . one massive platitude." Bosley Crowther, "'American Romance,' Big Scenic Film, with Brian Donlevy," *New York Times,* November 4, 1944.

116. Crowther, "'American Romance.'" Of course, King Vidor, who wrote this film, apparently would not know a Czech from a Martian. "Dangos" is a Lithuanian word, though not a name. The only other "dangos" would be Japanese dumplings, but even Vidor probably did not consider this Asiatic theme.

117. Ibid.

118. This was noted by, among others, Crowther, in ibid.

119. Alberni's one, very minor role as a Pole was in the 1939 Warner Brothers release *Naughty but Nice*. Alberni was usually cast as a Mediterranean because of his very dark features.

120. Muggs is Irish, and Irish references of all sorts are frequent in the East Side Kids films. No other nationality is mentioned.

121. Clements was a Pole born in Long Island, New York, whose real name was Stanisław Klimowicz. He portrayed Stash in at least three East Side Kids films: *'Neath Brooklyn Bridge* (1942), *Smart Alecks* (1942), and *Ghosts on the Loose* (1943). When the East Side Kids evolved into the Bowery Boys after World War II, Clements again was part of the gang but was now called Stanislaus "Duke" Covaleskie. There were several dozen Bowery Boys films, all quite formulaic and cheaply made. The Stash character reached costarring status by the end of the Bowery Boys series in the late 1950s. Clements, in this very minor role, thus created the most visible continuing Polish presence in American film. The Stash character was portrayed once by Dick Chandlee in the 1943 Monogram film *Clancy Street Boys*. A very small role with no discernible dialogue, it was Chandlee's only appearance in the series.

122. *The More the Merrier*, directed by George Stevens, screenplay by Richard Flournoy, Lewis R. Foster, Frank Ross, and Robert Russell, starring Jean Arthur, Joel McCrae, and Charles Coburn (Columbia, 1943). Coburn won an Academy Award for best supporting actor.

123. The antagonist, a repulsive child Nazi, gets into a fight with little Stan Dumbrowski. In this Polish-German struggle, the Pole bears the name of the famous Polish general, Jan Henryk Dąbrowski, whose exploits are celebrated in the Polish national anthem. For the film's goals of attacking racial prejudice, see Lardner, *I'd Hate Myself*, 8.

124. *The Talk of the Town*, directed by George Stevens, screenplay by Sidney Harmon and Dale Van Every, starring Jean Arthur, Cary Grant, and Ronald Coleman (Columbia, 1942).

125. Pulaski is portrayed, with excessive ethnic flourishes, by the Russian expatriate Leonid Kinskey. Tom Tyler, a real Pole, plays Clyde Bracken, an ethnic nondescript.

126. *We Were Dancing*, directed by Robert Z. Leonard, screenplay by

Claudine West, starring Nora Shearer, Melvyn Douglas, and Gail Patrick (MGM, 1942). The *New York Times* regarded it as one of the worst films of the year. Strauss, "Again the Ten Worst."

127. The film was adapted from the Coward play by Claudine West, who collaborated on a number of critically acclaimed films, including *Mrs. Miniver* and *Random Harvest.* Director Leonard had had a number of successes, including *Pride and Prejudice.* The cast was large and impressive. Nonetheless, the film was a major failure.

128. *Princess O'Rourke,* directed by Norman Krasna, screenplay by Norman Krasna, starring Olivia de Havilland, Robert Cummings, and Charles Coburn (Warner Brothers, 1943).

129. *Sing Another Chorus,* directed by Charles R. Lamont, screenplay by Marion Orth and Sam Robins, starring Johnny Downs, Jane Frazee, and Mischa Auer (Universal, 1941).

130. *Don't Get Personal,* directed by Charles R. Lamont, screenplay by Howard Snyder, starring Hugh Herbert and Mischa Auer (Universal, 1942).

131. Steve Fisher, "Destination Tokyo," *Liberty,* October 30, 1943, copy in folder 1, box 96, Warner Brothers Scripts; Steve Fisher, "Treatment," June 4, 1943, 5, folders 1, 2, box 96, Warner Brothers Scripts.

132. Steve Fisher, *Destination Tokyo* (New York: Appleton-Century, 1943), 30, 34, 180–85. A copy is in folder 10, box 95, Warner Brothers Scripts.

133. "Destination Tokyo: Temporary," May 1, 1943, folder 4, box 96, Warner Brothers Scripts.

134. "Destination Tokyo: Revised Treatment," May 13, 1943, folder 3, box 96, Warner Brothers Scripts.

135. Delmer Daves (screenplay) and Steve Fisher (story), "Destination Tokyo: Revised Temporary," May 14, 1943, folder 5, box 96, Warner Brothers Scripts.

136. See "Destination Tokyo: Second Revised Temporary," n.d., folder 6, and "Destination Tokyo," June 20, 1943, esp. 9, 20, folder 7, both in box 96, Warner Brothers Scripts.

137. *Destination Tokyo,* directed by Delmer Daves, screenplay by Delmer Daves and Albert Maltz, starring Cary Grant, John Garfield, and Alan Hale (Warner Brothers, 1943). Mike was played by Tom Tully. His role was considerably reduced from the prominence attached to the character in its original Polish manifestation.

138. Maltz, "Citizen Writer," 2:531–33.

139. *Lifeboat,* directed by Alfred Hitchcock, screenplay by Jo Swerling, starring Tallulah Bankhead, William Bendix, Walter Slezak, and John Hodiak (Twentieth Century–Fox, 1944).

140. Steinbeck wrote the story, at least in outline. He apparently produced another version in collaboration with Harry Sylvester. It was reworked for the screen, initially by MacKinlay Kantor, but Hitchcock did not care for the result. Kantor was dismissed, and Hitchcock rewrote the script at least in part. Ben Hecht made some changes to the final scenes. See Ryder W. Miller, "John Steinbeck: Publish Lifeboat," *Rain Taxi Online,* Summer 2002, http://www.raintaxi.com/online/2002summer/lifeboat.shtml. As far as Hitchcock was concerned, the final screenplay was written by Swerling. Alfred Hitchcock, interview by Andy Warhol, 1974, in *Alfred Hitchcock: Interviews,* ed. Sidney Gottlieb (Jackson: University Press of Mississippi, 2003), 201. Cf. *Hitchcock's Notebooks,* ed. Dan Auiler (New York: Avon, 1999), 128. Hecht was, be it noted, then a member of the party. Bernstein, interview, 47.

141. Koppes and Black, *Hollywood Goes to War,* 310. The name is also given as "Sheinkowitz" in Miller, "John Steinbeck." Donald Spoto claims that the character was clearly intended to be a "tough Communist." Donald Spoto, *The Art of Alfred Hitchcock: Fifty Years of His Motion Pictures* (Garden City, NY: Doubleday, 1976), 148.

142. Jay Parini, *John Steinbeck: A Biography* (New York: Holt, 1995), 279.

143. See Jackson J. Benson, *The True Adventure of John Steinbeck, Writer* (New York: Viking, 1984), 510–11, 542–43.

144. See John Steinbeck, "Lifeboat," March 23, 1943, 15, 31, 33–34, 38–39, 232, folder 351, Alfred Hitchcock Papers, Special Collections, Herrick Library.

145. Jo Swerling, "Lifeboat: Script," revised final, July 29, 1943, folder 353, Hitchcock Papers. The earliest version of the script by Swerling that transforms Sheinkowitz the Pole into Kovac the Czech seems to be dated April 30, 1943. See folder 3, "Lifeboat," Twentieth Century–Fox Collection. There is an intriguing possibility that the character spent some time in ethnic limbo, as it were. In November 1943 *Colliers* published a short story by Alfred Hitchcock and Harry Sylvester "based on an original screen story by John Steinbeck." Here the character's name is Kovac and he retains his violent dislike of the German, but he has, it seems, no specific nationality. There is nothing at all like the remarks concerning Czechoslovakia. These additions, which redefined the character, hence almost certainly came from Swerling. Though the story was published in November, it must have been completed earlier. See Alfred Hitchcock and Harry Sylvester, "Lifeboat," *Colliers,* November 13, 1943, a copy of which is in folder 354, Hitchcock Papers. The illustrations accompanying the story reflect the cast that appears in the film.

146. See Jo Swerling, script, June 3, 1943, folder 3, "Lifeboat," Twentieth Century–Fox Collection.

147. Miller observes that Kovac's desire to kill the German is inexplicable: "For some unnamed reason . . . [he] wants to throw the German overboard immediately." Miller, "John Steinbeck." Kovac's reaction is substantially explained if he is a Pole.

148. In June 1942 the Germans massacred the population of the small Czech town of Lidice, killing 172 people in reprisal for the assassination of Reinhold Heydrich, the German protector of Bohemia-Moravia. About 1,200 other Czechs were killed throughout the country as part of the same action. During the war the total Czech civilian casualties were about 60,000, or slightly more than 2 percent of the population. By comparison, Polish civilian deaths under occupation were approximately 2.2 million, or 16 percent of the population. Lidice was given enormous attention. As a Pole bitterly remarked at the time, "We have thousands of Lidices in Poland." Quoted in Richard C. Lukas, *The Forgotten Holocaust: The Poles under German Occupation, 1939–1944* (Lexington: University Press of Kentucky, 1986), 37. Roosevelt made a special reference to Lidice, a benediction precious to the Left. See Novick, *Holocaust,* 45.

149. *Variety* noted that Kovac was supposed to be a Czech but attached no significance to it. *Variety,* June 12, 1944, clipping in file "Lifeboat," MPAA-PCA.

150. See BMP, review, July 31, 1943; Warren H. Pierce to Eugene O'Neil, August 2, 1943; BMP, report, September 11, 1943; and Peg Fenwick, report, December 31, 1943, all in file "Lifeboat," box 3520, RG 208, National Archives.

151. *Margin for Error,* directed by Otto Preminger, screenplay by Lillie Howard, starring Joan Bennett, Milton Berle, and Otto Preminger (Twentieth Century–Fox, 1943). In the film Bennett befriends stalwart Gotham policeman Moe Finkelstein (Milton Berle, badly cast), and together they combat Nazism. See Jeff Gordon, "The World War II Films of 20th Century-Fox," *Films of the Golden Age* 42 (Fall 2005): 29. The film is very bad, simultaneously attempting to be comedy and drama and succeeding as neither.

152. *Lake Placid Serenade,* directed by Steve Sekely, screenplay by Dick Irving Hyland and Doris Gilbert, starring Vera Hruba Ralston, Eugene Pallette, and Vera Vague (Republic, 1944). We have two Hascheks, a Cermak, and a Benda, but also a Jiggers, who is Irish.

8. Why Hollywood Was at War with the Poles

1. The political affiliations of this group are discussed in previous chapters with the exception of Lewis Milestone. See Dick, *Radical Innocence,* 2–3. Milestone prepared a montage of Soviet combat footage in 1942 titled, significantly, *Our Russian Front.* In 1943 he directed both *Edge of Darkness* and *The North Star.* See Nicholas J. Cull, "Samuel Fuller on Lewis Milestone's *A Walk in the Sun* (1946): The Legacy of *All Quiet on the Western Front* (1930)," *Historical Journal of Film, Radio and Television* 20, no. 1 (2000): 79–80. Indeed, the long list of those denounced as Communists by Jack Warner in his October 1947 testimony before Congress may not all have been party members, but they were certainly very leftist, perhaps the best one can say for Warner's hapless performance. Warner, testimony, 14–15. Horne argues that "25 to 30 percent of the most regularly employed members of the Screen Writers Guild were members of the CPUSA." Horne, *Final Victim,* 132.

2. Ceplair and Englund, *Inquisition in Hollywood,* 437–38. Ceplair and Englund admit that the influence of radical Left politics in wartime Hollywood is difficult to gauge and rather vaguely note that the "insistence and articulateness of the film Communists altered the atmosphere of Hollywood and influenced film content and political behavior." Ibid., 323. For an extended discussion, see esp. chap. 9, "The Influence of Hollywood Communists on American Films and American Politics, 1930–47," in ibid., 299–324. An FBI survey in June 1944 counted among directors and producers "nine known Communist Party members and fifteen members of one or more Communist Party front groups." Among writers there were fifty-six party members; among actors there were five party members and twenty-four members of various front groups. This included Ida Lupino, who appeared in *In Our Time.* See "Communist Infiltration of Motion Picture Industry," May 24, 1947, pt. 3, [2], COMPIC. By July 1945 the FBI increased its count of Communists in the Writers Guild to "approximately 100." "Communist Infiltration of Labor Groups," 23.

3. Regarding Warner Brothers' reputation for "progressive" films, see Gianos, *Politics and Politicians,* 124. Jack Warner specifically singled out the film *In Our Time* in his denunciation of Howard Koch, claiming that Koch "always started out with big messages and I had to take them out." Warner, testimony, 14–15.

4. Patrick McGilligan and Paul Buhle, "Meet the People," introduction to *Tender Comrades,* xv; Billingsley, *Hollywood Party,* 67. The political domination of the Left in Hollywood is beyond question. See the useful discussion of Steven J. Ross's "Little Caesar and the HUAC Mob:

Edward G. Robinson and the Decline of Hollywood Liberalism" (presentation, Celebrity, Politics and Public Life seminar, Norman Lear Center, University of Southern California, Los Angeles, September 28, 2001) at http://www.learcenter.org/pdf/ross.pdf. Schwartz remarks, referring to the 1930s, "In Hollywood . . . the Communist Party was barely distinguishable in policy and activities to the noncommunist Left." Schwartz, *Hollywood Writers' Wars,* 82.

5. Buhle and Wagner, *Radical Hollywood,* 56.

6. Schwartz, *Hollywood Writers' Wars,* 86.

7. De Toth, *Fragments,* 282–83. De Toth provides examples of performers labeled "fascists" who were nothing of the kind but were simply not members of the Left. Ibid.

8. "Burnett: The Outsider," 73.

9. Ibid. The guild, as earlier noted, was founded by Communists. See McGilligan and Buhle, "Meet the People," xvi. Party member Maurice Rapf recalls that the party was able to "control an election" in the guild. Maurice Rapf, interview by Patrick McGilligan, in McGilligan and Buhle, *Tender Comrades,* 519. Though party members were only a minority of the total membership in the guild, they dominated the key offices. See "Summary on the Communist Infiltration," 81.

10. Gibney, interview, 157.

11. "Allen Scott: A Nice Life," interview by Pat McGilligan, in McGilligan, *Backstory,* 315.

12. Anne Froelick, interview by Paul Buhle and Dave Wagner, in McGilligan and Buhle, *Tender Comrades,* 255.

13. Jarrico, interview, 328.

14. Quoted in Billingsley, *Hollywood Party,* 58–59.

15. John Cogley quoted in ibid., 68.

16. Dunne, interview, 21, 38. For Dunne's role as a defender of radicals, see Dmytryk, *Odd Man Out,* 55.

17. Cole, *Hollywood Red,* 202.

18. This view, of course, reflects the argument of the party's "cultural head," V. J. Jerome, that "agitprop drama was actually better drama because Marxists better understood the forces that shaped human beings." Jerome quoted in Schwartz, *Hollywood Writers' Wars,* 44. Hence the Hollywood Communists were urged to conclude that their arguments, even if used to slander and misrepresent, were by definition not only politically but also aesthetically superior.

19. Alvah Bessie is a case in point. A vocal political radical and member of the Communist Party, Bessie went to Spain in the 1930s to fight in the International Brigades and returned to become the film reviewer for

the party's journal, *New Masses.* In 1943 he began a career as a Warner Brothers screenwriter responsible for such important wartime films as *Northern Pursuit, Objective Burma,* and *Hotel Berlin.* In 1945 he became involved in a nasty contretemps with fellow party member Albert Maltz, who enraged Bessie by having the audacity to suggest that the party should allow greater intellectual freedom. It is eloquent testimony to the sectarianism of the Hollywood Communists that Maltz's offense was suggesting that a Trotskyite might be a good writer. See McGilligan and Buhle, *Tender Comrades,* 46n.

20. Huggins quoted in Schwartz, *Hollywood Writers' Wars,* 88.

21. See Shein, *Analysis of Motion Pictures,* 81. Cf. McGilligan and Buhle, "Meet the People," xiv. Jules Dassin claims there were only a handful of Communists among the directors. Dassin, interview, 210.

22. McGilligan and Buhle, "Meet the People," xvi.

23. Alvah Bessie, interview by Patrick McGilligan and Ken Mate, in McGilligan and Buhle, *Tender Comrades,* 107.

24. Pt. 1, 74, COMPIC.

25. Billingsley, *Hollywood Party,* 64, 66. Cf. Dick, *Radical Innocence,* 191.

26. Radosh and Radosh, *Red Star,* 84.

27. Tuttle quoted in Billingsley, *Hollywood Party,* 228. Tuttle was a busy if not critically regarded director of a large number of films over several decades, mostly for Paramount, including *Hostages* (1942), set in Czechoslovakia. He directed several Bing Crosby musicals as well.

28. Horne, *Final Victim,* 160. Horne, however, specifically denies that this process was designed for ideological reasons and insists that it was "to make the scripts better." Ibid.

29. The network of party penetration of nonparty organizations is noted in Ceplair and Englund, *Inquisition in Hollywood,* 68.

30. *Once upon a Honeymoon* (1942) was directed by Leo McCarey, no leftist, from a screenplay he created in conjunction with Sheldon Gibney, who was indeed on the left. *Destroyer* was written by Borden Chase and Lewis Meltzer, whose politics I have been unable to reconstruct. The director was William A Seiter.

31. Schwartz, *Hollywood Writers' Wars,* 195.

32. Cohn quoted in ibid., 279.

33. Georgakas, "Hollywood Reds," 72.

34. Buhle and Wagner, *Radical Hollywood,* xvii.

35. Georgakas, "Hollywood Reds," 66.

36. Dunne, interview, 120, 264.

37. For Maltz's view of Poland, see "Citizen Writer," 1:296, 453–54, 2:760.

38. Ceplair and Englund, *Inquisition in Hollywood,* 239.

39. Billingsley, *Hollywood Party,* 26. In his 1947 testimony before Congress, Mayer was rather dismissive of the ideological content of his wartime films, describing them quite instrumentally. *Mrs. Miniver* was made after the fall of Tobruk to cheer up the British; *Song of Russia* was a "pat on the back" for their military efforts; etc. Louis B. Mayer, testimony, October 20, 1947, House Committee on Un-American Activities, *Hearings,* 71.

40. Warner seemed concerned about employing openly Communist writers as early as 1942. See Bessie, interview, 101. Zanuck was regarded by the radical Left as being essentially fair minded and apolitical. See Mickey Knox, interview by Patrick McGilligan, in McGilligan and Buhle, *Tender Comrades,* 379.

41. "Epstein: A King of Comedy," 181.

42. The description of pro-Russian films as "political accidents" is from Fuhrammar and Isaksson, *Politics and Film,* 64. The 1941 description to the U.S. Senate of the anti-Russian *Ski Patrol* as "no good any more" similarly reflects Hollywood's efforts to shape film's ideological content to geopolitical fashion. See Small, "Buffoons," 328–29.

43. Trumbo paraphrased in Small, "Buffoons," 330. Cf. Billingsley, *Hollywood Party,* 92–93. In 1947 *Variety* published an essay by Richard Macauley in which he noted that leftist writers in Hollywood would prevent any film from depicting, for example, the Warsaw Rising of 1944. Richard Macauley, "Who Censors What," *Variety,* October 14, 1946, reprinted in House Committee on Un-American Activities, *Hearings,* 201.

44. Froelick, interview, 257–58.

45. Robert Lees, interview by Paul Buhle and Dave Wagner, in McGilligan and Buhle, *Tender Comrades,* 423–24.

46. Lionel Stander, interview by Patrick McGilligan and Ken Mate, in McGilligan and Buhle, *Tender Comrades,* 609–18.

47. See Froelick, interview, 257–58.

48. Jarrico, interview, 328, 335.

49. Bernstein, *Inside Out,* 68, 227.

50. Collins made this remark in a 2001 conversation with Robert Mayhew. Mayhew, *Ayn Rand,* 27.

51. Howard Koch to Representative Thomas, June 10, 1947, folder 13, box 3, Koch Papers.

52. Some recent Russian scholarship has argued that American aid was considerably more important to the Soviet war effort than previously estimated; this remains a controversial topic. The most recent study by an American scholar overstates the importance. See Albert J. Weeks, *Russia's*

Life-Saver: Lend-Lease Aid to the U.S.S.R. in World War II (Lanham, MD: Rowman and Littlefield, 2004).

53. Jones and McClure, for example, deem *Mission to Moscow* "a rather crude attempt to sell Russia." Jones and McClure, *Hollywood at War,* 131.

54. Saverio Giovacchini, *Hollywood Modernism: Film and Politics in the Age of the New Deal* (Philadelphia: Temple University Press, 2001), 141–42.

55. Regarding the OWI's first principle, see Gianos, *Politics and Politicians,* 116.

56. Small, "Buffoons," 330.

57. Combs and Combs, *Film Propaganda,* 61.

58. The phrase "reinventing the Soviet Union" was coined by Gianos in *Politics and Politicians,* 123.

59. See Frank E. Beaver, *Bosley Crowther: Social Critic of the Film, 1940–1967* (New York: Arno, 1974), and *For the Love of Movies: The Story of America Film Criticism,* directed by Gerald Peary, written by Gerald Peary (AG Films, 2009). Phillip Dunne regarded Crowther as "one of the worst major film reviewers of all time" but one whose influence was nonetheless enormous because of his position at the *New York Times.* Dunne, interview, 28.

60. Crowther quoted in Koppes and Black, *Hollywood Goes to War,* 105.

61. Bosley Crowther, "Against a Sea of Troubles," *New York Times,* March 22, 1942.

62. Bosley Crowther, "The Screen," *New York Times,* February 12, 1944.

63. Of course, it would have been both more generous and more accurate for the film to be devoted to a Pole in the RAF, given the substantial role of Polish air crews in the defense of Britain, but that is perhaps to ask the impossible. On balance, the Tyrone Power role of the Yank is such a cad and an egomaniac that the Poles were well served by being omitted from this film.

64. Crowther, "'Mission to Moscow.'"

65. Dick, *Star-Spangled Screen,* 211; Bosley Crowther, "'Song of Russia,' Rich Musical Picture, with Robert Taylor and Susan Peters," *New York Times,* February 11, 1944. Jay Leyda, of *Mission to Moscow* fame, also served as technical adviser for this film. See Jay Leyda to William Wyler, November 27, 1943, folder "Wyler, Wm.," box 9, Leyda Papers. Wyler helped arrange Leyda's transfer to an air corps unit where he could be involved in filmmaking. See Howard Koch to William Wyler, December 1, 1943, folder 781, Wyler Papers.

66. Ayn Rand quoted in Small, "Buffoons," 334.

67. Bosley Crowther, "'The North Star,' Invasion Drama, with Walter Huston," *New York Times,* November 5, 1943.

68. Bosley Crowther, "New Film Surveys Soviet Role in War: 'The Battle of Russia,' Fifth in 'Why We Fight' Series," *New York Times,* November 15, 1943; Small, "Buffoons," 331.

69. This, of course, raises the intriguing question of why Slavs in general and Poles in particular have been traditionally portrayed negatively in American films. Gołąb has addressed this topic provisionally in "Stellaaaaaa," 135–55, but a thorough study would be most welcome.

70. Quite apart from the moguls, Gabler, for example, calculates that of eighty-six major producers in Hollywood in 1936, fifty-three were Jewish. Gabler, *Empire of Their Own,* 1–2.

71. David Desser and Lester D. Friedman note that whereas American entertainment has "been heavily Jewish since the turn of the century . . . nowhere is the Jewish contribution to show business more total than in the movie industry." David Desser and Lester D. Friedman, *American-Jewish Filmmakers: Traditions and Trends* (Urbana: University of Illinois Press, 1993), 27. Also see Ben B. Seligman, "They Came to Hollywood: How the Jews Built the Movie Industry," *Jewish Frontier* 20 (July 1953). Doneson writes of a "dominant" Jewish position in the film industry and even refers to "'Jewish' Hollywood." Doneson, *Holocaust in American Film,* 16. "Moviedom . . . was created by outsiders: Jews from Eastern Europe," conclude Lary L. May and Elaine Tyler May in "Why Jewish Movie Moguls? An Exploration in American Culture," *American Jewish History* 72 (1982): 6–7. They also note that the Jewish presence in Hollywood has been more noted than explained. Cf. McGilligan and Buhle, "Meet the People," xiv.

72. "Epstein: A King of Comedy," 189.

73. Alan Spiegel, "The Vanishing Act: A Typology of the Jew in the Contemporary American Film," in *From Hester Street to Hollywood: The Jewish-American Stage and Screen,* ed. Sarah Blacker Cohen (Bloomington: Indiana University Press, 1983), 260–61.

74. Gabler, *Empire of Their Own,* 1–2, 4. Cf. May and May, "Jewish Movie Moguls," 13.

75. Maltz, "Citizen Writer," 1:2–3.

76. Bernstein, *Inside Out,* 30.

77. John Howard Lawson, "Manuscripts, Autobiography," n.d., 15A, folder 1, box 93, Lawson Papers.

78. Bernard F. Dick, *Hal Wallis: Producer to the Stars* (Lexington: University Press of Kentucky, 2004), 14.

79. Ibid., 1, 2, 14.

80. Roth quoted in Novick, *Holocaust,* 32. Schwartz comments that "the Hollywood establishment didn't want to look back to the ghettoes, to their ethnicity and attendant vulnerability." Schwartz, *Hollywood Writers' Wars,* 45.

81. Anzia Yezierska, *Bread Givers: A Novel; A Struggle between a Father of the Old World and a Daughter of the New* (1925; repr., New York: Braziller, 1975), 277; Alice Kessler Harris, introduction to ibid., xii–xiii, xiv–xv. Yezierska, a Polish Jewish writer, was of the same generation as the moguls.

82. Maja Trochimczyk, "A Question of Identity: Polish Jewish Composers in California," in *Polish-Jewish Relations in North America,* ed. Mieczysław B. Biskupski and Antony Polonsky (Oxford: Littman Library of Jewish Civilization, 2007), 345–71.

83. De Toth, *Fragments,* 311.

84. Gabler argues that Jews in Hollywood shared remarkably similar biographies and values. See Gabler, *Empire of Their Own,* 1–7.

85. Lardner recalled that MGM's Mayer was hesitant to have anything even remotely Jewish in any of his films. Lardner, *I'd Hate Myself,* 108.

86. See Carr, *Hollywood and Anti-Semitism,* 159.

87. See Mieczysław B. Biskupski and Antony Polonsky, introduction to Biskupski and Polonsky, *Polish-Jewish Relations,* 45.

88. Novick, *Holocaust,* 51.

89. Jennifer Holt, "Hollywood and Politics Caught in the Cold War Crossfire (1947)," *Film and History* 31, no. 1 (2001): 8.

90. Howard Suber, "Politics and Popular Culture: Hollywood at Bay, 1933–1953," *American Jewish History* 68 (1979): 518.

91. Marsha Hunt, one of the stars of the film, remembers her "self-consciousness about showing anti-Semitism" in the film. Hunt, interview, 310.

92. There are some interesting comments on Hollywood's Jews' great reluctance to raise issues of anti-Semitism in films in Whitfield, "Our American Jewish Heritage," 330–40. Cf. Gabler, *Empire of Their Own,* 342–45, and Short, "Hollywood Fights Anti-Semitism," 159–60, 169.

93. Novick, *Holocaust,* 28–29, 40–41.

94. The danger of a public discussion of Poland's wartime plight is illustrated by a survey taken in early 1945 of schoolchildren in Los Angeles and Salt Lake City. The students were shown the film *Tomorrow the World* and then asked to complete a survey on issues of prejudice and discrimination. A black student from the poor Willowbrook section of Los Angeles commented that the film reminded him that "we Americans promised the Polish we would free them," and now another war might be neces-

sary to deliver them from Russian captivity. Another student from the same group noted the disturbing aspect of Germans' dislike of Poles in the film. A Jewish boy from Beverly Hills noted that people should see Poland to understand what Hitler had done. Scattered references to Poles appear in the comments of students from various Roman Catholic schools. This is hardly an exhaustive sample (it was confined to one thousand students in two large cities), but it suggests that the American public could very easily have been aroused to considerable sympathy for Poland's wartime travails. See "First Draft: The Democratic vs. the Nazi Way of Life; A Report on an Experiment with the Motion Picture 'Tomorrow the World' Conducted by the Committee on School and Screen with the Bureau for Intercultural Education," contained in Mildred J. Wiere to Margaret Gledhill (AMPAS), June 13, 1945, *Tomorrow the World* files, Vertical File Collection, Herrick Library.

   95. Harry's daughter Betty claimed the family had lived in Krasnosielc for "300 years." See Cass Warner Sperling and Cork Millner with Jack Warner Jr., *Hollywood Be Thy Name: The Warner Brothers Story* (Lexington: University Press of Kentucky, 1998), 17.

   96. *Forbes,* 1937, reprinted in Behlmer, *Inside Warner Bros.,* 56.

   97. Warner, *My First Hundred Years,* 15–20.

   98. Ibid., 65, 25.

   99. Betty Warner Sheinbaum, "Obligations Above and Beyond: Remembering Harry Warner," in *Warners' War: Politics, Pop Culture and Propaganda in Wartime Hollywood* (Los Angeles: Norman Lear Center, n.d.), 11. She even claims that the family left to "survive," implying that life in Poland was equivalent to the threat of death. See Sperling and Millner, *Hollywood Be Thy Name,* 17. In 1992 Harmetz wrote that Harry was "born in Poland and a victim of Anti-Jewish pogroms," an unfortunate formulation. Harmetz, *Making of* Casablanca, 67.

   100. Snow, "Confessions," 61.

   101. Harry's daughter recalled that her father "never talked about Russia [i.e., Krasnosielc]. Never." Sperling and Millner, *Hollywood Be Thy Name,* 177.

   102. Warner, *My First Hundred Years,* 20.

   103. Sperling and Millner, *Hollywood Be Thy Name,* 255. Harry also regularly explained that his family left Poland to avoid pogroms. See, for example, Birdwell, *Celluloid Soldiers,* 27, 83.

   104. *1930 United States Federal Census* and *1920 United States Federal Census* available online at http://www.ancestry.com/. In Jack Warner's memoirs, the only Polish references are a bad restaurant he frequented in Youngstown, where he apparently ate Polish sausage—a form of cultural

assimilation, to be sure—and an episode when a friend impersonated an obnoxious Pole. So much for the family's Polish traditions. Warner, *My First Hundred Years,* 103–4, 144–45.

105. Jack's marriage to a gentile damaged his already volatile relations with brother Harry. Freedland, *Warner Brothers,* 74. Cf. Birdwell, *Celluloid Soldiers,* 7.

106. Colgan, "Warner Brothers' Crusade," 53–54.

107. Carr, *Hollywood and Anti-Semitism,* 192.

108. Bessie quoted in Gabler, *Empire of Their Own,* 289.

109. *Sons of Liberty,* directed by Michael Curtiz, screenplay by Crane Wilbur, starring Claude Rains (Warner Brothers, 1939). In the other biographical film Warner Brothers produced about the Revolutionary era, *Alexander Hamilton* (1931), Kościuszko and Pułaski are also omitted. The Solomon biography was originally intended to be a full-length film with a major figure in the lead but was scaled down because of concern that it would be perceived as "Jewish propaganda." See Carr, *Hollywood and Anti-Semitism,* 209–10.

110. Birdwell, *Celluloid Soldiers,* 59.

111. Mordden, *Hollywood Studios,* 230.

112. Darryl F. Zanuck to Jack Warner, February 16, 1944, in *Memo from Darryl F. Zanuck: The Golden Years at Twentieth Century–Fox,* ed. Rudy Behlmer (New York: Grove, 1993), 72–73.

113. Birdwell, *Celluloid Soldiers,* 8.

114. In June 1932 Harry told FDR he was "offering prayers" for his nomination. In July the governor urged him to begin his campaigning efforts at once. By August Jack was very active in the campaign, which Harry reported to Roosevelt. Harry Warner to Franklin D. Roosevelt, telegram, June 30, 1932; Franklin D. Roosevelt to Harry Warner, July 9, 1932; Harry Warner to Franklin D. Roosevelt, August 8, 1932, including a telegram from Jack Warner; Franklin D. Roosevelt to Harry Warner, August 9, 1932, all in file 1050, President's Personal File. Jack's typically colorful version of the family's fascination with FDR is in Warner, *My First Hundred Years,* 207–8. For Harry's motives, see Freedland, *Warner Brothers,* 64. Harry's daughter attributes her father's support for the Democrats to the federal investigation of his stock manipulations during the Hoover presidency; the issue remains unclear. See Sperling and Millner, *Hollywood Be Thy Name,* 161.

115. Stephen T. Early (assistant secretary to the president) to Harry Warner, August 9, 1933; Harry Warner to Franklin D. Roosevelt, November 27, 1933, file 1050, President's Personal File. Jack Warner claims a large Warner role in electing FDR in 1932. Warner, *My First Hundred Years,* 215–17.

116. Warner, *My First Hundred Years,* 224. Jack's son later dismissed this as a fabrication. See Sperling and Millner, *Hollywood Be Thy Name,* 161.

117. See Sperling and Millner, *Hollywood Be Thy Name,* 210. Nonetheless, Warner Brothers provided FDR with a year's free pass to all its theaters, an odd gesture whatever the motivation. See Joseph Bernhard to Franklin D. Roosevelt, December 23, 1937, file 1050, President's Personal File.

118. Birdwell, *Celluloid Soldiers,* 10.

119. Jack Warner to Franklin D. Roosevelt, January 31, 1940, file 1050, President's Personal File.

120. Stephen Early to Jack Warner, February 3, 1941, file 1050, President's Personal File.

121. Harry Warner to Franklin D. Roosevelt, July 23, 1941, file 1050, President's Personal File.

122. Jack Warner to Marvin McIntyre, June 9, 1942; Harry Warner to Franklin D. Roosevelt, July 13, 1942, both in file 1050, President's Personal File.

123. Jack Warner to Marvin McIntyre, November 10, 1942, May 17, 1943, both in file 1050, President's Personal File.

124. Franklin D. Roosevelt to Jack Warner, October 24, 1944, file 1050, President's Personal File.

125. Warner, *My First Hundred Years,* 285. He recalls his putatively intimate association with FDR in ibid., 220–24, 238–39.

126. Writer John Wexley considered Jack Warner "a clown" who lacked the intellect to understand what the writers were doing. Wexley, interview, 711–12.

127. Bessie, interview, 101.

128. "Sherman: Actor Turned Writer," 99.

129. Ceplair and Englund, *Inquisition in Hollywood,* 279.

130. Behlmer, *Inside Warner Bros.,* 288–90. This version has been slightly edited; for the full text, see Warner, testimony, 38–39.

131. Jack Warner's professed innocence because of ignorance is the more objectionable because the documents reveal that he monitored the production of *Mission to Moscow* very carefully and was personally involved in the decisions to include issues he knew were controversial. He later exulted that he had "stir[red] up every Red baiter and Fascist elements" with the film. Jack Warner to Robert Buckner, May 22, 1943, folder 2785, *Mission to Moscow* Collection, Warner Bros. Archives. Regarding his intimate involvement with the script and its content, see Jack Warner to Howard Koch, November 24, 1943, folder 2085; R. J. Obringer to Walter Ebenstein, October 21, 1942, folder 2691; and Robert Buckner to Joseph E.

Davies, March 15, 1943, folder 2785, all in *Mission to Moscow* Collection, Warner Bros. Archives.

132. For the text of Harry Warner's September 25, 1941, statement before the Senate Subcommittee of the Committee on Interstate Commerce, see Behlmer, *Inside Warner Bros.*, 188–91.

133. That Harry consciously regarded Warner Brothers as being in the propaganda business is the thesis of Snow's "Confessions of a Hollywood Propagandist." There is no evidence that Jack dissented from this view until the congressional hearings of 1947 made that disposition awkward.

134. Birdwell, *Celluloid Soldiers,* 12.

135. See Kracauer, "National Types," 57.

136. Ring Lardner Jr., interview, "Episode 6: Reds," *National Security Archive,* November 1, 1998, http://www.gwu.edu/~nsarchiv/coldwar/interviews/episode-6/lardner1.html.

137. *The Life of Jimmy Dolan,* directed by Archie Mayo, screenplay by David Boehm and Erwin Gelsey, starring Douglas Fairbanks Jr., Loretta Young, and Aline MacMahon (Warner Brothers, 1933). Curiously, the film *How Many More Knights?* seems to have vanished without a trace. It was possibly retitled. However, no Warner Brothers film I have been able to locate has a character named Kościuszko. Similarly, the character of Pułaski that is supposedly in *The Life of Jimmy Dolan* cannot be found. The whole episode is very mysterious.

138. "Poles Bar Films of 3 Studios Here," *New York Times,* May 25, 1934. The Polish act was hardly unique; Harry Warner complained about other countries' banning Warner Brothers films for political reasons throughout the 1930s. Harry Warner to Harry Hopkins, March 6, 1939, folder "Motion Pictures," container 117, Hopkins Papers.

139. Warner quoted in Freedland, *Warner Brothers,* 89. Harry used the attribution "anti-Semitic" whenever he reckoned it was convenient for him. In 1935 he instructed his attorney to argue that as a Jew he was the victim of systematic anti-Semitic persecution in the United States. He thought this would gain him the jurors' sympathy—particularly that of one African American member—during an antitrust case. See Warner and Millner, *Hollywood Be Thy Name,* 211.

140. Colgan, "Warner Brothers' Crusade," 62–63, 127.

141. Carr, *Hollywood and Anti-Semitism,* 194.

Conclusion

1. Ceplair and Englund, *Inquisition in Hollywood,* 71.

2. Harmetz, *Making of Casablanca,* 238. Harmetz argues that Ameri-

can audiences have a lasting affection for *Casablanca* because it conjures such a simplified and comforting moral vision. All the war films, taken as a category, serve the same function.

3. Melvin Small's remark that Hollywood's efforts allowed FDR to be confident that the American people were pro-Russian when he went to Yalta is worth pondering in any reconstruction of the motives and methods of American policy regarding both Poland and Soviet Russia. Small, "Buffoons," 335.

Bibliography

Archival Materials

Margaret Herrick Library, Academy of Motion Picture Arts and Sciences, Los Angeles

Clipping Files

Desperate Journey
Destroyer
Edge of Darkness
Paul Henreid
In Our Time
Howard Koch
Melchior Lengyel
None Shall Escape
North Star
Ellis St. Joseph
To Be or Not to Be
Tomorrow the World

Special Collections

Alfred Hitchcock Papers
Lewis Milestone Papers
Motion Picture Association of America Production Code Administration
    Records
Marty Weiser Papers
William Wyler Papers

Vertical File Collection

Tomorrow the World

Oral History Collection
Phillip Dunne, interview by Douglas Bell, 1991

Federal Bureau of Investigation, Washington, DC
Communist Infiltration—Motion Picture Industry, file 100-138754
Lillian Hellman, file 100-28760
Hollywood Anti-Nazi League, file 100-6633

Franklin D. Roosevelt Presidential Library, Hyde Park, NY
Harry L. Hopkins Papers
Lowell Mellett Papers
President's Personal File
John Winant Papers

Howard Gotlieb Archival Research Center, Boston University, Boston
Gladys Hasty Carroll Collection
Albert Maltz Collection

Billy Rose Theatre Collection, New York Public Library for the Performing Arts, New York
Paul Muni Papers

Special Collections, Morris Library, Southern Illinois University, Carbondale
John Dewey Papers
John Howard Lawson Papers

Tamiment Library and Robert F. Wagner Labor Archives, Elmer Holmes Bobst Library, New York University, New York
Jay and Si-lan Chen Leyda Papers

United States National Archives, College Park, MD
Records of the Office of War Information, RG 208

Performing Arts Special Collections, Charles E. Young Research Library, University of California, Los Angeles
RKO Collection

Cinematic Arts Library, University of Southern California, Los Angeles
Performing Arts Archives
MGM Collection
Twentieth Century–Fox Collection
Warner Bros. Archives
Air Force Collection
In Our Time Collection
Mission to Moscow Collection

Wesleyan Cinema Archives, Wesleyan University, Middletown, CT
Frank Capra Collection
William Hornbeck Collection

Wisconsin Center for Film and Theater Research, Wisconsin Historical Society, Madison
Howard E. Koch Papers
Warner Brothers Scripts, United Artists Corporation
John Wexley Papers

Sterling Memorial Library, Yale University, New Haven, CT
Victor Jeremy Jerome Papers

Published Primary Materials

Ambler, Eric. *A Coffin for Dimitrios.* In *Intrigue: Four Great Spy Novels,* 146–294. New York: Knopf, 1960.

Barnes, Joseph. "Fighting with Information: OWI Overseas." *Public Opinion Quarterly* 7, no. 1 (1943): 34–45.

Barzman, Norma. *The Red and the Blacklist: The Intimate Memoir of a Hollywood Expatriate.* New York: Thunder's Mouth/Nation, 2003.

Behlmer, Rudy, ed. *Inside Warner Bros. (1935–1951).* New York: Viking, 1985.

———, ed. *Memo from Darryl F. Zanuck: The Golden Years at Twentieth Century–Fox.* New York: Grove, 1993.

Benny, Jack. *Sunday Nights at Seven: The Jack Benny Story.* New York: Time Warner, 1990.

Bernstein, Walter. *Inside Out: A Memoir of the Blacklist.* New York: DaCapo, 1996.

Capra, Frank. *The Name above the Title: An Autobiography.* New York: Macmillan, 1971.

Carroll, Gladys Hasty. *As the Earth Turns*. New York: Macmillan, 1942.

Ciliberti, Charles. *Backstairs Mission in Moscow*. New York: Booktab, 1946.

Cole, Lester. *Hollywood Red: The Autobiography of Lester Cole*. Palo Alto, CA: Ramparts, 1981.

Curie, Eve. *Madame Curie: A Biography*. Garden City, NY: Doubleday, Doran, 1938.

Davies, Joseph E. *Mission to Moscow*. New York: Simon and Schuster, 1941.

———. *Mission to Moscow*. Garden City, NY: Garden City, 1943.

———. *Mission to Moscow*. Edited by David Culbert. Madison: University of Wisconsin Press, 1980.

de Toth, André. *De Toth on de Toth: Putting the Drama in Front of the Camera; A Conversation with Anthony Slide*. Edited by Anthony Slide. London: Faber and Faber, 1996.

———. *Fragments: Portraits from the Inside*. London: Faber and Faber, 1994.

Dmytryk, Edward. *Odd Man Out: A Memoir of the Hollywood Ten*. Carbondale: Southern Illinois University Press, 1996.

Documents on Polish-Soviet Relations, 1939–1945. Vol. 1, *1939–1943*. London: Heinemann, 1961.

Dunne, Phillip. *Take Two: A Life in Movies and Politics*. New York: McGraw-Hill, 1980.

Fisher, Steve. *Destination Tokyo*. New York: Appleton-Century, 1943.

Francis, Patrick. "Wise Guys: A Virtual Roundtable with Three American Filmmakers of an Extremely Rare Vintage." *LA Weekly,* May 2, 2002, http://www.laweekly.com/2002-05-02/film-tv/wise-guys.

Gilpatric, Guy. *Action in the North Atlantic*. New York: Dutton, 1943.

Gottlieb, Sidney, ed. *Alfred Hitchcock: Interviews*. Jackson: University Press of Mississippi, 2003.

Henreid, Paul, with Julius Fast. *Ladies Man: An Autobiography*. New York: St. Martin's, 1984.

Hitchcock, Alfred. *Hitchcock's Notebooks*. Edited by Dan Aulier. New York: Avon, 1999.

House Committee on Un-American Activities. *Hearings Regarding the Communist Infiltration of the Motion Picture Industry*. Washington, DC: GPO, 1947.

Johnpoll, Bernard K., ed. *A Documentary History of the Communist Party of the United States*. 8 vols. Westport, CT: Greenwood, 1994.

Koch, Howard. *As Time Goes By: Memoirs of a Writer*. New York: Harcourt Brace Jovanovich, 1979.

————, comp. Casablanca: *Script and Legend.* Woodstock, NY: Overlook, 1973.

Lardner, Ring, Jr. *I'd Hate Myself in the Morning: A Memoir.* New York: Thunder's Mouth/Nation, 2000.

McClelland, Doug, ed. *Forties Film Talk: Oral Histories of Hollywood, with 120 Lobby Posters.* Jefferson, NC: McFarland, 1992.

McGilligan, Pat, ed. *Backstory: Interviews with Screenwriters of Hollywood's Golden Age.* Berkeley: University of California Press, 1986.

McGilligan, Patrick. *Film Crazy: Interviews with Hollywood Legends.* New York: St. Martin's, 2000.

McGilligan, Patrick, and Paul Buhle. *Tender Comrades: A Backstory of the Hollywood Blacklist.* New York: St. Martin's, 1997.

"The Meaning of the Non-aggression Pact." *Soviet Russia Today,* September 1939, 5–6.

Moscow Conference on American and British Cinema, August 21–22, 1942. Washington, DC: Embassy of the USSR, [1942].

Negri, Pola. *Memoirs of a Star.* Garden City, NY: Doubleday, 1970.

Poague, Leland, ed. *Frank Capra: Interviews.* Jackson: University Press of Mississippi, 2004.

Prokosch, Frederic. *The Conspirators.* New York: Harper, 1943.

Robinson, Edward G., with Leonard Spigelgass. *All My Yesterdays: An Autobiography.* New York: Hawthorn, 1973.

Sherman, Vincent. "Vincent Sherman: Actor Turned Writer Turned Director." Interview by Ronald L. Davis, 1981. In Ronald L. Davis, *Just Making Movies: Company Directors on the Studio System,* 83–101. Jackson: University Press of Mississippi, 2005.

Short, K. R. M., ed. "Washington's Information Manual for Hollywood." *Historical Journal of Film, Radio and Television* 3 (October 1983): 171–80.

Suid, Lawrence Howard, ed. *Air Force.* Madison: University of Wisconsin Press, 1983.

Wanger, Walter. "OWI and Motion Pictures." *Public Opinion Quarterly* 7, no. 1 (1943): 100–110.

Warner, Jack L., with Dean Jennings. *My First Hundred Years in Hollywood.* New York: Random House, 1965.

Watson, John O., from the screenplay by Dudley Nichols. *Air Force.* New York: Grosset and Dunlop, 1943.

Woods, William. *Edge of Darkness.* Philadelphia: Lippincott, 1942.

Dissertations and Theses

Coatney, Louis Robert. "The Katyn Massacre: An Assessment of Its Significance as a Public and Historical Issue in the United States and Great Britain, 1940–1993." Master's thesis, Western Illinois University, 1993.

Colgan, Christine Ann. "Warner Brothers' Crusade against the Third Reich: A Study of Anti-Nazi Activism and Film Production, 1933 to 1941." PhD diss., University of Southern California, 1985.

Published Secondary Materials

Ajnenkiel, Andrzej. "Z Problematyki polskiego czynu zbrojnego." In *Naczelni wodzowie i wyżsi dowódcy Polskich Sił Zbrojnych na zachodzie,* edited by Stefan Zwoliński, 7–28. Warsaw: Wojskowy Instytut Historyczny, 1995.

Balio, Tino. *Grand Design: Hollywood as a Modern Business Enterprise, 1930–1939.* Berkeley: University of California Press, 1993.

Barsam, Richard. "Why We Fight." In *Frank Capra: The Man and His Films,* edited by Richard Glatzer and John Raeburn, 149–54. Ann Arbor: University of Michigan Press, 1975.

Behlmer, Rudy. *America's Favorite Movies.* New York: Ungar, 1982.

Benson, Jackson J. *The True Adventure of John Steinbeck, Writer.* New York: Viking, 1984.

Billingsley, Kenneth Lloyd. *Hollywood Party: How Communism Seduced the American Film Industry in the 1930s and 1940s.* Rocklin, CA: Prima, 1998.

Birdwell, Michael E. *Celluloid Soldiers: The Warner Bros. Campaign against Nazism.* New York: New York University Press, 1999.

Biskupski, Mieczysław B., and Antony Polonsky, eds. *Polish-Jewish Relations in North America.* Oxford: Littman Library of Jewish Civilization, 2007.

Black, Gregory D., and Clayton R. Koppes. "OWI Goes to the Movies: The Bureau of Intelligence's Criticism of Hollywood, 1942–1943." *Prologue* 6, no. 1 (1974): 44–59.

Bondanella, Peter. *Hollywood Italians: Dagos, Palookas, Romeos, Wise Guys, and Sopranos.* New York: Continuum, 2004.

Bossak, Jerzy. "Ostrożnie—temat polski!" *Srebrny ekran,* nos. 13–14 (1938): 12–13.

Buhle, Paul, and Dave Wagner. *Blacklisted: The Film-Lover's Guide to the Hollywood Blacklist.* New York: Palgrave Macmillan, 2003.

———. *Radical Hollywood: The Untold Story behind America's Favorite Movies.* New York: New Press, 2002.

Bulgakowa, Oksana. "The 'Russian Vogue' in Europe and Hollywood: The Transformation of Russian Stereotypes through the 1920s." *Russian Review* 64, no. 2 (2005): 211–35.

Carr, Steven. *Hollywood and Anti-Semitism: A Cultural History up to World War II.* Cambridge: Cambridge University Press, 2001.

Ceplair, Larry, and Steven Englund. *The Inquisition in Hollywood: Politics in the Film Community, 1930–1960.* Garden City, NY: Anchor/Doubleday, 1980.

Chambers, John Whiteclay, II, and David Culbert, ed. *World War II, Film, and History.* New York: Oxford University Press, 1996.

Cienciala, Anna M. "Polityka mocarstw zachodnich wobec Polski i Powstania Warszawskiego." *Białostockie Teki Historyczne* 3 (2005): 261–89.

Combs, James E., and Sara T. Combs. *Film Propaganda and American Politics.* New York: Garland, 1994.

Cortés, Carlos E. "Italian-Americans in Film: From Immigrants to Icons. *MELUS* 14, nos. 3–4 (1987): 107–26.

Couvares, Francis G. "Hollywood, Main Street, and the Church: Trying to Censor the Movies before the Production Code." *American Quarterly* 44, no. 4 (1992): 584–616.

Crowther, Bosley. *The Great Films: Fifty Golden Years of Motion Pictures.* New York: Putnam, 1967.

Culbert, David. "Our Awkward Ally: *Mission to Moscow.*" In *American History/American Film: Interpreting the Hollywood Image,* edited by John E. O'Connor and Malcolm A. Jackson, 121–45. New York: Ungar, 1979.

Desser, David. "The Cinematic Melting Pot: Ethnicity, Jews, and Psychoanalysis." In Friedman, *Unspeakable Images,* 379–403.

Desser, David, and Lester D. Friedman. *American-Jewish Filmmakers: Traditions and Trends.* Urbana: University of Illinois Press, 1993.

Dick, Bernard F. *Hal Wallis: Producer to the Stars.* Lexington: University Press of Kentucky, 2004.

———. *Hellman in Hollywood.* East Brunswick, NJ: Farleigh Dickinson University Press, 1982.

———. *Radical Innocence: A Critical Study of the Hollywood Ten.* Lexington: University Press of Kentucky, 1989.

———. *The Star-Spangled Screen: The American World War II Film.* Lexington: University Press of Kentucky, 1985.

Doherty, Thomas. *Projections of War: Hollywood, American Culture, and World War II.* Rev. ed. New York: Columbia University Press, 1999.

Donati, William. *Ida Lupino: A Biography.* Lexington: University Press of Kentucky, 1996.

Doneson, Judith E. *The Holocaust in American Film.* 2nd ed. Syracuse, NY: Syracuse University Press, 2002.

Druxman, Michael B. *Paul Muni: His Life and His Films.* South Brunswick, NJ: Barnes, 1974.

Durgnat, Raymond, and Scott Simmon. *King Vidor, American.* Berkeley: University of California Press, 1988.

Eckstein, Art. "The Hollywood Left Revealed." *Front Page,* June 8, 2005, http://www.frontpagemag.com/articles/Read.aspx?GUID=B76A6172-16C9-419D-86C7-F4885925691D.

———. "The Truth about the 'Hollywood Ten.'" *Front Page,* April 18, 2005, http://www.frontpagemag.com/articles/Read.aspx?GUID=6DD1DC4-5CB0 -4729-A4D3-4DD8862DD785.

Erens, Patricia. *The Jew in American Cinema.* Bloomington: Indiana University Press, 1984.

Eyman, Scott. *Ernst Lubitsch: Laughter in Paradise.* New York: Simon and Schuster, 1993.

Freedland, Michael. *The Warner Brothers.* New York: St. Martin's, 1983.

Friedman, Lester D. "Celluloid Palimpsests: An Overview of Ethnicity and the American Film." In Friedman, *Unspeakable Images,* 11–35.

———. *Hollywood's Image of the Jew.* New York: Ungar, 1982.

———, ed. *Unspeakable Images: Ethnicity and the American Cinema.* Urbana: University of Illinois Press, 1991.

Fuhrammar, Leif, and Folke Isaksson. *Politics and Film.* New York: Praeger, 1971.

Fyne, Robert. *The Hollywood Propaganda of World War II.* Lanham, MD: Scarecrow, 1997.

Gabler, Neal. *An Empire of Their Own: How the Jews Invented Hollywood* (New York: Random House, 1988).

Garraty, John A., and Mark C. Carnes, eds. *American National Biography.* 24 vols. New York: Oxford University Press, 1999.

Georgakas, Dan. "The Hollywood Reds: 50 Years Later." *American Communist History* 2, no. 1 (2003): 63–76.

Gianos, Phillip L. *Politics and Politicians in American Film.* Westport, CT: Praeger, 1998.

Giovacchini, Saverio. *Hollywood Modernism: Film and Politics in the Age of the New Deal.* Philadelphia: Temple University Press, 2001.

Gordon, Jeff. "The World War II Films of 20th Century-Fox." *Films of the Golden Age* 42 (Fall 2005): 18–38.

Hammersmith, Jack L. "The U.S. Office of War Information (OWI) and the Polish Question, 1943–1945." *Polish Review* 19, no. 1 (1974): 67–76.

Harmetz, Aljean. *The Making of* Casablanca*: Bogart, Bergman and World War II.* New York: Hyperion, 2002.

Harvey, Brian D. "Soviet-American 'Cinematic Diplomacy' in the 1930s: Could the Russians Have Infiltrated Hollywood?" *Screen* 46, no. 4 (2005): 487–98.

Holmgren, Beth. "Cossack Cowboys, Mad Russians: The Émigré Actor in Studio-Era Hollywood." *Russian Review* 64, no. 2 (2005): 236–58.

Holt, Jennifer. "Hollywood and Politics Caught in the Cold War Crossfire (1947)." *Film and History* 31, no. 1 (2001): 6–12.

Horak, Jan-Christopher. "Sauerkraut and Sausages with a Little Goulash: Germans in Hollywood, 1927." *Film History* 17, nos. 2–3 (2005): 241–60.

Horne, Gerald. *Class Struggle in Hollywood, 1930–1950: Moguls, Mobsters, Stars, Reds and Trade Unionists.* Austin: University of Texas Press, 2001.

———. *The Final Victim of the Blacklist: John Howard Lawson, Dean of the Hollywood Ten.* Berkeley: University of California Press, 2006.

Howe, Irving, and Lewis Coser. *The American Communist Party: A Critical History, 1919–1957.* Boston: Beacon, 1957.

International Motion Picture Almanac, 1942–43. New York: Quigley, 1942.

Isserman, Maurice. *Which Side Were You On? The American Communist Party during the Second World War.* Urbana: University of Illinois Press, 1993.

Januszewski, David G. "The Case for the Polish Exile Government in the American Press, 1939–1945." *Polish American Studies* 43, no. 1 (1986): 57–97.

Jarvie, Ian C. "Stars and Ethnicity: Hollywood and the United States, 1932–1951." In Friedman, *Unspeakable Images,* 82–111.

Jensen, Richard. "'No Irish Need Apply': A Myth of Victimization." *Journal of Social History* 36, no. 2 (2002): 405–29.

Jones, Ken D., and Arthur F. McClure. *Hollywood at War: The American Motion Picture and World War II.* New York: Castle, 1973.

Juran, Robert A. *Old Familiar Faces: The Great Character Actors and Actresses of Hollywood's Golden Age.* Sarasota, FL: Movie Memories, 1995.

Kane, Kathryn. *Visions of War: Hollywood Combat Films of World War II.* Ann Arbor, MI: UMI Research Press, 1976.

Kelley, Beverly Merrill, John J. Pitney Jr., Craig R. Smith, and Herbert E.

Gooch III, eds. *Reelpolitik: Political Ideologies in '30s and '40s Films.* Westport, CT: Praeger, 1998.

Klehr, Harvey, John Earl Haynes, and Kyrill M. Anderson. *The Soviet World of American Communism.* New Haven, CT: Yale University Press, 1998.

Knock, Thomas J. "'History with Lightning': The Forgotten Film *Wilson.*" *American Quarterly* 28, no. 5 (1976): 523–43.

Koch, Stephen. *Double Lives: Stalin, Willi Münzenberg, and the Seduction of the Intellectuals.* Rev. ed. New York: Enigma, 2004.

Koppes, Clayton R., and Gregory D. Black. *Hollywood Goes to War: How Politics, Profits, and Propaganda Shaped World War II Movies.* Berkeley: University of California Press, 1990.

———. "What to Show the World: The Office of War Information and Hollywood, 1942–1945." *Journal of American History* 64, no. 1 (1977): 87–105.

Kracauer, Siegfried. "National Types as Hollywood Presents Them." *Public Opinion Quarterly* 13, no. 1 (1949): 53–72.

Larsh, William. "W. Averell Harriman and the Polish Question, December 1943–August 1944." *East European Politics and Society* 7, no. 3 (1993): 513–54.

Lawson, John Howard. *Film in the Battle of Ideas.* New York: Masses and Mainstream, 1953.

Leff, Leonard J., and Jerold L. Simmons. *The Dame in the Kimono: Hollywood, Censorship, and the Production Code from the 1920s to the 1960s.* New York: Grove Weidenfeld, 1990.

Lopez, Ana M. "Are All Latins from Manhattan? Hollywood, Ethnography, and Cultural Colonialism." In Friedman, *Unspeakable Images,* 404–24.

Lukas, Richard C. *The Strange Allies: The United States and Poland, 1941–1945.* Knoxville: University of Tennessee Press, 1978.

Manvell, Roger. *Films and the Second World War.* New York: Dell, 1976.

Marchetti, Gina. "Ethnicity, the Cinema, and Cultural Studies." In Friedman, *Unspeakable Images,* 277–307.

Marowitz, Charles. *The Other Chekhov: A Biography of Michael Chekhov, the Legendary Actor, Director, and Theorist.* New York: Applause Theatre and Cinema Books, 2004.

Matich, Olga. "The White Emigration Goes Hollywood." *Russian Review* 64, no. 2 (2005): 187–210.

May, Lary L., and Elaine Tyler May. "Why Jewish Movie Moguls? An Exploration in American Culture." *American Jewish History* 72 (1982): 6–25.

Mayhew, Robert. *Ayn Rand and* Song of Russia*: Communism and Anti-Communism in 1940s Hollywood*. Lanham, MD: Scarecrow, 2005.

McBride, Joseph. *Frank Capra: The Catastrophe of Success*. New York: St. Martin's Griffin, 2000.

McCarty, John. *Hollywood Gangland: The Movies' Love Affair with the Mob*. New York: St. Martin's, 1993.

McLaughlin, Robert L., and Sally E. Parry. *We'll Always Have the Movies: American Cinema during World War II*. Lexington: University Press of Kentucky, 2006.

Meyers, Jeffrey. *Gary Cooper: American Hero*. New York: Cooper Square, 1998.

Miller, Randall M., ed. *The Kaleidoscopic Lens: How Hollywood Views Ethnic Groups*. Englewood, NJ: Ozer, 1980.

Miller, Ryder W. "John Steinbeck: Publish Lifeboat." *Rain Taxi Online,* Summer 2002, http://www.raintaxi.com/online/2002summer/lifeboat.shtml.

Mitchell, Charles P. *The Great Composers Portrayed on Film, 1913 through 2003*. Jefferson, NC: McFarland, 2004.

Moran, Kathleen, and Michael Rogin. "'What's the Matter with Capra?' Sullivan's Travels and the Popular Front." *Representations* 71 (Summer 2000): 106–34.

Mordden, Ethan. *The Hollywood Studios: House Style in the Golden Age of the Movies*. New York: Simon and Schuster, 1988.

Murphy, William Thomas. "The Method of *Why We Fight*." *Journal of Popular Film* 1, no. 3 (1972): 185–96.

Musser, Charles. "Ethnicity, Role-Playing, and American Film Comedy: From *Chinese Laundry Scene* to *Whoopee* (1894–1930)." In Friedman, *Unspeakable Images,* 39–81.

Navasky, Victor S. *Naming Names*. New York: Viking, 1980.

The New York Times Film Reviews, 1913–1968. Vol. 3. New York: New York Times Books, 1970.

Novick, Peter. *The Holocaust in American Life*. Boston: Houghton Mifflin, 1999.

Parini, Jay. *John Steinbeck: A Biography*. New York: Holt, 1995.

Paris, Michael. "Lessons for Democracy: American Cinema, 1942–1945." *European Review of History* 5, no. 1 (1998). Northern Light Special Collection document BM19981102020053500.

Parish, James Robert, and William T. Leonard. *Hollywood Players: The Thirties*. New Rochelle, NY: Arlington House, 1976.

Parker, Matthew. *Monte Cassino: The Hardest-Fought Battle of World War II*. New York: Doubleday, 2004.

Paul, William. *Ernst Lubitsch's American Comedy.* New York: Columbia University Press, 1978.

Peck, Jeff. "The Heroic Soviet on the American Screen." *Film and History* 9 (September 1979): 54–63.

Pizzitola, Louis. *Hearst over Hollywood: Power, Passion, and Propaganda in the Movies.* New York: Columbia University Press, 2002.

Poague, Leland A. *The Cinema of Ernst Lubitsch.* South Brunswick, NJ: Barnes, 1978.

Radosh, Ronald, and Allis Radosh. *Red Star over Hollywood: The Film Colony's Long Romance with the Left.* San Francisco: Encounter, 2005.

Rainey, Buck. *Heroes of the Range: Yesteryear's Matinee Movie Cowboys.* Waynesville, NC: World of Yesterday, 1987.

Roddick, Nick. *A New Deal in Entertainment: Warner Brothers in the 1930s.* London: British Film Institute, 1983.

Samuels, Stuart. "The Evolutionary Image of the Jew in American Film." In *Ethnic Images in American Film and Television,* edited by Randall M. Miller, 23–34. Philadelphia: Balch Institute, 1978.

Schwartz, Nancy Lynn. *The Hollywood Writers' Wars.* New York: Knopf, 1982.

Seligman, Ben B. "They Came to Hollywood: How Jews Built the Movie Industry." *Jewish Frontier* 20 (July 1953): 19–29.

Sennett, Ted. *Warner Brothers Presents: The Most Exciting Years—from* The Jazz Singer *to* White Heat. New Rochelle, NY: Arlington House, 1971.

Shein, Russell Earl. *An Analysis of Motion Pictures about War Released by the American Film Industry, 1930–1970.* New York: Arno, 1970.

Sheinbaum, Betty Warner. "Obligations Above and Beyond: Remembering Harry Warner." In *Warners' War,* 10–13.

Shindler, Colin. *Hollywood Goes to War: Films and American Society, 1939–1952.* London: Routledge and Paul, 1952.

Shohat, Ella. "Ethnicities-in-Relation: Toward a Multicultural Reading of American Cinema." In Friedman, *Unspeakable Images,* 215–50.

Short, K. R. M. "Hollywood: An Essential War Industry." *Historical Journal of Film, Radio and Television* 5 (March 1985): 90–100.

———. "Hollywood Fights Anti-Semitism, 1940-1945." In *Film and Radio Propaganda in World War II,* edited by K. R. M. Short, 159–69. Knoxville: University of Tennessee Press, 1983.

Sklar, Robert. *Movie-Made America: A Cultural History of American Movies.* Rev. ed. New York: Vintage, 1994.

Slide, Anthony. *Selected Film Criticism, 1941–1950.* Metuchen, NJ: Scarecrow, 1983.

Small, Melvin. "Buffoons and Brave Hearts: Hollywood Portrays the Russians, 1939–1944." *California Historical Quarterly* 52, no. 4 (1973): 326–37.

———. "How We Learned to Love the Russians: American Media and the Soviet Union During World War II. *Historian* 36 (1974): 455–78.

Snow, Nancy. "Confessions of a Hollywood Propagandist: Harry Warner, FDR and Celluloid Persuasion." In *Warners' War,* 60–71.

Sobchack, Vivian. "Postmodern Modes of Ethnicity." In Friedman, *Unspeakable Images,* 329–52.

Sperling, Cass Warner, and Cork Millner with Jack Warner Jr. *Hollywood Be Thy Name: The Warner Brothers Story.* Lexington: University Press of Kentucky, 1998.

Spiegel, Alan. "The Vanishing Act: A Typology of the Jew in the Contemporary American Film." In *From Hester Street to Hollywood: The Jewish-American Stage and Screen,* edited by Sarah Blacker Cohen, 257–75. Bloomington: Indiana University Press, 1983.

Spoto, Donald. *The Art of Alfred Hitchcock: Fifty Years of His Motion Pictures.* Garden City, NY: Doubleday, 1976.

———. *Blue Angel: The Life of Marlene Dietrich.* New York: Doubleday, 1992.

Steele, Richard W. "The Great Debate: Roosevelt, the Media, and the Coming of the War, 1940–1941." *Journal of American History* 71, no. 1 (1984): 69–92.

Suber, Howard. "Politics and Popular Culture: Hollywood at Bay, 1933–1953." *American Jewish History* 68 (1979): 517–33.

Suid, Lawrence H. *Guts and Glory: Great American War Movies.* Reading, MA: Addison-Wesley, 1978.

"Survey of War Pictures." *Communiqué,* August 22, 1942, 6–7.

Swindell, Larry. *Charles Boyer: The Reluctant Lover.* New York: Doubleday, 1983.

———. *The Last Hero: A Biography of Gary Cooper.* Garden City, NY: Doubleday, 1980.

Sword, Keith. *Deportation and Exile: Poles in the Soviet Union, 1939–48.* London: St Martin's, 1994.

———, ed. *The Takeover of the Polish Eastern Provinces, 1939–41.* New York: St. Martin's, 1991.

Taylor, John Russell. *Strangers in Paradise: The Hollywood Émigrés, 1933–1950.* New York: Holt, Rinehart and Winston, 1983.

Thompson, Ewa M. "Nationalist Propaganda in the Soviet Russian Press, 1939–1941." *Slavic Review* 50, no. 2 (1991): 385–99.

Toczewski, Andrzej. "Cooperation between the Soviet Union and the Third

Reich in Exchanges of Polish Population and Prisoners of War in the Years 1939–1941." *Polish Review* 37, no. 2 (1992): 209–16.

Triplett, William. "Busting Heads and Blaming Reds: How Movie Producers Used the Blacklist to Crack Down on Hollywood Unions." *Salon,* January 11, 2000, http://archive.salon.com/ent/movies/feature/2000/01/11/blacklist/print.html.

Troyan, Michael. *A Rose for Mrs. Miniver.* Lexington: University Press of Kentucky, 1999.

Walsh, Francis R. "*The Callahans and the Murphys* (MGM, 1927): A Case of Irish-American and Catholic Church Censorship." *Historical Journal of Film, Radio and Television* 10 (1990): 33–45.

Warren, Spencer. "The 100 Best Conservative Movies." *National Review,* October 24, 1994, http://findarticles.com/p/articles/mi_m1282/is_n20_v46/ai_15905983/.

Whitfield, Stephen. "Our American Jewish Heritage: The Hollywood Version." *American Jewish History* 75 (1986): 322–40.

Winokur, Mark. "Improbable Ethnic Hero: William Powell and the Transformation of Ethnic Hollywood." *Cinema Journal* 27, no. 1 (1987): 5–22.

Warners' War: Politics, Pop Culture and Propaganda in Wartime Hollywood. Los Angeles: Norman Lear Center, 2004.

Wright, William. *Lillian Hellman: The Image, the Woman.* New York: Simon and Schuster, 1986.

Wollstein, Hans J. *Vixens, Floozies and Molls: 28 Actresses of Late 1920s and 1930s Hollywood.* Jefferson, NC: McFarland, 1999.

Vidor, King. *King Vidor on Film Making.* New York: McKay, 1972.

Youngkin, Stephen D. *The Lost One: A Life of Peter Lorre.* Lexington: University Press of Kentucky, 2005.

Zebrowski, Walter. "Poles in Gladys Hasty Carroll's *As the Earth Turns.*" *Polish American Studies* 20, no. 1 (1963): 17–21.

Index

Abroad with Two Yanks (film), 186–
  87, 189, 309n84
Action in the North Atlantic (film),
  71, 189, 219, 222, 227
  credits, 306n32
  discussed, 175–83
  Roosevelt is urged to view, 223
Actors' Laboratory of Hollywood,
  203–4
Air Force (film), 171–75, 219, 222,
  223, 304–5n10
Alberni, Luis, 24–25, 195, 243n67,
  314n119
Alexander Hamilton (film), 326n109
All through the Night (film), 189–90
Ambler, Eric, 127, 284n45
American Cavalcade (film), 78
American Communists. *See*
  Communist Party of the United
  States of America; radical Left
American Jewish Congress, 71
American Romance, An (film),
  193–94, 200, 313n115
Anders, Władysław, 130, 131
Andrews, Jack, 283n32
anti-Irish persecution, 242n52
anti-Semitism, 8, 213, 214–16, 217,
  226–27, 242n52
antitrust violations, 258n10
Appointment in Berlin (film), 77
Armia Krajowa (Home Army), 52
Arnold, Gen. H. H., 171

Arthur, Jean, 195
Assignment in Brittany (film), 78
As the Earth Turns (film), 32–34,
  246–47n111
Astor, Camille, 17, 239n24
Atlantic Charter, 67
Atlas, Leopold, 131, 201, 286n59
Atwill, Lionel, 85
Auer, Mischa, 18, 196
Australia, 153
Avengers (film), 78

Background to Danger (film), 78
Baclanova, Olga, 18
Ball, Ernest R., 187
Barasch, Stephen, 102–3
Barzman, Norma, 270n41, 284n37
Bassermann, Albert, 121, 161
Bataan (film), 190–91, 312n102
Battle of Britain, The (documentary),
  151, 285n53
Battle of China, The (documentary),
  295n151
Battle of Russia, The
  (documentary), 71, 151–52,
  212, 297nn170–171
Bazykin, Vladimir, 77
Beban, George, 24
Bell, Ulric, 72, 107, 146, 164
Bellamy, Ralph, 35
Bell for Adano, A (film), 16, 189
Bendix, William, 186

Beneš, Eduard, 75, 297n166
Bennett, Bruce, 128
Benny, Jack, 17, 84, 85, 87, 268n28
Bergquist, Lillian, 70, 77, 203,
    260n26
Berle, Adolf, 67
"Berlin Nightingale," 12
Berneis, Eleanor, 106, 164–65, 166
Bernstein, Walter, 206, 213
Bessie, Alvah, 203, 221, 223,
    319–20n19
Biberman, Herbert, 64, 261n48
Birdwell, Michael, 225
Bischoff, Samuel, 111, 217
Black Book of Poland, The, 279n163
Black Fury (film), 29–32, 245n90
"Black Hell" (screenplay), 29–30
    See also Black Fury
Black Legion (film), 40–43, 250n154
Bleeding Hearts, The (film), 242n58
Block Busters (film), 78
Blonde Fever (film), 78
Boeing, 172
Bogart, Humphrey, 40–43, 175, 189
Bohunk: A Melodramatic Comedy
    (play), 29
Bolesławski, Ryszard, 16–17
Bomber's Moon (film), 78
Bond, Ward, 43, 192
Boretz, Allen, 300n200
Boros, Ferike, 196
Bossak, Jerzy, 27–28
Bowery Boys, 314n121
Boyer, Charles, 16, 38
Boys from Stalingrad (film), 263n68
Brandon, Henry (Heinrich von
    Kleinbach), 42, 44, 251n167
Brazil, 153
Brecher, Egon, 251n163
Breen, Joseph, 21, 217, 275n113
Brennan, Frederick Hazlitt, 79,
    264n82
Brennan, Sandra, 133
Bressart, Felix, 86

Brewster, Ralph O., 296n158
Briskin, Samuel J., 147
Britain, Battle of, 52–53, 120
Browder, Earl, 61
Brown, Karl, 192
Buchman, Sidney, 164, 167, 201
Buckner, Robert, 74, 290n93
Buck Rogers (serial), 44
Buhle, Paul, 4, 202, 203
Bureau of Motion Pictures (BMP)
    Action in the North Atlantic, 182
    Air Force, 174
    concern for portrayals of ethnic
        Americans, 81
    concern for the positive portrayal
        of foreigners, 78–79
    Edge of Darkness, 133–34
    function of, 68
    indifference to Poles and Polish
        issues, 80
    leftist preferences of, 204
    Lifeboat, 199–200
    Madame Curie, 163–64
    None Shall Escape, 115–17
    The North Star, 146–47
    In Our Time, 105–7
    pro-Soviet attitude in, 5, 73, 74,
        76, 78–79
    recommendations to the film
        industry, 72–73
    review of scripts, 71, 77–78
    Song of Russia, 77
    A Song to Remember, 164–66
    Warner Brothers and, 75–76, 183
Burnett, W. R., 179, 202
Bzura, Battle of the, 46

Cagney, Jimmy, 23
Caldwell, Erskine, 289n88
Cameron, Kate, 143
Canada, 153
Capra, Frank, 75
    Jay Leyda and, 299–300n195
    Anatole Litvak and, 296n157

politics of, 205
on the Soviet invasion of Poland,
297n165
Soviet themes in films and, 18
Why We Fight, 147, 151, 152, 154,
296n160
Carey, Harry, 172
Carlisle, Harry, 58
Carnovsky, Morris, 133
Carroll, Gladys Hasty, 32, 34
Casablanca (film)
authoring of, 88, 269–70n34
credits, 300n198
as having a simplified moral
vision, 329n2
Paul Henreid in, 127
Jewish characters in, 222
omission of the Polish cause from,
155–56, 300n198
Victor László character and, 4, 75
Warner Brothers' concerns with
ethnicity and, 264n84
Cass, Maurice, 17, 239n24
Catholic Church, 21–22
cavalry, 49, 148
"celebratory nationalism," 64
Censor Forbids, The, 86
censorship, Production Code, 21, 81
"Century of Friendship, A"
(screenplay), 195
Ceplair, Larry, 6
Chałupiec, Apolonia. *See* Negri, Pola
Chandlee, Dick, 314n121
Chase, Borden, 185, 320n30
Chekhov, Michael, 18, 19, 89, 108,
270n44
Chesterfield Motion Picture
Corporation, 15
Chetniks (film), 283n32
Chicago, Halsted Street, 313n110
Chilston, Viscount, 138, 139
Chopin, Frédéric, 166
Ciechanowski, Jan, 69
Ciliberti, Charles, 137

Clancy of the Mounted (film),
238n16
Clancy Street Boys (film), 314n121
Clark, Dane, 175
Clark, Dennis, 241n45
Clarke, Estelle (Stanisława
Zwoliński), 12
Clements, Sidney (Stanisław
Klimowicz), 195, 314n121
Cobb, Lee J., 180
Coffin for Dimitrios, A (film), 127
Cohan, George M., 27
Cohens and Kellys, The (film), 22
Cohn, Harry, 111, 166, 216, 217
Cohn, Joe, 204
Colbert, Claudette, 234n25
Cole, Lester, 112, 113, 116, 201, 203
Coleman, Nancy, 132
Coleman, Ronald, 195
Collins, Richard, 206, 212, 261n48
Columbia, 202
None Shall Escape, 111–18
Combs, James and Sara, 210
Commandoes Strike at Dawn (film),
122–23, 282n22
Communist Party of the United
States of America (CPUSA),
235n35
condemns support of the war
against Nazi Germany, 60–61
German invasion of Russia and, 64
Hitler-Stalin pact and, 59–61
"Hollywood studio section," 57–58
Jewish section endorses the
Russian invasion of Poland, 62
John Howard Lawson and, 176
mission, 59
peak of membership, 59
position toward Poland, 61–63
propaganda and, 58
Comrade X (film), 261–62n50
Confession (film), 43
Confessions of a Nazi Spy (film), 39,
250n153

Conquest (film), 38–39, 249n143
Conspirators, The (film), 124–27, 283n30
Conspirators, The (Prokosch), 124
Cooper, Gary, 34, 35
Corbett, James J., 27
Corrigan, "Wrong Way," 27
Cortés, Carlos E., 24
Cossacks, 246n106
Cossacks, The (film), 18
Coulondre, Robert, 138, 139
Counter Attack (film), 131
Counter Espionage (film), 77
Count of Monte Cristo, The (film), 15
Coward, Noel, 196
CPUSA. *See* Communist Party of the United States of America
Crowther, Bosley
  on *An American Romance,* 194
  on *To Be or Not To Be,* 84, 211, 265n5
  on *Casablanca,* 262n52
  Phillip Dunne on, 322n59
  on *In Our Time,* 109–10, 211
  significance as a critic, 210–12
  Wilson and, 156
Cud nad Wisłą (film), 16
Culbert, David, 141
Cunningham, William S., 107
Curie, Eve, 160, 162
Curie, Pierre, 160
Curley, James, 258n6
Czechoslovakia
  film industry depiction of, 4, 75, 200, 233–34n22
  German occupation and, 50
  Lidice massacre, 317n148

Dąbrowski, Jan Henryk, 314n123
Daily Worker, 57, 60, 91, 206
Dancers in the Dark (film), 12
Dangerous Moonlight (film), 233n18
Daves, Delmer, 197

Davies, Joseph E., 135, 136, 139, 141
Davis, Elmer, 68
Days of Glory (film), 87
Deception (film), 43
Demarest, William, 189
DeMille, Cecil B., 18
Desert Fox, The (film), 255n13
Desperate Journey (film), 81, 123–24, 283n27
"Destination Tokyo" (Fisher), 196
Destination Tokyo (film), 196–97, 315n137
Destroyer (film), 79, 183–85, 189, 308n71
de Toth, André, 112, 113, 115, 202, 216, 277n142
Dewey, John, 142
Dick, Bernard F., 4, 88, 211–12, 291n134
Dieppe Raid, 80
Dietrich, Marlene, 16, 187
Dillingham Commission, 170
Dimitrov, Georgi, 48
Diplomatic Courier (film), 77
Dispatch from Reuters, A (film), 221
Disraeli (film), 221
Divide and Conquer (documentary), 150–51, 285n53
Dmytryk, Edward, 255n15
Dobrzański, Henryk, 48
Donat, Robert, 14–15
Donath, Ludwig, 191
Donati, William, 106
Donlevy, Brian, 193
Donnelly, Ruth, 189
Don't Get Personal (film), 196, 315n130
Dorn, Philip, 283n32
Dr. Ehrlich's Magic Bullet (film), 24, 221
Dugan, Tom, 85
Dunne, Phillip, 69–70, 202–3, 204, 256n23, 276n119, 322n59
Durgnat, Raymond, 36

Dvorak, Anna, 26
Dzisna, 46

Eagle Squadron, 280n7
Eagle Squadron (film), 53, 170
East of the River (film), 25
East Side Kids, 195, 314n121
Eder, Bruce, 87
Edge of Darkness (film), 81, 103,
  131–34, 193, 219, 262n59
Edward Small Productions, 186
Eichelbaum, Pearl, 219
Einfeld, Charles, 75, 104–5
Eisenstein, Sergei, 18
Emergency Quota Act, 170
Emperor's Candlestick, The (film),
  13, 38, 249n141
Endore, Guy, 58, 131, 201, 286n59
Englund, Steven, 6
Epstein, Julius, 88, 155, 213, 300n200
Epstein, Phillip, 88, 155, 300n200
Erickson, Carl, 30

Faust, Felix, 103
Faust, Frederick, 124
Fenwick, Peg, 166, 185
Fighting Sullivans, The (film), 222
Fighting 69th, The (film), 27
film attendance, 1, 231n2
film industry (prewar)
  fading of the ethnic theme in, 27
  films set in Poland, 38–39
  films with Russian themes, 17–18
  Irish characters and films, 20–23
  Italian characters and films, 24–25
  Jewish characters and films, 23–24
  lack of a Polish presence in films,
    26–28
  Polish actors, 11–16
  Polish characters and films, 28–38
  Polish directors, 16–17
  Polish Jews, 17
  pro-Russian/Soviet attitudes in,
    17–20

film industry (wartime)
  as an "essential war industry," 68
  communism and the radical Left,
    4–6
  depiction of occupied European
    countries, 3–4
  ethnic prejudice in, 194–95
  ethnic representation of Americans
    in, 188–89
  the Holocaust and, 217–18
  Irish films, 27
  Jewish presence and, 213–18
  lack of concern for Poland, 3
  negative portrayals of Poland and
    Poles, 4–5
  number of "war movies" made,
    232n16
  Roosevelt and, 258n10
  Warner Brothers and anti-Polish
    propaganda, 218–27
Finkel, Abem, 30, 31, 40, 41
Finland, 293n135
First National, 249n146
Fisher, Ham, 28, 29
Fisher, Steve, 196, 197
Fitzgerald, Edith, 37
Florentine Dagger, The (film), 25
Flying Irishman, The (film), 27
Flynn, Errol, 124
Forbes (magazine), 219
"Forced Landing" (screenplay), 123
Ford, Glenn, 184
Ford, John, 26, 251n167
Foster, William Z., 6
Four Jills in a Jeep (Landis), 237n9
Fourteen Points, 157
France, 4
Francen, Victor, 89, 127
Francis, Kay, 43
Franklin, Sydney, 163
Freedland, Michael, 22
free speech, 210–11
French resistance, 233n21
Friedman, Lester D., 22, 311n92

Froelick, Anne, 202, 206
Front Page (play), 119
Fuhrammar, Leif, 296n161
Fyne, Robert, 71, 231n1

Gable, Clark, 16
Gabler, Neal, 213
gangster films, 243n76
Gangway for Tomorrow (film),
    191–92, 312n103
Garbo, Greta, 17, 38
Garden of Allah, The (film), 16
Garfield, John, 171, 174, 175, 195,
    201, 305n11
Gargan, William, 243n73
Garson, Greer, 155, 160
Gąsiorowski, Wacław, 38
Gentleman Jim (film), 27
Georgakas, Dan, 7, 143, 204
George Washington Cohen (film), 24
George White's 1935 Scandals
    (film), 12
Gestapo, 51
Gibney, Sheldon, 320n30
Gibney, Sheridan, 202, 282n21
Gielgud, John, 15
Gilpatric, Guy, 176
Giovacchini, Saverio, 209
Girl and the Gambler, The (film), 15
Girl in Danger (film), 43, 251n168
Give Us This Night (film), 14,
    238n13
Gleason, Jackie, 189
Golden Boy (film), 25
Goldwyn, Samuel, 17, 35, 146
Gorcey, Leo, 195, 309n74
Gorney, Jay, 261n48
Granach, Alexander, 17, 239n24,
    285n50
Grant, Cary, 119, 121, 195, 197
Gray, Gilda (Marianna Michalska),
    11, 12
Great John L., The (film), 27
Great Waltz, The (film), 12

Greenstreet, Sidney, 126
Griffith, D. W., 22, 28, 243n76
Grinde, Nick, 192
Grodno, 46
Grzybowski, Wacław, 138, 139,
    291n100
Guernsey, Otis L., 109
Guinan, Mary Louise Cecilia, 27
Gustav Line, 130

Haines, William Wister, 41
Hale, Alan, 176, 189
Hall, Huntz, 195
Halsted Street (Chicago), 313n110
Halton, Charles, 85
Hangmen Also Die (film), 71, 78,
    234n22, 239n24
Harriman, Averill, 68
Harvey, Brian D., 18
Heart of New York, The (film), 24
Hecht, Ben, 147, 316n140
Held, Anna, 17, 239–40n24
Heller, Robert, 296n161
Hellman, Lillian
    Communist Party member, 201
    Arthur Kober and, 287n78
    The North Star, 144, 212, 294n136
    pro-Soviet actions of, 293n135
    visit to the Soviet Union, 294n140
Henie, Sonja, 134
Henreid, Paul, 201, 270n45
    Casablanca, 127, 155
    The Conspirators, 126, 127
    In Our Time, 88–89, 91, 108
"Heroes without Uniforms"
    (screenplay), 176
Heydrich, Reinhold, 317n148
Hi Diddle Diddle (film), 193,
    313n114
Higham, John, 170
High Pressure (film), 26
His Girl Friday (film), 119–20,
    280n1
Hitchcock, Alfred, 198, 316n140

Hitler—Dead or Alive (film), 192,
    313n109
Hitler's Madmen (film), 78
Hitler-Stalin pact, 45, 256n23
    the radical Left and, 59–61
Hodiak, John, 16, 199
Hollywood Anti-Nazi League,
    58–59, 63
Hollywood League for Democratic
    Action, 63
Hollywood Now (newsletter), 59
Hollywood Peace Forum, 63
Hollywood Writers Mobilization, 74,
    84–85, 147, 261n48
Holocaust, 8, 54–55, 71, 217–18
Home Army (Armia Krajowa), 52
Hopkins, Harry L., 69, 293n134
Hopkins, Miriam, 296n158
Horak, Jan-Christopher, 237n5
Hornbeck, William, 297n165
Hostages (film), 320n27
House Committee on Un-American
    Activities, 204, 224–25
House of Rothschild, The (film), 24
How Many More Knights? (film),
    226, 328n137
Huggins, Roy, 203
Hunt, Marsha, 113, 277–78n145, 324n91
Hunter, Kim, 192
"Hunyak," 246n107
Huston, Walter, 138
Huxley, Aldous, 163

I Hate Women (film), 26
I Married an Angel (film), 249n146
Incendiary Blonde (film), 27
In Our Time (film), 3
    the BMP and, 105–7
    cast, 88–89
    credits, 268n29
    Bosley Crowther on, 109–10, 211
    the Einfeld letter, 104–5
    examination of St. Joseph's
        treatments, 92–99

Victor Francen and, 127
Howard Koch and, 87–88, 99–102
    passim, 108, 136, 209, 273n78,
    273n89, 318n3
    origin of, 87–88
    plot, 89–91
    Polish response to, 103–5
    political implications, 107–8
    as a political indictment of Poland,
        110–11
    reactions to, 91, 108–10
    release date, 209
    studio research on, 102–3
    Jerry Wald and, 272n68
    Warner Brothers and, 80, 218–19,
        265n1
International Squadron (film),
    120–21, 280n3
Irish Americans, 20–23, 241n45
Irish Eyes Are Smiling (film), 187,
    310n85
Irish films
    before World War II, 20–23
    during World War II, 27
Irish-Jewish films, 20–21, 22–23
Iron Major, The (film), 27
Irving, Harry R., 29
Isaksson, Folke, 296n161
Isn't Life Wonderful (film), 28,
    244n84
Italian, The (film), 24
Italian films, 24–25
Italy, in World War II, 54
It's Great to Be Alive (film),
    288n79
Iturbi, José, 164

Jacobowsky and the Colonel
    (Werfel), 118
Januszewski, David, 3
Japanese Americans, 64
Jarrico, Paul, 73, 206, 212
Jarvie, Ian C., 236n1
Jazz Singer (film), 37

Jensen, Richard, 242n52
Jerome, Alice, 254n4
Jerome, V. J. *See* Jerome, Victor
  (Isaac Romaine)
Jerome, Victor (Isaac Romaine), 57,
  253–54n4, 319n18
Jessel, George, 23
Jewish Americans
  anti-Semitism, 213, 214–16, 217
  attitudes toward Poland, 8
  Polish immigrants, 169–70
  Polish-Jewish relations, 214–16
  rejection of the past, 213–14
  the wartime film industry and,
  213–18
Jewish films, 23–24
  See also Irish-Jewish films
Joan of Paris (film), 111, 276n135
Joelson, Asa. *See* Jolson, Al
"Joe Volkanik" (screenplay), 29–30
Jolson, Al (Asa Joelson), 17, 239n24
Jureko, Fr. J., 117
Justice Department, 258n10

Kac, Isser. *See* Katch, Kurt
Kaiser, Henry J., 182
Kalser, Erwin, 128
Kamieniec, 144, 294n139
Kane, Kathryn, 3
Kantor, MacKinlay, 316n140
Katch, Kurt (Isser Kac), 17, 239n24,
  285n48
Katyń massacre, 2, 51, 54, 68, 107,
  142
Katz, Otto, 58
Kaye, Sally, 146
Ketchel, Stanley (Stanisław Kiecał),
  187
Kiepura, Jan, 13–14, 237n12
King, Louis, 283n32
King of Alcatraz (film), 238n16
Kinskey, Leonid, 18, 314n125
Kleinbach, Heinrich von. *See*
  Brandon, Henry

Klimowicz, Stanisław. *See* Clements,
  Sidney
Knight, Eric, 147, 152–53, 299n190
Knock, Thomas J., 156–57
Knopf, Edwin, 37
Knox, Alexander, 112, 156
Kober, Arthur, 134, 201, 287–88n79,
  287n78
Koch, Anne, 88
Koch, Howard
  Casablanca, 155, 269–70n34
  defense of *Mission to Moscow* and
    pro-Soviet films, 207, 208
  on depicting Polish farmers, 273n82
  in the Hollywood Writers
    Mobilization, 261n48
  on John Lawson, 270n38
  leftist politics and, 201
  Jay Leyda and, 289–90n92
  Mission to Moscow, 75–76, 136–41
    passim, 143, 207, 288n86,
    289n87, 293n131
  In Our Time, 87–88, 99–102
    passim, 108, 139, 209, 272–
    73n78, 273n82, 273n89, 318n3
  politics of, 269n33
  Vladimir Pozner and, 284n41
  sees Poland as fascist, 205
  Jack Warner and, 268–69n32,
    318n3
Koestler, Arthur, 64
Korda, Alexander, 84, 87
Korjus, Miliza ("Berlin
  Nightingale"), 12–13
Kościuszko Squadron, 280n7
Kracauer, Siegfried, 9, 80
Krasnosielc, 219
Kubelsky, Benjamin. *See* Benny,
  Jack
Kucharski, Edward ("Raquello"), 15
Kunde, Al, 191

Lachteen, Frank, 251n169
Lady to Love, A (film), 243n70

LaFollette, Suzanne, 142
Lake Placid Serenade (film), 200,
    317n152
Lamarr, Hedy, 13, 126
Lamont, Charles R., 196
Landis, Carole, 13, 26, 237n9
landowners, 90
Lane, Richard, 310n91
Lantern for Jeremy, A (Jerome),
    254n4
Lardner, Ring, Jr., 62, 226, 236n39,
    261n48, 305n11
Lassie Come Home (film), 299n190
Last Mile, The (film), 26
Laughton, Charles, 25
Lawson, John Howard
    Action in the North Atlantic,
        176–82 *passim*
    Counter Attack, 131
    family past, 213–14
    on the Hitler-Stalin pact, 62,
        256n23
    as a Hollywood Communist,
        57, 58, 60, 176, 201, 255n13,
        255n15, 255n17
    in the Hollywood Writers
        Mobilization, 261n48
    Howard Koch on, 270n38
    on Louis Mayer, 261n46
    review of scripts for ideological
        uniformity, 204
    Sahara, 203
    Screen Writers Guild and, 202
    Jack Warner's accusations against,
        307–8n56
    "Women at War," 307n47
Łazienki Palace, 273n78
LeBaron, William, 135
"Lebensraum" (script outline), 115,
    117
Lebovics, Menyhert. *See* Lengyel,
    Melchior
Lees, Robert, 206
Left. *See* radical Left

Lengyel, Melchior, 87, 267–68n23
Leonard, Robert Z., 315n127
Lesinski, John, 69, 70
Leslie, Joan, 189
Les Miserables (film), 16
Leszczyński, Stanisław, 238n20
Letter from America (newsletter),
    14, 71
Levene, Sam, 176, 222
Leyda, Jay, 108
    Frank Capra and, 299–300n195
    Communism and, 201, 289n90
    Mission to Moscow, 136, 289n89,
        289n91, 290n92
    The North Star, 293n135
    Why We Fight, 147
Liberty (magazine), 196
Libkow, Marek, 117, 274n99
Lidice, 317n148
Lifeboat (film), 16, 197–200,
    315n139, 316n140, 316n145
Life magazine, 142
Life of Emile Zola, The (film), 221
Life of Jimmy Dolan, The (film), 226,
    328n137
Lissauer, Herman, 103, 104,
    290n93
Little Caesar (film), 26
Litvak, Anatole, 147–48, 151, 201,
    296nn157–158, 296n161
Litvinov, Ivy, 290n93
Litvinov, Maxim, 294n136
Loder, John, 186
Lombard, Carole, 84
Lopez, Ana M., 22, 80
Lord, Robert, 40
Lorre, Peter, 126, 195, 285n46
Los Angeles Times, 109
Lovell, Glenn, 114
Lubitsch, Ernst, 17, 84, 85, 86,
    257n18, 265n4
Luftwaffe, 49
Lukas, Richard C., 1–2
Lumet, Baruch, 17, 239n24

Lupino, Ida, 89, 318n2
Lynch, William, 241n45

Macauley, Richard, 321n43
Mackinder, Herbert, 296n162
Madame Curie (film), 160–64,
    260n33, 302n224
Majewski, Karen, 24
Maltz, Albert
    controversy with Alvah Bessie,
       320n19
    Destination Tokyo, 197
    Hollywood Communism and, 88
    In Our Time, 99
    perceptions of Poland, 204–5
    propaganda in films and, 6
    rejection of the personal past, 213
Man of the People (film), 26
manors, Polish, 90
Manvell, Roger, 121
March, Frederic, 16
March, Radetzky, 233n18
Margin for Error (film), 200,
    317n151
Markowski, Wincenty. *See* Tyler,
    Tom
Marshall, Gen. George C., 154
Martin, Richard, 192
Marx, Chico, 25
Marx Brothers, 25
Mask of Dimitrios, The (film), 127,
    239n24, 284–85n46
massacres
    Katyń, 2, 51, 54, 68, 107, 142
    Lidice, 317n148
    of Poles during World War II,
       46–47, 51
Massey, Raymond, 175
Mastny, Vojtech, 4
Mayer, Edwin Justus, 87
Mayer, Louis B., 205
    on the ideological content of
       wartime films, 321n39
    John Howard Lawson on, 261n46

Polish origins of, 17
    Song of Russia and, 73–74
    toleration of Communists, 277n140
Mayhew, Robert, 73, 74
Mayo, Archie, 41
Mazurka (film), 43
Mazurki, Mike (Michał
    Mazurkiewicz), 15–16
McCarey, Leo, 121, 280n9, 282n21,
    320n30
McClean, Albert, 24
McClure, Arthur F., 1
McGilligan, Patrick, 202, 203
McHugh, Frank, 189
McManus, Jack, 143
McManus, John T., 110
Mellett, Lowell, 68, 70, 71, 77
Meltzer, Lewis, 185, 320n30
Men in White (film), 16
Mexico, 153
MGM, 79, 163, 249n146
Michalska, Marianna. *See* Gray,
    Gilda
Milar, Adolph, 43
Milestone, Lewis (Lev Milstein), 18,
    19, 133, 201, 287n72, 318n1
Million Dollar Legs (film), 12
Milstein, Lev. *See* Milestone, Lewis
Miraculous Mandarin, The (film),
    268n23
Mission to Moscow (Davies), 137
Mission to Moscow (film), 111
    American pro-Soviet sentiment
       and, 2
    credits, 288n82
    Bosley Crowther on, 211
    depiction of Russian peasants in,
       95–96
    discussion of, 135–41
    Howard Koch and, 75–76, 136–41
       passim, 143, 207, 288n86,
       289n87, 293n131
    origin of, 135
    Nelson Poynter and, 75–76

reactions to, 141–43, 263n68
release date, 209
Roosevelt and, 223, 224, 288n86,
  289n87
Jack Warner and, 327n131
Miss V from Moscow (film), 78
Mitchell, Thomas, 190
Mitchum, Robert, 129
Molotov, Vyacheslav, 48
Monte Cassino, 54, 130–31, 286n57
Moon is Down, The (film), 71
Mordden, Ethan, 75, 222
More the Merrier, The (film), 195,
  314n122
Motion Picture Producers and
  Distributors of America
  (MPPDA), 81, 134
Mr. Winkle Goes to War (film), 188
Mrs. Miniver (film), 155, 211, 321n39
Muni, Paul
  as an Austrian Jew, 245–46n103
  Black Fury, 30–31, 32
  Commandoes Strike at Dawn, 122
  efforts for Polish relief, 240n25
  the FBI on, 304n248
  Polish origins of, 17
  politics of, 167
  Scarface, 26
  A Song to Remember, 164
  travels to Poland, 245n103
Münzenberg, Willi, 57
Murphy, George, 185, 189, 190
Musketeers of Pig Alley, The (film),
  243n76
Musmanno, Judge M. A., 29
Mysterious Pilot, The (serial), 251n169

Nachbar, Jack, 300n198
Naish, J. Carrol, 25, 243n69
names, nonsensical, 188
Narvik campaign, 53
Nasjonal Samling, 252n13
National Council of American-Soviet
  Friendship, 89

National Peace Week, 63
Naughty but Nice (film), 243n67,
  314n119
Navasky, Victor S., 5
Nazimova, Alla, 18, 89, 270n44
Nazi-Soviet pact, 45
Nazis Strike, The (documentary),
  148–50, 153, 154, 296n162,
  299n192
Negri, Pola (Apolonia Chałupiec),
  11–12, 43, 193, 236n2, 236n4
Nelson, Barry, 190
Neuman, Sam, 192
Neumann, Alfred, 115, 278n153
Never Say Goodbye (film),
  312n101
New York Daily News, 146
New Yorker, 109
New York Herald-Tribune, 109
New York Sun, 143
New York Times, 84, 109–10, 142,
  210, 226
Nichols, Dudley, 58, 172, 201
Niemo-Niemojowski, Lech, 104
Ninotchka (film), 87, 152, 268n23
NKVD (People's Commissariat of
  Internal Affairs), 51
None Shall Escape (film), 3, 83
  credits, 276–77n137
  denigration of Poles in, 80
  discussion of, 111–18
  Holocaust and, 217–18
Normandy invasion, 54
North Star, The (film), 71
  credits, 293n134
  Bosley Crowther on, 212
  depiction of Russian peasants in,
    95–96
  discussion of, 143–46
  OWI and, 146–47
  Production Code and, 81
  as a propaganda film, 76
  reactions to, 146, 263n68
  in the Soviet Union, 294n140

Norway, 3–4, 53, 233n19, 252–
    53n13
Novick, Peter, 8
Nowitzky, Herman, 219

Oakie, Jack, 185
Oberon, Merle, 164, 167
Oboler, Arch, 201
Office of Facts and Figures, 69
Office of War Information (OWI)
    Action in the North Atlantic, 182
    Air Force, 174
    allied with the Left, 69, 209–10
    attitudes toward Poland, 69–70, 74
    concern for the positive portrayal
        of foreigners, 78–79
    creation of, 68
    Destroyer, 184
    film treatment of the Holocaust
        and, 217
    Gangway for Tomorrow, 191
    Hitler—Dead or Alive, 192–93
    ideological guidelines for
        Hollywood, 70–71
    the importance of film in shaping
        public attitudes and, 71
    influence on movie production, 72
    Mission to Moscow, 141–42
    The North Star, 146–47
    Overseas Operations Branch,
        69–70, 72
    pro-Russian/Soviet bias, 5, 69,
        73–74, 76
    "Quota Girl" (script), 134–35
    reviews movie scripts for their
        treatment of the Allies, 78
    Since You Went Away, 234n25
    A Song to Remember, 166–67
    surveys of public opinion
        regarding the international war
        effort, 76
    Walter Wanger's denunciation of,
        71–72
O'Keefe, Dennis, 186

Once Upon a Honeymoon (film),
    121–22, 149, 218, 280n8,
    320n30
Operation Torch, 4
Orczy, Baroness, 38
Ordyński, Ryszard, 17, 87
Ornitz, Samuel, 58
Ouspenskaya, Maria, 18

Paderewski, Ignacy Jan, 122, 140,
    141, 157, 292n112
Painted Veil, The (film), 16
"palooka," 244nn87–88
Palooka (comic strip character),
    244–45n89
Palooka (film), 28–29, 244n86
Pani Walewska (Gąsiorowski), 38
Pan Tadeusz (film), 17
Paramount, 202
Parker, Jean (Lois Zelinska), 13
Parker, Mathew, 131
Paul, Elliot, 125
Peck, Jeff, 18
Perry, Gerald, 210
Pétain, Marshal, 4
Philadelphia Record, 156
Picon, Molly, 17
Pidgeon, Walter, 160
Piłsudski, Józef, 122
Pittsburgh (film), 187, 310n86
PM, 93, 110
Poland
    American public opinion, 1–2
    anti-Semitism and, 8
    complaints to the U.S. government
        about inattention to Poland in
        war propaganda, 69–70
    position of American Communists
        toward, 61–63
    Roosevelt's position toward, 67, 68
    Wilson's Fourteen Points and, 157
Poland (World War II)
    air force, 49, 148
    cavalry, 49, 148

composition of the government,
49–50
deportations, 51–52
extended fighting in, 47–48
factors in the defeat of, 48–49
German invasion, 45
German occupation, 50–51
government-in-exile, 52
Holocaust, 54–55
losses during the war, 48, 56, 153,
253n20, 253n23, 298n183
massacres in, 46–47, 51
military strategy, 46
Nazi-Soviet pact and, 45
organized resistance, 52, 55–56
Polish-Soviet relations, 54
soldiers abroad, 52–53
soldiers on the eastern front,
253n20
Soviet invasion, 46–47
Soviet occupation, 51–52, 56
treatment of Polish Jews, 51
Warsaw Rising, 54, 56
Polish actors, 11–16
Polish Americans
    BMP concerns for the sensibilities
    of, 81
demographics, 310n90
Polish directors, 16–17
Polish films, prior to World War II,
28–39
Polish immigrants
American responses to, 170
Jewish, 169–70
overview, 169
Polish Information Center, 103
Polish Information Service, 117
Polish Jews
attitudes toward Poland, 8
in Hollywood before 1939, 17
immigrants, 169–70
Polish Ministry of Information,
279n163
Polish Refugee Association, 104

Polish Roman Catholic Union of
America, 104
political activism, the radical Left
and, 201
Polonsky, Abraham, 261n48
Polonsky, Antony, 217
Poniatowski, Stanisław August, 95,
97, 271n54
Popular Front, 59, 61
Powell, William, 38
Poynter, Nelson, 261n41
    Action in the North Atlantic, 182,
    183
    Edge of Darkness, 262n59
    as head of the Hollywood office of
    the BMP, 70–76 *passim*
    Wilson, 159
Pozner, Vladimir, 126, 201, 283–
84n37, 284n41
Pravda, 60, 61
Pride of the Marines (film), 189
Princess O'Rourke (film), 196,
315n128
Private Izzy Murphy (film), 23
Production Code, 21, 81
Prokosch, Frederic, 124
propaganda
American Communists and, 58
anti-Polish, 218–27
Hollywood films and, 76
Albert Maltz and, 6
OWI and, 71
Public Enemy (film), 26
public opinion
on Poland, 1–2
pro-Soviet attitudes, 2
regarding the international war
effort, 76
on World War II in 1939, 232n8
Purple Heart, The (film), 188
Pyle, Ernie, 130

Quisling, Vidkun, 3
"Quota Girl," 134–35

Rachmaninoff, Sergei, 19
Racket, The (film), 26
radical Left
  allied with the OWI, 69, 209–10
  dislike of Poland, 204–5
  the Hitler-Stalin pact and, 59–61
  in Hollywood, 4–6
  presence and influence in
    Hollywood, 4–6, 201–4
  pro-Soviet films and, 205–10
  undermining of the Polish cause,
    6–7
Raft, George, 26
Rainer, Luise, 38
Rameau, Emil, 140, 291n109,
  292n111
Rand, Ayn, 129
Raquello. *See* Kucharski, Edward
Rasumny, Mikhail, 128
Ratoff, Gregory, 19
Reagan, Ronald, 120, 124, 189
Reardon, Jeff, 186
Redelings, Lowell, 109
Rennie, Michael, 233n18
Return of Jimmy Valentine, The
  (film), 26
Rich, Freddie, 17
Ridgely, John, 175
Riggs, Lynn, 163
Rise and Shine (film), 185, 309n81
Rivkin, Allen, 152, 154
RKO, 202, 242n52
Roberti, Lyda, 12
Robinson, Edward G.
  Destroyer, 183, 185, 201
  A Lady to Love, 243n70
  Little Caesar, 26
  physical size of, 195
  politics of, 308–9n72
Roddick, Nick, 42
Rogers, Ginger, 121
Roger Touhy, Gangster (film), 27
Romaine, Isaac (Victor Jerome), 57
Roman Catholic Church, 215

Roosevelt, Franklin Delano
  the film industry and, 258n10
  film treatment of the Holocaust
    and, 217
  Mission to Moscow and, 135, 143,
    288n86, 289n87
  position toward Poland, 67, 68
  position toward Russia, 67–68
  the Warner Brothers and, 222, 223,
    326n114
Rosenbloom, "Slapsie Maxie," 187
Rossen, Robert, 132, 133, 201, 205,
  261n48
Rosten, Leo C., 75
Roth, Phillip, 214
Rotterdam, 285n53
Royal Air Force, 120
Rozumny, Mikhail, 18
Rubinstein, Artur, 166
Ruman, Sig (Siegfried Rumann), 35,
  37, 84, 265n6
Russell, Rosalind, 119
Russia. *See* Soviet Union

Sahara (film), 203
Sailor Izzy Murphy (film), 23
Sakall, S. Z., 222
Samuels, Stuart, 20
Sandburg, Carl, 1
Sarny, 47
Scarface (film), 26
Scarlet Pimpernel, The (Orczy), 38
Schallert, Edwin, 109
Schary, Dore, 154, 299n190
Schmidlapp, Horace, 237n10
"scientist biographies," 302n222
Scott, Allen, 202
Screen Actors Guild, 206
Screen Readers Guild, 58, 203
Screen Writer, The (journal), 203
Screen Writers Guild, 58, 167, 202,
  318n1
Second Comintern Conference,
  235n35

Second Polish Corps, 130
Seiter, William, 185
Semels, Harry, 25
Seredzius, 239n24
Sergeant York (film), 311n94
serials, 43–44, 200
service films, 311–12n99
Sharin, Eugene, 280n8
Shearer, Norma, 196
Sherman, Vincent, 89, 94, 108,
    270n44, 271n59
Sherman Antitrust Act, 222
Shindler, Colin, 85
Shohat, Ella, 28, 311n92
Sikorski, Władysław, 50, 54, 107
Silvers, Phil, 189
Simmon, Scott, 36
Since You Went Away (film), 200,
    234n25
Sing Another Chorus (film), 196,
    315n129
Ski Patrol (film), 210, 321n42
Skłodowska, Maria, 160, 161–62
Sławoj-Składkowski, Felicjan, 121
Slezak, Walter, 121, 198
Slight Case of Murder, A (film), 26
Small, Melvin, 1, 2, 210, 231n2,
    329n2
So Ends Our Night (film), 128,
    285n50
Sokoloff, Vladimir, 18
Solomon, Haym, 221–22
Song of Russia (film)
    the BMP and, 77
    Louis Mayer on, 321n39
    Polish aspects of, 129
    as a propaganda film, 76
    reactions to, 211–12
    the Roosevelt administration
        pushes for the production of,
        73–74
    Russian-born actors in, 19
    screenwriter, 131, 261n46
Song of Russia (Jarrico), 73

Song of the City (film), 25
Song to Remember, A (film), 16, 160,
    164–67
Sons of Liberty (film), 326n109
Sons of Steel (film), 43
Soubier, Clifford, 42
South of Panama (film), 15
Soviet Russia Today (journal), 60
Soviet Union
    importation of Hollywood films,
        294n140
    invasion of Poland, 46–47
    occupation of Poland, 51–52, 56
    Roosevelt's position toward, 67–68
Spellman, Francis Cardinal, 67
Spiegel, Alan, 213
Spigelgass, Leonard, 152, 296n161
Średniki, 239n24
St. John, Robert, 265n1
St. Joseph, Ellis, 88, 90, 92–99
    passim, 111, 201, 205
Stack, Robert, 85
Stalin, Joseph, 6, 51, 53
Stander, Lionel, 206
Starzyński, Stefan, 98–99, 272n75
Steele, Freddie, 171, 304n9
Steinbeck, John, 197, 198, 316n140
Steinke, Hans, 43
Sten, Anna (Anel Sudakevich), 35,
    249n137
Stevens, George, 195
Stevenson, Philip, 131, 201, 286n59
Stewart, Donald Ogden, 64
Stone, George E., 17
Story Analysts Guild, 203
Story of G.I. Joe, The (film), 54,
    129–31, 170–71, 286n56
Stranded (film), 43
Strassoff, Olga, 26
Strauss, Theodore, 84
Stripling, Robert, 224–25
Strzelecki, T., 103, 104
Submarine Base (film), 129, 239n24,
    285–86n54

Submarine Raider (film), 190,
    312n100
Sub Patrol (film), 26
Sudakevich, Anel. *See* Sten, Anna
Suicide Squadron (film), 232–33n18
Sullivan, John L., 27
Sullivans, The (film), 27
Swerling, Jo, 147, 198–99
Sylvester, Harry, 316n140
Sztandar wolnošci (film), 17

Talk of the Town, The (film), 167,
    195–96, 314n124
Tamiroff, Akim, 18
Tanks Are Coming, The (film), 193,
    313n112
Taxi! (film), 23
Taylor, Robert, 12–13
Tehran conference, 55
Tender Comrade (film), 192,
    313n107
Than, Joseph, 115, 278n153
They Knew What They Wanted (film),
    25
39 Steps, The (film), 15
This Is the Army (film), 189
Thorsen, Marjorie, 163
Three Russian Girls (film), 88
Thurber, James, 185
Time magazine, 84
To Be or Not To Be (film), 3
    credits, 265n2
    Bosley Crowther on, 84, 211,
        265n5
    discussion of, 83–87
    the Holocaust and, 218
    reactions to, 266n7, 266n11
    reference to the Polish
        underground, 56
Tobias, George, 180
    Air Force, 174, 175, 222
    names of screen roles, 313n113
    The Tanks Are Coming, 193
    This Is the Army, 189

Tomorrow, the World (film), 81, 131,
    195, 324–25n94
Tone, Franchot, 16, 238n20
Touhy, Roger, 27
Travers, Henry, 113
Triplett, William, 5, 6
Trochimczyk, Maja, 215
Trotti, Lamar, 157, 158, 159
Trumbo, Dalton, 203, 206
Tucker, Forrest, 190, 312n101
Tuttle, Frank, 204, 320n27
Twentieth Century–Fox, 118
Tyler, Tom (Wincenty Markowski),
    14, 238n14, 238nn16–17,
    314n125

U-Boat Prisoner (film), 128–29,
    285n52
United Artists, *The Wedding Night*
    and, 34–38
United Jewish Welfare Fund, 221
United States
    film attendance, 1, 231n2
    Polish population, 310n90
    pro-Soviet attitudes, 2
    public opinion on Poland, 1–2
U.S. Army, *Why We Fight* and, 147
Universal, 202

vaudeville, 21
Veidt, Conrad, 155
Veiller, Anthony, 152, 296nn160–161
Vichy regime in France, 4
Vidor, King, 35, 37, 248n135,
    314n116
Vinson, Helen, 34
Visaroff, Michael, 18
Vorska, Jesse de, 17
V1 rocket, 55
V2 rocket, 55

Wake Island (film), 128, 193
Walasek, Janina. *See* Wallace, Jean
Walbrook, Anton, 233n18

Wald, Jerry, 94, 104, 272n68
Walker, Helen, 186
Wallace, Jean (Walasek, Janina), 16
Wallis, Hal, 214
Wanger, Walter, 71–72
War Comes to America
    (documentary), 152, 295n151
War Department, *Why We Fight* and,
    147
Warm Springs Foundation, 222
Warner, Ben, 219
Warner, Harry
    attitude toward Poland, 226–27
    the BMP and, 75
    claims of anti-Semitic persecution
      and, 226–27, 328n139
    denial of the past, 214
    ideological use of film and, 225
    Mission to Moscow, 135
    opposition to Nazism, 39
    Polish origins, 17, 220–21
    politics, 222–23
    religion, 221
    Roosevelt and, 222, 223, 326n114
Warner, Jack, 17, 22
    accusations against John Lawson,
      307–8n56
    Air Force, 171–72
    the BMP and, 75
    denial of the past, 214
    Sheridan Gibney and, 282n21
    ideological use of film and, 225–26
    Howard Koch and, 268–69n32,
      318n3
    memoirs and, 325–26n104
    Mission to Moscow, 135, 140, 143,
      327n131
    In Our Time, 88, 99, 104, 105
    Polish origins and, 219–20, 221
    politics, 205, 222, 224–25
    promotion of the Jewish image in
      America, 222
    religion, 221
    Roosevelt and, 222, 223, 326n114

Warner, Pearl (née Eichelbaum), 219
Warner Brothers
    Air Force, 171–75
    anti-Polish propaganda and,
      218–27
    Black Fury, 29–32
    Black Legion, 40–43
    the BMP and, 75–76, 183
    casting of Poles, 271n50
    As the Earth Turns, 32–34
    film depiction of Poland and,
      201–2
    films dramatizing Jewish triumphs,
      221–22
    ideological use of film, 225–26
    Irish animosity toward, 21, 22
    Jewish characters and, 222
    Marek Libkow and, 274n99
    opposition to the Nazis and
      fascism, 39–40
    In Our Time, 87–111, 265n1
    Pride of the Marines, 189
    pro-FDR politics and, 205
    stops war films, 206
Warsaw, fall of, 47
Warsaw, 1943 Jewish uprising in,
    160
Warsaw Rising, 54, 56
Watch on the Rhine (film), 239n24
Watson, John O., 174
Waugh, Evelyn, 300n197
Wead, Frank, 185
Weber, John, 58, 203, 261n48,
    283n37
"We Can Do Business with Russia"
    (memorandum), 72–73
Wedding Night, The (film), 34–38,
    248n130
Wengraf, John, 138, 139
We Refuse to Die (film), 234n22
Werfel, Franz, 118
West, Claudine, 315n127
We Were Dancing (film), 196,
    314–15n126

White, Leo, 17
"White Cliffs, The" (screenplay), 80
Whitfield, Stephen J., 21
Why We Fight (documentary series),
    206
    The Battle of Britain episode, 151,
        285n3
    The Battle of China episode,
        295n151
    The Battle of Russia episode, 71,
        151–52, 212, 297nn170–171
    Divide and Conquer episode,
        150–51
    exaggeration of German forces,
        297n164
    Eric Knight and, 152–53
    The Nazis Strike episode, 148–50,
        153, 154, 296n162, 299n192
    overview, 147–48
    reactions to, 154
    script writing for, 296n160
    unproduced segments, 153–54
    War Comes to America episode,
        152, 295n151
Wieluń, 285n53
Wilde, Cornel, 16, 164
William Morris Agency, 283n37
Wilshire Boulevard Temple, 221
Wilson (film), 156–59, 301n204
Wilson, "Dooley," 301n203
Wilson, Woodrow, 157, 170
Winchell, Walter, 110
Windheim, Marek, 17, 90, 193,
    239n24, 271n50
Winokur, Mark, 310n92
Winterset (film), 25
Wintertime (film), 134–35, 288n81
"Women at War" (screenplay),
    307n47
Woods, Donald, 34
Woods, William H., 133
World War II
    American public opinion in 1939,
        232n8

Battle of Britain, 52–53, 120
German bombing of Rotterdam,
    285n53
German invasion of Poland, 45
German invasion of Russia, 53
Katyń massacre, 2, 51, 54, 68, 107,
    142
Lidice, 317n148
Monte Cassino, 54, 130–31,
    286n57
Nazi-Soviet pact, 45
Soviet invasion of Poland, 46–47
Tehran conference, 55
Warsaw Rising, 54, 56
Western front, 53–54
See also Poland (World War II)
Wright, Virginia, 108–9
Wyler, William, 146, 294n136

Yankee Doodle Dandy (film), 27
Yank in Libya, A (film), 234n22
Yank in the R.A.F., A (film), 211
Yezierska, Anzia, 214
York, Alvin, 311n94
You and Me (film), 26
Youth on Parade (film), 239n24

Zanuck, Darryl F., 152, 156, 205,
    214, 222
Zbyszko, Władysław, 43
Zelinska, Lois. *See* Parker, Jean
Zwoliński, Stanisława. *See* Clarke,
    Estelle